A Galaxy Here
and Now

D1217314

A Galaxy Here and Now

Historical and Cultural Readings of Star Wars

Edited by PETER W. LEE

McFarland & Company, Inc., Publishers

Jefferson, North Carolina

LIBRARY OF CONGRESS CATALOGUING-IN-PUBLICATION DATA

Names: Lee, Peter W., 1980– editor.
Title: A galaxy here and now : historical and cultural readings of Star
    wars / edited by Peter W. Lee.
Description: Jefferson, N.C. : McFarland & Company, Inc., Publishers,
    2016. | Includes bibliographical references and index.
Identifiers: LCCN 2015049160 | ISBN 9781476662206 (softcover : acid
    free paper) ∞
Subjects: LCSH: Star Wars films—History and criticism.
Classification: LCC PN1995.9.S695 G33 2016 | DDC 791.43/75—dc23
LC record available at http://lccn.loc.gov/2015049160

BRITISH LIBRARY CATALOGUING DATA ARE AVAILABLE

© 2016 Peter W. Lee. All rights reserved

*No part of this book may be reproduced or transmitted in any form
or by any means, electronic or mechanical, including photocopying
or recording, or by any information storage and retrieval system,
without permission in writing from the publisher.*

Front cover image of alien planet © 2016 Sylphe_7/iStock

Printed in the United States of America

*McFarland & Company, Inc., Publishers
    Box 611, Jefferson, North Carolina 28640
    www.mcfarlandpub.com*

For Clare and Helen Wong,
who introduced me to space opera,
and to Lai Goon Lee, who never wanted to hear the odds.

Table of Contents

Preface:
Galactic Graffiti

Star Wars needs no introduction.

From its initial release in 1977, George Lucas's franchise has captured the hearts, imaginations, and wallets of three generations of moviegoers. Comic book adaptations, novels, video games, and television shows have created an "Expanded Universe," extending the Skywalker mythos and perpetuating its fan culture into other media beyond the confines of celluloid film. *Star Wars* hinted at a larger galaxy than the one on screen. Shortly after the 1977 premiere, the universe took a giant leap forward in developing a fan base, marketing characters such as Snaggletooth, R5-D4, and Dodonna—names never mentioned and sometimes even barely seen on screen, but became collectible action figures among fans. The word "Force" means more than simple pressure, but connotes an entire lifestyle combination of meditation and martial arts. Although nearing middle age and despite the dynamic shifts in the United States since the waning Seventies, *Star Wars* is very much a relevant cultural phenomenon.

Less so in academic circles. Popular culture, while generally accepted as a legitimate source of scholarly attention, still contains a stigma of low-brow, disposable junk—merely fads for the masses, and surely not on equal footing as "high" culture. Nevertheless, the $32 billion of sold merchandise in 2014 speaks to the adaptability and prevalence of Lucas's universe on the world stage (Taylor). Escaping its Cold War roots, side-stepping the embarrassing shuffles of Jar-Jar Binks, erupting debate over "who shot first," and building a next generation in spinoffs, followers continue to flock around the adventures of Luke Skywalker with reverence. When Disney spent $4.05 billion to acquire Lucasfilm in 2012, the Mouse probably wasn't after the filmic rights to *Howard the Duck* (Taylor 393).

Juxtaposed against the ubiquitous presence of Star Warriors on Main Street, the libraries in the Ivory Tower display a noticeable dearth in Darth Vader analyses. Recent works have examined *Star Wars* primarily through a philosophic lens; Paul F. McDonald, Caleb Grimes, Douglas Brode, and Leah

Deyneka discuss the mythology and multimedia contexts within film genres. Within a historical and cultural context, recent studies have drawn comparisons between the filmic galaxy to what happened on Earth a long time ago. Steven A. Galipeau and Mary Henderson point to the original trilogy's plot as evidence of continuing tropes of classic myths, Arthurian lore, and visual imagery from World War II. Nancy Regain's and Janice Liedl's *Star Wars and History* relies primarily on visual comparisons without noting the dynamic shifts in the political, social, and cultural contexts. Kevin J. Wetmore, Jr., positions the film as a continuation of white colonialism writ large. Recent anthologies by Carl Silvio and Tony M. Vinci have explored facets of the films' connections with American cultural identities.

Star Wars's resonance with American audiences reflects more of the recent past than classical antiquity. George Lucas drew from the vast collective memory of American history, his own background, his experimental days in film school at the University of Southern California, the unhappy future depicted in his first feature-length production *THX-1138*, followed by his tribute to his hot-rod past (Kaminski). *Star Wars*, an accumulation of his cinematic visions of the past and future, hit audiences with strokes of celluloid graffiti uniquely American.

Fittingly, the film, like the nebulous term "American culture," eludes a specific meaning. *Star Wars* embraces a mechanical future both on the screen and off even as it champions the age-old tropes of knights and princesses. Even as the original *Star Wars* film negative recedes into the past, the various spinoffs, sequels, prequels, alternate realities, and a fan-based Expanded Universe across the entire spectrum of visual and audio media, continue to update a galactic history supposedly far away. George Lucas's universe, contrary to the opening title cards, is very much a living one.

Given *Star Wars*'s evolving relationship with modern times, the historical and cultural (F)orces underpinning *Star Wars* are much more complex than the film's simple binary "light" versus "dark." The essays in this volume reflect those multiple points of view—a concept which stumped Luke Skywalker in *Return of the Jedi*, but such complications no doubt make film and cultural analyses so much fun.

George Lucas re-introduced Twentieth Century–Fox's opening fanfare, which has become a part of the movie soundtrack, segueing into John Williams's score. Music is the audience's first exposure to Lucas's cinematic universe and, appropriately, also starts this collection, even though Tom Zlabinger surveys the music *beyond* the cinematic universe. Looking at/hearing the different interpretations, Zlabinger analyzes how shifting tastes in music—such as from disco to rock—altered the musical adaptations of John

Williams's iconic score. *Star Wars* has become a coded language connecting audiences to artists beyond the mere sights and sounds of the franchise. While some musicians paid homage to the nostalgia the film evokes, other interpretations suggest larger critiques against socio-political norms and raises issues of identity construction.

After hearing John Williams's iconic introduction and Industrial Light and Magic's opening battle sequence, viewers come across the ethereal image of Princess Leia. Far from a typical damsel-in-distress, yet the original trilogy's sole prominent female, Leia has attracted much critical attention as an anchor to a deeper discussion of feminism within Lucas's mythos. Karin Hilck's essay contextualizes Leia's representation within NASA and the American space program's role in the Cold War. Hilck argues Leia failed to appeal to NASA as a cultural spokesman. In contrast to NASA's appropriation of *Star Trek*'s Uhura as a model for feminism and multiculturalism, the Alderaanian senator/princess duality complicated the image NASA wanted to project as well as the organization's own internal gender politics. In recent years, however, this relationship has become noticeably warmer to suit NASA's changing public profile.

Mara Wood expands on the conflicting image of female characters as cultural icons. In close readings of the main female leads in the six movies, Wood argues Leia Organa and Padmé Amidala represent strong characterizations, subverting the traditional image of helpmates and damsels imposed in the largely male-dominated movies. She extends this strength to the more recent television shows *Clone Wars* and *Rebels* with the programs showcasing non-white, non-human female characters' emotional growth and leadership abilities during times of galactic unrest.

Erin C. Callahan examines the men in Leia's life, drawing out the contentions between forms of masculinity through the princess's brother, father, and future husband. Using the western frontier as a parallel mythology, Callahan argues the "return" of the Jedi heralds a masculinity replacing the dominant patriarchy that fell out of favor in the late 1970s. Luke's growth and Han's transformation from space cowboy to the ranks of general suggest the future of Lucas's mythos rests upon "the importance of non-violence, peace, cooperation, connection to and serving others."

Leia's capture also coincides with Darth Vader's introduction. Popular and scholarly criticisms have examined the Dark Lord's presence as a racial stand-in, running the gamut of African to Asian heritages. Gregory E. Rutledge forcefully argues that, rather than accept a straight black/white dichotomy, the films appropriate the cultures of non-western peoples in a form of modern day minstrelsy, a process which he coins "epic mimicry."

Specifically, Rutledge addresses the movies' borrowing motifs from the African American civil rights movements of the 1960s and 1970s as vehicles for white resistance against the Empire while also representing a "cool" norm within Lucas's celluloid milieu.

The action moves from space to the first planetary environment: the desert. Paul Charbel's essay addresses the ethnic identities and appropriations involved in Lucas's conception of desert inhabitants. Charbel argues the *Star Wars* films have capitalized on long-standing racial caricatures of the Middle East in their depiction of Jawas and Tusken Raiders while situating the human colonists as heroes. Contextualizing the native inhabitants—especially the Tuskens—in Bedouin culture, Charbel powerfully punctures the negative constructions of Tatooine's "others" as desert barbarians and scavengers and inverses the relationship between the desert planet's human and non-human dwellers.

The last three essays focus on the film's own mythologized reputation in a historical and revisionist narrative. Peter W. Lee's essay focuses on the film's Cold War context. The film evoked a specific nostalgic reading, one conforming to a Cold War consensual history of social progress, consumerism, and a valorization of technology. Alternate readings contesting that narrative—as evidenced in the ill-fated *Star Wars Holiday Special* and the Ewok movies—sparked controversy as to their inclusion within the filmic canon. This celebration ultimately shaped the public rhetoric surrounding Cold War policy, notably President Ronald Reagan's Strategic Defense Initiative.

Jessica K. Brandt examines the relationship between *Star Wars* radio adaptation and Cold War radio. With a running time of over six and a half hours, the radio program expanded the filmic narrative. However, as Brandt argues, Lucas intended the national public radio program to "elevate" his movie from associations of crass commercialism. Situating the program within the Cold War context and the radio industry's struggles to stay culturally relevant, Brandt acutely observes the producers' hopes in celebrating *Star Wars* within a revived "middlebrow" mix of entertainment and cultural sophistication.

Just as George Lucas has continually updated the films to suit his taste, Michael Fuchs and Michael Phillips argue the fans have likewise responded in kind. This complex relationship between creator, fanbase, and the texts have resulted in an explosion of competing versions over the "official" and "definitive" structures of narrative. Conflicting yearnings for nostalgia and inspirational impulses to bring balance to a true version of *Star Wars* have Balkanized the movies. As Fuchs and Phillips point out, the lines separating authorship, authority, and auteur have blurred considerably. The recent jettison of much of the Expanded Universe and J.J. Abrams's ascension to the director's chair demonstrate the fluctuating nature of storytelling and, as a suitable conclusion to this anthology, questions the sustainability of definitive narratives.

From "official" music interpretations in the late 1970s to complete fan-made edits in an online marketplace of ideas, *Star Wars*'s filmic circle is far from complete. In 1982, director Richard Marquand, having just finished helming *Return of the Jedi*, offered a glimpse into upcoming installments in the galaxy from long ago. "Some characters are bound to reappear but they'll be older. Luke will be fifty, or whatever. It will be a long time hence; so I think in a way they will be here, but they will ... by then they'll be the springboard for a whole series of new adventures that will take place" (Tuchman). Marquand, who died in 1987, never found out. But despite the obvious changes that the passage of time will bring to the growing Skywalker clan, and the shifts and reflections within American culture in the here and now, the filmic episodes maintain a consistent theme to entertain mass audiences worldwide. No matter what dark force awakens to further the numeric episodes, a new hope will always emerge to meet the challenge.

Works Cited

Brode, Douglas, and Leah Deyneka, eds. *Myth, Media, and Culture in Star Wars: An Anthology.* Lanham, MD: Scarecrow Press, 2012. Print.

Galipeau, Steven A. *The Journey of Luke Skywalker: An Analysis of Modern Myth and Symbol.* Peru, IL: Open Court, 2001. Print.

Henderson, Mary. *Star Wars: The Magic of Myth.* New York: Bantam Books, 1997. Print.

Kaminski, Michael. *The Secret History of Star Wars: The Art of Storytelling and the Making of a Modern Epic.* Kingston, Ontario: Legacy, 2008. Print.

Silvio, Carl, and Tony M. Vinci. *Culture, Identities, and Technology in the Star Wars Films.* Jefferson, NC: McFarland, 2007. Print.

Taylor, Chris. *How Star Wars Conquered the Universe: The Past, Present, and Future of a Multibillion Dollar Franchise.* New York: Basic Books, 2014. Print.

Tuchman, Mitch. Interview with Richard Marquand. December 12 and 14, 1982. Mitch Tuchman transcripts. Margaret Herrick Library, Academy of Motion Picture Arts and Sciences.

Wetmore, Kevin J. *The Empire Triumphant: Race, Religion and Rebellion in the Star Wars Films.* Jefferson, NC: McFarland, 2005. Print.

Hearing the Force

Manifestations and Transformations of Music from Far, Far Away

Tom Zlabinger

Music is an enormous part of the *Star Wars* universe. George Lucas's space opera would not have had the same emotional impact without John Williams's ingenious musical contribution. After the premiere of *Star Wars* [*Episode IV: A New Hope*] in 1977, the film's symphonic soundtrack was immensely popular. Not only did Williams's musical themes become part of our shared culture in the United States and beyond, the music of *Star Wars* became a touchstone that would be musically referenced, reinterpreted, and transformed. This essay surveys some of these musical echoes heard beyond the galaxy far, far away.

On a personal note, I was the perfect age growing up in the United States in the late 1970s and early 1980s when *Star Wars* and other space-themed music, merchandise, and video games seemed to be everywhere. Like many kids, I collected *Star Wars* figures and boogied to disco versions of Williams's music. At the time, I thought it was normal and that everyone had a childhood filled with lightsabers, spaceships, and robots. And as a result, I associated the *Star Wars* phenomenon with being a kid. Later in high school, I realized just how much *Star Wars* had become part of our greater social consciousness after witnessing the famous stolen-car scene in John Hughes's movie *Ferris Bueller's Day Off* (1986). With no references or markers to *Star Wars* or anything space-related before, during, or after the scene, the main musical theme to *Star Wars* is heard as Cameron's father's limited-edition 1961 Ferrari GT California flies over a hill piloted by the two garage attendants to whom Ferris and Cameron had entrusted the car earlier. The underscoring of the freedom the two men felt with the music of *Star Wars* was one of the funniest moments in movie history that I have ever witnessed as a fifteen-year-old or since. The scene from *Ferris Bueller's Day Off* has become legendary among many Gen

Xers. But the fact that the *Star Wars* theme had completely transcended its original context is a testament to the power of the film and, more specifically, Williams's music.

This essay will trace the many echoes heard beyond the official *Star Wars* universe. The music of the films (1977–2005), the television specials *The Star Wars Holiday Special* (1978), *Caravan of Courage: An Ewok Adventure* (1984) and *Ewoks: The Battle for Endor* (1985), the television series *Star Wars: The Clone Wars* (2008–2014) and *Star Wars Rebels* (2014–), and the many video games based on the *Star Wars* franchise are not the main focus of this survey. Rather, the music beyond the official *Star Wars* universe is worthy of examination because we can begin to see and hear the extent of the reach of *Star Wars* and its music beyond the galaxy far, far away. And in doing so, we may better understand how the *Star Wars* universe has become part of our shared culture.

After combing several articles and performing countless internet searches, I propose to categorize the many echoes of Williams's music beyond the original *Star Wars* galaxy into eight strains: disco/electronic echoes, jazz echoes, rock/pop echoes, hip-hop/nerdcore echoes, comedic/parodistic echoes, anomalous echoes, movie/television echoes, and ocular echoes. I will explore each chronologically. My goal is not to critique or judge any of these manifestations, interpretations, and transformations. Instead, I hope to share these musical discoveries as a fan and to provide further enjoyment to other fans of the *Star Wars* continuum.

Disco and Electronic Echoes

Without a doubt, the most-remembered and most-loved transformation of the music of *Star Wars* is the disco hit "Star Wars/Cantina Band" from Meco's *Music Inspired by Star Wars and Other Galactic Funk* (1977). The single became a number one on Billboard's pop charts and rose to the top ten in the R&B, dance, and UK charts. This success sparked a phenomenon that Patrick Reed termed "starwarsploitation." Several musicians and producers attempted to repeat the success of the Meco original and thus capitalize on the *Star Wars* craze.[1] Many of the recordings also included transformations of music from other successful space-themed movies and television shows like *Star Trek* (1966–1969), *2001: A Space Odyssey* (1968), *Barbarella* (1968), *Space: 1999* (1975–1977), *Logan's Run* (1976), *Close Encounters of the Third Kind* (1977), among others. So the exploitation was not limited to the *Star Wars* franchise, but the *Star Wars* recordings remain the most memorable.

Meco (the band credited for *Music Inspired by Star Wars and Other Galactic Funk*) is simply one person: producer Domenico "Meco" Monardo. Before recording the album, Monardo had a successful career as a jazz and pop trombonist. In addition to producing records based on other space-themed movies after his initial success, Monardo continued working with music from the *Star Wars* universe. Coinciding with the release of the *Star Wars* sequel *The Empire Strikes Back* (1980), Monardo produced a more rock-influenced record entitled *Meco Plays Music from the Empire Strikes Back* (1980). According to Monardo, the change from disco to rock was intentional:

> 1977 was the height of disco. 1980 was—disco sucks! Simple as that.... There was this big backlash against disco and a return to pop. I didn't want to repeat that sound because I knew the commerciality was gone, so we purposely went for a harder, more rock and roll beat and that's what you hear on the record. More rock and roll guitar, but still with the Meco orchestrations, which was my signature, but with a harder beat to it. And that was cool because Darth Vader's theme was dark, it's thick. A rock and roll beat suits Darth Vader a lot better than a disco beat. So it was really, really nice how it all came together like that [TheForce.net].

In addition, Monardo was able to collaborate with Lucasfilm and incorporate the official sounds of R2-D2, Chewbacca, laser fire, ships, and lightsabers clashing, provided by original *Star Wars* sound designer Ben Burtt.

Later that same year, Monardo continued to capitalize on the *Star Wars* craze with the album *Christmas in the Stars: Star Wars Christmas Album* (1980). As opposed to the earlier disco and rock remakes of Williams's music, Monardo produced original holiday music written by Yale University professor and Broadway composer Maury Yeston, featuring the original voice of C-3PO by Anthony Daniels. Monardo explained how he was able to expand Lucasfilm's involvement, including how Lucas kept an eye on the project from a distance:

> I had made contact earlier with Lucasfilm and so I wrote a letter, nine pages long. It starts: "Dear George, you don't know me personally but you know who I am…" and I reiterated all the things I had done with Star Wars, blah blah blah, and then I said, "You have some characters who are so much like all the Christmas characters that we all love…" I went into great detail, eventually saying, "I think we should do a Christmas album together."
>
> And then I had the one and only telephone conversation I ever had with George Lucas. Whoa man! I was I thrilled … excited … nervous! We spoke for probably an hour and in that hour conversation when you would imagine that Meco would speak for 30 minutes and George would speak for 30 minutes, Meco spoke for 54 minutes and George spoke for maybe 6 minutes. He's the type of guy who listens a lot and doesn't say too much. I remember the one thing he said to me, "These are the things you can do, and these are the things

you cannot do, but the one thing you must not do is kiss the Wookiee." [laughs] So, I was excited, it was going to be fun. They flew in Anthony Daniels from London for a weekend to do his part, but of course he's not a singer so he basically talks the part.

The biggest surprise of all with that album was on the day we were recording the horn section, which was assembled in the recording studio Power Station. Suddenly the door opens up and none other than Darth Vader was standing there! He strides ominously through the door! And oh my God, we were like … well, nobody said a word. We were speechless!! Nobody knew what to do! Here was Darth Vader. And after a minute or so I understood! Lucasfilm had sent Darth Vader to make sure we did everything right…

He stayed around for the strings session and it just was a lot of fun [TheForce. net].

This was one of the very rare occasions that Lucas collaborated with a musical project outside the official *Star Wars* franchise. Nevertheless, through humorous orders (unlike Leia, Monardo could not "kiss the Wookiee") and veiled threats (Darth Vader), Lucas contained the project strictly within bounds. Also worth noting about *Christmas in the Stars*, the song "R2-D2 We Wish You a Merry Christmas" featured the voice of a then unknown singer Jon Bon Jovi (credited as John Bongiovi). The album has no connection with the infamous *Star Wars Holiday Special*.

Monardo also produced an album after the final movie of the original *Star Wars* trilogy *Return of the Jedi* (1983), entitled *Ewok Celebration* (1983). Since Williams did not write as much new music for *Return of the Jedi* as he did for *The Empire Strikes Back*, Monardo only produced Meco versions of "Ewok Celebration," "Lapti Nek" (the song performed by Sy Snootles at Jabba the Hutt's palace), and a medley entitled "Themes from *Star Wars*." The rest of the album featured the musical themes from the movies and television shows *Simon & Simon* (1981–1989), *Superman III* (1983), *The Twilight Zone: The Movie* (1983), and *WarGames* (1983). The two new Williams compositions "Ewok Celebration" and "Lapti Nek" were ideal for Meco's danceable production. "Ewok Celebration" featured a rap in Ewokese by famous Sugar Hill Records producer Duke Bootee.

More recently, Monardo produced *Star Wars Party* (2005). Although released after the prequel trilogy, the album referenced only the original trilogy. The album was a mix of R&B and dance tracks featuring real and imitation dialogue samples from the original trilogy. Most of the music is original, but does include some of the more famous musical themes by Williams. Unlike the previous *Star Wars* endeavors by Monardo, the tracks on *Star Wars Party* lean more toward songs and are not solely instrumentals. Monardo explained:

My current work is not like my older work. There is no "disco beat." It doesn't reek of "Oh my God, it's like 30 years old." It's a contemporary beat…. The *Star Wars* characters are saying lines from the film, but they're saying them to the tempo of the music. And the other thing is, it's not instrumental. Again, they are songs which are about the world of *Star Wars* from which I've chosen a lot of the great, great scenes. So for a younger person who maybe hasn't seen all of the films, this is a way for everybody to remember those scenes and maybe bring a smile to their faces [TheForce.net].

Star Wars Party is more of a montage of musical themes and sound bites from the *Star Wars* universe. But there is more of Monardo and less of Williams on the album. Instead of only transforming Williams's original music, Monardo has created additional music built on the *Star Wars* continuum.

In addition to disco echoes, other electronic echoes were heard reverberating from the *Star Wars* universe. The same year the first *Star Wars* movie was released, the Electric Moog Orchestra released *Music of Star Wars* (1977), performed on Moog synthesizers augmented by electric guitar, drum set, and tympani. The futuristic synthesizers had been all the rage the previous decade with Wendy Carlos's *Switched-On Bach* (1968) and subsequent recordings of Bach translated to the Moog synthesizer. Patrick Gleeson also recorded an entire album based on the *Star Wars* universe entitled *Patrick Gleeson's Star Wars* (1977). But Gleeson obviously included his name in the album's titles to indicate that many of the tracks are significantly lengthened and modified compared to the Williams original score. In addition, Japanese musician Isao Tomita recorded a version of the *Star Wars* theme on his album *Kosmos* (1978) that was very reminiscent of Gershon Kingsley's famous Moog recording "Popcorn" (1969). Tomita's version features a comedic, wordless dialogue by two robots based around Beethoven's Bagatelle No. 25 in A minor (1867), more commonly known as "Für Elise."

More recently, the music of *Star Wars* has been retrofitted and reimagined as 8-bit music (also known as chiptune). Starting in the mid–2000s, several musicians like Beck, The Killers, and No Doubt revisited technology from the 1980s and 1990s to create music reminiscent of the music heard in arcade games and video game consoles. Afterwards, a larger group of musicians began to create entire albums of 8-bit music. In 2014, both Joe Jeremiah and the band 8-Bit Universe created 8-bit versions of Williams's music from *Star Wars*. Given that many *Star Wars* video games created in the 1980s and 1990s contained simple, electronic versions of Williams's elaborate score, there is an irony that Jeremiah and 8-Bit Universe created new "low res" versions of the music of *Star Wars*. On comparison, the newer versions are longer and more complex than their video game predecessors. But that should not be a surprise, given the limited memory space in the older games. The 8-bit tracks tap into the listeners' nostalgia while "personalizing" the iconic score, thus reconstructing *Star Wars*'s music to fit their childhood memories.[2]

Many remember the disco transformation of the music of *Star Wars*, as it was ubiquitous in the late 1970s and early 1980s. In addition, the Electric Moog Orchestra, Gleeson, and Tomita took electronic transformation further and cleverly used synthetic sounds to recast Williams's music into the future. Jeremiah and 8-bit Universe paradoxically returned Williams's music to what many fans would have remembered while playing *Star Wars* video games in the arcade or at home on consoles at the time of the original trilogy's release. All three waves of disco or electronic echoes play upon *Star Wars*'s distinct aural universe. For listeners, the shared collective experience from the films remains: regardless of the music's transformation, they are still *Star Wars*, which strengthens the bonds between listeners, producers, and the performances.

Jazz Echoes

In many ways an extension of disco and electronic echoes, several jazz musicians reimagined the music of *Star Wars*. Jazz had gone electric in the late 1960s and 1970s with the birth of fusion. Many jazz musicians and their groups (like Miles Davis's bands, Herbie Hancock, John McLaughlin's Mahavishnu Orchestra, Chick Corea's Return to Forever, Weather Report, and others) used current electronic instruments and funk elements. So by 1977, such electronic sounds were the norm and *Star Wars* was ideal material.

Several jazz musicians included a solitary *Star Wars* selection on their albums to capitalize on the "starwarsploitation" phenomenon. Maynard Ferguson recorded his version of "Star Wars (Main Title)" on his album *New Vintage* (1977). Richard "Groove" Holmes ingeniously fused two of Williams's most famous themes into one track entitled "Themes from Star Wars and Close Encounters of the Third Kind" on his album *Star Wars / Close Encounters* (1977). And more recently (and coinciding with the third and final *Star Wars* prequel film), Chris Walden recorded a big band version of "Star Wars (Main Title)" on his Hollywood-inspired album *Home of My Heart* (2005) that relied more on swing and African rhythms rather than funky rhythms and instruments.

But a few jazz musicians recorded more than one track and even entire albums based on *Star Wars*. Don Ellis included "Star Wars (Main Title)" and

"Princess Leia's Theme" on his funky big band album *Music from Other Galaxies and Planets* (1977), along with other cosmic-inspired explorations like "Orion's Sword," "Pegasus," "Ursa," and "Vulcan." David Matthews recorded "Star Wars (Main Title)" and "Princess Leia's Theme" on his electronic album *Dune* (1977) that also included a four-movement suite based on Frank Herbert's *Dune* book series (1965–1985), music from the science fiction movie *Silent Running* (1972), and David Bowie's "Space Oddity" (1969).

After the initial success of *Star Wars*, at least three more jazz musicians made *Star Wars*-dedicated albums. The same year that *The Empire Strikes Back* was released, Ron Carter recorded *Empire Jazz* (1980), which boasted an album cover depicting Darth Vader in the audience of a jazz club listening to a quartet featuring Chewbacca on piano, C-3PO on bass, R2-D2 on drums, and a stormtrooper on saxophone. The recording featured more traditional jazz combo arrangements of Williams's "The Imperial March (Darth Vader's Theme)," "The Asteroid Field," "Han Solo and the Princess (Love Theme)," "Lando's Palace," and "Yoda's Theme." The recording also featured many jazz legends, including Billy Cobham, Jon Faddis, Hubert Laws, and Frank Wess. In traditional jazz combo form, the melody of each piece is stated and then the soloists improvise during the middle section before restating the melodic theme, with either straight ahead swing or Latin accompaniment instead of a funky backbeat. Under Carter's direction, Williams's music provided multiple avenues for virtuosic flights of fantasy for these jazz legends.

Coinciding with the release of the special editions of the original trilogy and the twentieth anniversary of the first *Star Wars* film, Terry Trotter recorded *Sketches on Star Wars* (1997), featuring piano trio arrangements from all of the movies of the original trilogy. Though without horns, the arrangements are similar in spirit to Carter's jazz combo arrangements. But Trotter has the added advantage of *Return of the Jedi* for inspiration and therefore includes the quirky "Ewok Celebration" and the down low "Jabba The Blues (Han Solo at the Court of Jabba the Hutt)." The album concludes with a haunting ballad entitled "May the Force Be with You."

More recently, organist Andrew Allen released the album *Live! From the Cantina: A Star Wars Jazz Tribute* (2015). The album reimagines the music of *Star Wars* in mostly an organ trio setting with electric bass and drums, plus a guest saxophonist on a few tracks. Allen's recording is easily the most adventurous of all the jazz echoes. Famous melodies are altered in very exciting ways. For example, "Princess Leia's Theme" is not presented traditionally as a ballad, but rather as an up-tempo vehicle for high-powered improvisation. "Parade of the Ewoks" is performed in a haunting, odd meter. And "Duel of the Fates" closes the album as a call to prayer that quickly breaks down into a breakbeat groove with solo sections for both the bass player and drummer. Allen has taken the possibilities of *Star Wars* and jazz into a more nontraditional direction.

Jazz musicians picked up where disco/electronic echoes left off, further funkifying and electronifying the music of *Star Wars*. But some jazz musicians returned to more traditional modes of expression in jazz. Both the funky/electric and the swing/Latin recordings by jazz musicians further emphasize the strength and malleability of Williams's compositions.

Rock and Pop Echoes

It was only a matter of time before kids raised on *Star Wars* movies in the 1970s and 1980s would start rock bands and the *Star Wars* universe would appear in their music in some shape or form. One of the earliest manifestations was "Chewbacca" by the band Supernova, featured in Kevin Smith's debut *Clerks* (1994). The mostly instrumental song is a love letter to the universe's most famous Wookiee, complete with growls. The song is included in *Clerks* at a crucial moment as main characters Dante Hicks and Randal Graves discuss the ethics of the destruction of the Death Star at the end of *Return of the Jedi,* as many innocent contractors were killed on the uncompleted battle station. The use of Supernova's homage to Chewbacca underscores Gen Xers' obsession with the culture of their childhood. Smith continued to refer to *Star Wars* in other films, most notably in *Jay and Silent Bob Strike Back* (2001), which (along with the movie's referential title) included appearances by *Star Wars* actors Carrie Fisher and Mark Hamill. In that same year, guitar legend (and sometime Guns N' Roses member) Buckethead included a rendition of "Star Wars (Main Title)" on his album *Giant Robot* (1994).

Homage to the *Star Wars* universe by rock bands would become more frequent during the end of the 1990s. The band ash included the scream of a TIE fighter to open their album *1977* (1996), entitled after the year of the first *Star Wars* film. Their promotional single "Girls from Mars" (1995) also featured a raucous, guitar-driven version of "Cantina Band" as a bonus track. The band Blink-182 recorded "A New Hope" on their album *Dude Ranch* (1997), which told the story of a boy falling asleep and dreaming of dating Princess Leia, only to wake up alone the next morning. The nostalgia for the original trilogy continued in the song "Goodnight" (1999) by Coheed and Cambria (at the time known as Shabütie), which told the tale of getting together as kids and playing with *Star Wars* toys. Another example (though the song is not originally about *Star Wars*) is the video for Salacious Crumb's

"The Ultimate Song" (1998), which depicts karaoke night at Mos Eisley. And as final testament to the intersection of rock music and the *Star Wars* universe in the late-1990s, famous *Star Wars* artist Hugh Fleming created the *Star Wars Rocks!* poster (1998) for The *Star Wars* Fan Club, which depicted a rock band with Chewbacca on drums, Darth Vader on bass, C-3PO and R2-D2 on keyboards, Han Solo and Luke Skywalker on guitar, and Princess Leia as the lead singer on stage in front of an audience.

The 2000s featured more rock and pop echoes, possibly fueled by the prequel trilogy. The ska band The Taj Motel Trio paid homage to the Dark Lord with "Vader" (2000), one of the first rock or pop echoes to reference the prequel films. The song tells the tale of the evolution of Anakin Skywalker. The comic video for the song featured a shirtless Vader dancing around a pool with a lightsaber. And an entire compilation of *Star Wars*-themed songs by punk bands was released, appropriately entitled *A Punk Rock Tribute to Star Wars* (2000).

The 80s-centric band Radio Star recorded two songs with *Star Wars* references on their album *1.21 Jigowatts* (2003), its title a nod to the iconic movie *Back to the Future* (1985). The song "80's Girlfriend" depicts the pleading and struggles involved in courting Princess Leia. The next song on the album, "Jedi Princess," tells the story of the denial and self doubt that may result in finally winning the affections of someone like Leia.

But one of the most surreal rock or pop echoes was the band Gnarles Barkley's performance at the MTV Film Awards in 2006. Before the band performed, lead singer CeeLo Green walked onstage dressed as Darth Vader accompanied by Vader's famous breathing. During the performance of their song "Crazy" (which contained no references to the *Star Wars* universe), members performed dressed as imperial officers, Jango Fett, a non-descript Jedi knight, stormtroopers, and X-wing fighter pilots, while Chewbacca played drums.

Two more rock or pop echoes are worth noting. The Dutch symphonic metal band Epica recorded "The Imperial March" as part of their live album *The Classical Conspiracy* (2009), which included other classical/metal fusions plus original material. And the singer-songwriter Ryan Adams recorded an original song entitled "Star Wars" (2010) that detailed his desire for someone who loves ninjas, wizards, and *Star Wars* like he does.

Finally, as an epilogue to proper rock and pop echoes, Wilco released their latest album as a surprise and for free on the internet. In addition, the album was simply titled *Star Wars* (2015) and featured the painting of a white cat as its album artwork. Wilco's leader Jeff Tweedy explained the decision of the title and artwork:

That painting of that cat hangs in the kitchen at the [Wilco] loft, and every day I'd look at it and go, "You know, that should just be the album cover." Then I stared thinking about the phrase "Star Wars" recontextualized against that painting—it was beautiful and jarring. The album had nothing to do with *Star Wars*. It just makes me feel good [32].

Tweedy admitted he was unaware that a new *Star Wars* movie was soon to be released, until his lawyer alerted him and advised against the use of the *Star Wars* name as it was protected by a trademark. Tweedy obviously ignored his lawyer's advice. But the use of the title and Tweedy's good feelings toward the title are yet again another testament to the staying power of the *Star Wars* universe.

The above rock and pop echoes are just a few examples. Except possibly the Gnarls Barkley performance on MTV, the above-mentioned echoes are not part of the more-dominant culture in the United States. Nevertheless, their presence begins to show the extent to which *Star Wars* has become part of our shared culture. While some performances may have been simple jests, each new interpretation demonstrates the fluidity of Lucas's universe as artists leave their personal stamps on the product. If music is a global conversation, then *Star Wars* heightens the dialogue, as artists and audiences understand the re-imagined characters and sounds. Interacting through the same source material, producers and listeners share a coded communication beyond the mere surface music.

Hip-Hop and Nerdcore Echoes

Star Wars has frequently been part of hip-hop for decades, which has been written about elsewhere.[3] In addition to everyone from LL Cool J to the Wu-Tang Clan to Eminem constructing rhymes based on *Star Wars*, Cibo Matto rapped about meeting Obi-Wan Kenobi in "Sci-Fi Wasabi" (1999) and Nas warned us about violence in the street in his "Star Wars" (2004), taking the "wars" to urban decay. Nerdcore has also unsurprisingly included lyrics based on the *Star Wars* universe. As the name suggests, these musicians identify as nerds and draw heavily upon hip-hop culture. Although Lucas had maintained a strict control with Mondaro's early arrangements, the proliferation of technology has enabled musicians to unofficially take license with Williams's music and the iconic special effects. *Star Wars*'s "democratic" diffusion has allowed the franchise to spread into multiple music genres beyond Lucas's grasp (or even his knowledge).

The band 2 Skinnee J's recorded a trio of songs that were based on *Star*

Wars references: "Mindtrick" (1995), "Irrestible Force" (1997), and "Friends Don't Let Friends Listen to Rap Metal" (2003). In addition to quotes and allusions to dialogue from the *Star Wars* films, the songs also included samples of Williams's music. But the more famous nerdcore echoes are the songs written by MC Chris (Christopher Brendan Ward's stage name) for each of the bounty hunters in *The Empire Strikes Back* and the vehicles they drive: "Fett's Vette" (2001), "IG 88's '57 Chevy," "Zuckuss' Prius," "Dengar's Dumptruck" (all 2009), and "Bossk on a Segway" (2010). Ward worked on several television shows on Cartoon Network in the early 2000s, and all five songs are founded in humor (as is much of nerdcore), but Ward's recordings are legitimate. Ward did not quote any of Williams's music in the recordings. But in addition to the characters from *Star Wars* universe, he uses fragments of dialogue and *Star Wars* vocabulary. An examination of hip-hop and nerdcore echoes would not be complete without MC Frontalot's "Yellow Lasers" from his album *Nerdcore Rising* (2005), which tells the satirical tale of an encounter between two *Star Wars* fans at a convention gone horribly wrong. Though self-identifying more as rap than nerdcore (and leaning more toward punk ska bands like No Doubt or Sublime), the single *Star Wars Toys* (2015) by Norwegian group Subway Safari depicts the singer reminiscing about the bitterness and violation he felt the day his mother threw away his "useless" toys, a childhood tragedy to which more than one fan could relate.

2 Skinnee J's, MC Chris, MC Frontalot, and Subway Safari all have genuine love for the *Star Wars* universe. All four use *Star Wars* references as a signifier of the nerdiness. But a non-humorous fusion of hip-hop and nerd culture is different from the previous disco or rock/pop manifestations. Rather than portray a straight mixing of "geeks" with mainstream culture through *Star Wars*, these musicians are serious fans. This is not exploitation per se, but rather identification: negotiation of identity in the social milieu through *Star Wars*. Loving *Star Wars* is part of who they are, where they come from, and the music serves as a conduit for listeners to identify with.

Comedic and Parodistic Echoes

The longest strain and the most frequently heard echoes from the galaxy far, far away are the reverberations that are intended to be humorous and evoke laughter. These comedic and parodistic echoes have sounded for decades since the beginning of the *Star Wars* franchise. The Rebel Force Band's *Living in These Star Wars* (1977) may have contained some serious attempts at soft rock and some ballads in the midst of the countless disco recordings. But songs with titles like "Don't Fall in Love with an Android" and "A Respirator for Darth Vader" prevents any serious consideration of the album. Listening to the album as a humorous endeavor, the album quickly becomes a novelty.

Another humorous song, "Bertha Butt Encounters Vader" (1978) by Jimmy Castor, depicts the continuing story of Castor's recurring character Bertha Butt. Known for her dance moves, Bertha Butt has appeared in Castor's songs since 1972, and in this latest incarnation, Bertha Butt made Vader and other members of the galaxy dance and scream.

But the most famous comedic and parodistic echoes are undeniably "Weird Al" Yankovic's contributions: "Yoda" (1985) and "The Saga Begins" (1999). Based on the Kinks' "Lola" (1970), "Yoda" tells the story of Luke Skywalker meeting and training with master Yoda. The ode to Luke's teacher is still performed by Yankovic as the final song of his encore during live performances. During the encore before "Yoda," Yankovic performs "The Saga Begins," which summarizes *Episode I: The Phantom Menace* (1999) and is based on Don McLean's epic "American Pie" (1971). During both songs, Yankovic and the members of his band perform dressed as a Jedi knights and accompanied by a dancing Darth Vader and stormtroopers (Yankovic 2000 and 2011). In true Yankovic form, both songs and their performances are as much a comedic endeavor as a love letter to the entire *Star Wars* universe.

Since the turn of the twenty-first century there have been a handful of jazz/Latin/lounge comedic echoes based on *Star Wars*. The Evil Genius Orchestra recorded *Cocktails in the Cantina* (1999) full of cheesy renditions of Williams's music, complete with finger snaps. And The Swingtips and Richard Cheese each recorded additional lounge versions of "Cantina Band" (2000) and "The Imperial March" (2007), respectively. But some of the most unexpected comedic echoes came from the Brobdingnagian Bards and their "Jedi Drinking Song" (2005) and "Jedi Drinking Song Prequel" (2008). Their Celtic drinking songs are well crafted and would be ideal for any over-21 *Star Wars* party.

One of the most creative comedic echoes was Moosebutter's four-part, a cappella "Star Wars" (2002) which told the original *Star Wars* story using musical themes Williams wrote for *Close Encounters of the Third Kind, E.T.: The Extra-Terrestrial* (1982), *Jaws* (1975), *Jurassic Park* (1993), *Raiders of the Lost Ark* (1981), and *Superman* (1978). The song ends praising Williams. Corey Vidal would become an internet sensation with his version, entitled "Star Wars (John Williams Is the Man)," in which he recorded all four parts himself.

After the release of the prequel trilogy, the number of comedic and parodistic echoes increased. For example, the band King released "She's into Star Wars" (2005), which depicts the virtues of dating a woman who appreciates

Star Wars and even knows all the lingo. The band Hot Waffles (consisting of brothers Chris and Tim Waffle) recorded possibly the first critical (though obviously satirical) song about *Star Wars,* entitled "George Lucas Raped Our Childhood" (2005). The song complained that the original trilogy was desecrated when altered and released as a special edition in 1997. And the content of the prequel trilogy caused further trauma to the previously devout fans. In addition, a live performance of Wesley Willis's song "Jar Jar Binks" surfaced on the *Funny or Die* website in 2009, six years after the singer's death. Willis was known for his short songs about popular culture. But this ode to one of the most unpopular characters in the *Star Wars* universe clearly embodies how many fans felt about *The Phantom Menace* sidekick. In contrast a few years later, Marc with a C released the nostalgic "Chicken Pox & Star Wars Guys" (2009), which tells the tale of a kid waiting to get over his chicken pox so he can go back outside and play with his *Star Wars* toys again. UFO Phil penned the song "Dear George Lucas" (2011), which satirically stated that the prequel trilogy was so wonderful that Lucas should make another movie between the prequels and the original trilogy entitled *Star Wars 3.5,* detailing the story of Luke Skywalker as he grows up from a baby. UFO Phil offered to write the storyline, which could include Luke levitating out of his crib, his issues concerning teething, and his diapers stinking like the Dark Side.

On their album *Ramming Speed* (2009), the band Sci-Fried included several songs with references to *Star Wars.* One could consider Sci-Fried the progeny of "Weird Al" Yankovic, as they take songs by famous bands and musicians and give them new, humorous lyrics. For example, "Join the Empire" is a parody of Suicidal Tendencies's "Join the Army" (1987). "Tatooine" is a parody of Eric Clapton's "Cocaine" (1977). "Land Speeder" is a parody of War's "Low Rider" (1975). And "Star Wars Idiot" is a parody of Green Day's "American Idiot" (2004). A few years later, Sci-Fried joined forces with Marc with a C and released "Star Wars Christmas" (2012), which depicts a holiday season saved by Yoda and other Jedi Knights from the clutches of the Empire. All of Sci-Fried's parodies are both comedic and reverential to the *Star Wars* universe.

Comedic echoes continued to resonate as the production team Teddie Films released several parodies as music videos. Their first video "Ke$ha Tik Tok Star Wars Spoof" (2010) was an entry to a contest to win a shopping spree with the Ke$ha. The members of Teddie Films made a video for her song "Tik Tok" (2010) featuring several *Star Wars* characters. Although the production team did not win the contest, they continued with "Primeday" (2011), a parody of Rebecca Black's "Friday" (2011) also featuring *Stars Wars* characters plus rewritten words about the Rebellion's adventures. And finally, the production team created its most famous video "The Star Wars I Used to Know" (2012) based on Gotye's "Somebody I Used to Know" (2011). Not only did the video feature *Star Wars* characters, the parody also incorporated the unique body paint and wallpaper techniques seen in the original. Similar to "George Lucas Raped My Childhood," "The Star Wars I Used to Know" was very critical of Lucas's revisions to the original trilogy and the content of the prequel trilogy.

In recent years, many musicians have continued to pay homage to *Star Wars*. The classical musicians known as The Piano Guys created an internet sensation with "Cello Wars" (2012). The comedic video depicted a Jedi and Sith cellist performing and fighting with lightsabers as bows. The two are interrupted by Darth Vader performing "Cantina Band" on an accordion. Luckily, the Jedi and Sith cellists use the Force to vanquish Vader and continue with their performance and duel. "Cello Wars" featured music from both the original and prequel trilogies. Jack Black's band Tenacious D recorded "Deth Starr" (2012), which told the story of how a Death Star would save humanity from self-destruction. For Black, the Death Star would transport humanity into space where everyone could escape natural disasters and overpopulation. But the salvation would only be temporary: in order to survive, multiple Death Stars would have to be created that, like a chain reaction, would then have to find new resources on other planets to exploit. The Tenacious D song is a not-so-subtle comment on humanity's abuse of technology and the environment. Neko Chase included "These Aren't the Droids" on the OneKid OneWorld benefit compilation *2776* (2014), which critiqued that the future was designed by teenage guys and felt more like a Comic Con that does not cater to female needs and wishes.

Finally, there are not one, but two different creations entitled *Star Wars: The Musical.* In 1999, Timothy Edward Smith and Hunter Nolen created a full-fledged musical based on the story and some of the music of the original *Star Wars* trilogy. In the Broadway tradition, the music contains some of the most conventional humor, camp, and vital clichés of musicals, like comedic case music, overly romantic ballads, and multiple characters singing simultaneously about different topics or issues. For example in the song "Do You Speak Bocce?" when Luke's uncle Owen is shopping for droids from the Jawas, Owen, Aunt Beru, Luke, and C-3PO each sing a section that then culminates in a climax where all four characters are singing interwoven parts, reminiscent of musicals like *Les Misérables* (1980). On their website, Smith and Nolen have carefully taken stills from the first *Star* Wars film and synchronized them combined with scrolling and close-ups to construct a compelling version of their musical.

In 2014, film composer George Shaw created a music video also entitled *Star Wars: The Musical* (with "the musical" written in the famous Disney font) that depicted *Star Wars* as a Disney animated musical. Shaw brilliantly combined Williams's music with musical themes and references from Disney films, like *Pinocchio* (1940), *Peter Pan* (1953), *Little Mermaid* (1989), *Beauty and the Beast* (1991), *Aladdin* (1992), *Lion King* (1994), and *Mulan* (1998). He admitted the creation of the musical was inspired by Disney's acquisition of *Star Wars* in 2012 (Shaw, "Star Wars Force Awakens Recording Session"). Throughout the video, there are several nods to The Mouse and the greater Disney empire. For example, the double sunset on Tatooine is now a triple sunset in the shape of the iconic Mickey Mouse ears and head. Wall-E makes a cameo. And in the climactic finale, Han Solo requests, "Please buy more toys...," Obi-Wan Kenobi adds "...and DVDs...," Luke sings "...so Disney can...," Princes Leia continues with "make more movies...," and the entire *Star Wars* cast (plus several Disney princesses) sings "...for you and me," all in a not-so-subtle jab at the commercialism of Disney's acquisition of *Star Wars*.

Comedic and parodistic echoes have arrived as satirical, critical, reverent, and irreverent manifestations. This is again a testament to the story and music of *Star Wars*'s presence in American culture. And the fact that comedic and parodistic echoes are more frequent than other strains illuminates that *Star Wars* and its music are loved not only as a franchise, but also as something that can bring happiness beyond the original films, while critiquing the marketplace and culture which allowed it to blossom.

Anomalous Echoes

While researching the echoes of the music from a galaxy far, far away, there were several recordings that did not fall neatly into any of the above five strains and are therefore anomalies. For example, John Rose made a solo organ recording of the original *Star Wars* films' music in 1977. Rico Rodriguez recorded a ska version of "Star Wars (Main Title)" on his *Man From Wareika* (1977).

In addition, several musicians recorded music that was obviously connected to the starwarsploitation of the late 1970s, but did not include Williams's music. For example, the band War's title track to their album *Galaxy* (1977) is obviously a result of the space craze at the time. Sarah Brightman (who would later be associated with Andrew Lloyd Webber) recorded the single "I Lost My Heart to a Starship Trooper" (1978), which included an accompanying video featuring futuristic dancers, references to droids, and a melodic fragment from *Close Encounters of the Third Kind*. A man who defies category, Lawrence Welk, even recorded "Star Wars (Main Title)" as part of his album *Live at Lake Tahoe* (1979). The band Jefferson Starship released "Light the Sky on Fire," featured in *The Star Wars Holiday Special* and on their greatest hits compilation *Gold* (1979). Country singer Tim Hall recorded "May the Force Be with You Always" (1977) and James Brown/George Clinton alumnus Bootsy Collins recorded "May the Force Be with You" (1978), neither of which contained references or melodic content from *Star Wars*. Amidst the excitement of upcoming *Star Wars* movies, the band Jamiroquai released "Use the Force" (1996). And there is an all-ukulele compilation of *Star Wars* music entitled *Ukulele Force: Star Wars Best Covers* (2005). When summarizing the last three hundred years of music, pianist Ingolf Wunder recorded "Star Wars (Main Title)" on his album *300* (2012), including Williams among some of greatest composers of all time like Chopin, Debussy, Liszt, Mozart, Rachmaninov, and Scarlatti. Finally and more recently, Williams's music has been converted into lullabies by Baby Wars on *Star Wars Lullaby Version* (2015), performed on toy pianos, chimes, and synthesizers.

The above recordings may not fit neatly into the previous categories, but they all deserve consideration. In addition to making us dance, swing, rock out, and laugh, the *Star Wars* universe has leaked into less direct and more obscure areas of our culture.

Movie and Television Echoes

Several movies have been made about the *Star Wars* films. There are documentaries about the films and its surrounding culture, like *From Star Wars to Jedi: The Making of a Saga* (1983), *Jedi Junkies* (2010), *The People vs. George Lucas* (2011), and *Plastic Galaxy: The Story of Star Wars Toys* (2014), among others. Several fictional films have been released, like *George Lucas in Love* (1999) and *Fanboys* (2009). Additionally, countless fan films have been made, most notably *Stuck on Star Wars* (2002) and the series *Chad Vader: Day Shift Manager* (2006–2012). Carrie Fisher's one woman Broadway show *Wishful Drinking* (based on the 2008 book of the same name) included reminiscences about *Star Wars* and was filmed and broadcast on HBO in 2010. And numerous movies and television shows contain references to the *Star Wars* universe.[4] In addition to the above, a few films and television shows deserve an examination regarding important musical echoes made possible by the galaxy far, far away.

Spaceballs (1987) poked fun at the *Star Wars* universe in an irreverent manner that only Mel Brooks could get away with. The movie includes music by some of the most popular musicians and bands at the time, like Berlin, the Pointer Sisters, and Van Halen, among others. Worth noting, Jon Bon Jovi returns to the *Star Wars* universe seven years after his *Christmas in the Stars* contribution with the inclusion of "Raise Your Hands" (1986) from Bon Jovi's hit album *Slippery When Wet*. The use of popular music of the time punctures the original *Star Wars* esthetic of timelessness.

The television series *Family Guy* featured three episodes dedicated to *Star Wars*: "Blue Harvest" (2007), "Something, Something, Something, Dark Side" (2010), and "It's a Trap!" (2011). All three episodes would later be packaged as DVD and Blu-ray box sets entitled *Laugh It Up, Fuzzball: A Family Guy Trilogy* (2010). *Family Guy* included references to *Star Wars* in previous episodes, but the *Star Wars* episodes are retellings of each of the original trilogy films. Music has always played a huge part in *Family Guy* and the *Star Wars* episodes are no exception. In "Blue Harvest" (which was the working title of *Return of the Jedi*), after looking at the binary sunset Chris (who plays Luke Skywalker) draws attention to Williams and the London Symphony Orchestra (who happen to be performing right next to him) and then asks Williams to perform the funky opening theme to television show *People's Court* (1981–2015). Later, Williams and the entire London Symphony Orchestra are killed along with Uncle Owen and Aunt Beru and Chris laments that the soundtrack has to be finished by Danny Elfman. The Mos Eisley scene is mocked when it turns out that the Cantina Band only knows one song and plays it over and over. And before he says goodbye to Chris for the last time, Herbert (Obi-Wan) sings "(I've Had) The Time of my Life" from *Dirty Dancing* (1987), complete with dancing stormtroopers and choreography from the final scene of the iconic 1980s film. In "Something, Something, Something, Dark Side," the crew of the *Millennium Falcon* encounter The Beatles when Peter (Han Solo) says to Princess Leia (Lois) that the option of going into an asteroid field is better than going to the Strawberry Fields. And during his torture scene, Peter is forced to listen Paula Cole's hit "Where Have All the Cowboys Gone?" (1997). In "It's a Trap!" there is an additional jab at 90s popular music with a VH1 special to singers of the era entitled "Why They All Needed to Turn Every Vowel into the Letter 'A.'" These are just a few of the musical moments in the *Family Guy* tributes to *Star Wars*.

The television series *Robot Chicken* also dedicated three episodes to *Star Wars* entitled appropriately "Star Wars Episode I" (2007), "Star Wars Episode II" (2008), and "Star Wars Episode III" (2010). Each episode consisted of several shorts featuring *Star Wars* characters from both trilogies. Primus bassist

Les Claypool, who wrote the original theme music for *Robot Chicken*, created a special *Star Wars* theme based on the famous Williams theme, but in the style of the original *Robot Chicken* theme. In a segment from the first episode, Lobot from Cloud City dances as he listens to a disco version of the *Star Wars* theme on his cybernetic headgear. There is also a commercial for a greatest hits album by Max Rebo (who performed for Jabba the Hutt with Sy Snootles), which features a duet with 'N Sync's Joey Fatone entitled "Neither of Us Is an Elephant" plus other blue and elephant-themed songs. The first episode concludes with a performance of *Empire on Ice*, which features all the major characters from *The Empire Strikes Back* in ice skates and singing their dialogue. In the second episode, the original lyrics to the Cantina Band's song are rejected for an Admiral Akbar Cereal commercial and the band decides it is better to leave the song as an instrumental. And in the third episode, The Emperor explains to Darth Vader what the first 65 orders before the famed Order 66 to kill all the Jedi to the tune of "Turkey in the Straw," complete with straw hat and a violin. The number of musical moments is not as many as in *Family Guy*, but these (and a few others) are too hilarious to ignore.

Finally, a recent episode of *Phineas and Ferb* was based on *Star Wars* and simply entitled "Phineas and Ferb: Star Wars" (2014). Before the famous opening crawl, the additional title reads "Episode IVa: May the Ferb Be with You." The *Phineas and Ferb* episode is different from *Family Guy* and *Robot Chicken* in that instead of simply creating material based on *Star Wars*, Phineas, Ferb, and others play characters within the *Star Wars* universe whose lives happen to intersect with the original *Star Wars* film storyline. Characters from the original *Star Wars* appear as themselves while Phineas, Ferb, Candace, Perry, and Dr. Doofenschmirtz are part of another story. But most of the *Phineas and Ferb* characters are re-imagined as characters appropriate to the *Star Wars* universe. Phineas and Ferb are residents of Tatooine similar to Luke. Candace is a stormtrooper. Dr. Doofenschmirtz is a Darth Vader–like villain. Perry is himself, but is also a secret agent who stole the plans of the Death Star and gave them to Princess Leia. During the interwoven story, the characters sing five original songs, making the episode a musical. Instead of being just a parody, the *Phineas and Ferb* episode adds new story to the *Star Wars* canon in its own way.

Spaceballs and the three television shows above are again more proof that *Star Wars* continues to be shared across our culture as both fan creations and in mainstream media. The acquisition of the *Star Wars* franchise by Disney solidifies *Star Wars* as part of our culture for now and in the future. But the incorporation of *Star Wars* into other franchises is further proof of the strength and malleability of *Star Wars*.

Ocular Echoes

The echoes of *Star Wars* are so strong that they must also include another strain, musical echoes that are embedded in films and videos that are void of Williams's original music. These ocular echoes can be heard despite the absence of the original *Star Wars* score.

For example, the video production team the Auralnauts created "Star Wars Minus Williams—Throne Room" (2014). During the famous throne room footage of Luke, Han, Chewbacca, and Leia at the end of the first *Star Wars* film, Williams's music has been replaced by nothing but background noise, Luke and Han's footsteps, Chewbacca's screams, and a few bleeps from a repaired R2-D2. The video is part of a greater internet phenomenon known as "shreds" where humorous videos are created by replacing the soundtrack of a musical performance or famous movie scene with an alternate soundtrack. The Auralnauts explain that there is a purpose to their altered videos:

> The Auralnauts are like graffiti artists, only we use sound instead of spray paint in order to deface things that other people made. When we watch movies, sometimes things will happen that don't make sense to us, like a half finished robot being turned on while still missing most of his face.
> When that happens, we stop paying attention to the movie and come up with a story that makes us feel better, like said robot being irreparably traumatized by the experience. Sometimes these jokes are more interesting to us than the stories themselves, and we feel compelled to share them ["About"].

This phenomenon is relevant to this essay, as it is the omission of the *Star Wars* echoes that makes the video possible. And the Auralnauts are obviously creating the videos as homage to something they love, while, like "graffiti artists," possibly critiquing the original creation.

Several *Star Wars* fans have taken footage from the films and other branches of the franchise to create entries into what was the Star Wars Music Video Festival (2011 and 2012) hosted by GalacticBinder.com. Several categories were created, including Best Use of a Song, Best Use of an Instrumental Song, Best Editing, Best Original Trilogy Video, Best Prequel Trilogy Video, Best Clone Wars Video, Best Video Game Video, Fan Favorite Video (strictly voted by the fans), and Best Video. The first year "Star Wars ACDC" featuring "Thunderstruck" (1990) by AC/DC won Best Video, which effectively condenses the first *Star Wars* film to less than five minutes. And the second year "Star Wars Battle Tribute" featuring "Voodoo People (Pendulum Remix)" (2005) by Prodigy won Best Video, which features battle scenes on Endor, Hoth, and outside the second Death Star accompanied by electronica. Every entry is archived on the website. The festival did not continue after 2012. But the festival is just another testament to the importance of music within the *Star Wars* universe.

Probably the earliest occurrence of an ocular echo was Neil Young's film *Rust Never Sleeps* (1979), which promoted the album of the same name released the same year. In the concert film, Young's roadies are dressed as Jawas and known as "road eyes." The Jawas are seen moving over-sized equipment, including towering amplifies and tall microphone stands with huge microphones. Recordings of stage announcements from the legendary Woodstock concert (which Young performed at ten years earlier) underscore the *Star Wars*–inspired choreography between songs. The spectacle, with the Jawas as little more than junk dealers, presents a commentary on the absurdity and over-commercialization of rock 'n' roll in the 1970s.

Other ocular echoes to be considered are the films by Lucas that do not include Williams's music. Coincidently, the echoes from all of the non-Williams films arguably include a "long time ago in a galaxy far, far away..." esthetic, as Lucas never sets a movie or script within the present. All his films take place in the past or future or are without historical context. Lucas's films are never set within the historical context they are created. And the choice of music further emphasizes this phenomenon. For example, the dystopian *THX 1138* (1971) features an eclectic score composed by Argentinean composer Lalo Schifrin that includes futuristic, avant garde sounds, Baroque-inspired choral works, and bossa nova jingles. The nostalgic *American Graffiti* (1973) creates a distant feeling by using some of the most iconic music of 1950s and early 1960s rock and roll, including music by the Beach Boys, Chuck Berry, the Big Bopper, Fats Domino, Bill Haley, and Buddy Holly, among others.

After the original *Star Wars* trilogy, many of the movies Lucas produced or wrote contained a sonic esthetic of temporal distance or contrast. Granted, a large part of 1980s movies and culture contained futuristic elements, but this was obviously a product of the success of such movies like *Star Wars*, the popularity of video games, the arrival of the personal computer, and the revitalization of the U.S. space program. But it was the prevalence of futuristic culture that opened creative avenues in some of Lucas's post-original trilogy films. Best known for his hit "She Blinded Me with Science" (1982), Thomas Dolby created a synthetic and synthesizer-heavy soundtrack of original music for the science fiction comedy *Howard the Duck* (1986). The synthetic sounds of Dolby's songs create an otherworldly contrast to the other jazz and orchestra underscoring heard in the film. The movie concludes with Howard rocking out with Beverly (Lea Thompson) and her band Cherry Bomb, very much like the Ewok celebration at the end of *Return of the Jedi*.

Lucas also collaborated with Michael Jackson on the 3D futuristic short film *Captain EO* (1986), which debuted exclusively at Disney World's Epcot. The film stars Jackson as the captain of a spaceship with a crew of robots and other creatures similar to those found in *Star Wars* flying through space and through a landscape reminiscent of the Death Star. Jackson performs both "We Are Here to Change the World" (which is exclusive to the film) and a shortened version of "Another Part of Me" from *Bad* (1988). For *Willow* (1988), James Horner created a soundtrack inspired by classical composers like Bartók, Grieg, Mozart, and Schumann. And the original music heard in *Radioland Murders* (1994) is reminiscent of the movie's historical context of 1930s radio plays.

Lucas's post-prequel trilogy films continued with anachronistic soundtracks. Appropriate for its setting, the World War II film *Red Tails* (2012) featured an original jazz score by trumpeter Terrence Blanchard, plus a few jazz standards. Though criticized as one long episode of *Glee* (2009–2015) set in a fantasy land, the animated musical *Strange Magic* (2015) includes a mixed soundtrack dominated by covers of classic rock and early rock hits (by musicians and bands like Badfinger, David Bowie, Deep Purple, the Doors, Electric Light Orchestra, the Four Tops, Heart, Whitney Houston, Bob Marley, Robert Palmer, Elvis Presley, and Queen) contrasted by covers of more-current hits (by musicians and bands like Beyoncé, the Black Eyed Peas, Kelly Clarkson, and Lady Gaga). All the above movies contain anachronistic uses of music that create a far, far away feeling that transports audiences to another time and place. Like Williams's original score, Lucas's non-*Star Wars* projects used the music to enhance the escapism from the present, while concurrently playing off facets of American cultural/musicological history.

Finally, *Star Wars: The Clone Wars* (2008–2014) must be examined as one unique ocular echo. Though based on Williams's music, Kevin Kiner's music for *The Clone Wars* is more than a reinterpretation. Kiner teases the famous Williams theme, but quickly veers off into other sonic spaces, using sounds not usually heard in the music of *Star Wars*, like electric guitars, synthesizers, and non-Western instruments. He also uses fragments of Williams's music that are re-engineered harmonically and with the augmented instrumentation evolve into new musical moments. Kiner's music is a perfect parallel to the fact that *The Clone Wars* was created completely with computer animation as opposed to using live action characters mixed with CGI. The "rock" music also parlays into the series's appeal: although not strictly for kids, as a cartoon, the music echoes and updates the Saturday matinee movie experience of Lucas's childhood, bringing the "far away" closer to home.

These ocular echoes (as most of the previously discussed echoes) are evidence of the shared cultural worth of the *Star Wars* universe in the United

States and beyond. Except for *The Clone Wars*, the ocular echoes are the most distant use of *Star Wars* outside of the official franchise. And *The Clone Wars* can be seen as a completion of a greater processorial circle. The *Star Wars* universe that was first introduced in 1977 has become so enmeshed in our shared culture that it can be fractured and redefined without losing its potency.

Conclusion

After exploring and investigating all the echoes generated by the *Star Wars* films and their music, we can see that the use of *Star Wars* in music and other spaces beyond the galaxy far, far away has changed over the years. Initially, starwarsploitation was all the rage in disco, funk, and jazz. Later, musicians who grew up with the films naturally incorporated the movies as subject matter, if not musically. And in addition to the *Star Wars*-themed band names mentioned above, *Star Wars* continues to be an inspiration for many other band names.[5] While the comedic and parodistic echoes remain the most numerous, additional anomalies have manifested over the years outside the musical strains described. The strength of the *Star Wars* franchise is also so strong that echoes from the *Star Wars* universe can be heard and seen in several major movies and television shows. And the ocular echoes are a further testament to the cultural weight of Lucas's franchise, as echoes of *Star Wars* can be heard even in media void of Williams's music. Hopefully, this survey of some of the musical and other echoes emanating from the galaxy far, far away will entertain and delight other fans of the films. And with the coming of the sequel trilogy (2015–2019), more echoes will surely be created.

May we hear the Force, always.

Notes

1. For example, see Bang Bang Robot's "Star Wars (Main Title) / Star-Robot System" (1977), Galaxy 42's "Star Wars (Disco-Theme) / She's Dynamite" (1977), the Planet Robots' *Disco Music Inspired by Star Wars and Other Soul Music* (1977), the Wonderland Singers and Orchestra's *Theme from Star Wars* (1977), A.D.'s "Return of Vader" (1978), the Force's "Star Wars Disco / Funky Hat" (1978), the Galactic Force Band's *Spaced Out Disco* (1978), Geoff Love's *Close Encounters of the Third Kind and Other Disco Galactic Themes* (1978), and Osamu Shoji's *Star Wars* (1978).

2. See Michael Fuchs's and Michael Phillips's essay on fan "reconstructions" in this volume.

3. See Galbraith.

4. For example, *Raiders of the Lost Ark* (1981), *Airplane II: The Sequel* (1982), *E.T.:*

The Extra-Terrestrial (1982), *Back to the Future* (1985), *Cocoon* (1985), *Mallrats* (1995), *Chasing Amy* (1997), *South Park: Bigger, Longer & Uncut* (1999), *Spaced* (1999–2001), *Clerks: The Animated Series* (2000–2001), *Team America: World Police* (2004), *Clerks II* (2006), *Zack and Miri Make a Porno* (2008), and *The Lego Movie* (2014).

    5. For example, AeroSith, Anchorhead, Bossk, DJ Jedi, DJ Yoda, Eisley, Ewok, Hoth, Jedi Mind Tricks, Nerf Herder, and WookieFoot.

Works Cited

A.D. "Return of Vader." T.K. Disco, 1978. 12" single.

Adams, Ryan. "Star Wars." *III/IV.* PAX AM, 2010. CD.

Allen, Andrew. *Live! from the Cantina: A Star Wars Jazz Tribute.* Self-released, 2015. CD.

ash. "Cantina Band." *Girl from Mars.* Infectious, 1995. CD.

_____. *1977.* Infectious, 1996. CD.

Auralnauts. "About: Now We Will Tell You Things." *Auralnauts.* Auralnauts, 2014. Web. 20 Aug. 2015.

_____. "Star Wars Minus Williams—Throne Room." Online video. *Auralnauts.* Auralnauts, 10 Sept. 2014. Web. 20 Aug. 2015.

Baby Wars. *Star Wars Lullaby Version.* Tam-Tam Media, 2015. MP3.

Bang Bang Robot. "Star Wars (Main Title) / Star-Robot System." 20th Century, 1977. 7" single.

Blink-182. "A New Hope." *Dude Ranch.* MCA/Cargo, 1997. CD.

Brightman, Sarah. "I Lost My Heart to a Starship Trooper / Do, Do, Do." Ariola Hansa, 1978. 7" single.

Brobdingnagian Bards. "Jedi Drinking Song." *Brobdingnagian Fairy Tales.* Mage, 2005. CD.

_____. "Jedi Drinking Song Prequel." *Real Men Wear Kilts.* Mage, 2008. CD.

Buckethead. "Star Wars." *Giant Robot.* SONY/CyberOctave, 1994. CD.

Caravan of Courage: An Ewok Adventure. ABC. 25 Nov. 1984. Television.

Carter, Ron. *Empire Jazz.* RSO, 1980. LP.

Case, Neko. "These Aren't the Droids." *2776.* OneKid OneWorld, 2014. CD.

Castor, Jimmy. "Bertha Butt Encounters Vader." *Let It Out.* Drive, 1978. LP.

Chad Vader: Day Shift Manager. Seasons 1, 1.5, 2, 3, and 4. Blame Society Productions, 2006–2012. DVD.

Cheese, Richard. "Darth Vader's 'Imperial March' Theme (Live in the Derby)." *Dick at Nite: Your Favorite TV Themes Loungified!* Coverage, 2007. CD.

Cibo Matto. "Sci-Fi Wasabi." *Stereo * Type A.* Warner Bros., 1999. CD.

Coheed and Cambria [Shabütie]. "Goodnight." *Plan to Take Over the World.* Self-released, 1999. EP.

Collins, Bootsy. "May the Force Be with You." *Bootsy? Player of the Year.* Warner Bros., 1978. LP.

8-Bit Universe. "Star Wars Cantina Theme" and "Star Wars Imperial March." *8-Bit Universe, Vol. 10.* Self-released, 2014. MP3.

_____. "Star Wars (Main Theme)." *8-Bit Universe, Vol. 11.* Self-released, 2014. MP3.

The Electric Moog Orchestra. *Music from Star Wars.* Musicor, 1977. LP.

Ellis, Don. *Music from Other Galaxies and Planets.* Atlantic, 1977. LP.

Epica. "The Imperial March." *The Classical Conspiracy.* Live. Nuclear Blast, 2009. CD.

The Evil Genius Orchestra. *Cocktails in the Cantina.* Arrangements by Carvin Knowles. Oglio, 1999. CD.

Ewoks: The Battle for Endor. ABC. 24 Nov. 1985. Television.

Fanboys. Weinstein, 2009. Film.

Ferguson, Maynard. "Star Wars (Main Title)." *New Vintage*. Columbia, 1977. LP.

Fisher, Carrie. *Wishful Drinking*. New York: Simon & Schuster, 2008. Print.

_____. *Wishful Drinking*. HBO. 12 Dec. 2010. Television.

The Force. "Star Wars Disco / Funky Hat." Splash, 1978. 7″ single.

From Star Wars to Jedi: The Making of a Saga. PBS. 3 Dec. 1983. Television.

The Galactic Force Band. *Spaced Out Disco*. Springboard, 1978. LP.

Galaxy 42. "Star Wars (Disco-Theme) / She's Dynamite." Derby, 1977. 7″ single.

Galbraith, Alex. "Top 15 Star Wars References in Hip-Hop." *HotNewHipHop*. HotNewHipHop, 21 Jan. 2015. Web. 20 Aug. 2015.

George Lucas in Love. MediaTrip, 1999. Film.

Gleeson, Patrick. *Patrick Gleeson's Star Wars*. Mercury, 1977. LP.

Gnarls Barkley. *MTV Film Awards*. MTV. 8 June 2006. Television.

Green, Seth. "Star Wars Episode I." *Robot Chicken*. Cartoon Network/Adult Swim. 17 June 2007. Television.

_____. "Star Wars Episode II." *Robot Chicken*. Cartoon Network/Adult Swim. 16 Nov. 2008. Television.

_____. "Star Wars Episode III." *Robot Chicken*. Cartoon Network/Adult Swim. 19 Dec. 2010. Television.

Hall, Tim. "May the Force Be with You Always." *New Train—Same Rider*. RCA, 1977. LP.

Holmes, Richard "Groove." *Star Wars / Close Encounters*. Versatile, 1977. LP.

Hot Waffles. "George Lucas Raped Our Childhood." *Ready to Laugh? We Don't Care*. Hot Waffles, 2005. CD.

Jamiroquai. "Use the Force." *Travelling Without Moving*. Sony, 1996. CD.

Jedi Junkies. New Video, 2010. Film.

Jefferson Starship. "Light the Sky on Fire." *Gold*. Grunt, 1979. LP.

Jeremiah, Joe. "A-Bit of Star Wars." *A-Bit of 8-Bit: Vol. 3*. Self-released, 2014. MP3.

_____. "A-Bit of Star Wars 2." *A-Bit of 8-Bit: Vol. 5*. Self-released, 2014. MP3.

Kiner, Kevin. *Star Wars: The Clone Wars*. Sony, 2008. CD.

King. *She's into Star Wars*. Microhits, 2005. CD.

Love, Geoff. *Close Encounters of the Third Kind and Other Disco Galactic Themes*. Music for Pleasure, 1978. LP.

Lucas, George. *American Graffiti*. Universal, 1977. Film.

_____. *Captain EO*. With Michael Jackson. Buena Vista, 1986. Film.

_____. *Episode I: The Phantom Menace*. 20th Century Fox, 1999. Film.

_____. *Episode II: Attack of the Clones*. 20th Century Fox, 2002. Film.

_____. *Episode III: Revenge of the Sith*. 20th Century Fox, 2005. Film.

_____. *Episode V: The Empire Strikes Back*. 20th Century Fox, 1980. Film.

_____. *Episode VI: Return of the Jedi*. 20th Century Fox, 1983. Film.

_____. *Howard the Duck*. Universal, 1986. Film.

_____. *Radioland Murders*. Universal, 1994. Film.

_____. *Red Tails*. 20th Century Fox, 2012. Film.

_____. *Star Wars [Episode IV: A New Hope]*. 20th Century Fox, 1977. Film.

_____. *Strange Magic*. Walt Disney, 2015. Film.

_____. *THX 1138*. Warner Bros., 1971. Film.

_____. *Willow*. Metro-Goldwyn-Mayer, 1988. Film.

MacFarlane, Seth. Fox. "Blue Harvest." *Family Guy*. Fox. 23 Sept. 2007. Television.

_____. "It's a Trap!" *Family Guy*. Fox. 22 May 2011. Television.

_____. *Laugh It Up, Fuzzball: The Family Guy Trilogy*. 20th Century Fox, 2010. DVD/Blu-ray.

_____. "Something, Something, Something, Dark Side." *Family Guy*. Fox. 23 May 2010. Television.

Marc with a C. "Chicken Pox & Star Wars Guys." *Losing Salt*. Self-released, 2009. CD.

Matthews, David. *Dune*. CTI, 1977. LP.

MC Chris [Christopher Brendan Ward]. "Bossk on a Segway." *Goes to Hell*. Self-released, 2010. CD.

_____. "Dengar's Dumptruck." *Part Six Part Three*. Self-released, 2009. CD.

_____. "Fett's Vette." *Life's a Bitch and I'm Her Pimp*. Self released, 2001. CD.

_____. "IG-88's '57 Chevy." *Part Six Part One*. Self-released, 2009. CD

_____. "Zuckuss' Prius." *Part Six Part Two*. Self-released, 2009. CD.

MC Frontalot. "Yellow Lasers." *Nerdcore Rising*. Level Up, 2005. CD.

McPadden, Mike. "Cosmic Connections You Probably Never Noticed Between Hard Rock + *Star Wars*." *VH1*. VH1, 25 May 2015. Web. 20 Aug. 2015.

Meco [Domenico Monardo]. *Christmas in the Stars: Star Wars Christmas Album*. RSO, 1980. LP.

_____. *Ewok Celebration*. Arista, 1983. LP.

_____. Interviewed by Shane Turgeon. *TheForce.net*. TheForce.net, May 2005. Web. 20 Aug. 2015.

_____. *Meco Plays Music from Empire Strikes Back*. RSO, 1980. 10" EP.

_____. *Music Inspired by Star Wars and Other Galactic Funk*. Millennium, 1977. LP.

_____. *Star Wars Party [Music Inspired by Star Wars]*. Mecoman, 2005. CD.

Moosebutter. "Star Wars." *see dee*. Moosebutter Music Group, 2002. CD.

Nas. "On The Real / Star Wars." Columbia, 2004. EP.

Newbold, Mark. "*Star Wars*-Inspired Music Guide (Including, Yes, Pipe-Organ Albums)." StarWarswww. Lucasfilm, 20 Mar. 2014. Web. 20 Aug. 2015.

_____. "*Star Wars* Music Guide, Part 2: Ewok 'n' Roll." StarWarswww. Lucasfilm, 1 May 2014. Web. 20 Aug. 2015.

The People vs. George Lucas. Lions Gate, 2011. DVD.

"Phineas and Ferb: Star Wars." *Phineas and Ferb*. Disney Channel. 26 July 2014. Television.

The Piano Guys. "Cello Wars." *The Piano Guys*. Sony/Masterworks, 2012. CD.

The Planet Robots. *Disco Music Inspired by Star Wars and Other Soul Music*. Harmony, 1977. LP.

Plastic Galaxy: The Story of Star Wars Toys. X-Ray Films, 2014. Film.

Radio Star. "80's Girlfriend" and "Jedi Princess." *1.21 Jigowatts*. Nerd Rock, 2003. MP3.

The Rebel Force Band. *Living in These Star Wars*. Bonwhit, 1977. LP.

Reed, Patrick. "Starwarsploitation Sounds: Star Wars On Record, 1977–1979 [Revised and Expanded]." *Depth of Field Magazine*. Depth of Field Magazine, 29 July 2012. Web. 20 Aug. 2015.

Rodriguez, Rico. "Ska Wars." *Man From Wareika*. Blue Note, 1977. LP.

Rose, John. *Star Wars*. Towerhill, 1977. LP.

Salacious Crumb. "The Ultimate Song." *Brainwash*. TWA, 1998. EP.

Sci-Fried. *Ramming Speed*. Self-released, 2009. CD.

_____. "Star Wars Christmas." With Marc with a C. *Free Tracks*. Self-released, 2009. MP3.

Shaw, George. "Star Wars Force Awakens Recording Session with John Williams in LA." *George Shaw Music*. George Shaw Music, 4 June 2015. Web. 20 Aug. 2015.

_____. *Star Wars: The Musical*. Online video. *George Shaw Music*. George Shaw Music, 17 June 2014. Web. 20 Aug. 2015.

Shoji, Osamu. *Star Wars*. Warner Bros., 1978. LP.

Smith, Kevin. *Clerks*. Mirimax, 1994. Film.

_____. *Jay and Silent Bob Strike Back*. Mirimax, 2001. Film.

Smith, Timothy Edward, and Hunter Nolen. *Star Wars: The Musical*. Infauxmedia, 1999. MP3.

Spaceballs. Metro-Goldwyn-Mayer, 1987. Film.

The Star Wars Holiday Special. CBS. 1978. Television.

Star Wars Rebels. Disney XD. 2014–2015. Television.

Star Wars: The Clone Wars. Cartoon Network/Netflix. 2008–2014. Television.

Stuck on Star Wars. Mental Ward Productions, 2002. DVD.

Subway Safari. "Star Wars Toys." Subway Safari, 2015. MP3.

Supernova. "Chewbacca." *Clerks: Music from the Motion Picture.* Columbia/Chaos, 1994. CD.

The Swingtips. "Cantina Band." *Roswell.* Ghost Note, 2000. CD.

The Taj Motel Trio. "Vader." *Feels the Force.* Self-released, 2000. MP3.

Teddie Films. "Ke$ha Tik Tok Star Wars Spoof." Online video. *YouTube.* YouTube, 20 Feb. 2010. Web. 20 Aug. 2015.

_____. "Primeday." Online video. *YouTube.* YouTube, 7 Apr. 2011. Web. 20 Aug. 2015.

_____. "The Star Wars I Used to Know." Online video. *YouTube.* YouTube, 27 June 2012. Web. 20 Aug. 2015.

Tenacious D. "Deth Starr." *Rize of the Fenix.* Columbia, 2012. CD.

Tomita, Isao. "Star Wars (Main Title)." *Kosmos.* RCA, 1978. LP.

2 Skinnee J's [Too Skinnee J's]. "Friends Don't Let Friends Listen to Rap Metal." *Sexy Karate!* Dolphins vs. Unicorns, 2003. CD.

_____. "Irresistible Force." *Sing, Earthboy, Sing!* AJS, 1997. CD.

_____. "Mindtrick." *Return of the New & Improved.* AJS, 1995. CD.

Trotter, Terry. *Sketches on Star Wars.* Varese Sarabande, 1997. CD.

Tweedy, Jeff. "On Anarchy at the Dinner Table, Touring with Dylan, and Why the Hell he named Wilco's album 'Star Wars.'" Interviewed by Patrick Doyle. *Rolling Stone* 27 Aug. 2015: 32. Print.

UFO Phil. "Dear George Lucas." *Gravity Brings Me Down.* Catapult, 2011. MP3.

Various. *A Punk Rock Tribute to Star Wars.* Lame, 2000. 7" single.

_____. *Ukulele Force: Star Wars Best Covers.* Pioneer, 2005. CD.

Vidal, Corey. "Star Wars (John Williams is the Man)." Online video. *YouTube.* YouTube, 27 Oct. 2008. Web. 20 Aug. 2015.

Walden, Chris. "Star Wars." *Home of My Heart.* Origin, 2005. CD.

War. *Galaxy.* MCA, 1977. LP.

Welk, Lawrence. "Star Wars." *Live at Lake Tahoe.* Ranwood, 1979. LP.

Wilco. *Star Wars.* dBpm, 2015. MP3.

Willis, Wesley. "Jar Jar Binks BLUE SCREEN CHALLENGE." Online video. *Funny or Die.* Funny or Die, 2014. Web. 15 Aug. 2015.

Wonderland Singers and Orchestra. *Theme from Star Wars.* Wonderland, 1977. LP.

Wunder, Ingolf. "Star Wars." *300.* Deutsche Grammophon, 2013. CD.

Yankovic, "Weird Al." "The Saga Begins." *Running with Scissors.* Volcano, 1999. CD.

_____. "The Saga Begins" and "Yoda." *"Weird Al" Yankovic Live!* Volcano, 2000. DVD.

_____. "The Saga Begins" and "Yoda." *"Weird Al" Yankovic Live! The Alpocalypse Tour.* Comedy Central, 2011. DVD.

_____. "Yoda." *Dare to be Stupid.* Rock 'n' Roll, 1985. CD.

Young, Neil. *Rust Never Sleeps.* BMG, 1979. Film.

_____. *Rust Never Sleeps.* Reprise, 1979. LP.

The Space Community and the Princess

Reworking the American Space Program's Public Image from "Miss NASA" to Princess Leia

KARIN HILCK

Thirteen-years-old and resigned to bed due to illness, my angry and annoyed self had nothing better to do than watch TV. Of course, there was nothing good on that particular Friday evening in 1999. Between German game shows and crime procedurals, a movie called *Star Wars* seemed like the best option, although it was from the "ancient" 1970s. How good could such an old movie be, my teenage self wondered. Two hours later I had the answer—it was a work of genius! My mind was blown; I had discovered the best movie of all times. When I told my parents about it, I was shocked to learn they already knew the movie and there were more films. So I waited desperately for the next two Fridays and the screenings of *The Empire Strikes Back* and *Return of the Jedi*. Two weeks later I had joined the club of die-hard *Star Wars* fans. Being a "Star Warrior" heavily influenced my decision to write a PhD dissertation in the field of space history. My dissertation project focuses on the interdigitation of technology, military, culture and politics in the United States in the context of the Cold War. Using the American spaceflight program as a unique entry point into the field, the dissertation aims to analyze the exclusion and inclusion of women in the American space community from the 1960s to 1990 as well as the significance of the gender, technological, and political correlations for American social and Cold War history.

I figured the topic of *Star Wars* would sooner or later come up in my research—perhaps as a funny cultural reference or as a public relations opportunity. However, this was not the case. As my research developed, I wondered if the *Star Wars* hype just passed by the entire space community? This question is especially interesting in regard to the female members of the space sector. With Princess Leia, *Star Wars* provided one of the first strong, shrewd, and powerful female characters in science fiction. In the late 1970s, she was a potential cultural icon for women and second wave feminism, particularly for those in the space community or young aspiring female spacefarers.[1] However, this incorporation took place among the space program's attempts to keep relevant with political and social developments. Therefore, this essay highlights NASA's shifting public image to suit the changing times with a focus on the interaction of the space community and *Star Wars* with a special emphasis on female participation and perspectives.

"Huntsville, Endeavor. All hailing frequencies are open": A Star Trek *Context*

While I could not find a single *Star Wars* reference in my research about women in the space sector, I stumbled upon a number of references to *Star Trek* at the National Aeronautics and Space Administration (NASA); conversely, the *Star Trek* television shows and movies feature many references to NASA. Several NASA images, like a picture of the Titan rocket, various satellite images, and Gemini photos, appear in several episodes. In the original series episode "Court Martial," for example, the background of Commodore Stone's office on Starbase 11 featured some NASA shots. The franchise also used NASA technology in their storylines. In the 1979 movie *Star Trek: The Motion Picture*, the crew encounters a machine planet that had developed from NASA's tiny "Voyager" satellite launched in 1977. Sometimes *Star Trek* acknowledged NASA or its astronauts in its end credits, such as those in *Star Trek II: The Wrath of Khan* (1980), or *Star Trek IV: The Voyage Home*'s (1986) opening dedication to the *Challenger* astronauts who died when their space shuttle exploded that year. Other times the *Star Trek* producers named spaceships after astronauts.[2] *Star Trek* even included NASA astronauts in its cast. The first African American woman to fly into space in 1992, Mae Jemison, had a guest role as a transporter officer in *Star Trek: The Next Generation* (Penley 20; Hillebrand). Jemison belongs to a quite sizeable group of NASA employees who consider themselves "Trekkies" and who credit Gene Roddenberry's cultural phenomena as their inspiration in pursuing a career in the space sector (Kevles 130–131; Nichols).[3]

Indeed, *Star Trek* enjoyed a healthy relationship with NASA. NASA employees unofficially named their computers or other space related equipment after beloved characters, dressed up as *Star Trek* characters, and frequently made *Star Trek*-related puns.[4] Jemison, for example, began every shift on the space shuttle mission STS-47 with a variation of *Star Trek*'s communication officer Lt. Uhura's trademark greeting: "Huntsville, Endeavor. All hailing frequencies are open" (Jemison 177). NASA also invoked *Star Trek* in official terms. In 1976, they named the first space shuttle *Enterprise* after a letter writing campaign by Trekkies and invited many of the show's cast members to the inauguration ceremony at the public unveiling at Edwards Air Force Base. They even played the *Star Trek* theme tune at the *Enterprise* premiere to emphasize the fusion of NASA and *Star Trek* (Penley 17; Star Trek's Nichelle). NASA also carried *Star Trek* creator Gene Roddenberry's and Scotty actor James Doohan's ashes into space—twice (White; Penley 17).

In 1976 NASA was looking for new astronauts for the shuttle program. For the first time in the agency's history, they actually wanted women and minorities to apply because NASA badly needed to reconnect to pressing public issues of the American people (Kay 114). For that purpose, NASA Assistant Administrator for Public Affairs John P. Donnelly suggested in 1974, "it may be time for us to go out and get ourselves a black astronaut from the Air Force or Navy…. I think from a public affairs standpoint the announcement of a black astronaut would by far be the most visible means of demonstrating NASA's commitment to EEO [Equal Employment Opportunity]" (Atkinson and Shafritz 137–138). However, NASA did not opt for a "token" minority astronaut but wanted to include women and minorities properly. They started to map out a new gender and minority friendly astronaut program but only a few answered NASA's call. After six months only ninety-three women had actually applied because NASA's reputation as a white, male agency was engrained in people's minds and most eligible women or minorities did not even consider making a bid for an astronaut position. Therefore, NASA had to quicken the interest of women and various minority communities in a more deliberate manner. NASA asked Nichelle Nichols, the actress who played Uhura in *Star Trek*, to do consulting work for them in 1977. Nichols advised NASA to work with prominent minority figures like Bill Cosby or Coretta Scott King to encourage women and minorities to fill out applications. In the end, NASA convinced her to do it herself. Nichols went on university tours giving lectures and appeared in TV commercials dressed like an astronaut. Her pitch was:

> Oh, Hi! I'm Nichelle Nichols. It kind of looks like when I was Lieutenant Uhura on the starship *Enterprise*, doesn't it? Well, now there's twentieth century *Enterprise*, an actual space vehicle built by NASA and designed to put us in the business of space—not merely space exploration. NASA's *Enterprise* is a space shuttlecraft, built to make regularly scheduled runs into space and back. Now,

the shuttle will be taking scientists and engineers, men and women of all races, into space—just like the astronaut crew on the starship *Enterprise*. That is why I'm speaking to the whole family of humankind—minorities and women included. If you qualify and would like to be an astronaut, now is the time! This is your NASA! [Phelps 63–64].

After the NASA-*Star Trek* crossover, NASA received 1500 applications and selected six women, three blacks, and one Asian male, along with twenty-five white males (Kevles 60–65; Atkinson and Shafritz 150–157; Phelps 62–66; Michaud 128; Penley 16–17; Foster, "The Gendered Anniversary" 158). According to Nichols, she took on this role as a NASA spokesperson out of her own personal conviction and she remains involved with NASA up to this day. As a professional, a black American, and a mother, she felt that the future of space exploration belonged to all Americans and that it

> is scientifically unsound to continue an elitist, chauvinistic attitude when the need is so great. If a mind is a terrible thing to waste—and mind is energy, then isn't it dangerous to the ecological balance to waste energy so flagrantly as we have in the past, because of race and sex? It is scientifically sound to draw from every source possible for the success of any experiment or project. NASA needs minds, and minds are out here waiting to be used. If what NASA promises is indeed what NASA delivers, then the success of what I call "Project Equality" will bring this Agency its most shining hour [Nichols].

These examples show NASA partly unconsciously but also consciously merged with *Star Trek* to promote space exploration and gain advertency and support from women and minority groups. Indeed, women of NASA and its fictional counterpart, notably the close association between Mae Jemison and Nichelle Nichols, stress this unique bond. According to Mary Jo Deegan, the women in the original *Star Trek* series are rather secondary figures who lack command authority and mainly provide romance (209). Given their limited agency, it is quite interesting that women of the space community turned to Lt. Uhura as a spokeswoman and not to Princess Leia, a leader of the Rebel Alliance, who made her first fierce appearance on the silver screen during the time when NASA was looking for its first female astronauts in 1977.

Constance Penley observed that NASA and the *Star Trek* franchise had formed a reciprocal relationship because the two fed off of each other. Unlike most American science fiction, *Star Trek* has a utopian outlook on the future and space exploration in particular. It made sense for them to join forces and promote a positive space exploration scenario together. In this relationship, *Star Trek* provided an idealized vision of beautiful and exciting utopian images for twentieth century humans in the midst of counter-culture and the beginnings of Cold War disillusionment. NASA was able to project a real-life counterpart to *Star Trek*'s visions; this rosy future overcame damaging reports to NASA's credibility due to public project failures and media cover-ups.[5] This bond between NASA and *Star Trek* worked so well because "this new entity NASA/TREK shapes our popular and institutional imaginings about space exploration by humanizing our relation to science and technology. It also gives us a language to describe and explain the world and to express yearnings for a different and better condition; it is, then, a common language for utopia" (16).

Space Station: Expedition XLV—The Science Continues

While *Star Trek* presents a harmonious United Federation of Planets, *Star Wars* cannot account for a similar "common language for utopia." Although, *Star Wars* is a classic good versus evil story, there is no special emphasis on exploration and it is certainly not utopian science fiction. Creator George Lucas compared his movies to the Brothers Grimms' fairytales and emphasized his movies were not science fiction but space fantasy ("Star Wars. The Year's Best Movie; Fun in Space").[6] *Star Trek*, with its allusions to realism and hard science, would seem a logical choice for NASA to align itself with. Gene Roddenberry's creation had an optimistic, positive outlook but despite its fictional setting, still sojourns from Earth as its center, thus appearing within America's reach. In contrast, lightsabers, Jedi Knights, Alderaanian princesses or "the Force" in a galaxy far, far away seemed fantastic and unrealistic by scientific standards. Considering *Star Wars*'s fantasy backdrop and the fact that *Star Trek* was ten years old by 1977 and had amassed a large following, the NASA/Trek bond remained secure. At that point, NASA needed a public relations boost to make up for technological snafus and *Star Trek* aptly delivered its positive spin.

However, *Star Wars*'s cultural power did not lie idle. A financial smash among a media blitz, it was later seized upon by the proponents of the Strategic Defense Initiative (SDI) proposed by U.S. President Ronald Reagan on March 23, 1983. The advocates of SDI wanted to use both ground-based and space-based systems to hamstring ballistic strategic nuclear weapon attacks against the United States. The ambitious initiative was supposed to replace the doctrine of mutual assured destruction (MAD) that had been in place since the start of the Cold War. SDI was dubbed "Star Wars" in the mainstream media because Senator Edward Kennedy had compared SDI to the film. Kennedy accused Reagan of "misleading Red Scare tactics and reckless

Star Wars schemes" (Krämer 43). The pointed remark failed to do its job of discrediting SDI; Reagan's supporters embraced the term and harnessed *Star Wars* for their purpose. Although George Lucas filed a lawsuit because he did not like the use of his franchise in this context, the name stuck (Desloge; Butrica).[7] This use of *Star Wars* shows its narrative resonated with Cold War topics of its time, such as proxy wars, espionage, and, most obviously, nuclear annihilation through an "evil empire." Considering that the U.S. space program was fashioned in response to the Sputnik shock in the late 1950s and remained an important factor in the Cold War power play between the Soviet Union and the United States via the space race, the good versus evil story of *Star Wars* should also have been attractive as a public relations tool to NASA. However, this was not the case until the twenty-first century.

Despite the historic lack of association between *Star Wars* and NASA, there are several *Star Wars* homages at NASA today. However, these modern links reflect the fandom of *Star Wars*, and do not have any similarities with the Cold War space race. Mark Byrnes hypothesized NASA has always adjusted its image according to the political environment of its time because all agencies

> must have political support to function; that simple fact underlies virtually all agency activity. The fates of agency programs—and of the agencies themselves— are determined in the political arena, where political support is a prerequisite for success. Bureaucratic agencies need political support because it enables them to obtain the two resources all agencies must have: the authority to run programs and the money to pay for them. Agencies seek political backing from numerous sources: Congress, the president, other bureaucratic agencies, interest groups, and the general public [2].

Therefore, Byrnes identified three distinctive "image" periods at NASA in the twentieth century: the nationalism phase in the 1950s and early 1960s, the romantic period during the Johnson administration, and the pragmatic era during the 1970s and 1980s. To these three, I would add NASA adopted an "entertainment" outlook at the end of the millennium.

Due to the panic that the little Soviet satellite Sputnik triggered amongst the American public and in Congress in 1957, NASA worked in the first years after its foundation in a Cold War–defined framework. The American public feared the Soviet Union was ahead of the United States in space and missile technology and might use their advantage to destroy the United States from space. Thus, NASA was created and the agency put an emphasis on national pride, prestige, and strength through the use of symbols or patriotic names for their space crafts or programs. NASA also positioned itself in opposition to the Soviet space program and declared an American leadership in space.

President John F. Kennedy's famous declaration in 1961, to fly Americans to the moon and return them safely back to earth before this decade ended, also fits perfectly in this period (Kennedy). If *Star Wars* had debuted in the late 1950s or early 1960s alongside the various "space cadet" television shows, NASA might have taken advantage of *Star Wars*'s cultural power to polish its image. Byrnes calls those years the period of "Nationalism" at NASA.

The "Romanticism" period in the middle to late 1960s replaced the Nationalism period. The Cold War definition in the conceptualization of space policy lost its political persuasiveness as the majority of the American people no longer felt that threatened by the Soviet space program due to American successes in space, like the successful completion of the Mercury and Gemini missions. Because a deceitful Soviet attack from space no longer appeared an immediate threat, NASA had to come up with a new way to market themselves to the American public. The Romanticism phase therefore emphasized the enthralling aspects of space exploration and invited the public to come along for the ride and to participate in the adventure. It stressed four major romantic themes: exploration, heroism, curiosity and the emotional reward. All of those themes are emphasized in the then-new *Star Trek* television series as well, with Captain Kirk leading an Americanized group of astronauts around the "final frontier." In this light, NASA's merge with *Star Trek* seems even more compelling and comprehensible.

On the other hand, *Star Wars* premiered during NASA's "Pragmatism" period in the 1970s and 1980s. In this period, NASA's space activities were depicted as reliable and routine activities with the potential to improve life on earth, in various direct and indirect ways, through technological and economical stimuli such as satellite technology.[8] NASA had to change its marketing strategy because it needed to convince Congress and the American public that space exploration was still important to people's lives on a daily basis, even after the moon landing it planned for other ventures into space. However, in times of social upheavals, disillusionment with the Cold War, and especially the failure in Vietnam, NASA could not fall back on its previous agency branding of nationalism. Therefore, NASA emphasized the benefits of space exploration for every American citizen on earth like telecommunications or weather satellites or spin-off inventions (Byrnes; Kay). In this down-to-earth period of NASA, a good versus evil space fairytale may have garnered record-breaking ticket sales, but in NASA's eyes, this simplistic "fantasy" storyline was just not attractive for the promotion of the American space program.

The Pragmatism period blew up with the explosion of the space shuttle *Challenger* in 1986 due to porous O-rings. The televised death of the six astronauts, including one school teacher, demonstrated the space shuttle was not a reliable "space truck" and space flight was not as routine as a worker's commute that NASA had made it appear. The end of the pragmatic period has led NASA to again try to remake its image. In the twenty-first century, it seems NASA wants to rebrand itself to appeal to the new generation's technological prowess.[9] For the lack of a better name, I am calling it the period of "Entertainment."[10] NASA has increasingly catered to a generation of digital natives who have grown up immersed in technological social media, seemingly inseparable from Twitter, Facebook, Google+, Snapchat or Pinterest.[11] Besides goofy animal videos, witty jokes about iconic movies and TV shows have proliferated via "official" releases and fan-made renditions. Undoubtedly, Star Wars has become one of the most iconic movie franchises with a very loyal fan base. Even people who have not seen the movies or read books from the Expanded Universe would recognize cultural references to Star Wars. The characters and many homages to Star Wars in popular TV shows such as The Big Bang Theory or How I Met Your Mother can attest to that ("Star Wars in HIMYM"; "Star Wars in TBBT"). George Lucas's franchise has become such an important part of the cultural repertoire of this generation it can be used to pretty much endorse anything, including cars, beverages, non-profit organizations, toys or discount retailing companies ("Star Wars Pepsi"; "The Best Star Wars Commercials").[12] This iconic status also gave Star Wars an "in" at NASA. After decades of disassociation, NASA and Star Wars have bonded. That does not mean Star Trek was replaced with Star Wars. With its long association with NASA since the early 1970s, Star Trek is still highly regarded as NASA's fictional twin but the Force has now joined the Vulcan IDIC as a cultural partner.

Unlike the NASA/Trek relationship, the NASA/Wars relationship is more of a one-way street. Centered in another galaxy than our own, Star Wars has not evoked NASA themes in the movies or its Expanded Universe. However, NASA has made several references to Star Wars in the recent years. For instance, NASA has a commercial crew and cargo program called C3PO, which wants to "extend human presence in space by enabling an expanding and robust U.S. commercial space transportation industry" ("Commercial Crew & Cargo Program"; Taylor 400–402). Furthermore, astronomers of NASA have dubbed the planet Kepler 16-b "Tatooine" because it is close to two suns. NASA even refers to Tatooine in its official description of Kepler 16-b. NASA let the world know "the existence of a world with a double sunset, as portrayed in the film Star Wars more than 30 years ago, is now scientific fact" ("NASA's Kepler Mission"; Taylor 400–402). NASA also honored Star Wars with a commemoration of the thirtieth anniversary of the first movie by carrying Luke Skywalker's lightsaber into space. There are also several astronauts who have recently outed themselves as *Star Wars* fans. Mission Specialist Scott Parazynski, who flew on STS-120 to the International Space Station (ISS), was surprised when NASA played John Williams's soundtrack as his wakeup call on November 3, 2007. Parazynski also used his time in space to call his son, who is named "Luke," and advise him "to use the Force" (Taylor 400–402).[13] Other astronauts followed suit. For example, Flight Engineer Kjell Lindgren, who will participate in the ISS Expedition 45 at the end of 2015, mused about the influence of *Star Wars* on his career:

> *Star Wars* is definitely the first movie I remember seeing. I must have been three or four at the time. I'm also just a big fan of science fiction and speculative fiction, in general. And my father was in the Air Force, and I grew up on Air Force bases. I think all those things, taken together, influenced my desire to become an astronaut. It's what I wanted to do for as long as I can remember. I think *Star Wars*, just the story, of course, captures the imagination. And then also, the technology and the idea of living in space and doing all those things is very exciting, as well. I've never let go of that. It's interesting, because *Star Wars* is a cultural touchstone, and we're in a generation of astronauts now that saw *A New Hope*, *The Empire Strikes Back*, and *Return of the Jedi* when they were little kids. Star Wars is one of the many reasons that I became interested in space flight [Brooks].[14]

Lindgren even proposed the idea of a *Star Wars* themed mission poster and NASA gave its approval. The official mission poster now features the crew dressed as Jedi Knights with lightsabers in hand. The backdrop shows a starfield with an X-wing-like satellite. The official name of the mission is also a spoof of *Star Wars*'s "episode" format. It is named: *Space Station: Expedition XLV—The Science Continues* ("Poster for Star Wars"). The *Star Wars*-themed mission poster is only one of many cultural references NASA has done in recent years to appeal to younger generations. From *Pirates of the Caribbean* or the *Hitchhiker's Guide to the Galaxy* to *The Matrix*, the agency continues to incorporate Hollywood and show business to gain attention and amuse its advocates and possible sponsors ("SFA Products"). In its attempt to project entertainment and a laid-back image, NASA even bent its rules and allowed astronaut Leland Melvin to "sneak in" his dogs, Jake and Scout, into the NASA portrait shoot. Melvin's official portrait now features him in astronaut garb with two excited canines trying to jump on their owner's lap. One of the dogs even licks Melvin's ear in the picture (Konstantinides).[15]

These examples show NASA is trying to position itself as a fun, modern agency.[16] Forgotten are the Cold War times of "serious" mission posters and mission names such as "Mercury," "Apollo," or "Magellan" bristling with national pride with nautical and frontier imagery based on Greek and Roman mythology. NASA even took it a step further in its attempt to appeal to the current generation of digital natives. Even though it has nothing to do with any of its missions, NASA published a collection of "Star Wars Day Shareables" on its homepage and in social media on "Star Wars Day," May the Fourth, in 2014 and 2015. The date is a play on words on the iconic Jedi expression and, as one of the favorite puns among *Star Wars* fans, NASA did not want to miss out on the fun. In a public broadcast, the agency let the world know: "NASA invites you to join in the fun of 'Star Wars Day' by sharing these images with your friends and followers online. May the Fourth Be with You!" ("Star Wars Day Shareables"; Mastracchio). The images NASA provided for its supporters were NASA/Wars puns intended to be shared on social media, such as one shot of Saturn's moon Mimas, a Death Star look-alike. The picture was captioned with the pun: "That's no moon. It's a space station.... Nope, you're right. It's a moon. It's Saturn's moon Mimas and its large Herschel Crater. May the 4th be with you!" ("Star Wars Day Shareables"). NASA has extended its reach not only through online fan bases, but through a real world presence. The agency, for example, now has booths at *Star Wars* conventions. Representatives chatted with *Star Wars* fans about the nature of space exploration today. NASA was especially interested in the technology featured in *Star Wars*. Fans were asked what kind of *Star Wars* tech they would like to see NASA work on. Many of the fans wanted NASA to bring hyperspeed to the world of real-life space exploration (Siceloff). The point of this exchange was not to advance science per se, since faster-than-light travel remains outside modern technology. Nevertheless, the dialogue between NASA's visionaries and sci-fi fanboys provided an amusing way for NASA to position itself in the pop culture realm and score PR points for the American space program.

NASA has clearly jumped on the *Star Wars* bandwagon in recent years in order to cater to an increasingly interactive digital media-savvy generation. Not only do they gain a heightened public portrayal, their social approval leads to political backing from the American public. Like NASA/Trek crossovers, NASA/Wars connections mainly produce positive responses from the traditional media as well as social media outlets. The winning over of space enthusiasts from the science fiction/fantasy realm into lifelong careers is another advantage for sustaining the American space program. The increasing blending of the real life space community and the *Star Wars* community leads to the benefit of both. But how have women fit into this fan-based space culture? Did *Star Wars*, especially the character of Princess Leia, also influence female members of the space community in the same way as Uhura did in the late 1970s and 1980s? Or did NASA's attempts to recruit women into the space sector clash with the idea of "space princesses" as a setback to the progressive portrayals presented in *Star Trek*?

A Princess Paradox

There are two major issues one has to consider when pursuing the topic of women and *Star Wars*. Both revolve around Leia and her royal status and the paradox that a "princess" connotes when her character is juxtaposed against the larger women's movement. Let us have a look at her character first. There are two opposing groups concerning Leia's character in fan circles as well as in academia. Basically, there are those who criticize Leia as a weak character who cannot serve as a feminist role model. Conversely, Leia's champions advocate she is a strong and witty trailblazer for female characters in science-fiction as well as women everywhere, despite being the token female of the franchise in the original trilogy; her mother, Queen Amidala, takes Leia's place as the token female in the prequels.[17] Both groups agree Leia initially started out as an intense character who defied Darth Vader's torture—including the destruction of her home planet—to protect the Rebellion in *A New Hope*. She was introduced to the audience as a strong-willed woman who took charge in her own rescue mission, employing both a blaster and a smart mouth. The first words she said to her "rescuer" Luke Skywalker, dressed in stormtrooper uniform, were not words of gratitude and submissiveness, but the sassy remark: "Aren't you a little short for a stormtrooper?" (Lucas *A New Hope*). This remark has become so iconic it has appeared in various movies such as *Mulan* (1998), *Shrek* (2001), and *Tangled* (2010) as a source of female empowerment (Merlock 80). The re-creation of this moment in other movies shows how impressed men and women alike were with Leia's sharp tongue. It became obvious she was not a fairytale princess, a damsel in distress.[18] The minute she opened her mouth, she made clear she was an outspoken and bossy rebel, not afraid to literally dirty herself in the garbage disposal and to figuratively get dirty by taking up a gun herself, shooting at the enemy with the same skill as the men who came to her rescue. Leia's first appearance in the movie was so impressive because it seemed she had revoked the rules of the fairytale world. Fairytales had acquired a reputation for having male heroes: they "indicate repeatedly that active adventure is a male activity, and that if a woman is to embark on such endeavors, she must at least dress like a man" (Gilligan 13).

There are two conclusions one can draw from Leia's scenes in the first movie. The "pro–Leia" faction who celebrate Leia as a trailblazer for women in and outside of science fiction conclude the princess in her feminine, white flowing gown with a gun in hand rewrote the role for women in fairytales, movies, and the real world (Hatton). When they saw Leia for the first time in the movie theaters, the pro–Leia group was amazed to see "a woman who could play *like* and *with* the boys, but who didn't have to become one of the boys and who could, if and when she wanted to, show she *liked* the boys, a woman who is outspoken, unashamed, and, most importantly, unpunished for being so" (Dominguez 115–116; emphasis in original). They cheered Leia's continuing leadership abilities in the sequels.

In contrast, the "contra-Leia" faction feels Leia's initial power was broken by sexual abjection and belittlement. They are convinced George Lucas did not give the character of Leia enough thought as a fully-formed individual. In their opinion, Leia serves multiple incompatible functions in the narrative; her fractioned and inconsistent behavior gives her a "Rorschach Quality" (Miller and Sprich 218; Gordon 201). As the only female in the main cast she has to be a "composite woman, Leia is Goddess, Whore, Lover, Mother, Sister, and Castrating Bitch all at once: tempting but taboo" (Miller and Sprich 216–217).

The contra-Leia group admits Leia's character is a breakthrough for female heroes in some aspects, but they also point out the limitations of that breakthrough. Leia, for example, uses the symbol of the male hero—the gun. However, in *Star Wars* guns are considered "crude" and "clumsy" weapons which anyone can pick up. The actual heroic weapon in *Star Wars* is the lightsaber, an "elegant weapon" which takes much training. Although the trilogy ends before audiences see her use a lightsaber, in the early Expanded Universe, for example in author Timothy Zahn's "Thrawn trilogy," she is not comfortable using one. Luke took up his training right away, but, five years after *Return of the Jedi*, Leia is still a basic trainee, despite the fact she is one of the few people qualified to use a lightsaber due to her descent (Cavelos 324). The Skywalker bloodline theoretically entitles Leia to use the Force but the audience does not really see her using it and she is reluctant to use it in the early Expanded Universe. The trailer for *The Force Awakens* entices fans with Carrie Fisher picking up a lightsaber, perhaps for the first time, decades after her last appearance. The contra-Leia group traces her limited agency to the love triangle between Luke, Leia, and Han. Although she falls in love with Han Solo, she is ultimately denied a choice between Solo and Skywalker. Han-as-protector also sidelines her growth as a strong character: he continually pokes fun at her royalty, calling her "worshipfullness" and other mock titles. Contra-Leia groups contend she does not need to actively use the Force because she is only in possession of the Force to preserve the Skywalker bloodline and pass this gift on to her offspring (Cavelos 309; Simpson 117).

On the other hand, the pro–Leia group is convinced Leia does use the Force but on a more subtle level. In *The Empire Strikes Back*, Leia, Chewbaca and C3PO flee from Bespin and on their escape they turn around because

Leia senses Luke was wounded and needs her help (Merlock 82). In addition, they emphasize Leia eventually receives formal Jedi training in the stories of the expanded Star Wars universe. In the novel *The Joiner King* by Troy Denning, which was released in 2005, Leia finally picks up the lightsaber as a standard weapon (Spangler 332–334; Dennings). The pro–Leia group also celebrates Leia as a sophisticated woman with leadership responsibilities. She is a Senator, a Princess and a Commander in the Rebellion and, later, a leader in the Expanded Universe (Spangler 331; Merlock 80–81).

The contra-Leia group, however, perceives the *Star Wars* movies are structured "around male relationships and male-oriented viewpoints. Women exist primarily to provide motivations for male activity" (Rubey). They point out Leia's titles are irrelevant because that's all they are—titles. There is no power attached to the titles because being a Senator of a dissolved Senate or a Princess of a destroyed planet negates the responsibilities and privileges Leia had. Although Leia is still a Commander in the Rebel Alliance, in the minds of the contra-Leia group, the sexualization of Leia by becoming Han's love interest diverts her from her role as she turns from rebel leader to "passively suffering woman in a romantic tragedy" (Simpson 119–120; Cavelos 308). Indeed, in *The Empire Strikes Back* she makes the hard decisions and oversees the evacuation on the ice planet Hoth; in *Return of the Jedi*, she spends the second half of the movie following Han's haphazard leadership, surrounded by smitten Ewoks.

According to the contra-Leia group, her sexual surrender becomes obvious when she infiltrates Jabba the Hutt's palace to rescue her lover from his carbonite prison instead of standing by her responsibilities to the galaxy and leading the rebellion to a victorious end (Simpson 121). This romantic entanglement contrasts sharply with her stoic façade as her entire planet is blown to bits. Even then, Leia did not completely succeed in freeing Han because she was captured shortly after and enslaved by Jabba the Hutt. He forces her to wear a neck chain, dress in a tiny metal bikini, and sit for his amusement. Therefore, Leia is the only character in the movie who suffers outright sexual victimization. During the battle on his sail barge, the contra-Leia group dismisses her actions as almost inconsequential. She kills Jabba, but they point out he is just "a defenseless slug" (Cavelos 310). After that, she did not take charge but needed directions from Luke on what to do next (Cavelos 310). Luke's only injury during his fight against Jabba's men occurred when he was instructing Leia. Considering how Luke was effectively mowing down Jabba's henchmen, he could have accomplished everything himself.

The pro–Leia group interprets the situation very different. They emphasize Leia did not fall apart when Han Solo was put into carbonite. She defied the princess stereotype and stayed determined, much like male action heroes. In *Return of the Jedi*, she reverses the typical fairytale storyline of the knight saving the princess by being the one who frees Han from the carbonite (Merlock 83; Dominguez 117). Jabba certainly enslaves her, but he had also objectified Han Solo when his body was put on display in his carbonite prison as his ultimate trophy for all to see. They applaud Leia for freeing herself from her captivity by strangling Jabba the Hutt with the very chains the slug intended to enslave her. This is quite the achievement given the difference in size of Leia and Jabba and, of course, it is also an accomplishment in the figurative sense as an act of self-liberation (Dominguez 117; Spangler 332). They rebut the contra-Leia group, arguing,

> one cannot blame Leia for being weak just because she escapes while wearing a string bikini. The image of slave girl, sex object, and victim turning on her captor has its own connotations and logic, especially since the act carries with it not only vengeance but the value of ridding her comrades of Jabba's sadistic presence and ongoing interference with their more important mission. Leia's supporting the others does not end with her slaying of Jabba. At Luke's direction, she takes command of a pivoting machine gun and gives them cover [Merlock 83].

Although Luke could have conceivably rescued them single-handedly, Leia's actions demonstrate her continued agency, not a passive figure. Regardless of their interpretation, however, both sides saw Leia primarily through a lens of violence. As discussed, her immersion in the "war" in *Star Wars* tainted her as a spokesperson for NASA's exploration-oriented outlook. Uhura could communicate with aliens; Leia blows them up.

Another major issue surrounding Leia's character is her lack of emotional depth and complexity. According to Jane Cavelos, audiences should have seen Leia suffering and dealing with internal turmoil after being tortured by Darth Vader, after her entire planet was destroyed, and after the revelation that Darth Vader, a man who had tortured her twice, who had put her lover in carbonite, cut Luke's hand off, annihilated her home Alderaan and killed countless people, was actually her father. She should have had a strong reaction to the pain of being tortured but the audience does not see her suffering because she becomes sidelined in favor of the male characters' struggles. When Han and Chewbacca are tortured on Cloud City, the audience witnesses their heroic acts of suffering. Same with Luke: when he loses his aunt, uncle, and Obi-Wan, the audience is allowed to feel with him. However, Leia is denied that part of being a hero. The audience cannot share her pain over her multiple losses because the audience never sees her suffering. In particular, the revelation that Darth Vader is Leia's father in *Return of the Jedi* should have triggered a strong reaction. Instead of expressing any sort of emotion at her new-found brother, such as curiosity, and asking him some questions about his certainty or adamantly emphasizing that the man who raised and loved her, Bail Organa, will always be her true father rather than that mechanical monster, she reacts like a zombie, stating she has kind of always known about it. For the contra-Leia party, her reaction—or rather, lack thereof—shows the development of depth and complexity of Leia's character was not a priority for the narrative (Cavelos 311–313). Indeed, after Luke exits the scene, she seeks comfort with Han Solo. After the night ends, all is forgotten in the climactic battle.

The pro–Leia group defends Leia's reactions as a reversal of the "fairy-tale" stereotype. According to them, Leia did not have a strong reaction to the evil tidings and exploitations from Darth Vader because

> it is not in Leia's character to be hysterical but rather unflappable and duty-bound because her problem is less with Vader as her enemy and more with the empire itself as her enemy. She is concerned with the larger chess game of Republic vs. Empire, while Luke is trying to find his father (who identifies Luke by his last name more than by the Force) and learn to grow up from his country-boy childhood [Merlock 85].

The arguments surrounding Leia's character definitely show there are inconsistencies open to interpretation. From a feminist perspective, the character of Leia appears to be a paradox. She was constructed to be a universal motif; as "all things to all people" (Millner 218). Hence, some people who watch the movies see a strong, independent and heroic warrior princess, while others see a virginal princess in distress in a patriarchal fairytale world and another group sees all of the above. Like Diana Dominguez, I did not see this princess paradox when I watched *Star Wars* for the first time. For Dominguez and me, "Leia was someone I could identify with at seventeen. She was part of that crowd of girls who said what they felt, when they felt it, and put people in their places when they needed to be ... and even managed to get the good-looking guy in the end, who didn't seem to mind it so much if she was a little bit bossy" (Dominguez 120–121). I was impressed with this pro-active, yet elegant woman. However, other girls and women could not feel as inspired by Leia because they stood on the other side of the conflict, mainly seeing a sophisticated and well-educated princess playing second fiddle to a naïve farm boy and a smug smuggler.[19] Those women had to look for inspiration elsewhere, either in another science fiction universe or they had to find other characters in *Star Wars* to identify with. Usually, women can better identify with characters of their own gender, but other than Leia, there are almost no female characters in the original trilogy. However, there are a couple of characters open to an interpretative gender reading. Female *Star Wars* fans broke gender stereotype by stressing that Jedi could be female as well, a concept that was validated in the *Phantom Menace*, even as they appeared as "extras." They also claimed androgynous characters, such as Boba Fett, for themselves, a concept refuted in *Attack of the Clones* but appears to be acknowledged in *The Force Awakens*. Gwendoline Christie will portray Captain Phasma—a Boba-esque, male appearing character (Rich; Robinson; Brooker 14–19; Bacon-Smith 18). Thus, they reappraise the movies' assumption about gender.

Astronaughty Space Gals

The women of the space community faced the same paradox as all the other female members of the *Star Wars* audience—a princess in distress verses a distressing princess. So how did *Star Wars* and Princess Leia in particular influence the women who chose a career in the space sector? Apparently, there are very few Princess Leia fans among the female members of the space community. The most readily identifiable Leia fan is Holly Griffith, a former mission control flight controller for the Space Shuttle and the ISS. The strong, independent and elegant warrior princess impressed her as much as she used to impress me. She passionately summarized her childhood feelings:

> At the ripe old age of probably four or so, I wanted to be Princess Leia when I grew up. I was going to travel the galaxy in Corellian Corvettes, wear my hair in funny ways, and just be generally awesome. She was my hero. She was smart, funny, and a great leader. I'd never seen anything like her before and I was instantly enamored. I proudly and matter-of-factly explained all of this to my grandfather; I had it all planned out—surely by the time I was 18 this technology would exist, right? [Griffith].

Even though the *Millennium Falcon* failed to make the Kessel Run to corvette car lots, Griffith did not lose hope. She chose the next best thing: NASA.

> Princess Leia always stuck with me throughout school and, well, since we weren't going to be building X-wings or Super Star Destroyers anytime soon, I figured the closest thing was NASA. I thought about what degree I should major in if my final destination was to work in human spaceflight. I did my research, and Mechanical Engineering seemed like a good choice…. Would I have stayed in engineering if Princess Leia hadn't led me to dream about going to the stars? I would like to think so, but honestly, I can't say. But I do know for certain that strong female characters like Leia and now Ahsoka do influence the young girls who watch them [Griffith].

Clearly, Griffith is a full-blown *Star Wars* enthusiast who traced her professional career back to Princess Leia. However, there appear to be not many more female devotees of both *Star Wars* and Princess Leia, even on a smaller scale, among the women of the American space community. Despite NASA's recent public relations bonanza emphasizing "Entertainment," there has been no emphasis on women in the *Star Wars* references in its social media and general promotion. Princess Leia-themed references at NASA do not exist at the time of this writing. Furthermore, until Griffith "outed" herself, NASA's women employees do not participate in the *Star Wars* puns promoted by NASA: in all the PR material I reviewed, the "fanboys" in the space program are just that—men. The absence of female *Star Wars* and Leia fans in that particular community reflects Leia's complicated position as a feminine "paradox," especially the fact that she is a princess.

The Leia's "fairytale" princess presents an obstacle for the non-royal NASA workforce. The definition of a "princess" belies this negative portrayal: it does not matter how hard a woman tries, she cannot become a princess through her own merit. She is either born a princess or marries a prince but hard work and determination will not get her there. In contrast, NASA and actress Nichelle Nichols played up the accessibility and equality in the workplace for *all* women, such as becoming a chief communications officer. As presented on television and in NASA's promotional material, Lt. Uhura's job on the *USS Enterprise* is a position any young girl can dream of with the hope of actually achieving something like it in the space program. Princess Leia was born into her position but Lt. Uhura had to work for it and won the respect and admiration of her shipmates. This is an important difference that made Lt. Uhura more appealing to aspiring women who also work hard to achieve their spots within the male-dominated space sector. Furthermore, it has to be noted that Uhura, and the *Star Trek* Universe in particular, catered to the American "melting pot" with its multicultural crew. Uhura is a commissioned officer and a spacefaring woman of African descent in a non-menial position. In the 1960s, she was—and still is—an inspiration to many women, especially African American women like Mae Jemison (and, in another context, Whoopi Goldberg), to stretch their space legs, either in the real world or on television. The role of Uhura was so culturally important to African Americans, Martin Luther King, Jr., personally convinced Nichelle Nichols to continue with the show when, in 1967, Nichols had planned to leave *Star Trek* after its first season to pursue another project (Colman; Nishi).

The characters of *Star Wars* lack the multicultural inclusiveness and the optimistic vision of *Star Trek*: when aliens get together, they are clustered in seedy bars or in Jabba's palace (a decade later, the prequels made clear a "Federation" is a bad thing and a "Republic" of aliens is rife with corruption). Leia, as the only female lead in the original trilogy, is not as liberating as Uhura. She is pretty, slim, white, and privileged. She embodies the type of woman American society valued throughout the twentieth century. Therefore, contemporary magazines and newspapers did not concern themselves overtly with an analysis of Leia's overburdened and paradoxical character, but only commented on Leia's looks when the movie was released. *Newsweek*, for example, wrote: "Carrie Fisher is adorable with her big, clean spunky features and her great figure, which is the embodiment of the friendly voluptuousness we all remember in girls like *Buck Roger*'s Wilma, *Flash Gordon*'s Dale and *Mandrake the Magician*'s Princess Narda" ("Fun in Space" 61; Isaacs).

Leia's diminution to her appearance is not surprising considering it was common practice to evaluate a woman's worth in such terms, especially a leading actress in a movie. One might expect the treatment of Leia to already be different because *Star Wars* premiered in 1977 during the second wave of feminism in the United States. Women were fighting for their equal rights, inter alia to be judged based on their character and professional skills. However, the media coverage of Leia and the ambivalent character development of Princess Leia Organa in the *Star Wars* franchise, as well as women who tried to professionally establish themselves in the space community in the 1960s and 1970s, show that the women's struggle for equal treatment in life, professional careers, as well as in movies was an ongoing process.[20]

Given Leia's troublesome image, it should come as no surprise the female trailblazers in the space community had to battle the same gender biases concerning their physical appearances in the space community, the media, as well as the general public. The first American women who tried to venture into space were tested by the Lovelace Foundation for Medical Research, NASA's de-facto medical department, albeit without NASA's permission in 1960 and 1961. Dr. Randolph Lovelace and his associates wanted to find out how far women were capable of spaceflight for their possible usage in future space missions. Thirteen out of nineteen women passed the tests, and they were joined by two other accomplished female aeronautics champions, Betty Skelton and Ruth Nichols, who were tested by *Look* magazine and air force researchers during the same time (Weitekamp; Kevles; Ackmann). The female pilots underwent the same physical and psychological tests the Mercury astronauts had to pass, and the published test results generated a discussion about women in space.

The public discussion surrounding those women pilots, now known as the Mercury 13, was multifaceted.[21] One of the most popular reactions simply made fun of women's bodies and their appearance. Women were described as vain and simple-minded who could pass the long hours of spaceflight simply by applying make-up and take joy in being weightless ("Sex and Space"). The press asked the readers: "Can you imagine a woman locked up for weeks or months in space with no telephone to jabber over all day long? But perhaps they'll line the inside of the spaceship with mirrors and she can be happy admiring herself" (Reader's comment in Welch). Another way the press used the female body against the women to deny the determined female astronauts-to-be credibility and respectability in the technical field of space flight was to degrade them as sex objects. The press frequently quoted snide comments of male, mostly anonymous, NASA employees like "Well, there IS an allowance of 125 pounds for recreation equipment aboard the Apollo spacecraft" (United Press International; emphasis in original). The women who wanted to become astronauts were even declared to be "astronaughty" for not expressing qualms about flying to space with a man in the confined isolation of the space capsule for long periods of time ("No. 1 Space Gal"). The results of this line of thinking were mostly one-dimensional: women should stay on Earth and stick to blow drier helmets at the hair salon instead of donning space helmets ("First Blonde in Space").[22] Friendly legislation to the widespread women's movement and the persistent demonstration of skills by the few women who were already part of the space community encouraged the American public, media, and male members of the space community to retain their negative opinions about women in space between the early 1960s and 1977, the year *Star Wars* was released and the first female astronauts were selected. However, the media's emphasis on Leia's looks and the treatment of the first female astronauts demonstrate the concept of women taking part and taking charge in important space missions was still off-putting to many people (Ross-Nazal 23).[23] The media frequently asked the six selected women who became the United States' first female astronauts gender specific questions. The press mused about the astronauts' menstrual periods, if they wanted to have children, if they will start crying in space when things do not go well, if they ever wanted to be boys, or if they were planning on shaving, using make-up, or wearing bras in space. Like the Mercury 13 before them in the 1960s, the six astronauts also became the punchline of various jokes. When the launch date for the mission of America's first female astronaut, Sally Ride, was pushed back for two months in 1983 due to technical delays, *The Tonight Show* host Johnny Carson joked the mission was delayed because Ride had to find a purse to match her shoes first (Lipman; Sherr 282–289; Ross-Nazal 29–31). Because the media put such an emphasis on the astronauts' femininity, the first female astronauts always emphasized this aspect was not important. They insisted they were just "one of the guys," thus denying their femininity as a crucial part of their identity. Judy Resnik, for example, described herself in gender-neutral terms: "I am an astronaut. Not a woman astronaut. Not a Jewish astronaut. An astronaut" (Kevles 97). However, not all of them were content with their way of dealing with the press and their colleagues. In 2004 Rhea Seddon noted, "The thing that bothered me a lot and occasionally still bothers me is that you have to act like a man or you have to look like a man or you have to be like a man in order to do your work. I am a 'female' female, and a lot of times you lose credibility by being that way" (Foster, *Integrating Women* 146). Within this context, a close association to "Princess" Leia was counterproductive to NASA's social progress.

Queen of Outer Space and Other Space Princesses

As was mentioned earlier, there are two major issues one has to consider pursuing the topic of women and *Star Wars* within the space community. The oxymoronic character of Princess Leia and its mostly resultant abrasive or indifferent attitude of the women in the space community have been analyzed. However, Leia's royal title and its connection to the women in the space sector have yet to be looked at. The princess theme is the epitome of femininity or rather "girliness," thanks to Disney's largely popular connection of princesses with cuteness for young girls—of which *Star Wars* and thus Princess Leia is now a part of (Fisher).[24] A Google search of "Disney and Princess Leia" shows how fans of Disney and/or *Star Wars* imagine Leia situated among the other Disney princesses—in an off-the-shoulders poufy white gown with big doe-like eyes and her signature buns hairstyle.[25] Her Disney-ficated portrayal in the fan-fiction demonstrates the associations most people have in their mind when thinking about a princess. A princess is supposed to be a very feminine woman adorned with at least one of these items: a dress, long hair, elaborate hairstyles, jewelry, and a tiara. Princess Leia, even without being Disney-ficated, possesses most of these attributes at one point or the other in the movies: from the concluding ceremonial scene after Luke blows up the Death Star to the idol of Ewoks. Furthermore, the mere knowledge of the fact that Leia is not just any other woman but a "princess" and a prospective crowned head, lingers in the back of the minds of the audience— especially the female audience. In comparison, Mon Mothma may be the leader of the Alliance, but her sole appearance relegates her as a non-entity compared to the Rebel's Princess. She seemingly does not even play a part in the battle. Being a princess does not necessarily exclude Leia as a role model for women in the space community. However, her title presumably detracts from her possible appeal for women who want to be active participants in space exploration because the title "princess" is too charged with expectations about beauty standards and female etiquette. The first six women to become the United States' first female astronauts certainly did not want to be associated with these assumptions. As noted above, they wanted to be genderless members of the astronaut choir—a common attitude of women who entered the workforce in the 1970s and 1980s.

Considering the gendered practices previously exercised in the space community, this approach is quite understandable. Throughout its history, NASA reinforced strict roles for women. The agency issued clothing guidelines for the astronauts' wives in the early 1960s. The mockingly called "Astrowives" were instructed by NASA as well as *Life* magazine, which had an exclusive contract with the astronauts and their families, to wear "prim and proper tailored pastel shirtwaist dresses" for their first magazine photoshoot (Koppel 43). Henry Robinson Luce, owner of *Life* magazine, used its publication to support his political point of view and to promote patriotism in the United States. Therefore, not only the astronauts but also their wives had to fit the all-American extraordinary "ordinary" image *Life* and NASA tried to depict. They even airbrushed the wives' real lipstick color from a Mamie Eisenhower pink to a patriotic red (Koppel 50; Kauffman 68–86; Sherrod). Even worse, NASA also crowned space princesses (O'Donnell 34–35). Several NASA installations continued the practice of their predecessors or started their own tradition and held beauty pageants between 1952 and 1973. The Jet Propulsion Laboratory, the Lewis Space Center (later renamed Glenn Research Center), and the Johnson Space Center each respectively crowned the "Queen of Outer Space,"[26] "Miss NASA," and, "Lunar Landing Festival Queen" out of a selection of their female employees (O'Donnell; "Mystery Photo"; Meyer).

With the passing of time and the rise of the women's movement, many women did not approve of this type of "female activity" any longer. In 1973, the Johnson Space Center held an election for a "Queen" and her "Court" to reign over the Lunar Landing Festival activities in Houston. A group of anonymous feminists (most likely they were NASA employees, given the enclosed environment; however, the identity of the group members remains unknown) wanted to protest against NASA's discriminatory employment practices and swapped the official ballot with a mock ballot that listed forty-five male NASA employees who could become "King (or Queen)" or one of the "boys" of the court. The notification for the mock selection announced: "Selection should not be based on merit. Vote for a pretty face & a good bod"

(Meyer 38). The men of NASA were shocked and called in the security police. Inspector Glenn L. McAvoy investigated and all the ballots were collected. However, the pageant saboteurs still managed to distribute the results of the mock ballot overnight along with caricatures that portrayed the male winners in typical beauty pageants poses. Furthermore, there were caricatures that showed women as, for example, a "moon maid" or as a crowned queen on the moon about to be crushed by the foot of an astronaut who is taking the "giant step for mankind" (Sams). The announcement of the winners finished with the proclamation: "Let us now, Kings and Queens, pledge ourselves to overcoming that immortal statement by Astronaut, Patriot, and National hero, James Lovell, which was reported recently in *Play Boy* [sic] Magazine: 'We fully envision that in the near future we will fly women into space and use them the same way we use them on earth—for the same purpose'" ("The Winners"). The NASA men who won the beauty king election were embarrassed. Only one of them took it with humor, asking "when he was going to get a fitting for his dress" (Meyer 39). The other NASA installations had already discontinued the contests due to political reforms and the Johnson Space Center followed suit.

This particular incident reveals that being a space princess is a thankless job in a galaxy not so far away in the 1970s. The women of America's space community were no longer willing to accept to be reduced to their appearance and most certainly did not appreciate having to wear a crown for their diminution. As the mock pageant revealed, the nomination to be part of space royalty was even an affront to men in the space community. Being belittled to a "pretty face & a good bod" insulted the men so much they turned to the security police for help instead of just laughing it off (Meyer 38). Indeed, the sole man who took his victory in good humor associated royalty with "girlie dress-ups," asking for a fitting of a flattering outfit. Therefore, when Leia, a princess with "big, clean spunky features" and a "great figure," appeared four years later, she was a throwback to a less socially progressive era. The space community could not overcome her paradoxical status as a witty powerful leader juxtaposed against a traditional subordinate damsel. Women in NASA ultimately rejected both role models, preferring to integrate themselves in the space community as "one of the guys" in the 1970s and 1980s ("Fun in Space" 61). Considering NASA has increasingly referenced *Star Wars* in recent years, and as second wave feminism recedes further back in historical memory, it is likely the new female members of the space community will take part in those references in the future. Indeed, *Star Wars*'s new owner, Disney, seems willing to play up the "princess" angle as a modern role model for young girls. Now situated in a new cultural empire, future episodes are in a unique position to bestow the women of the space community, and all other women, with a storyline that includes newer, modern, self-reliant female lead character(s) of non-royal descent whose sole purpose should not be to only provide romance for a smug smuggler or a boy who is gifted with the Force.

As of this writing, the latest astronaut group selected by NASA to fly to an asteroid and Mars are a perfectly gender balanced group of four men and four women ("2013 Astronaut Class"). Although science-fiction often inspires real-life, maybe this time art can imitate real-life and *Star Wars* will present its audience with more leading ladies in the vein of Uhura. Watching the *Star Wars: The Force Awakens* trailers, the possibility is definitely there, although, once again, there seem to be disproportionately more male characters ("Star Wars: The Force Awakens Official Teasers"). However, the thirteen-year-old teenager in me who had to stay home sick will still love *Star Wars* and its daring imagination no matter what—but more so if there is a butt-kicking, strong, shrewd woman who is a new and improved Leia.

Notes

1. For an analysis of Leia in the context of second wave feminism, see Mara Wood's chapter in this collection.

2. A shuttlecraft on *Star Trek: The Next Generation* was named "Onizuka" after astronaut Ellison Onizuka and in *Star Trek: The Search for Spock* (1984) the spaceship *USS Grissom* was named in honor of Virgil "Gus" Grissom. He was one of the group of seven men who became the United States' first astronauts, today known as the Mercury 7. He tragically died in a fire onboard the first Apollo spacecraft in 1967. Ellison Shoji Onizuka was the first Asian American astronaut who successfully flew to space with the Space Shuttle *Discovery* on STS-51-C. He died in the *Challenger* explosion in 1986.

3. Jemison was not the only real-life astronaut who appeared on *Star Trek*. Astronauts Michael Fincke and Terry Virts were part of the cast of the series finale of *Star Trek: Enterprise*. Both astronauts consider themselves Trekkies and credit *Star Trek* for their interest in space and their careers at NASA ("NASA—Final Frontier Astronauts").

4. The most recent example: Astronaut Sam Cristoforetti in a *Star Trek: Voyager* uniform on board the ISS (Cristoforetti).

5. Such as malfunctioning rockets or astronauts who kicked over the traces (Makemson).

6. While science fiction and space fantasy are both set in futuristic surroundings, science fiction eschews the supernatural, and works with futuristic science and technology instead. This is not the case in the genre of fantasy where magic and supernatural elements are important pillars within the genre. *Star Wars*'s use of the magical Force and other fantasy elements makes the film, despite its futuristic settings and use of technology, space fantasy, a fantasy story with elements of science fiction.

7. For more information about SDI and *Star Wars* see also Peter Lee's and Jessica Brandt's chapters in this collection.

8. NASA keeps spin-off records up to this day. For more information see: Lockney.

9. TV was *the* space age media. However, NASA is switching more and more its media use in favor of the internet and social media in order to stay in touch with the American public.

10. The "Entertainment" period was not framed by Mark Byrnes. Building upon his hypotheses, I have transferred his arguments onto the twenty-first century NASA branding effort.

11. The characterization of NASA's public relations as being in an "Entertainment" phase refers solely to its marketing and branding efforts of the agency. It does not apply to NASA's work in the field of human and robotic space exploration.

12. This is not the case for the astronaut brand. From the very beginning of NASA, the astronauts were used as cultural ambassadors for their country. They represented the American national brand, as opposed to the Soviet national brand embodied by the Soviet cosmonauts. They were even sent on domestic and international tours to win the hearts and minds of the public for their country. While the Soviet space travelers had to represent the qualities of socialism, the American space travelers had to have "the right stuff." This referred explicitly to the qualities that American frontier pioneers were supposedly made of: white, brave, honest, married, and God-loving middle class men. Young boys and men were supposed to aspire to attain these qualities in abundance and women were supposed to want them. This astronaut image, the brand of the astronauts, was established in the very beginning of the American space program. Although there is a racially integrated and gender balanced astronaut corps in place in this century, the original astronaut brand is not dead, yet. Like *Star Wars*, astronauts are also used to endorse consumer products; such as the powder drink Tang or the German beer and vodka mix Astra Rakete. Granted, the commercials do not use "real" astronauts, but they use the image of the astronaut. Unlike *Star Wars*, however, the astronaut brand is mainly used to endorse products which cater to traditionally male stereotypes such as beer drinking, men's deodorants, or farting. Those commercials are homage to the original astronaut brand and they still resonate with people. See Rentz; Einmal Schub, bitte; "Axe Apollo: Firefighter"; "Axe Apollo: Lifeguard"; Haynes. Baked Beans.

13. NASA has provided its astronauts with wake-up calls since the Gemini missions. For more information about the wake-up calls, see Fries.

14. Flight engineer Rick Mastracchio delivered a "Star Wars Day" felicitation from the International Space Station on May the Fourth 2014 (Mastracchio).

15. There are also other examples, such as the "singing astronaut" (Hadfield).

16. For more information regarding the importance of social media and entertaining the public in the space sector, see Beuth.

17. There are similar discussions about the characterization and the relevance of Queen Amidala (see Wood in this collection). However, in her case, the range of opinions is not as broad. Generally speaking, there is a consensus George Lucas should have paid less attention to her hair, make-up and wardrobe and should have concentrated more on the continuance of Amidala as being a strong diplomatic leader. However, the prequel narrative broke down her power by type-casting her into a love interest of Anakin Skywalker and who dies of a broken heart: the ultimate subversion of her initially strong character who was dedicated to higher ideals for an entire world and for the whole galaxy. See Cavelos; Simpson; Dominguez; Merlock.

18. Indeed, she even mouths off at Darth Vader when he captures her ship and tells Tarkin off right before he blows up her planet.

19. A point of view I can understand today.

20. I hereby do not want to suggest that the goal of the feminist movement has been reached in this century. The character of Leia's and Luke's mother, Queen Padmé Amidala, in the *Star Wars* prequel trilogy which premiered between 1999 and 2005, can attest to that fact. See Simpson; Cavelos; Dominguez; Merlock. Merlock even suggests Amidala's demise of character represents the post–1970s backlash against feminism (85).

21. The program had no official attachment to NASA and the Mercury program in particular. Journalists retroactively dubbed those women the "Mercury 13" in the late

twentieth century. The 1960s journalists called the women: moon maid, astronautess, astro-eves, lady astronauts, spacewoman, astronautix, astronette, female astronaut, spacegirl, woman astronaut, astrodoll, spacegal or astrotrix. See "Moon Maid's Ready"; "Sex and Space"; von Braun; Johnson; Marshall; Thompson; McCullough.

22. See also several newspaper caricatures that poke fun at women in space due to their appearance: *Washington Daily News* (17 Apr. 1963). James E. Webb Papers, John F. Kennedy Presidential Library, Box 5, Current News 1962/1963, Apr. 1963: caricature about a group of women who want to hear more about weightlessness from a NASA official; unknown newspaper (1960–1963). Jerrie Cobb Collection, unprocessed collection, Schlesinger Library, Radcliffe Institute, Harvard University: caricature about the NASA men in mission control having to stop the countdown because Jerrie Cobb (one of the women who had been successfully tested by Lovelace) is fixing her lipstick; *The Evening Bulletin* (15 Sept. 1960). Jerrie Cobb Collection, unprocessed collection, Schlesinger Library, Radcliffe Institute, Harvard University: caricature about space officials agreeing women would be better suited for space travel than men while two female astronauts stand in the background giggling and doing their makeup. The caption below reads: "Our tests show that women have better resources for space flight than men.... They can pass the long hours in orbit by fixing their hair, doing their nails and dabbling with makeup!"; *Fort Lauderdale News* (27 Mar. 1963). Jerrie Cobb Collection, unprocessed collection, Schlesinger Library, Radcliffe Institute, Harvard University: caricature about a woman who can't fit her curlers under her space helmet; *The Phoenix Gazette* (22 Aug. 1960). Jerrie Cobb Collection, unprocessed collection, Schlesinger Library, Radcliffe Institute, Harvard University: caricature shows a female astronaut in a miniskirt running to a rocket with a "to bring on spaceship-list" in hand. The list included a lipstick and a comb. The news about women eventually flying to space produced an array of different opinions in the early 1960s. The ones presented here were among the most popular. However, there were also people, including men, who supported the idea of women in space. For more information, see Hilck.

23. The announcement of the first astronaut class that included women and minorities was in January 1978. Out of the thirty-five selected astronauts, six women made the cut in the new astronaut position "mission specialist": Anna L. Fisher, Sally K. Ride, Shannon W. Lucid, Margaret Rhea Seddon, Judith A. Resnik, Kathryn D. Sullivan.

24. Princess Leia can now also be seen and greeted in Disney World, alongside the other Disney princesses. Sometimes, Minnie Mouse even dresses like her (Leia Organa).

25. A Google search about "princesses" depicts a similar result. The first couple of pages are solely about Disney princesses.

26. The beauty pageant was called "Miss Guided Missile" from 1952 to 1958. It changed its name in 1959 when the Jet Propulsion Laboratory transitioned from missiles to space crafts.

Works Cited

Ackmann, Martha. *The Mercury 13: The Untold Story of Thirteen American Women and the Dream of Space Flight.* New York: Random House, 2003. Print.

Atkinson, Joseph D., and Jay M. Shafritz. *The Real Stuff: A History of NASA's Astronaut Recruitment Program.* New York: Praeger, 1985. Print.

"Axe Apollo: Nothing Beats an Astronaut: Firefighter." *YouTube* 11 Jan. 2013. Web. 24 Mar. 2015.

"Axe Apollo: Nothing Beats an Astronaut: Lifeguard." *YouTube* 3 Feb. 2013. Web. 24 Mar. 2015.

Bacon-Smith, Camille. *Enterprising Women: Television Fandom and the Creation of Popular Myth.* Philadelphia: University of Pennsylvania Press, 1992. Print.

"The Best *Star Wars* Commercials." *YouTube* 31 Jan. 2012. Web. 19 Mar. 2015.

Beuth, Patrick. "Wir müssen uns immer wieder selbst übertreffen. Als Mohawk Guy wurde NASA-Ingenieur Bobak Ferdowsi während der Landung des Mars-Rovers Curiosity zur Netzberühmtheit. Retten Stars wie er und Astro-Alex die Raumfahrt? Interview." *Zeit Online* 2 June 2015. Web. 9 June 2015.

Brooker, Will. *Using the Force. Creativity, Community and* Star Wars *Fans.* New York: Continuum, 2002. Print.

Brooks, Dan. "Interview with Kjell Lindgren of NASA: The Expedition 45 Astronaut Discusses His Crew's Popular *Star Wars*-Themed Poster and Much More." *Star Wars* 23 Feb. 2015. Web. 12 Mar. 2015.

Butrica, Andrew J. "The Right Stuff: The Reagan Revolution and the U.S. Space Program." *Remembering the Space Age.* Ed. Steven J. Dick. Washington, D.C.: U.S. Government Printing Office, 2008. 121–134. Print.

Byrnes, Mark E. *Politics and Space: Image Making by NASA.* Westport, CT: Praeger, 1994. Print.

Cavelos, Jane. "Stop Her, She's Got a Gun! How the Rebel Princess and the Virgin Queen Became Marginalized and Powerless in George Lucas' Fairy Tale." *Star Wars on Trial: Science Fiction and Fantasy Writers Debate the Most Popular Science Fiction Films of All Time.* Ed. David Brin and Matthew Woodring Stover. Dallas: BenBella, 2006: 305–327. Print.

Colman, Dan. "Nichelle Nichols Explains How Martin Luther King Convinced Her to Stay on *Star Trek.*" *Open Culture and the Archive of American Television* 21 Jan. 2013. Web. 12 Mar. 2015.

"Commercial Crew & Cargo Program." *NASA* 27 Apr. 2012. Web. 19 Mar. 2015.

Cristoforetti, Samantha. "There's Coffee in That Nebula." *Twitter* 17 Apr. 2015. Web. 28 Apr. 2015.

Deegan, Mary Jo. "Sexism in Space: The Freudian Formula in *Star Trek.*" *Eros in the Minds's Eye: Sexuality and the Fantastic in Art and Film.* Ed. Donald Palumbo. New York: Greenwood Press, 1986. 209–224. Print.

Dennings, Troy. *The Joiner King.* New York: Del Rey, 2005. Print.

Desloge, Nick. "Star Wars: An Exhibition in Cold War Politics." *Sex, Politics, and Religion in* Star Wars: *An Anthology.* Eds. Douglas Brode and Leah Deyneka. Lanham, MD: Scarecrow Press, 2012. 55–62. Print.

Dominguez, Diana. "Feminism and the Force: Empowerment and Disillusionment in a Galaxy Far, Far Away." *Culture, Identities and Technology in the* Star Wars *Films: Essays on the Two Triologies.* Eds. Carl Silvio and Tony M. Vinci. Jefferson, NC: McFarland, 2007. 109–133. Print.

"Einmal Schub, bitte." *Astra Shop* Mar. 2015. Web. 24 Mar. 2015.

"First Blonde in Space? Should a Woman Take the Risks?" Unknown newspaper (ca. 1960–1963). Jerrie Cobb Collection, unprocessed collection, Schlesinger Library, Radcliffe Institute, Harvard University.

Fisher, Luchina. "Leia Latest Disney Princess? Stars Sound Off on Disney Buying Lucasfilm." *ABC News* 31 Oct. 2012. Web. 17 Apr. 2015.

Foster, Amy. "The Gendered Anniversary: The Story of America's Women Astronauts." *The Florida Historical Quarterly* 87.2 (2008): 150–73. Print.

_____. *Integrating Women into the Astronaut Corps. Politics and Logistics at NASA, 1972–2004.* Baltimore: Johns Hopkins University Press, 2011. Print.

Fries, Colin. *Chronology of Wakeup Calls.* NASA 13 Mar. 2015. Web. 28 Apr. 2015.

"From Aviatrix to Astronautrix." *Time* 29 Aug. 1960: 41. Print.

"Fun in Space." *Newsweek* 30 May 1977: 60–63. Print.

Gilligan, Carol. *In a Different Voice: Psychological Theory and Women's Development.* Cambridge: Harvard University Press, 1993. Print.

Gordon, Andrew. "The Power of the Force: Sex in the *Star Wars* Trilogy." *Eros in the Mind's Eye: Sexuality and the Fantastic in Art and Film*. Ed. Donald Palumbo. New York: Greenwood Press, 1986. 193–207. Print.

Griffith, Holly. "How *Star Wars* Inspires Real Scientists and Engineers." *Star Wars* 10 Oct. 2012. Web. 12 Mar. 2015.

Hadfield, Chris. "Space Oddity." *YouTube* 12 May 2013. Web. 24 Mar. 2015.

Hatton, Lois. "*Star Wars Heroes* Slay Stereotypes." *USA Today* 1 July 2005: 13a. Print.

"Haynes. Baked Beans Commercial." *YouTube* 7 Apr. 2014. Web. 24 Mar. 2015.

Hilck, Karin. *The United States' Portrayal of Women in the Field of Manned Space Travel during the Cold War*. Stage & Performance—Theatricality in International History since 1500, Berlin 2014. Unpublished conference paper.

Hillebrand, Jörg, Mike Okuda, and Bernd Schneider. "NASA References in *Star Trek*." *Ex Astris Scientia* 6 Apr. 2015. Web. 8 May 2015.

Isaacs, Bruce. "A Survey of Popular and Scholarly Reception of the *Star Wars* Franchise." *Finding the Force of the* Star Wars *Franchise: Fans, Merchandise & Critics*. Eds. Matthew Wilhelm Kapell and John Shelton Lawrence. New York: Peter Lang, 2006. 265–281. Print.

Jemison, Mae. *Find Where the Wind Goes*. New York: Scholastic Press, 2001. Print.

Johnson, Lyndon B. Letter to Jerrie Cobb (23 Apr. 1962). Jerrie Cobb Collection, unprocessed collection, Schlesinger Library, Radcliffe Institute, Harvard University.

Kauffman, James L. *Selling Outer Space: Kennedy, the Media, and Funding for Project Apollo, 1961–1963*. Tuscaloosa: University of Alabama Press, 1994. Print

Kay, W. D. *Defining NASA: The Historical Debate Over the Agency's Mission*. Albany: State University of New York Press, 2005. Print.

Kennedy, John F. Address before a Joint Session of Congress. John F. Kennedy Presidential Library, 25 May 1961. Web. 8 Jan. 2015.

Kevles, Bettyann Holtzmann. *Almost Heaven: The Story of Women in Space*. Cambridge: MIT Press, 2006. Print.

Konstantinides, Anneta. "Is this NASA's Best Ever Official Portrait? Coolest Astronaut Sneaks His Dogs into Photo Shoot." *Mail Online* 30 Jan. 2015. Web. 12 Mar. 2015.

Koppel, Lily. *The Astronaut Wives Club*. New York: Grand Central, 2013. Print.

Krämer, Peter. "*Star Wars*: Peter Krämer Tells How the Popularity of the Sci-Fi Epic Proved Timely for Ronald Reagan and the Strategic Defense Initiative." *History Today* (March 1999): 41–7. Print.

"Leia Organa." *Wikia* 5 Mar. 2015. Web. 17 Apr. 2015.

Lipman, Julia C. "Technology's Glass Ceiling." *The Tech* 119/30 (1999). Web. 17 Apr. 2015.

Lockney, Dan. "Technology Transfer Program. Bringing NASA Technology Down to Earth." *Back Issues Archive 1976–2013*. Web. 10 July 2015.

Makemson, Harlen. *Media, NASA, and America's Quest for the Moon*. New York: Peter Lang, 2009. Print.

Marshall, Ann. "Spacewoman's Hopes Crushed by Tragedy." *Nairobi East African Standard* 8 June 1967. Technical Files Wally Funk, CF-833200–01, United States Air and Space Museum.

Mastracchio, Rick. "A *Star Wars* Day Message from NASA." *YouTube* 28 Apr. 2014. Web. 12 Mar. 2015.

McCullough, Joan. "The 13 Astronauts Who Were Left Behind." *Ms.* 3/3 (1973): 41–45. Print.

Merlock, Ray, and Kathy Merlock Jackson. "Lightsabers, Political Arenas, and Marriage for Princess Leia and Queen Amidala." *Sex, Politics, and Religion in* Star Wars*: An Anthology*. Eds. Douglas Brode and Leah Deynek. Lanham, MD: Scarecrow Press, 2012. 77–88. Print.

Meyer, Wendy Haskell. "The Decline and Fall of Lunar Royalty." *Texas Monthly* (Jan.

1974): 38–39. National Organization for Women Collection, MC 496 Carton 44, Folder 5, Schlesinger Library, Radcliffe Institute, Harvard University.

Michaud, Michael A. G. *Reaching for the High Frontier: The American Pro-Space Movement 1972–84*. New York: Praeger, 1986. Print.

Miller, Martin, and Robert Sprich. "The Appeal of *Star Wars*: An Archetypal-Psychoanalytic View." *American Imago* 38.2 (1981): 203–220. Print.

"Moon Maid's Ready." *Oklahoma City Press* (24 Aug. 1960). Jerrie Cobb Collection, unprocessed collection, Schlesinger Library, Radcliffe Institute, Harvard University.

Mystery Photo. Beacon Information/Jet Propulsion Laboratory Feb. 2011. Web. 17 Apr. 2015.

"NASA—Final Frontier Astronauts Land on *Star Trek*." *NASA* 13 May 2005. Web. 20 Mar. 2015.

"NASA's Kepler Mission Discovers a World Orbiting Two Stars." *NASA* 15 Sept. 2011. Web. 19 Jan. 2015.

Nichols, Nichelle. *Trekking NASA from Mars or What's in It for Me?* (19 Aug. 1976). Ruth Bates Harris Papers, unprocessed collection, Manuscript Division, Moorland-Spingarn Research Center, Howard University.

Nishi, Dennis. "'*Star Trek's*' Nichelle Nichols on How Martin Luther King, Jr. Changed Her Life." *Wall Street Journal* 17 Jan. 2011. Web. 12 Mar. 2015.

No. 1 Space Gal Seems A Little Astronaughty. Unknown newspaper (ca. 1960–1963). Jerrie Cobb Collection, unprocessed collection. Schlesinger Library, Radcliffe Institute, Harvard University.

O'Donnell, Franklin. "Explorer I." *California Institute of Technology* 2007. Web. 17 Apr. 2015.

Penley, Constance. *NASA/Trek: Popular Science and Sex in America*. New York: R.R. Donnelley & Sons, 1997. Print.

Phelps, J. Alfred. *They Had a Dream: The Story of African-American Astronauts*. Novato, CA: Presidio, 1994. Print.

"Poster for *Star Wars Episode VII*? No, Just a Space Station Crew." *NBC News* 12 Feb. 2015. Web. 12 Mar. 2015.

Rentz, Ingo. "Astra Rakete: Philipp und Keuntje schickt neues Biermischgetränk in die Umlaufbahn." *Horizont* 17 Feb. 2015. Web. 24 Mar. 2015.

Rich, Katey. "*Star Wars* Spin-Off Will Be a Boba Fett Origin Story." *Vanity Fair Magazine* 4 May 2015. Web. 4 May 2015.

Robinson, Joanna. "First Official Look at Game of Thrones Star Gwendoline Christie in *Star Wars: The Force Awakens*. Meet Captain Phasma." *Vanity Fair Magazine* 4 May 2015. Web. 4 May 2015.

Ross-Nazal, Jennifer. "Pioneering Women of Today: Space Travellers." *Sound Historian* 13 (2011): 23–32. Print.

Rubey, Dan. "*Star Wars*: Not So Long Ago, Not So Far Away." *Jump Cut* 18 (1978). Web. 22 Mar. 2015.

SFA Products. NASA 17 Apr. 2015. Web. 20 Apr. 2015.

Sams, Anastasia. *Several Lunar Landing Festival Queen Caricatures*. National Organization for Women Collection, MC 496 Carton 44, Folder 5, Schlesinger Library, Radcliffe Institute, Harvard University.

Sex and Space. Unknown newspaper (ca. 1963). Jerrie Cobb Collection, unprocessed collection, Schlesinger Library, Radcliffe Institute, Harvard University.

Sherr, Lynn. *Sally Ride: America's First Woman in Space*. New York: Simon & Schuster, 2014. Print.

Sherrod, Robert. "The Selling of the Astronaut." *Columbia Journalism Review* 12.1 (1973): 16–25. Print.

Siceloff, Steven. Star Wars *Fans to NASA: Build a Hyperdrive*. NASA 16 Aug. 2010. Web. 12 Mar. 2015.

Simpson, Philip L. "Thawing the Ice Princess." *Finding the Force of the* Star Wars *Franchise: Fans, Merchandise & Critics.* Eds. Matthew Wilhelm Kapell and John Shelton Lawrence. New York: Peter Lang, 2006. 115–130. Print.

Spangler, Bill. "Fighting Princesses and other Distressing Damsels." Star Wars *on Trial. Science Fiction and Fantasy Writers Debate the Most Popular Science Fiction Films of All Time.* Eds. David Brin and Matthew Woodring Stover. Dallas: BenBella, 2006. 329–338. Print.

"*Star Trek*'s Nichelle Nichols' Warp-Speed Visit to Dryden." *NASA* 11 Jan. 2012. Web. 12 Mar. 2015.

"*Star Wars* Day Shareables." *NASA* 4 May 2014. Web. 12 Mar. 2015.

"*Star Wars* in *How I Met Your Mother.*" *Wikia* 26. Sept. 2013. Web. 19 Mar. 2015.

"*Star Wars* in *The Big Bang Theory.*" *Wikia* 9 Sept. 2013. Web. 19 Mar. 2015.

"*Star Wars* Pepsi Commercial." *YouTube* 31 Jan. 2011. Web. 19 Mar. 2015.

"*Star Wars: The Force Awakens* Official Teaser." *YouTube* 28 Nov. 2014. Web. 20 Apr. 2015.

"*Star Wars: The Force Awakens* Official Teaser #2." *YouTube* 16 Apr. 2015. Web. 20 Apr. 2015.

"*Star Wars*: The Year's Best Movie." *Time* 30 May 1977: 56–62. Print.

Taylor, Chris. *How Star Wars Conquered the Universe: The Past, Present, and Future of a Multibillion Dollar Franchise.* New York: Basic Books, 2014. Print.

Thompson, Anne V. "Equality of Sexes Ends Where Outer Space Begins." *Tulsa Daily World* 1 Oct. 1967. Jerrie Cobb Collection, unprocessed collection, Schlesinger Library, Radcliffe Institute, Harvard University.

"2013 Astronaut Class. NASA Selects 2013 Astronaut Candidate Class." *NASA* 1 May 2015. Web. 4 May 2015.

United Press International. *Scoffs, Bravos Aim At Woman in Orbit.* Unknown newspaper (ca. June 1963). Jerrie Cobb Collection, unprocessed collection, Schlesinger Library, Radcliffe Institute, Harvard University.

von Braun, Wernher. Letter to Jerrie Cobb (9 May 1962). Jerrie Cobb Collection, unprocessed collection, Schlesinger Library, Radcliffe Institute, Harvard University.

Weitekamp, Margaret A. *Right Stuff, Wrong Sex: America's First Women in Space Program.* Baltimore: Johns Hopkins University Press, 2004. Print

Welch, Douglass. "Girls Best the Men, Again." *Pittsburgh Post-Gazette* 16 Sept. 1960. Jerrie Cobb Collection, unprocessed collection, Schlesinger Library, Radcliffe Institute, Harvard University.

White, Steve. "*Star Trek Creator Gene Roddenberry's Ashes to be Blasted into Deep Space.*" *Mirror* 21 June 2013. Web. 12 Mar. 2015.

The Winners!!! … Lunar Landing Festival King (or Queen) Contest…. National Organization for Women Collection, MC 496 Carton 44, Folder 5, Schlesinger Library, Radcliffe Institute, Harvard University.

Feminist Icons Wanted
Damsels in Distress Need Not Apply

Mara Wood

Feminism is a hot-button issue in media. Movies, television shows, and books are often criticized for their portrayal of female characters. The number and quality of those characters are assessed by measures like the Bechdel test and are analyzed by blogs and popular entertainment sites. Media inspires fandoms on sites like tumblr, where viewers can connect to and understand a character. Ideas of equality, autonomy, and respect are increasingly becoming standards to measure a good female character. In the case of *Star Wars*, the official canon's women embody traits important to feminism and can be considered as feminist icons.

Central to the ideals of feminism is autonomy and choice. Female characters who act as agents of change within stories are regarded as icons of feminism. In many science fiction and action-oriented tales, that narrative is missing. Women are often presented as love interests, sidekicks, or background noise. *Star Wars* gives us a different narrative despite the limited number of prominent female characters. The original trilogy introduced us to a princess who prefers to rescue herself. The prequels presented a troubled senator fighting for the rights of the galaxy. The animated series *Clone Wars* allow viewers to grow up with a Padawan and experience her heartbreak as she matured. The newest, ongoing television series, *Rebels*, gives us a ground-level portrayal of two women trying to make a difference in the lives of others. What *Star Wars* lacks in quantity is certainly made up in quality.

Defining Feminism

Describing anyone, real or fictional, as a feminist icon presents a bit of a challenge. There is no single "best" example of a feminist. Feminists themselves are not always in agreement on what is feminist. For example, some see "girlie" characters such as Miss Piggy, who was honored at the Elizabeth A Slacker Center in 2015, as a necessary feature of the feminist movement, arguing their heightened femininity translates into a source of empowerment. Others view these women as succumbing to the pressures of society rather than transcending them (Purvis). There seems to be little agreement on what makes an icon an icon.

Further, the various movements of feminism elude a single definition. Some describe them as waves; others view them as more of a constantly evolving and shifting perspective (Showden). Regardless, feminism is often characterized as having three historic "waves." Each wave spotlighted different challenges and perspectives. The first wave is often attributed as the spark of feminism despite the obvious ignoring of minority populations (Kinser). Those who benefitted the most from this movement were white women of privilege, such as suffragettes in the United States during the Progressive era. During the Civil Rights movements in the 1960s and 1970s, the second wave sought to empower women of color who had long struggled for rights and liberation (Kinser). The third wave presents even more confusion. There is a current strive for individuality and autonomy, sexual freedom and equality. Women who grew up in the third wave of feminism are accustomed to a sense of entitlement to rights (Kinser). They also, to an extent, embrace contradictions within feminism better than the previous generations (Kinser). Third wave feminism sets us up for a wide variety of icons and role models, each different and important as the last. Because the ideals of feminism are so entwined in this generation's culture, it is easy to see the diversity in representation of feminist icons in media.

The relationship between third wave feminism and media cannot be separated. The generation who grew up in the third wave also grew up with MTV, the Harry Potter saga, *Twilight*, and *Sailor Moon*. Media is no longer consumed in a vacuum; websites and blogs are dedicated to analyzing new fiction within the context of feminism and representation. Social media in particular creates spaces to discuss feminist issues in pop culture. Through media, third wave feminists demand recognition and respect through characters portrayed in fiction. Media that does not incorporate the ideals of feminism is often heavily criticized; in 2014, video game fans were incensed that the Assassin's Creed franchise did not acknowledge the desire for playable female characters (Baker-Whitelaw). Current television shows like *Agent Carter* and movies such as *Mad Max: Fury Road* succeed in furthering the inclusivity of third wave feminism. Both of these examples of popular media feature a gender-diverse cast of characters and fans have responded in kind.

Even media with praise for diversity are not perfect—it should be noted that, after the second season of *Agent Carter* was announced in 2015, there was a vocal call for more racial diverse characters that was echoed by the cast and crew of the show (Cox).

Media offers people a safe way to view the world. It can be easier to digest the issues of the world through a third party. Media has been used to explain real-world phenomena, such as Travis Langley's use of the comic book character Batman to explain abnormal psychology without violating the privacy and rights of those experiencing mental illness (Langley). Media also has the power to change and influence cultural perspectives. Debbie Stoller of *BUST* magazine believes "changing the pop culture and critiquing the pop culture is a perfectly valid way to effect change in people's ideas and values, and these changes trickle down to the government" (Showden 184). While there are a number of political changes that have yet to be made, Stoller is on to something. Media culture permeates our lives, and it can be a way to teach people, especially children, about equality and rights.

Enter a New Galaxy

Star Wars, in particular, is an interesting medium to explore gender and feminism. The original trilogy has three named women (Leia, Beru, and Mon Mothma), two of which barely have a speaking role. The prequel trilogy has far more named women, but the majority lack screen time and storytelling power. In fact, the deaths of two women (Padmé and Shmi) in the prequels are used to motivate Anakin to turning to the Dark Side of the Force. As much as the films lack in female and racial representation, the *Star Wars* television series make up for it in spades. *The Clone Wars* features Ahsoka Tano and Padmé Amidala heavily, the former created just for the show, often with one or both of these women as the driving force in a story. Female Jedi are regularly shown, such as Master Luminara and her Padawan Barriss Offee, as well as Aayla Secura, Shaak Ti, and Adi Gallia—many of whom were introduced in the movies, but featured as silent "filler." We also cannot forget the villains, like the powerful Aurra Sing and Asajj Ventress who wrecked havoc in the galaxy. *Star Wars Rebels* may have two male Force-users as the primary characters, but the ensemble cast includes two well-received women: Hera Syndulla and Sabine Wren, neither of whom are portrayed as white women. The television shows, which are marketed to a wide variety of ages, help redefine *Star Wars* as a franchise that welcomes women and strives to make them more visible in a number of roles.

The limited number of women shown onscreen in the films belies a form of sexism in the *Stars Wars* movies' narrative. This could be intentional on the part of the producers, or it could be the sad result of the contextual lack of women in films. Due to the nature of the overall story—an unending battle for liberty—those women who are portrayed are in positions of power and influence. Regardless of their origins, their impact is noticeable. For instance, no character faults Leia or Padmé as leaders solely because of their gender. Both enjoy prominent positions of power without being ridiculed for being feminine. The exception, of course, comes from Han Solo in *Star Wars* as he remarks the trouble with female advice (Lucas *Star Wars*).[1]

In contrast to the inclusive heroic side, sexism is presented in the original trilogy as associated with evil (like Jabba's slave dancers) or morally ambiguous (like the "cad" Lando who shamelessly flirts with Leia while betraying her to Darth Vader). Indeed, the Empire seems to have banned women from the armed services entirely. As discussed below, Leia's actions and role in the original trilogy speak volumes about the way the "good guys" perceive her.

Leia's mother, Padmé Amidala, also commands enormous respect. Her transition from queen to senator is not marked by sexist opinions. Her peers respect her primarily for her fight against the tyrannical Trade Federation in *The Phantom Menace* and against the Separatists during the Clone Wars. *The Clone Wars* television series does a magnificent job of showcasing Padmé's diplomatic skills, reinforcing just why she was so important to the Republic. The women in *The Clone Wars* especially do not seem to face sexism barriers in education, careers, politics, or military leadership (Stephanie). Women serve on the Jedi Council as Masters as well, although their presence in the films is limited; in *Revenge of the Sith* they exist primarily to be executed and horrify the viewers (Lucas *Revenge of the Sith*).

It is obvious that Lucas is telling a male-driven story in his films. Anakin is "The Chosen One" and the women he encounters in the prequels are supplementary to his story at best or plot devices at worst. His son, Luke, is "The Hero" whose main journey is to become a Jedi and save his father. The women in Luke's journey aid him along the way. However, those who explore the *Star Wars* universe through comics, novels, video games, and television have introduced a number of female characters who help highlight the richness of gender dynamics in the Star Wars universe and enrich the contexts barely hinted at in the films.

The *Star Wars* Legends universe is full of fleshed-out, diverse female characters. Who could forget Mara Jade Skywalker or Jaina Solo? The flexibility of multiple creators, a wider time frame, and diverse media platforms allowed female characters to flourish. While they are important to the overall narrative of the *Star Wars* universe, only those main female characters that appear in the canon prior to *The Force Awakens* will be addressed here. These are the women primarily important to the tone and direction of *Star Wars* as the series grows under the direction of Lucasfilm and Disney. Their impact on overall story, interactions with other characters, and representation of feminist ideals will be explored as we determine the role of each woman as a feminist icon.

The Distressing Damsel

When it comes to women in science fiction, Princess Leia Organa set the feminist bar high. Her appearance in the 1977 *Star Wars* film redefined what it means to be a woman in the science fiction universe. Before her, women characters in fantasies were portrayed as victims and damsels in distress, such as Ann in *King Kong* (1933). Leia's presence flipped the notion of a woman's assumed role in a mythological tale.

Carrie Fisher, the actress who portrayed Leia, once said Leia was not a damsel in distress; rather, she was a distressing damsel (Roller).[2] Leia did not fit the mold for a princess. Her presence challenged the cultural perception of a "princess." There is an expectation from women in films, thanks in part to her introduction in *Star Wars*. Leia is distressing, her outright refusal to conform as the source. Leia's lifelong training primed her for the position of the most powerful woman in the Rebel Forces (Waid *Princess Leia No. 2*). Further, she embraces wisdom and compassion as she helps lead the Rebellion in their war against the Empire.

SOMEBODY'S GOT TO SAVE OUR SKINS

Until Luke arrives on the Death Star, he holds a preconceived notion of who the mysterious princess was. He first sees her as a projection from R2-D2: she is tiny, clad in white and begging for help. His sense of chivalry evoked, Luke, the heroic errant (Jedi) knight in the making, feels the call to aid her by any means possible. His purpose is to rescue Leia.

This assumption is one readers and fans are familiar with. A damsel in distress, and an unlikely hero. Through bravery and ingenuity, the hero manages to devise a plan to rescue the princess and save the day. However, this motif goes out the window when Leia and Luke first meet and the princess famously dismisses him as her heroic savior:

LUKE: I'm Luke Skywalker, I'm here to rescue you.
LEIA: Who? [Lucas *Star Wars*].

Indeed, she does not seem to take him seriously until he mentions Ben Kenobi, the aged warrior to whom she originally sent the message. Even then, her next question is "Where is he?" Concerned about the plans and the fate of Rebel Alliance at stake, she remains all business.

Although we do not see any real scars, she had been tortured, physically and emotionally, during her imprisonment on the Death Star. She witnessed her entire culture, family, and home get wiped out by an unbelievable weapon. Leia, at this point of the rescue, is fed up with being out of control of her life. In the course of her rescue, Leia takes charge of the situation and helps Han, Luke, Chewbacca, and the droids escape the Death Star. In the climatic battle, she is the center figure in the control room, monitoring the battle (even though there is little she can do). As the leader on Yavin, she awards Luke and Han at the end. Leia continues to aid in her rescue and others' in the original trilogy. In *The Empire Strikes Back*, she tells Han "they" need him as an ally and the smuggler responds by calling her ice-cold for not being a romantic woman. She participates in the initial rescue of Han and goes back for Luke on Bespin (Kershner). In *Return of the Jedi*, Leia disguises herself as a ruthless bounty hunter to free Han from carbonite. On Endor, she is again in the heart of the battle to destroy the shield generator (Marquand). Leia refuses to be helpless in any situation in which she finds herself.

THE ICE PRINCESS

One of Leia's most interesting moments in *Star Wars* is her reaction to Tarkin's destruction of Alderaan. Onscreen, she is visibly upset. Afterwards, her loss of homeworld is never brought up onscreen again, with the exception of a quickly brushed off condolence on Yavin, where she has "no time for sorrows" (Lucas *Star Wars*). In a comic book story exploring this moment, however, Leia deals with her grief in a much different way than most, one that centers on her role as a princess. Leia formally honors the loss of Alderaan with the Rebels, but her sincerity is questioned by some members (Waid *Princess Leia No. 1*). She seems to put aside her need to mourn the death of her planet and family in favor of protecting the Rebellion. Luke puts Leia on the spot by noting her lack of grief. General Dodonna is blunter about Leia's current role in the Rebellion: her duty is to grieve, not to lead. Further, as princess of a now-dead planet, she is a walking target, "too valuable an asset to be unguarded" (Waid *Princess Leia No. 1*). Therefore, he wants her to take a back seat in the Alliance's leadership.

Not satisfied to site back in hiding, Leia partners with an Alderaanian X-Wing pilot named Evaan Verlain. Unfortunately, Evaan's initial opinion of

Leia is less than flattering. Instead of seeing Leia's dedication to the Rebellion as a sign of her unwavering strength of leadership, she outright calls her an ice princess for failing to adhere to the social norms for grieving (Waid *Princess Leia No. 1*).

Evaan further resents having Leia as the surviving member of the royal House Organa and the embodiment of the deceased planet's culture. Evaan was directly instructed by Queen Breha of Alderaan and internalized the characteristics expected of an Alderaanian woman—that of wisdom, grace, and femininity. Leia, on the other hand, rejects her prescribed role as a royal official, including the lessons of politics and culture she took as a child—she much preferred the physical training her father made sure she received in order to ensure her own protection. Although Evaan and Leia are at odds, it is Evaan's devotion to Alderaanian culture that inspires Leia to hijack a ship and explore the galaxy searching for survivors. Leia explains her actions to Dodonna:

> What is my alternative? To collapse in grief, as everyone seems to wish? To keep my head down and hide? To rule over nothing? I reject that. The last royal of Alderaan must be too strong to cower. Too certain to despair. And more than that, she must be too stubborn to quit—if her subjects—and her culture—are to survive. If you will not allow me to aid the Rebellion, I can do this [Waid *Princess Leia No. 1*].

In one speech, Leia demonstrates the need to continue saving others while also acting as a worthy leader.

Leia's mission to save Alderaanian survivors is also an act of redemption. She feels personally responsible for the planet's death, and protecting the last of her subjects is the only course of action she sees fit for her (Waid *Princess Leia No. 3*). By personally rescuing her people, Leia is conveying to them her understanding of their loss while simultaneously being proactive in her position as a leader.

That Damn Metal Bikini

When talking about *Star Wars* and feminism, there is an elephant in the room. Namely, the slave outfit Leia wears in *Return of the Jedi* (Marquand). As Karin Hilck notes in her essay in this volume, the jury is still out on whether the bikini and its layered meanings are empowering or demeaning to Leia personally, women in the *Star Wars* universe, or feminist movement outside theaters. Like feminism itself, it is subjective, dependent on the on the personal opinion and experience of the individual.

The bikini and its connotation of Leia's hopelessness and helplessness are problematic, but the bikini offers a unique commentary on the power of women. After her daring attempted rescue of Han fails, Leia is stripped and placed under the control of Jabba the Hutt, much to her revulsion. She is his trophy, and she is meant to be sexually provocative to the viewer. Indeed, in her first appearance in the bikini, the camera focuses on one of Jabba's stooges gazing at her bare leg. His gaze becomes the viewer's who wants to see more. The next shot shows Leia entirely, sleeping near Jabba; her skimpy outfit has clear implications. As a chained slave, she loses her agency. She becomes more or less eye candy for Jabba's court and the audience.

Even in this demeaning position, Leia can still be an icon of feminism. As Barr puts it on fangirlblog, "fortune or circumstance can take away everything, but only you can give away your dignity." Leia retains her dignity as Jabba's slave, even looking defiant at times. However, Leia once again proves she is no damsel in distress. During the battle, she kills Jabba, strangling him with the chains around her own neck. Leia's weakness becomes her weapon of choice in securing her freedom.

In terms of character, the outfit and position offer viewers a new perspective on the princess. Until this moment, Leia had consistently shown masculine-heavy traits, such as her commanding presence and action-driven attitude. Both Evaan and Han Solo had commented on her coldness. Leia's portrayal as a slave reminds fans that she is feminine. Despite her masculine-dominant personality, men find her attractive: even in the first film, Han and Luke trade barbs whether she will settle down "with a guy like me." (Lucas *Star Wars*). Conversely, women are able to sympathize with her powerless position and cheer when she takes charge and kills her oppressor (Barr).

Yes, Leia is highly sexualized in this moment, but she never loses her importance to the overall story of *Star Wars*. The others never treat her differently, and she continues to be an effective leader in the Rebellion. The bikini and slavery act as an example of oppression that can be overcome through strength of character and determination to mete out justice. In this, Leia's reaction to her short-lived stint as an overgrown slug's play-thing offers women and men an example of triumph over setbacks.

The Problem with Padmé

In the prequel trilogy, Padmé Amidala, on the surface, is presented as an exemplar of feminism. She rules a planet at a young age—actress Natalie Portman was in her late teens when she first played the role. She repairs the relationship between the human culture and that of the Gungans on her home planet of Naboo. She speaks out time and time again against the escalating Clone Wars, citing the damage and death caused to the citizens of the galaxy. She is, in many parts of the prequels and *The Clone Wars*, the driving force of the story. Underneath it all, however, Queen Amidala has a problem that affects the presentation of the characters and her effectiveness as a feminist icon.

Padmé is the primary female character in the *Star Wars* prequels. She is the "Leia" of the millennial generation, a character meant to satisfy the changing social norms of third wave feminism. From the beginning, there are many parallels between the mother and daughter. Both are leaders, as well as royalty. Both are introduced as women who need to be saved from plot contrivances. And, both women show themselves capable of their own rescue. Unlike Leia, though, Padmé falls short in many areas despite an impressive record in the first prequel, *The Phantom Menace*. In part, her relationship with Anakin Skywalker sets her up for failure. She is, as feminist Diana Dominquez describes her, a tragic heroine that possesses the traits of a warrior-hero. The most frustrating aspect of Padmé's character is the inconsistency of her actions and the gradual diminishing of her agency as the series progresses. What start out as a hands-down feminist icon is reduced to a plot device to further the male character's development.

Child Prodigy

The ruler of the planet Naboo is a fourteen-year-old girl in *The Phantom Menace* (Lucas *The Phantom Menace*). You would never know looking at her. Padmé makes her first appearance onscreen in a holographic image. She is forceful, commanding, and calm. She speaks to the Trade Federation as their equal, not as a child. Her team of advisors respects her decisions; there are no remarks made about her course of action or of her age or experience. Curious about Tatooine, she has no qualms "slumming" down to mingle with the locals. As queen, she confronts the Senate about their lack of leadership in resolving the blockade surrounding her planet and calls for a voice of no confidence to replace an indecisive chancellor. In the end, she masterminds the plan to re-take her palace and leads the charge herself. Padmé, upon reflection of her office, is aware of the limitations she had as a young woman: "I wasn't the youngest queen ever elected. But now that I think back on it, I'm not sure I was old enough. I'm not sure I was ready" (Lucas *Attack of the Clones*). If that is what Padmé truly felt during the course of *The Phantom Menace*, she never let that slip. She exudes confidence and leadership, two things her people needed in their most desperate hour.

What is interesting about Padmé's situation is that she was never the youngest queen to serve her people. In *Attack of the Clones*, Padmé confesses to Anakin that she does not see herself as special or apart from the other queens of Naboo, certainly not by age (Lucas). She brushes off his comment about the people of Naboo desiring to extend her term. This brief exchange highlights Padmé's uncanny leadership, respect for tradition and law, and humility. Padmé sees herself as a servant of the people, a servant that can make a difference in a variety of settings outside of the elected office of queen.

PROMINENT SENATOR

When Padmé left her position as queen, she was not ready to abandon her position as a political leader. The next queen recognizes that need and requested that Padmé serve as a Senator to the Galactic Republic (Lucas *Attack of the Clones*). The Senate is a forum in which Padmé is accustomed to performing. Much like her daughter Leia, Padmé was groomed for her role as a political leader since childhood. Padmé's father had connections to political figures, and Padmé participated in the Legislative Youth Program. She was always meant to be a leader, and she performs her job splendidly in the last years of the Republic.

Padmé's skills as a Senator are highlighted in her activity in *The Clone Wars*. She is intimately familiar with the problems of absolute control through the Trade Federation blockade the devastation caused by war. In any conflict, Padmé's gut reaction is to look for a peaceful solution. She recognizes the validity of the argument on the Separatists' side and makes an effort to teach Anakin the dangers of absolute power in *Attack of the Clones* but he refuses to listen. Later, she tries to teach his Padawan apprentice Ahsoka to listen to those who oppose her, and Ahsoka learns that people's reactions based on their beliefs are not simply black and white, but have layers of complexity ("Heroes on Both Sides"). When it comes to the people of the galaxy, Padmé fights hard to protect their rights and lives. She joins Bail Organa on Alderaan to host a conference to discuss how to protect refugees from the Clone Wars ("Assassin"). Even knowing her life was in explicit danger, Padmé makes efforts to be present and deliver her message. Even for aliens who were not outright citizens of the Republic, namely the Zillo Beast of season two ("The Zillo Beast Strikes Back"), Padmé believes it is her duty to defend those who have no voice.

Padmé constantly fights for the rights of others at the expense of her own reputation and likability. Where Leia is generally respected by those around her, Padmé is seen as a troublemaker and a traitor to the Republic.

She admits she is partisan and against the war, but she also recognizes the power of having an ally that is widely accepted by others in the Senate. Bail Organa, who shares many of the same views as Padmé, is far less polarizing (Dunham). Padmé is aware that she is abrasive to others in the Senate, which in turn may impact the attitude towards her causes. Senator Organa, who is just as passionate but more sensitive to others in the Senate, often aids Padmé in her quest to protect the Republic.

Romantic Death

The driving force behind Anakin's acceleration to the Dark Side is his desire to protect Padmé from death, either from assassins or from her troubled pregnancy. The thought becomes all-consuming, causing Anakin to turn his back on the Jedi, kill children, and become Darth Vader. In her final story arc in the prequels, Padmé is a plot device, doing little other than giving birth to Luke and Leia.

It can be argued that Padmé's arc throughout *Star Wars* is a reflection of the death of the Republic (Dominguez). This positive spin excuses her limited presence in *Revenge of the Sith*. Padmé's power and influence as a Senator greatly diminishes as the Empire begins to form. Indeed, viewers can foreshadow her decline from *The Phantom Menace* as Palpatine manipulates her and her court in his bid for power. However, her death is not presented as an analogy to the structure of the Republic to the casual viewer; it is framed as a romantic death, a woman so torn by her love that she cannot continue to live. This romanticized death—complete with petals arranged around her funeral procession—heightens the tragedy of Anakin's failure to "save" her (from himself, as it turns out). Padmé Amidala's death has little purpose than a prop for Darth Vader's rise.

After the events of *The Clone Wars* television series, Anakin and Padmé's relationship is strained. During the series, she is hurt by his accusations of cheating and betraying him ("The Rise of Clovis"). This leads to the events in the last prequel, where Padmé comes to Anakin and reveals her pregnancy (Lucas *Revenge of the Sith*). She spends much of the movie in her own home, far from the politics and adventure viewers have witnessed up to this point. From a narrative standpoint, she hides her pregnancy because of her secret relationship with her husband. She fears a scandal would lead to her dismissal from her political position if anyone found out, and she wants to protect Anakin's position as a celibate Jedi. She makes fewer public appearances, and her power as a Senator and former queen is nonexistent by the time the film concludes.

Padmé's waning power makes her death even more troublesome. Padmé, who had spent her entire career as a politician fighting for the rights of others, dies of a broken heart shortly after childbirth. This is the same character who put her career before her marriage, the safety of others before herself ("Hostage Crisis"). In contrast, Leia's position reflected her strong stance in second wave feminism: even with the demise of her planet, the princess never wavers. However, Padmé is not her daughter's mother. If there was ever a time that the Republic needed her expertise, it was at the moment when Palpatine declared the formation of a Galactic Empire. Instead, Padmé loses the will to live.

What is most disheartening about Padmé's death is the thought that occupies her mind at the very end. After giving birth to two children, she spends her final moments pleading with Obi-Wan to look for the good in Anakin. She has little remorse for the Republic's demise—a far cry from the champion in her first appearance. Rather, *Revenge of the Sith*'s swansong for Padmé shows she was never meant to be a fully-realized character in *Star Wars*; her function was a piece of Anakin's story, the driving force behind him turning to the Dark Side and helping facilitate the rise of the Empire. To add insult to injury, *Star Wars* suffers from a paternal narrative. Luke's legacy and motivation is shaped by the knowledge of his father Anakin. He defines himself as similar to Anakin, then as a foil to Vader, then as Anakin's son and savior. There is only one instance where he acknowledges the existence of his mother. In his brief conversation with Leia about their parentage, they describe Padmé's legacy as "kind, but sad" (Marquand). He does not ask about her relationship with the Force. Even after death, Padmé is presented only as a woman who fell in love with a man who became a monster.

The Wrong Jedi

Anakin Skywalker's Padawan, Ahsoka Tano, offered a brand-new perspective to the *Star Wars* universe. Prior to her introduction, the only insight into the Master-Padawan relationship was limited to the brief interactions between Luke, Obi-Wan, and Yoda; Obi-Wan and Qui-Gon Jinn; and the strained "brother" relationship between Anakin and Obi-Wan. With Ahsoka, fans get to see the trials and tribulations of becoming a Jedi and the stress of growing up in the middle of a war. Ahsoka matures before our eyes; the beginning of the *Clone Wars* television show portrays her as a know-it-all teenager; by the end of the show she departs from the Jedi Temple as a mature young woman determined to not let the mistakes of her idols change her identity.

Ahsoka arguably has the most character growth and development of all the women in the *Star Wars* canon while still retaining her position as a character of influence and agency.

AHSOKA THE LEADER

What makes Ahsoka a compelling feminist icon is how she combats her faults. Ahsoka is put in a position of power early in life. Her Master takes her to the front lines with him and uses the Clone Wars as a classroom to teach the Force. She is not merely a bystander or foot soldier; Ahsoka learns early in her life to become a leader. Multiple times she is called to devise plans and order troops on the field. At times, that pressure feels immense. At one point, Ahsoka's desire to perform well as a leader costs her the life of many troopers and endangers the mission ("Storm over Ryloth"). She is not given much time to grieve her loss; Anakin requires her to perform a risky plan that could kill him if it goes wrong. Reluctant at first, Ahsoka overcomes her fear of failure and performs her part beautifully. She learns to trust her instincts in battle and be confident in her training as a commander and a Jedi.

Ahsoka leads more than just clones. In one episode, the ruler of her home world, Duchess Satine of Mandalore, suspects corruption in the planet's government ("The Academy"). She requests the aid of a Jedi and Anakin hides his mission's true purpose from Ahsoka. Instead of outright telling Ahsoka the purpose, he sends her to teach Mandalorian youth about leadership, corruption, and civic lessons. At first, Ahsoka believes the mission to be beneath her. However, she faithfully instructs the youth to the best of her abilities. She eventually aids the Mandalorian youth as they uncover corruption in their own government. Ahsoka demonstrates the ability to lead and inspire people outside of battle as they strive to make their world a better place.

Throughout *The Clone Wars*, Ahsoka demonstrates her growing capacity for leadership. Part of that capacity centers on treating her followers with respect. An ongoing theme in *The Clone Wars* deals with the individuality and purpose of the clones beyond their creation for war. Several episodes explore this theme and strive to show the troopers' humanity. Ahsoka follows her Master's example and refers to the clones by the names they chose for themselves. She takes risks to save their lives when they encounter danger. She earns their respect on and off the field. At one point, Ahsoka is framed for a murder. Although the majority of the people she knows believe her guilt, the troopers do not. Rex, one of her loyal comrades, comments he does not believe his leader could ever be capable of mass murder (Keller *The Jedi*

Who Knew Too Much). Although his observation falls on deaf ears, it is an example of the level of respect she earns from her troopers.

AHSOKA THE JEDI

It is no secret Anakin is an untraditional Jedi. From his immaculate conception to his late admittance to the Jedi Order, Anakin Skywalker is anything but normal. It follows, then, that anyone Anakin personally trains and mentors would have different notions about the role of the Jedi and the nature of the Force, particularly his recklessness and headstrong demeanor. Obi-Wan goes as far as stating, "Why do I get the feeling that you're going to be the death of me?" (Lucas *Attack of the Clones*). He proves prophetic: when they meet decades later, Kenobi's circle becomes complete.

Despite her teacher's questionable training and eventual turn to the Dark Side of the Force, Ahsoka develops a deeper understanding of the Force and how it impacts everything around her. Ahsoka understands the Force as a weapon of the Jedi, something to be harnessed and used to enact the will of the Republic for the benefit of all, not just a preconceived notion of justice. Through the interactions with her fellow Jedi, Ahsoka learns the Force is much more than a weapon. Further, she discovers key characteristics of the Jedi that are necessary for that connection.

One notable example occurs in season two of *The Clone Wars* when Ahsoka pairs up with Jedi Barriss Offee to infiltrate and destroy a weapons factory ("Weapons Factory"). Ahsoka initially sees Barriss Offee's teachings a waste of time: having been trained by Anakin, she often relies on her gut feeling rather than intense preparation. She slowly comes to respects Barriss's different perspective of being a Padawan. Ahsoka understands the Force is multifaceted and Barriss's calmer approach is just as valuable her own. Ahsoka values Barriss's opinion and insight, even as she is later betrayed and framed for the attack orchestrated by Barriss herself.

As Ahsoka grows in the series, she integrates key elements of the Force into her approach towards life. While helping Prince Lee-Char of Mon Calamari, Ahsoka shares a perspective that deserves a second look: "If you make decisions out of fear, you're more likely to be wrong" ("Gungan Attack"). She delivers this short sentence with more insight than can be expected from a budding apprentice not fully learned in the way of the Jedi. Ahsoka is briefly referencing the path to the Dark Side. As Yoda had said to young Anakin regarding his emotions, "Fear leads to anger, anger leads to hate, hate leads to suffering. Fear is the path to the Dark Side" (Lucas *The Phantom Menace*). Anakin clearly did not take the lesson to heart: his fear of losing loved ones—from his mother to his wife—will eventually damn him and the galaxy. Yet his apprentice seems to pick up on this vital lesson her teacher cannot comprehend. Without diving unnecessarily into why Prince Lee-Char needs to be careful with his next course of action, Ahsoka provides the advice and guidance the Jedi were always meant to provide to world leaders.

Anakin's apparently one-dimensional mindset contrasts sharply with Ahsoka's growth. At times, it appears her strength was equal to her teacher's. Just as she understood fear and its consequences more than Anakin, Ahsoka has other abilities exceeding her Master's. She could sense things he could not, such as Plo Koon's survival ("Rising Malevolence"). She has legitimate visions she further cultivates with mediation while Anakin's impatience prohibits him from doing the same ("Assassin"). Her physical prowess and skill with her lightsabers makes her a formidable opponent throughout the Clone Wars.

AHSOKA THE WOMAN

One of Ahsoka's biggest challenges in *The Clone Wars* is establishing independence from Anakin. Ahsoka's first episode of *The Clone Wars* ("Rising Malevolence") shows her mildly annoyed by Anakin's nonchalant attitude about the war, yet she depends entirely on him to guide her. Even though Ahsoka gains experience as a leader, her teacher continually inhibits her growth. In the episode "Weapons Factory," Anakin undermines Ahsoka during her briefing of the clones, generating resentment on both sides and endangering the mission. Gradually, Ahsoka is recognized for her innate leadership skills and deep understanding of being a Jedi. More importantly, Ahsoka comes into womanhood during the Clone Wars, signified by her becoming an equal to her peers in the Jedi Order and the Republic's command structure.

Ahsoka encountered a crucial turning point at the end of season five of *The Clone Wars* ("To Catch a Jedi," "The Wrong Jedi," "The Jedi Who Knew Too Much," "Sabotage"). Framed for a murder she did not commit, Ahsoka was hunted down by the very people she trusted most—the Jedi, including doubts of her innocence by her own Master. To make matters worse, nobody takes the time to listen to her without making pre-determined judgment calls. Rather than allow the charade to carry on, Ahsoka decides to uncover the mystery of the murder herself with the aid of a former enemy, Asajj Ventress—who had gave the Jedi much grief. This final arc demonstrates Ahsoka becoming a woman by shedding the dependent childhood she once had. The Jedi, the ones who protected and taught her for years, were in the wrong. She is forced to reconsider everything she learned in a short period of time and decide how to approach the rest of her life. In a sense, Ahsoka has to suddenly grow up very fast. Her choice to leave the Order and become fully independent is one of the most heartbreaking moments of *The Clone Wars*. She set aside the familiar and safe training to experience the world through her own eyes is a choice that many women make as they age. She makes her decision after careful consideration and contemplation, a prime example of maturity and wisdom. In her final interaction with Anakin before leaving, Ahsoka reinforces the decision as her own choice:

> ANAKIN: The Jedi Order is your life. You can't just throw it away like this. Ahsoka, you are making a mistake.
> AHSOKA: Maybe, but I have to sort this out on my own, without the Council and without you ["The Wrong Jedi"].

Ahsoka's leadership and Jedi training prepares her for her greatest role: she assumes a new identity as "Fulcrum," a leader in the Rebellion against the Empire ("Fire Across the Galaxy"). Fulcrum's identity is a mystery throughout the first season of the *Star Wars Rebels* series, but one thing is clear: Fulcrum is a person to be trusted. Time and time again, Ahsoka as Fulcrum provides the heroic crew of the *Ghost* with much-needed intelligence and guidance.

What makes Ahsoka such an effective feminist icon is her devotion to herself and her principles. At times, she falters. She loses confidence in her abilities, and she questions the motives of those in her many battles. But, in the end, Ahsoka always comes back to what she knows: She wants to embody the Jedi way of life and find balance and harmony in the galaxy and her place in it. As shown by the end of *The Clone Wars*, she will go at any length to achieve that dream, even if it means forsaking everything she has ever known.

Space Mom

Hera Syndulla, captain of the transport ship *Ghost* on *Star Wars Rebels*, is the daughter of Ryloth's freedom fighter Cham Syndulla (Miller). It is easy to see his impact on her; with her ship and crew, Hera dedicates her life to defeating the Empire and helping others, all while keeping a rag-tag group in line. Like her Greek goddess namesake, Hera is the default mother figure for the crew, and arguably the first prominent mother figure featured in the *Star Wars* canon. Hera is a great example of a feminist icon because of her ability to fully embrace the spectrum of classically feminine and masculine traits. A non-human, she leads a "melting pot" cast of characters to battle the Empire. She is fierce and forgiving, compassionate and kind, and possessing of both direction and drive.

IF YOU ONLY FIGHT FOR YOUR LIFE, YOUR LIFE IS WORTH NOTHING

Hera's appearance in the novel *A New Dawn* and the television show *Rebels* signifies a continued dedication to presenting strong female characters in the continuing *Star Wars* saga. She is the driving force behind the *Ghost's* mission to make things difficult for the Empire during the early years of the Rebellion. A guerrilla fighter, she convinces her shipmate Kanan that their skills are better used on a larger scale than personal vendettas (Miller). She helps the main hero, the teenage Ezra, realize that he cannot merely sit back while others suffer (Kinberg). For both men, she emphasizes the importance of fighting for others and their well-being and safety.

Hera genuinely believes people are decent (Miller). She holds faith that, one day, people of the galaxy would see the horrors of the Empire and rise up collectively. This belief help drive her forward in her goal to bring down the Empire. Hera is careful to weigh her options before every action. She takes calculated risks, but always errs on the side of protecting people.

MY SHIP—MY RULES

At times, it is hard for viewers to tell who exactly is in charge on the *Ghost*. Kanan, a Jedi outcast, has an authoritative presence, but often defers to Hera's judgment. Rightly so—he would still be meandering around the galaxy if she had not saved him from Imperial troops. Kanan is smitten by Hera, but he treats her as an equal. He openly acknowledges Hera's skill as a pilot and owner of the *Ghost*. In fact, he emphasizes in *A New Dawn* time and time again her skill in handling a variety of ships (Miller). Further, he trusts her judgment, and he understands her mission to protect the galaxy, one person at a time.

Hera's authority is recognized throughout the fist season of *Rebels*. While Ezra has a problem, he often seeks out Hera's advice. As owner and pilot of the *Ghost*, she is the person to convince to perform risky missions. She is also the person you do not want to upset, as her anger often leaves the crew feeling shamed. Hera's authority and presence as a female character is crucial in this youth-oriented animated show. She shows that women can be equal partners with men without sacrificing any of their values.

The Artist

Sabine Wren, much like Ahsoka, is a young woman just trying to find her place in the galaxy. An ex-academy student, Sabine is aware of the horrors the Empire is capable of committing. Her rebellious activity becomes a way to atone for her brief alignment with the Imperial military as well as a personal mission to bring down those who oppress.

Sabine is a unique combination of destruction and creation. As the weapons expert of the crew, Sabine is known for her effective explosives. However, she uses every resource at her disposal to put the Empire on edge beyond weapons. She creates colorful works of art that conflict with the standard Imperial drab monochrome schemes. On a symbolic level, her use of vibrant colors adds complexity to the Empire's single-minded quest for order. She expresses an individuality that contradicts the Empire's anonymous stormtroopers and uniform appearance. Even Hera regards Sabine's spray-painting her quarters not as graffiti or vandalism, but as an expression of self. As a feminist icon, Sabine has the ability to connect to younger women and girls while emphasizing the importance of representation of female characters with a direct influence on the storyline.

Not Your Romantic Interest

Sabine could have easily been written off as a romantic interest for Ezra: they are both young and relatively insecure despite a tough exterior. However, it is established early in the series that Sabine just is not interested in him. She often refers to him as a child, noting his inexperience and youth. In their first encounter, Sabine initially wanted to leave Ezra behind and continue on with *Ghost's* original plan; battling the Empire was not a kid's game. She did not greatly dislike Ezra, but she did not see his addition to the team significant until after Hera and Kanan's argument (Kinberg). She turns down Ezra's romantic advances, and season one ends with the two of them becoming more like friends.

Sabine's status as a non-romantic interest is further highlighted by the arrival of Lando Calrissian. Lando, a known smooth-talker, flirts openly with both Hera and Sabine ("Idiot's Array"). It is unsettling to see a grown man flirt with a teenager, but Sabine handles the interaction with style. She appreciates the conversation, but she does not lead him on. Much like the way she treats Ezra, Sabine affirms her status as a women with a choice in her romantic pursuits, and those around her respect her decisions.

TRUST ISSUES

Sabine admirably deals with wannabe hot-shots Ezra and Lando. However, despite her self-sufficiency, she is still a teenager. It is hard to remember that fact at times, especially when she is shown exuding both confidence and skill. But, like many other teenagers, Sabine is dealing with issues of independence. Part of independence is gaining relevant knowledge as she matures. In Sabine's case, she develops an obsession to uncover Ahsoka's identity as "Fulcrum." On a psychological level, Sabine needs to verify for herself that Fulcrum is a trusted member of the crew. Uncovering Fulcrum's identity becomes Sabine's subplot: she learns Hera knows this secret and Sabine sees Hera's refusal to part with this as an example of the *Ghost*'s "mother" treating her like a child ("Out of Darkness"). She insists forcefully that she "needs to know," likening her ignorance in the missions to her experience with the Empire and the unquestioning loyalty they demanded.

Sabine goes about obtaining the information in an immature way. Rather than cooperate and prove herself capable of handing important information, she puts her life at risk. In the episode "Out of Darkness," Sabine recklessly insists on joining Hera in hopes of meeting Fulcrum. In the end, she matures and accepts Hera's position and judgment on this issue. Hera stresses it is not that she cannot trust Sabine, but that she will reveal her secret when the stakes are lower; as the captain of the *Ghost*, she will not compromise their safety. Hera points out she has trusted her life to Sabine continuously and reminds Sabine of her importance to the overall mission and the crew of the *Ghost*. The interaction between these two women is crucial to the future direction of *Star Wars* and feminism. Not only are two women part of an ensemble cast, but they fill different roles in the show and interact in meaningful ways. Together, they demonstrate the complexities of feminism in the unfolding *Star Wars* universe.

Representation Matters

Star Wars is not viewed in a vacuum. Lucas made that clear early on with the heavy reliance on mythology and the influence of Joseph Campbell's *Hero's Journey* (Larsen). Today, *Star Wars* is a recognizable cornerstone of popular culture. The saga has been studied and analyzed in a number of settings, and for good reason. In the case of understanding the main women as icons of feminism, it is essential to understand the importance of representation and the influence this representation has on culture and psychology.

The degree to which a consumer is absorbed into a medium is defined as transportation. It blends attention, imagery, and feelings into one all-encompassing experience (Green and Brock). The consumer focuses on the events of the medium, momentarily losing touch with reality around them. This can be seen in "getting lost in a book"; the reader is so entranced with the reading material that time passes differently. Transportation can occur in video games, television shows, and movies—essentially any medium that has a story can carry an audience across space and time (Kaufman).

In the case of fiction, readers can engage in identity play and high degrees of transportation can facilitate their experimentation with possible textual "selves" (Kaufman). Identification is the process in which the reader lives vicariously through the character and reacts to the experiences of the character as if they were happening directly to the reader (Cohen). Through identity play, readers can "try on" different identities they encounter in material (Kaufman) and take on the character's cognitive and emotional perspective in the fictional environment (Tukachinsky). When a person identifies with a character from media, they are able to experience social reality from a different viewpoint (Cohen). While transportation focuses on the narrative's environment, identification centers on one particular character or element. Both transportation and identification involve an emotional response and a suspension of reality in combination with absorption through imagery (Tukachinsky).

In regards to attitude change, identification can lead to a temporary adoption of a viewpoint and allow for the consumer to see cultural and social phenomena or issues from a different perspective (Cohen). Although *Star Wars* has few prominent female characters, the quality and presentation of those women set the stage for viewers to transport and identify with the five characters analyzed here. Transportation through the vehicles of feminist icons in the *Star Wars* universe can allow for deeper examinations of personal beliefs, real-world problems, and the effects of media on cultural understandings of women's roles.

As a cultural phenomenon, *Star Wars* offers us a look into our own understanding of gender roles and allows us to evaluate how flexible those roles truly are. Each of these five women subverts the traditionally female stereotype and presents a character that is relatable to a number of women. In doing so, they are icons for generations not only in a galaxy far away, but in the here and now.

Notes

1. See Erin C. Callahan's essay in this volume.
2. See Karin Hagen's essay in this volume.

Works Cited

"The Academy." *Star Wars: The Clone Wars*. Writ. Cameron Litvack. Dir. Giancarlo Volpe. Cartoon Network. 15 Oct. 2010. Television.

"Assassin." *Star Wars: The Clone Wars*. Writ. Katie Lucas and Drew. Z. Greenberg. Dir. Kyle Dunlevy. Cartoon Network. 22 Oct. 2010. Television.

Baker-Whitelaw, Gavia. "Gamers Angry Over Lack of Women in the New 'Assassin's Creed' Game." *The Daily Dot* 2014. Web. 25 July 2015.

Barr, Tricia. "Does Slave Leia Weaken or Empower Women?" *Fangirl Blog* 2011. Web. 25. July 2015.

Cohen, J. "Defining Identification: A Theoretical Look at the Identification of Audiences with Media Characters." *Mass Communication & Society* 4.3 (2001): 245–64. Print.

Cox, Carolyn. "Do as Peggy Says: Hayley Atwell Hints at More Diversity in Agent Carter Season 2." *The Mary Sue* 2015. Web. 25 July 2015.

Dominguez, Diana. "Feminism and the Force: Empowerment and Disillusionment in a Galaxy Far, Far Away." *Culture, Identities, and Technology in the* Star Wars *Films: Essays on the Two Trilogies*. Eds. Carl Silvio and Tony M. Vinci. Jefferson, NC: McFarland, 2007. 109–33. Print.

"Fire Across the Galaxy." *Star Wars: Rebels*. Writ. Simon Kinberg. Dir. Dave Filoni. Disney XD. 2 Mar. 2015. Television.

Green, Melanie C., and Timothy C. Brock. "The Role of Transportation in the Persuasiveness of Public Narratives." *Journal of Personality and Social Psychology* 79.5 (2000): 701–21. Print.

"Gungan Attack." *Star Wars: The Clone Wars*. Writ. Jose Molina. Dir. Brian Kalin O'Connell. Cartoon Network. 16 Sept. 2011. Television.

"Heroes on Both Sides." *Star Wars: The Clone Wars*. Writ. Daniel Arkin. Dir. Kyle Dunlevy. Cartoon Network. 19 Nov. 2010. Television.

"Hostage Crisis." *Star Wars: The Clone Wars*. Writ. Eoghan Mahony, Brian Larsen, and Drew Z. Grennberg. Dir. Giancarlo Volpe. Cartoon Network. 20 Mar. 2009. Television.

"Idiot's Array." *Star Wars: Rebels*. Writ. Kevin Hopps. Dir. Steward Lee. Disney XD. 19 Jan. 2015. Television.

"The Jedi Who Knew Too Much." *Star Wars: The Clone Wars*. Writ. Charles Murray. Dir. Danny Keller. Cartoon Network. 15 Feb. 2013. Television.

Kaufman, Melanie C., Timothy C. Green, and Geoff F. Brock. "Understanding Media Enjoyment: The Role of Transportation into Narrative Worlds." *Communication Theory* 14.4 (2004): 311–27. Print.

Kershner, Irvin. *The Empire Strikes Back*. Twentieth Century-Fox, 1980. Film.

Kinser, Amber E. "Negotiating Spaces for through Third Wave Feminism." *National Women's Studies Association Journal* 16.3 (2004). Print.

Langley, Travis. *Batman and Psychology: A Dark and Stormy Knight*. Hoboken, NJ: John Wiley & Sons, 2012. Print.

Larsen, S. and R. Larsen. *Joseph Campbell: A Fire in the Mind*. Rochester, VT: Inner Traditions, 2002. Print.

"Lightsaber Lost." *Star Wars: The Clone Wars*. Writ. Drew Z. Greenberg. Dir. Giancarlo Volpe. Cartoon Network. 22 Jan. 2010. Television.

Lucas, George, dir. *Attack of the Clones*. Twentieth Century-Fox, 2002. Film.

_____. *The Phantom Menace*. Twentieth Century-Fox, 1999. Film.

_____. *Revenge of the Sith*. Twentieth Century-Fox, 2005. Film.

_____. *Star Wars*. Twentieth Century-Fox, 1977. Film.

Marquand, Richard. *Return of the Jedi*. Twentieth Century-Fox, 1983. Film.

Miller, John Jackson. *Star Wars: A New Dawn*. New York: Del Ray, 2014. Print.

"Out of Darkness." *Star Wars: Rebels.* Writ. Kevin Hopps. Dir. Steward Lee. Disney XD. 3 Nov. 2014. Television.

"Pursuit of Peace." *Star Wars: The Clone Wars.* Writ. Daniel Arkin. Dir. Duwayne Dunham. Cartoon Network. 3 Dec. 2010. Television.

Purvis, Jennifer. "Grrrls and Women Together in the Third Wave Embracing the Challenges of Intergenerational Feminism." *National Women's Studies Association Journal* 16.3 (2004): 93–123. Print.

"The Rise of Clovis." *Star Wars: The Clone Wars.* Writ. Christian Taylor. Dir. Danny Keller. Netflix. 7 Mar. 2014. Web. 25 Jul. 2015.

"Rising Malevolence." *Star Wars: The Clone Wars.* Writ. Steven Melching. Dir. Dave Filoni. Cartoon Network. 3 Oct. 2008. Television.

Roller, Pam. "Life After Leia." *Star Wars Insider* 23 (Fall 1994): 38–41. Print.

"Sabotage." *Star Wars: The Clone Wars.* Writ. Charles Murray. Dir. Brian Kalin O'Connell. Cartoon Network. 9 Feb. 2013. Television.

Showden, Carisa R. "What's Political About the New Feminisms." *Frontiers* 30.2 (2009). Print.

"Spark of Rebellion." *Star Wars: Rebels.* Writ. Simon Kinberg. Dir. Steward Lee, Steven G. Lee, and Dave Filoni. 3 Oct. 2014. Disney Channel. Television.

Stephanie. "Star Wars, Gender, and the Bechdel Test." *The Feminist Fangirl* 2011. Web. 25 July 2015.

"Storm over Ryloth." *Star Wars: The Clone Wars.* Writ. George Krstic. Dir. Brian Kalin O'Connell. Cartoon Network. 27 Feb. 2009. Television.

"To Catch a Jedi." *Star Wars: The Clone Wars.* Writ. Charles Murray. Dir. Kyle Dunlevy. Cartoon Network. 23 Feb. 2013. Television.

Tukachinsky, R. "Transportation and Identification as Two Modes of Involvement with Fictional Texts." *Conference Papers—National Communication Association* 1 (2007). Print.

Waid, Mark (w), Dodson, Terry (p). *Princess Leia No. 1.* Princess Leia. Ed. Jordan D. White. New York: Marvel Worldwide, 2015. Print.

_____. *Princess Leia No. 2.* Princess Leia. Ed. Jordan D. White. New York: Marvel Worldwide, 2015. Print.

_____. *Princess Leia No. 3.* Princess Leia. Ed. Jordan D. White. New York: Marvel Worldwide, 2015. Print.

"Weapons Factory." *Star Wars: The Clone Wars.* Writ. Brian Larsen and Drew Z. Greenberg. Dir. Giancarlo Volpe. Cartoon Network. 13 Nov. 2009. Television.

"The Wrong Jedi." *Star Wars: The Clone Wars.* Writ. Charles Murray. Dir. Dave Filoni. Cartoon Network. 2 Mar. 2013. Television.

"The Zillo Beast Strikes Back." *Star Wars: The Clone Wars.* Writ. Steven Melching. Dir. Steward Lee. Cartoon Network. 10 Apr. 2010. Television.

Jedi Knights, Dark Lords and Space Cowboys

George Lucas's Re-Imagined and Redefined Masculine Identities

ERIN C. CALLAHAN

It is clear that when he released *Star Wars Episode IV: A New Hope* in 1977, George Lucas re-imagined the American Western, fusing it with science-fiction to create a new genre of the "space western." Andrew Gordon contends that, "in an era when most Americans had lost heroes in whom to believe, Lucas created a myth for our times, fashioned out of bits and pieces of twentieth-century American popular mythology—old movies, science fiction, television, and comic books" ("Myth"). Similarly, the Wild West depicted in the American Western genre had been "an exhilarating region of adventure and comradeship in the open air" (Smith 52). This genre presented the Frontier as an untamed wilderness that challenged men to conquer, tame, and civilize it. Although the West had long been settled, popular imagination continued to "win" the West through cultural media. In particular, John Wayne's longevity on screen became a reminder of the masculinity the genre presented. When the Duke died in 1979, his legacy was assured not only in the west, but spread into the "final frontier."

In the mid-twentieth century, outer space captured the American imagination as an uncharted frontier to explore through NASA's numerous space exploration programs. As a result, science fiction dominated the American consciousness in books, comic books, television, and movies. The success of Lucas's movie, its sequels, prequels, and the associated merchandising, books, cartoons, in popular culture capitalized on the familiarity of the Western and created a mythology that has made it equally influential on American culture and society. However, this new mythology presented masculinity in a way that aligned with the changing social, cultural, and political mores of the time. It projected dominant masculinity through Jedi Knights like Luke Sky-walker, a reinforcement of patriarchal masculinity through characters like Han Solo occupying the space as the modern cowboy, and Darth Vader as the representation of an exaggerated masculinity within the Force.

Consequently, the newly-created space-western genre also re-imagined hegemonic masculine gender development and performance in alignment with gender theory from the period. Gender discourse in the 1970s, the decade in which *Star Wars* was released, "offered a complete biological-reductionist theory of masculinity based on the idea that we are descended from a hunting species" (*Masculinities* 46). This places the locus of gender in the body or that one's biology determines one's gender. Not only does one's genitalia define the gender appropriated to a child at birth, but developed musculature and physical stature connote masculinity. In contrast, physical stature that suggests weakness or dependence is considered feminine. Connell continues, "we inherit with our masculine genes tendencies to aggression, family life, competitiveness, political power, hierarchy, territoriality, promiscuity, and forming men's clubs" (*Masculinities* 46). In the original *Star Wars* trilogy, the Force-sensitive heroes, Luke Skywalker and Ben Kenobi, are not the locus of traditional patriarchal masculinity. The dominant masculine identity performance is the one that is most recognizable in North American culture and is reinforced by Lucas's development of the brash, gun-toting Han Solo. However, it is challenged by the development of the Jedi Knight masculinity as Lucas develops the Jedi Knight, most notably through Luke Skywalker's character, as the hegemonic masculinity within his universe.

Biological gender attribution and gender socialization share many attributes in their designation of dominant masculinity. Successfully socialized men seek power, and are aggressive, violent, and competitive (Devor 430). However, social construction theory argues "masculinities are neither programmed in our genes, nor fixed by social structure, prior to social interaction" (*The Men and the Boys* 12). As a learned behavior, socialized gender construction is dependent upon cultural and social influences. Further, Devor labels the broader influence on a child's gender development as a "generalized other" who "functions as a sort of monitoring or measuring device with which individuals may judge their own actions against those of the generalized conceptions of how members of society are expected to act" (426–427). These "generalized conceptions" are products of media representations and cultural and social cues. Children learn that the behaviors exhibited by generalized others have been established as benchmarks of their gender. They are encouraged to internalize and mimic those attributes. Devor continues, "[a]ny person is available to become part of one's 'generalized other'" (427). For many boys, the masculinities presented in the *Star Wars* canon provide a generalized other on which they base their ideals of masculinity. Similarly, Leia's relationship with the male characters in the films establishes a generalized other for girls. Further, Devor labels those who have close relationships with children and directly influence their gender development as "significant others," who "become prominent in the formation of one's self-image and one's ideals and goals" (427). The *Star Wars* canon provided generalized others for viewers, but also for characters within the films. In addition, within the context of the world that Lucas created, there are characters that assume the role of "significant other" and foster the development of other characters. Regardless of the nature of the influence, both the "generalized other" and the "significant other" serve as role models of behaviors, dress, and speech.

In Lucas's fictional universe, traditional male dominance is still the most powerful expression of masculinity and is performed by those who learn the ways of the Force, all of whom are men in the original trilogy. This is reinforced when Luke affirms the patrilineal nature of the Force in the Skywalker family. He expresses this first when he begins his journey with Obi-Wan when he asserts that he wants to become a Jedi like his father had been. The importance of this relationship is further supported when Luke tells the Emperor he is a Jedi "like my father before me" at the end of *Return of the Jedi* (Marquand). Skywalker omits his sister, Leia, who displays some Force sensitivity in the original trilogy, but there are no female Jedi Knights. Indeed, Luke's statement assumes his mother, whom he knows nothing about, but whose description as being "kind, but sad" suggests passivity, was not a Jedi (Marquand). Therefore, the Jedi Knight is established as the hegemonic masculinity in the Star Wars canon. The characteristics of the Jedi masculinity signify a shift away from the traditional representation of Han Solo's "cowboy" masculinity or Darth Vader's hyper-aggressiveness. As Connell further asserts, "'hegemonic masculinity' is not a fixed character type, always and everywhere the same. It is, rather, the masculinity that occupies the hegemonic position in a given pattern of gender relations, a position always contestable" (*Masculinities* 76). The Jedi Knight's performance of masculinity is counter to the masculinity that John Wayne's heroes—and, by connotation, the average North American viewer—was accustomed to.

Lucas both contests and redefines North American archetypical hegemonic masculinity gender identity through Jedi Knights, who exhibit "body postures, speech patterns, and styles of dress which demonstrate and support the assumption of dominance and authority" and "convey an impression of masculinity" (Devor 430). In all six films, Jedi Knights maintain a consistent costume, of brown pants, an off-white tunic tied off with a belt, boots, and a cloak. The costume is a signifier of their position as Jedi Knights within their society. The only variations of this are Anakin's black garbs in *Attack of the Clones* and *Revenge of the Sith*, signifying his eventual turn to the Dark Side, and Luke's black tunic in *Return of the Jedi* to connote his mastery of the Force and his connection to Darth Vader and the Dark Side. Further, when a Jedi, like Mace Windu, Yoda, Qui-Gon, or Obi-Wan, speaks, he is generally non-confrontational, assertive, and soft-spoken. A Jedi uses logic, rather than aggression or coercion, to make his point. The tone of their voices and the logic they use asserts their authority. However, Lucas also assigns recognizably feminine attributes to the Jedi, challenging the accepted North American masculinity. Rather than expressing outward aggression, Jedi Knights use their powers to defend and protect, rather than to attack. A successful Jedi-in-Training or padawan must learn to control his aggressive tendencies and use the Force to bring peace where there is conflict.

The Dark Side of the Force, however, is a hyperbolic performance of hegemonic masculinity and exists in opposition to the Jedi Knights. Traditional patriarchal masculinity focuses on "some level of proficiency at some or all" of the aforementioned characteristics of masculinity: "'toughness, confidence, and self-reliance,' and 'the aura of aggression, violence, and daring'" (Devor 430). The Sith Lords' performance of these attributes is exaggerated in their patterns of speech, action, physicality, and costumes. They also tend towards reactionary and heightened emotional responses such as anger, hate, impetuousness, and even love that would traditionally be associated with the feminine. However, their performance of these attributes suggests the "aggression, violence, and daring" of dominant masculinity (Devor 430). The prequels depict Senator, and later Chancellor, Palpatine, who is also the Sith Lord Darth Sidious, manipulating Padmé and other members of the Senate to ensure his rise into a position of supreme power. To achieve this goal, he first employs Darth Maul to eliminate the threat that Obi-Wan and Qui-Gon pose to his plan. Darth Maul is aggressive and violent, and ultimately, he kills Qui-Gon in their "Duel of the Fates"—the title has allusions to the struggle between masculinity types as the Sith and Jedi slug it out. Subsequently, in *Attack of the Clones*, Count Dooku aids in assembling a drone army to start a war to ensure Palpatine's ascent to power. As the epic continues, *Revenge of the Sith* depicts Palpatine manipulating Anakin and the senate to the fruition of his plan to dissolve the power of the senate and acquire it himself. The original trilogy portrays Darth Vader performing that role. He leads the Empire's war against the Rebellion and plans complete domination of the universe. Darth Vader controls conversations through interruption and intimidation and uses the Force to persuade, injure, attack, or kill those who question, disobey, or disappoint him.[1] It is Palpatine, however, who emerges as the Emperor of the Galactic Empire, attempting to lure Luke to the Dark Side in the same way he did the elder Skywalker in the prequels. The Sith Lords' clearly demonstrate a performance of masculinity that seeks power as a marker of success and does so through aggressive and violent means. However, Lucas establishes these masculine traits as negative or evil. In contrast, the Jedi Knight, who demonstrates many characteristics that would generally be interpreted as feminine within a patriarchal gender schema.

These two masculine identities form a binary of how the characters perform this identity within Lucas's universe and their use of the Force. The characters of Luke Skywalker and Anakin Skywalker provide the clearest examples of socialization of gender performance across both trilogies as they follow their respective developments and progressions through their heroes' journey. Devor asserts "gender identities act as cognitive filtering devices guiding people to attend to and learn gender role behaviors appropriate to their statuses" (424). Without their biological fathers present to serve as their primary same sex gender role model or significant other, both Anakin and Luke are dependent upon secondary characters or generalized others to serve as role models for gender construction. Luke believes he has been orphaned and, because of that, he has been raised by his aunt and uncle on their moisture farm. Furthermore, his uncle has denied him the truth about his heritage. As a result, he has internalized his role as a farmer, though he dreams of leaving Tatooine and becoming a pilot. Similarly, as a slave without a father, Anakin has idealized podracing pilots as the identity to which he aspires. Once Luke and Anakin learn that they have the Force or a high midichlorian count, they begin to learn the appropriate "gender role behaviors" for young padawans from their mentor or significant other. Initially, Qui-Gon assumes the role for Anakin. After Qui-Gon's death, Obi-Wan Kenobi performs the role of Master. Obi-Wan will not be Luke's Master, but he will be Luke's initial significant other.

From Farm Boy to Jedi Knight

Before Luke begins his hero's journey, he is clearly restless on Tatooine. Delayed by a sense of filial duty to his aunt and uncle and his work on their farm, Luke remains though he is desperate to leave and he feels left behind by his contemporaries, like Biggs, who have departed for their own adventures and commitments with the Rebellion. As previously noted, at this point in his narrative, he has been denied his biological father as a model for gender construction and he has been influenced by his Uncle Owen who assumes that role. When Luke meets Obi-Wan Kenobi, and learns his father was a Jedi, Luke finds a generalized other on which to develop his gender identity and performance. This is heightened by Obi-Wan giving his father's lightsaber to him. Through this association, Luke has also found a significant other on whom he will begin his gender identity construction. Gordon notes that "despite the Oedipal nature of the conflict, he is finally accepted by the parent figures and thus discovers his true identity and attains his true powers, which he realizes were with him all the time." Further, Waller argues that, as Luke's mentor, the first signifier of Obi-Wan's ideology as authority figure is located in his name, explaining, "The paradoxical formation of his name ... characterizes the double nature of his authority, his first name [Obi-Wan] ... calling attention to the extent to which authority is constituted by the needs and desires of others ... while his second name [Kenobi] ... voices an appropriate response to that position" (64). While Obi-Wan encourages Luke to be his own man or to "be one," he also teaches Luke that reality is impossible or "can no be" because his fate is connected to the service of those around him (64). His position as Luke's authority figure translates to the gender performance behaviors Luke learns from Obi-Wan. He is compassionate and engenders trust by providing Luke with a link to his paternal history, a trust which Luke feels is ultimately betrayed when he learns that Obi-Wan lied to him.

After he and Luke watch the message Leia stored on Artoo, Obi-Wan attempts to recruit Luke, recognizing him as the next generation of Jedi and that he must begin his training if he is going to be socialized appropriately to his role. Luke would also provide the assistance Obi-Wan needs to fulfill Leia's request. He tells Luke he must "learn the ways of the Force if you are to come with me to Alderaan," thus setting up the condition to enable Luke to join a larger universe (Lucas *Star Wars*). Luke's provincial response that he cannot go with Obi-Wan because he has work to do at home and the conflict with the empire is so far away echoes his Uncle Owen's fears. When Luke addresses Leia's recording, his Uncle demands that he take Artoo to have his memory erased and ends the discussion. Uncle Owen also dismisses Luke's interest in finding Obi-Wan, telling him that he died the same time that Luke's father did. He redirects the conversation to focus on the farm and Luke's responsibilities. Similarly, Luke's response to Obi-Wan indicates he has internalized his Uncle's gender performance. He has a sense of domestic duty, a sense of loyalty, and a rejection of the Rebellion's goals against the Empire. Obi-Wan's response, "that's your uncle talking," acknowledges Uncle Owen's obvious influence on Luke's reaction (Lucas *Star Wars*). Luke rejects Obi-Wan's offer initially, but accepts it after he is personally affected by the Empire when they kill Uncle Owen and Aunt Beru. With his home destroyed and his family murdered, Luke decides there is nothing left on for him on Tatooine and that he will accompany Obi-Wan. At this moment Obi-Wan assumes the role of Luke's mentor and significant other. This is the beginning of Luke's training as a Jedi Knight.

It must be noted, however, Obi-Wan's immediate influence on Luke during his Jedi training is transitional. The aspects of the Force he teaches to Luke and his brief explanation of Luke's paternal heritage provides Luke's initial understanding of the Jedi ethos and his socialization into it. When Luke learns his father was a Jedi, it is the first sense of filial connection he feels towards a father he never knew. This is where the idea of the Jedi Knight as a potential generalized other merges with a significant other of the newly idealized lost father. Luke has discovered a legacy that he can continue through his Jedi training. Consequently, as a more present significant other, Obi-Wan exhibits behavior that is patient, responsive, helpful, and kind, and he uses his powers for defense rather than attack. These are signifiers of the Jedi ethos and behaviors Luke will ultimately emulate. For example, in Mos Eisley, Luke witnesses Obi-Wan use the Force to get past the guards and sees him cut off the arm of a criminal who threatened Luke at the cantina bar. Most notably is Obi-Wan's reaction just after Governor Tarkin destroys Alderaan. Luke asks his mentor what is wrong and Obi-Wan replies he "felt a great disturbance in the Force, as if millions of voices cried out in terror and were suddenly silenced" (Lucas *Star Wars*). In this scene, Obi-Wan's connection to all things through the Force is exemplified for Luke. Just following this scene, Obi-Wan teaches Luke to feel the Force and trust his instincts during his lightsaber training, then reinforces the lesson by putting a helmet on Luke so he cannot see. After Obi-Wan's death, he becomes part of the Force and mentors Luke through the completion of his mission to destroy the Death Star. Mirroring the earlier scene, Obi-Wan's voice compels Luke to turn off his computer guidance system and rely on the Force. Self-reliance and successful completion of the mission are part of Luke's training, but they are also signifiers of the dominant masculinity into which he is being socialized.

The first time viewers see Luke use his lightsaber in *The Empire Strikes Back* demonstrates his progress with the Force and, subsequently with his gender performance as a padawan. The scene depicts Luke hanging upside down in the carnivorous wampa's cave. Though Luke seems helpless, he steadies himself and focuses. When he does, he is able to use the Force to move his lightsaber from a nearby snow bank just in time to cut the wampa's arm off. This parallels the scene in the Mos Eisley cantina from *A New Hope* when viewers first see Obi-Wan use his lightsaber to cut off the criminal's arm in self-defense. Appropriately, Obi-Wan's apparition appears in the blizzard instructing Luke to go to Dagobah to complete his training with Yoda. If the scene in the Mos Eisley cantina serves as an initiating incident for Luke's development, his time in Dagobah provides both a second Jedi Master as a significant other, Yoda, and the location for his continued training to become a Jedi Knight.

Yoda serves as an interesting model for Luke's gender development, but is an appropriate mentor for his continuing Jedi Knight training. Although Yoda is not human, he is male and a master of the Force who has trained Jedi for eight hundred years. Luke's training on Dagobah displays the physical fitness and prowess most often associated with dominant masculinity. However, Luke must also learn to quiet his mind and find the calmness, peace, passivity that allows him to know the Force. When Yoda tells Luke, "You must unlearn what you have learned," he is not referring to Obi-Wan's earlier teachings, but to Luke's initial gender socialization that would lead toward continued normative masculine behaviors and attitudes (Kershner). The effects of Luke's primary gender socialization were evident in the first film when Luke echoed his Uncle Owen's views on work, helping Obi-Wan, and getting involved in the Rebellion. They are also present in Luke's consistent struggle to control his anger, aggression, and violence. Jedi masculinity performance counters these behaviors. At the pivotal moment before Luke enters the cave, Yoda cautions him not to bring his weapons, symbols of his masculine aggression. Although Yoda tells him that the cave will present only what he brings with him, Luke brings his weapons belt. When he faces the image of Darth Vader, Luke responds violently, cutting Vader's head off with his lightsaber. Luke's response is counter to Yoda's assertion that "a Jedi uses the Force for knowledge and defense, never to attack" (Kershner). When the mask on Vader's helmet dissolves, it reveals Luke's face, suggesting the lesson of the cave was that a Jedi Knight rejects aggression and violence, and that anger leads to one's demise. The path of the Jedi, Yoda argues, is much more challenging than giving in to the fear and anger of the Dark Side.

Luke's inner conflict is emphasized in his first face-to-face battle with Darth Vader. Leaving his training before its completion in an effort to save his friends, Luke has not yet mastered the calm, peace, or passive nature of the Force. Therefore, he remains vulnerable to succumbing to his anger, fear, and aggression and, ultimately, to the Dark Side. Because of this, Luke enters into the trap Darth Vader has set for him. During the course of their battle, Luke demonstrates his acumen with a lightsaber, illustrating his power within the Force. Darth Vader entreats Luke to join the Dark Side and rule the universe with him. However, Luke heeds Yoda's assertion that Dark Side and

Sith Lords are not stronger than the Force and Jedi Knights. The battle results in Darth Vader cutting Luke's hand off and revealing the truth that he is Luke's father. These events complicate the conflict that Luke feels. When he began his training, he declared he wanted to carry forth his family's legacy and follow the path of his father by becoming a Jedi Knight. However, the knowledge that his father turned to the Dark Side destroys the image he had of the ideal generalized and significant other as a Jedi Knight. Symbolically, the loss of his hand, which is replaced by a robotic hand, represents Luke becoming more like Darth Vader.

In the opening scenes of *Return of the Jedi*, Luke is almost fully actualized in his masculine performance as a Jedi Knight. Upon entering Jabba the Hutt's dessert palace, he is met by Jabba's henchman, who refuses him entry. Luke uses the Force to control the henchman's thoughts and gains entrance to the palace. This scene's similarity to the scene in which Obi-Wan uses the same methods to bypass the stormtrooper guards in Mos Eisley signifies that Luke has achieved a parallel level of mastery of the Force. The control that Luke exhibits in his actions and speech is derived from his skill as a Jedi and demonstrates his dominant masculine identity, despite initially demonstrating passivity by bargaining with Jabba for his friends' freedom. Jabba attempts to assert dominance over Luke through both his resistance to Luke's use of the Force and through pejorative language, calling him "boy." Luke maintains his authority, defeats the monster in the pit and rescues Han, Threepio, Leia, Lando, and Artoo from death. But, as later scenes prove, Luke still cannot fully control his anger and aggression. Although Luke does not require further training from Yoda, Yoda fears that because Luke's training was incomplete and he "rushes to confront Vader" he is not ready for the burden of killing him (Marquand). However, Luke must confront Darth Vader and the Dark Side of the Force as the last step to becoming actualized as a Jedi. This will restore balance to the Force. After Yoda dies, Obi-Wan's spirit returns completing Darth Vader's origination story, asserting, "He's more machine now than man. Twisted and evil" (Marquand). This is a clear statement about technology and humanity, but also about Vader's gender performance. To be identified as "man," as he was when he was Anakin, he would follow and adhere to the Jedi's use of the Force. As Darth Vader, the majority of his body composition is a machine. However, Luke recognizes the conflict between the Jedi ethos and the Dark Side in Darth Vader and, out of filial duty, will not kill his father. Killing Darth Vader would be an act of violent aggression rather than the use of the Force for defense, knowledge, or peace.

Once Luke is on the Death Star with the Emperor and Darth Vader, the symbolic confrontation between the two oppositional masculine identities is brought to its fruition. This places Luke in a binary against his father, who was manipulated to the Dark Side by his own fear and anger. Prior to Luke and Darth Vader engaging in combat, the Emperor attempts to manipulate Luke into abandoning the Jedi, insisting that he "use [his] aggressive feelings" and "let [his] hate flow through [him]" (Marquand). The Emperor encourages Luke to embrace aggression and violence to gain power and save his friends in the same way he manipulated Anakin to embrace the Dark Side to save Padmé. During the course of the battle, Luke viciously attacks Darth Vader and cuts his hand off. The Emperor's response, "Your hate has made you powerful," signifies to Luke allowed himself to be manipulated by the Emperor. This echoes Yoda's warning, "Do not underestimate the powers of the Emperor or suffer your father's fate you will" (Marquand). Indeed, Luke exhibits behaviors characteristic of a Sith Lord in these scenes. However, he has an epiphany after he cuts Darth Vader's hand off and considers his own mechanized hand. Just as Obi-Wan paralleled Darth Vader's loss of humanity to the robotics comprising the majority of his body, Luke realizes that his mechanized hand represents a potential transition to the Dark Side. This results in Luke's reconciliation of his conflict through which he saves Darth Vader and returns balance to the Force.

Turning to the Dark Side

In the original trilogy, Darth Vader has already accepted the path of "anger, fear, aggression" that led him to the Dark Side, but this concept is not developed until the prequels (Kershner). Early in *The Phantom Menace*, it is clear that, despite being a friendly and helpful little boy, the innate anger Anakin carries within him as a result of being a slave differs greatly from Luke's adolescent frustration. This anger and his inability to control it ultimately lead to Anakin becoming the Sith Lord Darth Vader. Anakin's anger stems from his feeling a lack of power and his feeling that he is viewed and treated as less than human. Regardless, he also demonstrates an innate kindness and protective instincts in his introduction as he takes in Qui-Gon, Padmé, and Obi-Wan during a sand storm. Later, he tells Padmé that when he is freed, he will become a Jedi and come home to free the slaves especially his mother.

Similar to Luke, Anakin Skywalker embarks on a journey of gender construction in *The Phantom Menace* when he is discovered by Qui-Gon. Anakin echoes Luke's desire to leave Tatooine; he believes his destiny will take him away from his home planet. The Jedi recognize that Anakin has one of the highest midicholrian levels ever recorded, higher than Yoda, and acknowledges that he might be the "Chosen One," the one who would bring balance back to the Force. Anakin's mother tells Qui-Gon that Anakin did not have a father, alluding to a virgin birth of a savior, but also signifying the absence of a father-figure or same sex gender role model. Through the first ten years of his life, Anakin's generalized others have been images of free men, Jedi Knights, or pod racers. His closest male influence was Watto, who owns him and his mother. Anakin resists Watto's influence because Watto is outwardly dishonest and opportunistic. If Qui-Gon and Obi-Wan can secure Anakin's freedom, his Jedi training would fulfill his destiny as the "Chosen One" and provide both significant and generalized others for him. After Anakin earns his own freedom by winning in the pod races, he feels a sense of power and pride. Those emotions are quickly diminished by his realization that he has not been able to fulfill the masculine role of protector and free his mother as well. Anakin's path will allow him to be socialized into his gender identity performance as a Jedi Knight. However, the loss of his mother and his lingering attachment to her will haunt him and be a major component of the development of his anger, aggression, and violence.

Anakin continues Jedi training in the prequels as Obi-Wan's padawan, but his latent fear and anger disrupt the full actualization of him becoming a Jedi. Because Anakin does not have a father, his Jedi Master mentor Obi-Wan occupies that role for him. Several times throughout *Attack of the Clones*, Anakin refers to Obi-Wan as his father figure. For example, as Anakin and Obi-Wan search for bounty hunter Zam Wesell, Obi Wan tells Anakin that he's being reactionary and that he's not using the Force. Anakin's recognition that he did not follow his Jedi training is apparent. He responds like a child who fears disappointing his father when he says, "Don't say that, Master. You're the closest thing I have to a father" (Lucas *Attack*). After Obi-Wan sends a message from the planet Geonosis requesting help, Anakin agrees to go; despite his anger towards his mentor, he says that Obi-Wan is "like my father" (Lucas *Attack*). This trope of the father-son relationship between Obi-Wan and Anakin is significant in his training and development as a Jedi, but also contributes to his eventual turn to the Dark Side. As much as Anakin reveres and cares for Obi-Wan, his adolescence and ego lead to a rebellion against his figurative father. This dynamic of their relationship mirrors the Oedipal aspects of Luke's relationships with his paternal figures, but Luke does not display the same level of hostility and rebellion. Rather, despite his dreams of adventure, Luke had accepted his place as a "normal" farmer under his aunt and uncle. Anakin, knowing from an early age he is the "Chosen One," views Obi-Wan as a barrier to his ascension to the Jedi council and achieving full Jedi status. Obi-Wan's control over Anakin's advancement produces in him similar feelings of powerlessness over his own future that he felt as a child slave on Tatooine. This causes him to resent Obi-Wan and become closer to Senator/Chancellor Palpatine, who seemingly understands Anakin's resentment and does not try to correct his misbehavior.

As Anakin's training continues, his powers allow him to see his feelings or the future in his dreams and this ability intensifies his fear for his mother. In *Attack of the Clones*, he dreams of his mother being tortured, in pain, and in danger. Because of this, he returns to Tatooine to rescue and free his mother only to learn that she has been sold, married, and abducted by Tusken Raiders. He finds her and she dies in his arms. This is the first time he allows his fear and anger to consume him. In his grief and rage, he slaughters the entire village, including the women and children, without remorse.[2] When this happens, Yoda feels the pain, suffering, and death, noting that something terrible has happened with Anakin. The manifestation of Anakin's anger results from his being unable to save his mother. He vows that he will one day "be the most powerful Jedi" and that he will be able to save people from death (Lucas *Attack*). Although he understands the anger he feels is counter to the Jedi ethos, he exhibits highly developed protective tendencies towards his mother, which he will translate to an obsession with protecting Padmé. In *Revenge of the Sith*, Anakin's dreams predict Padmé's death. The Jedi advise him that fear of loss is a path to the Dark Side. However, Palpatine explains his view of the Sith Lords' similarities to the Jedi Knights in their quest for power and tells Anakin the legend of Darth Palgueis the Wise, a powerful Sith Lord who could save people from death. Anakin's faltering trust in the Jedi Council and his fear for Padmé's life make him vulnerable to Palpatine's manipulation and to turn to the Dark Side.

As Anakin finalizes his transition to the Dark Side, he is the representation of fear and anger leading to the negative aspects or the more traditionally masculine aspects of the Force. In this process, his significant other also transitions from Obi-Wan to Senator Palpatine. The first two prequels establish the relationships Anakin has with both men. However, the third episode closely examines Anakin's conflict between his performance of the Jedi Knight masculinity and his acceptance of the Dark Side of the Force. Anakin has been socialized as a Jedi through his training as a padawan, which requires him to let go of his anger and fear. In contrast, Senator Palpatine encourages Anakin's ego, his aggression, and his violence, leading him to become a Sith Lord. Anakin makes the full transition; just as Senator Palpatine is revealed as Darth Sidious, Anakin mimics his mentor and is renamed Darth Vader. This renaming is a figurative death, but it sets in motion the events lead to Anakin killing Mace Windu, slaughtering the Younglings, using the Force to strangle Padmé, and battling Obi-Wan. These acts of aggression lead to the end scene in which the Emperor literally rebuilds Anakin with mechanized body parts. This scene signifies the death of the Jedi Anakin Skywalker and the true birth of Darth Vader as the full actualization of Dark Side masculinity. As he is depicted in the original trilogy, Darth Vader will seek to control the universe with the Empire through aggressive and violent means.

When Darth Vader's journey concludes in *Return of the Jedi*, he has the same conflicted feelings of anger and love with which he began in the first prequel when he was a young boy. In the end, Vader's paternal instincts or his love for Luke are what ultimately lead him away from the Dark Side of the Force and to accept the hegemonic masculinity within the *Star Wars* gender schema, that of the Jedi Knight. As a Jedi Master, Luke can feel there is still good in Vader, and Vader's conflict leads him toward empathy or sympathy for his son when he sees the Emperor, Darth Sidious, using his powers to electrocute Luke. Luke's pleas for Vader to help him, "Father, please," engender this sympathy in Vader, bringing him to make the ultimate paternal sacrifice (Marquand). To defend his son, Vader lifts the Emperor and throws him to his death. In the process, Vader is mortally wounded. The electricity highlight Anakin's skull revealing that there is still a human under among the machinery. As warning alarms sound for the evacuation of the Death Star, Luke struggles to take the ailing Vader with him. Vader asks his son to help "take this mask off" (Marquand). Despite that doing so will ultimately kill Vader, removing the mask is symbolic of Vader's final rejection of the Dark Side. In the final scenes of *Revenge of the Sith*, application of the mask is the final step in Anakin's transition to the Dark Side. In this scene at the end of *Return of the Jedi*, father and son are reunited in the Force. Further, when Vader implores Luke to leave him behind, Luke refuses. He tells his father he will not leave him behind because "I'm going to save you" (Marquand). Vader's response, "You already have," signifies that the son's influence on the father has allowed him to fulfill his potential (Marquand). Vader/Anakin dies, but the movie shows Vader's helmet burning in a funeral pyre. In contrast, Anakin's spirit (either in his older or younger forms, depending on the version) appears next to Obi-Wan and Yoda.[3]

Lucas's Re-Imagined Masculinities

Within the good versus evil binary that Lucas creates, the characters that learn the way of the Force do so in a way that adheres to or conflicts with heteronormative gender socialization, as previously addressed. However, Luke's gender socialization does initially include heteronormative tendencies prevalent in patriarchal societies. His initial "significant other" was his uncle Owen Lars, who is married to Beru and serves as head of their household. Upon seeing Leia on the partial recording Artoo plays in Luke's garage, he asks and observes, "Who is she? She's beautiful" (Lucas *Star Wars*). His inquiry and masculine gaze in which he objectifies Leia's physical appearance are part of his gender socialization, development, and performance up to this point. Viewers perceive Luke's attraction to Leia as "normal" because it reinforces their own ideas about gender performance as a component of heterosexuality. It also positions heterosexuality as a natural completion of gender socialization or development. This is further reinforced when Luke opens the door to cell 2187 and immediately assumes the role of hero or protector when he tells her he's "here to rescue you" (Lucas *Star Wars*). As Mara Wood and Karin Hilck note in their essays in this collection, Leia isn't a stereotypical damsel in distress. However, Luke attempts to fulfill traditional gender roles of physically and emotionally strong male who rescues a passive and physically and emotionally frail female. Although Luke does rescue Leia from the cell, his role as hero is undercut by Leia's quip, "Aren't you a little short for a stormtrooper?" and her active role in her own rescue (Lucas *Star Wars*).

Before he commits fully to his Jedi training and learns that she is his sister, Luke challenges Han for Leia's romantic attention in an effort to bring a heterosexual relationship to fruition. After Luke and Han rescue Leia and they escape the Death Star in, the men's exchange regarding Leia demonstrates the competitive nature of heterosexual masculine identity. Luke asks Han what he thinks of Leia, to which Han responds, "I'm trying not to, kid" (Lucas *Star Wars*). Luke's response of "Good," while looking away indicates competition for Leia's attention and his defensive jealousy. Han continues, asking Luke, "You think a princess and a guy like me" (Lucas *Star Wars*). Luke interrupts Han's train of thought with "no," a sign of his asserting his role in competition for Leia's affection. One of the characteristics of dominant masculinity that Devor outlines through speech patterns specifies that "people who attempt to control the direction of conversation seem more masculine. Those who tend to speak more loudly, use less polite and more assertive forms, and tend to interrupt the conversations of others more often communicate masculinity to others" (431). In this instance, Luke attempts to assert a position of dominance over Han through verbal cues. Han's smirk and laugh in response to Luke's interruption indicates his own assertion of dominance through aggression and competition. However, as Gordon notes, in *The Empire Strikes Back*, "while Luke appears asexual, and seems to regard Leia as a mother figure, Han woos her passionately" ("Id" 315). Han will compete with Luke for Leia's attention and affection throughout the movies and will fully earn them by the end of the original trilogy.

As stated earlier, binary gender socialization assumes that heterosexuality is the normal progression and performance of gender identity and roles that results in heterosexual relationships or marriage and culminates in childbirth. In addition to Anakin Skywalker's display of anger and aggression, he also violates the Jedi code of celibacy through his relationship with Padmé. This relationship begins in *The Phantom Menace* when ten-year-old Anakin establishes a crush on the Naboo queen and gives her a totem necklace that he carved for her. Anakin's one-sided crush is extended ten years later in next prequel. Upon first seeing Padmé, he is introduced as her part of her new security detail with his mentor Obi-Wan; they are both placed in the role of protector, but Anakin's performance in the role is accentuated as he feels it is his personal responsibility to apprehend those threatening her life. Further, Anakin is disappointed that she responds to him as she did the last time she saw him when he was a boy. Exemplifying aggression and the masculine gaze and mirroring Luke's reaction to Leia, Anakin tells Padmé that she has "grown more beautiful" (Lucas *Attack*). Her response, "Ani, you'll always be that little boy I knew on Tatooine," communicates that she does not initially consider him as a potential partner or a romantic interest (Lucas *Attack*). Jar Jar attempts to comfort Anakin by telling him that he had not seen the Naboo senator as happy as she was with Anakin in quite some time.

Later in *Attack of the Clones*, Anakin foils Zam Wesell's second assassination attempt, which sets in motion the plan for Obi-Wan to investigate the assassination attempts further and for Padmé to return to Naboo with Anakin as her escort and bodyguard. This provides the opportunity for Anakin to develop his relationship with her, fulfilling his masculine heterosexual gender construction. While Padmé is packing for Naboo, she acknowledges that Anakin has transitioned from boyhood to manhood, but he makes her uncomfortable with the way he looks at her. He apologizes, but his expression indicates a sense of self-satisfaction and ego. En route to Naboo, Anakin attempts to justify his growing interest in pursuing a relationship with Padmé by telling her that "attachment is forbidden. Possession is forbidden. Compassion, which I would define as unconditional love, is central to a Jedi's life. You might say we are encouraged to love" (Lucas *Attack*). Anakin's tortured logic attempts to manipulate the Jedi ideology to justify his interest in her. Once on Naboo, they become closer, but agree not to fall in love because it would violate the commitments they have already made; Anakin to the Jedi and Padmé to the Senate. Anakin betrays her trust and their agreement when he tells Padmé that he loves her. Padmé refuses to reciprocate and reinforces their agreement to maintain a platonic relationship. However, after they are captured on Geonosis in their failed attempt to save Obi-Wan. Facing execution in the coliseum, Padmé confesses her love for Anakin, "I truly, deeply love you" (Lucas *Attack*). Padmé's delayed acceptance of a relationship with Anakin places him in the dominant role of pursuer and her in the subordinate role of the pursued. Ultimately, *Attack of the Clones* concludes with Anakin and Padmé's wedding, signifying recognizable gender performance since "romantic heterosexual love [is] the basis for marriage" (*Men and Boys* 43). This relationship is brought to its culturally and socially significant completion at the end of the prequels when Padmé gives birth to Luke and Leia. The way that Anakin fulfills his destiny as the "Chosen One" and brings balance to the Force is through his children, the fruition of his heterosexual gender development.

Scoundrel in the Mix

In the original trilogy, Han Solo exemplifies the traditionally heteronormative masculine traits of physicality, aggression, power, and control. These characteristics are portrayed through the modernization of the cowboy masculinity with which audiences were familiar, a figure that remains central to the American mythos and imagination because of its place within American history. The myth of the cowboy "represents America's westering experience to the popular mind" and its figure "remain[s] the corner stone of American culture" (Savage 3). Subsequently, cowboys have served as generalized others for generations of boys who view them as rugged, independent, and tough— all qualities to be emulated. The figure, as it appeared and continues to appear in American popular culture, was that of a physically fit and handsome man, who was confident and self-sufficient. Lucas's inclusion of Han Solo provided American audiences with a recognizable masculine identity in the new gender identity schema that he created.[4]

The first and most notable alignment between Han and the cowboy archetype is his costume. The cowboy is usually depicted in leather or denim pants, with a vest, boots, cowboy hat, and a holster. Han's costume mirrors that portrayal, creating a familiar image with which audiences can identify. He is dressed in dark pants, boots, and a vest. His blaster holster mirrors the cowboy's holster for his six-shooter. The costume Han wears remains consistent throughout the original trilogy. There are slight alterations to accommodate the climates of Hoth and Endor. When he is on Hoth, he is depicted with a parka over his recognizable costume because of the planet's sub-zero temperatures. In Endor's forested environment, however, Han's costume also includes a duster. The duster coat is an allusion to the coat a rancher would wear. Han's performance of this identity extends beyond superficial traits; his behavior also suggests that he has internalized the cowboy masculine identity.

Han, as the cowboy, also signifies an idealized vision of the pioneering and independent American spirit and represents an average "everyman." This is what makes him most identifiable to male movie-goers as a generalized other to emulate and to female viewers as a romantic figure to admire. Further, Smith asserts that "the Wild Western hero as cowboy, who in the twentieth century has become the dominant type, first appeared in the wake of Buffalo Bill in the 1880's," the cowboy reached a hyperbolic performance. Smith traces the origin of this cowboy figure to Daniel Boone and James Fennimore Cooper's Leatherstocking character (109). This character embodies and promotes behaviors and attitudes that are anti-civilization, anti-institutions, and fiercely independent. Smith argues that Leatherstocking was similar to the figure of Daniel Boone in that he "was a symbol of anarchic freedom, an enemy of law and order" (60).

In the original trilogy, Han fulfills this role. Savage argues, "the cowboy was a wage earner, not a capitalist, and only occasionally did he—or could he—rise above that economic to acquire land or cattle of his own" (6). Han's earns his primary income through smuggling goods throughout the universe in the *Millennium Falcon*. Although Han owns the ship, he did not purchase it. He won it in a card game against Lando Calrissian. The ship is essential, as it compliments his "cowboy" image. Like Han's western costume, the *Millennium Falcon* takes the place of the cowboy's horse. Han proudly boasts his ship's prowess—it travels faster than lightspeed, cuts corners on the Kessel Run, and he has made many "special modifications" himself. Thus, although he was not the ship's original owner, his improvements have left his personal stamp on the ship. The *Millennium Falcon* maneuvers past and outruns his adversaries in it and "the old trick of hiding behind a rock as the posse rides by reappears when Han Solo attaches his ship to the aide of the Imperial Cruiser and effectively disappears" (Wright 121).[5]

Han's contrast to Jedi masculinity is apparent from the start. Just before Han is introduced, Obi-Wan and Luke stand on a cliff overlooking the port city Mos Eisley. Obi-Wan observes and cautions Luke, "You will never find a more wretched hive of scum and villainy" (Lucas *Star Wars*). There, Luke and Obi-Wan stand in the wilderness setting standard to the Western genre, looking off to the nearest civilized town, which parallels the Wild West City.

Winkler contends that, "it need hardly be stressed that most, if not all, of the historical Western heroes were of rather dubious, even criminal nature, in real life" (517). That they find Han Solo in this place is indicative of his role of an outlaw on the fringe of society. As a smuggler who is wanted by crime boss, Jabba the Hutt for unpaid gambling debts, Han reinforces those negative attributes. His involvement with Luke and Obi-Wan is that of a mercenary as he is only concerned with the reward that he was promised. In his May 26, 1977, review of the film, Vincent Canby of *The New York Times* defined Han Solo as "a free-booting freelance, space-ship captain who goes where he can make the most money." Similarly, in a May 1977 review from *The Hollywood Reporter,* Ron Pennington described Han Solo as "a smug and cynical space smuggler whose ship and services they entice with promises of great riches." These assessments of Han's character align with the romanticized outlaw rogue aspect of his character that connote strength, adventure, and virility. Han is further described as "an unprincipled, wandering rogue who must reluctantly be drawn into the good fight" (Wright 121). Once Han is in "the good fight," he will remain loyal to Leia and Luke and the cause of the Rebellion. His masculine demeanor becomes secondary to the Jedi's form.

Throughout the films, Han exhibits paternal behavior, assuming the role of guardian despite his self-interested motivation of paying off his debt to Jabba the Hutt. Quoting Henry King in in *Virgin Land,* Henry Nash Smith argues, "King also suggested that the cowboy had some virtues despite his violence: he was generous, brave, and scrupulously honest, with 'a strange, paradoxical code of personal honor, in vindication of which he will obtrude his life as though it were but a toy'" (qtd. in 109). Han first demonstrates this first when he is introduced in cantina scene. His initial interaction with Greedo shows Han shooting first, killing Greedo. This aggression and arrogance are the hallmarks of Han Solo's character, establishing him as the identifier of dominant patriarchal masculinity to audiences.[6] This is further exemplified through Han's erratic behavior during Leia's rescue on the Death Star. His code of honor is what triggers his highly-developed protective tendencies. At the beginning of the rescue sequence when Luke, Leia, Han, and Chewbacca are pinned down by stormtroopers, Han assumes the role of protector. He tells Chewbaccca to stay behind him so he won't get shot, and he provides cover so the others can safely escape into the garbage shoot, before jumping down himself.

Other moments confirm Han's protective role. At the end of the movie, Vader prepares to shoot Luke's X-wing down, but Han arrives in the *Millennium Falcon* like the cavalry in a Western film, complete with a "sunset" illumination as he swoops down. He sets Vader off course, allowing Luke to hit the target and destroy the Death Star. This scene establishes the primary masculine relationships in the canon. Luke is clearly the hero who must complete the task at hand. Han performs the role of protector and rescuer. This is revisited at the beginning of *The Empire Strikes Back* when Luke is captured by the wampa. Han disregards his personal safety and well-being and leaves the comfort of the base to confront sub-zero temperatures to rescue Luke. When he finds Luke, Han conquers nature, or the wilderness as a cowboy would, by building an ice shelter for himself and Luke, keeping them both alive until the search party finds them the next morning. He similarly assumes the role of protector and hero in *Return of the Jedi* as he leads the Endor team to disarm the force shield of the Death Star so that the Rebels can destroy it.

Although Han has become part of the group of rebels by the *Return of the Jedi*, eschewing his "solo" status for a greater cause, he maintains his self-serving, competitive, and aggressive attitude, projecting "a degree of emotional insensitivity of feelings of hurt and loss in defeated others, and a measure of emotional insularity to protect [him]self from becoming vulnerable to manipulation by others" (Devor 430). Gordon recognizes that "Solo is always torn between being for himself or being for the group" ("Id" 315). Han asserts his singularity and emotional distance through his speech patterns and linguistic cues. Thus, his use of language affirms his verbal authority through arrogance and through witty and sarcastic remarks. When he first meets Leia, he resents her attempt to take the lead to save them in the garbage shoot, which ultimately put them in further danger. Once they are safe, Han dismisses her attempt at authority, announcing, "if we just avoid any more female advice, we ought to be able to get out of here" (Lucas *Star Wars*). He communicates his masculinity, his supremacy, and his own authority when he announces, "I take orders from one person, me" (Lucas *Star Wars*). His unrefined speech patterns communicate his thoughts and emotions simply and directly. Moreover, he consistently refers to Luke with diminutive language like "kid" and "junior," and he uses sarcastic monikers like "your worship" to address Leia.

The most significant demonstration of Han Solo's heteronormative masculinity is evident in his romantic pursuit of Princess Leia. Though their relationship does not culminate in a marriage or children, it establishes the promise of both at the end of the original trilogy and explored in the Expanded Universe. The presence of a woman creates the opportunity for a heterosexual relationship. In the original movie, Han initially expresses his attraction for Leia through aggression because he is unable to communicate his emotions. After he meets her, he tells Luke, "Wonderful girl. Either I'm going to kill her or I'm beginning to like her" (Lucas *Star Wars*). Though

Han and Luke will continue to compete for her through the beginning of *The Empire Strikes Back*, Han establishes his claim to her through his linguistic aggression in this scene.

The Empire Strikes Back depicts Han continuing his pursuit of Leia through the pattern of attraction and aggression. On the cusp of Han's departure from the station on Hoth, he visits her to say goodbye. His farewell is tinged with undercurrents of sexual tensions masked in aggression. His vulnerability and desire for her attention are apparent when he physically follows her through the station, though his language remains antagonistic. She says she's sorry to see him go because the rebellion needs him. His response, "We need. What about you need," again demonstrates his need for her to verbalize her affection and his inability to soften his approach (Kershner). However, when the Empire attacks and Darth Vader has entered the building, Han is able to assert his authority in the role of protector by saving Leia, helping her escape on the *Millennium Falcon*. This bravado is successful in wooing her when they are hiding out from the Imperial forces on the asteroid and share their first kiss after she calls him a "scoundrel."[7] Following this, in one of the most iconic scenes in the film, Leia finally professes her love to him, and Han responds by saying "I know" in what *Rolling Stone's* Timothy White calls "crowd-pleasing arrogance" (Kershner). His response both reinforces the rugged masculinity that defines him, but continues to assert his claim on Leia. This scene is inverted on Endor when Leia is shot, but is ready to shoot the approaching stormtroopers. Han tells Leia that he loves her, to which she responds, "I know" (Marquand). This reversal indicates Han's acceptance of his vulnerability with Leia. The culmination of Han's heteronormative gender development occurs at the end of the original trilogy when he and Leia solidify their love and commitment to each other.[8]

George Lucas's imaginary universe is a pastiche of familiar traditions from American history and culture, mythology, and religion. The release of *Star Wars* came during the decline of the popularity of the Western genre, partially caused by political and social changes precipitated by the women's movement for equal rights. The release of the subsequent films corresponded with shifts in gender roles and relationships in America. While the cowboy remains a popular masculine identity in American culture, its expression of masculinity was, in many ways, antiquated by the late 1970s. Devor's argument that "gender role characteristics reflect the ideological contentions underlying the dominant gender schema in North American Society" is apropos to the *Star Wars* films (431). Although the binary positive and negative masculinities are represented through Luke Skywalker and Darth Vader in the original trilogy and Anakin in the prequels, Han Solo emerges in the role of the traditional cowboy. His presence in the film creates an association between North American audiences and a familiar gender identity. However comfortable audiences were with Han Solo's gender performance, he was not the hero and did not represent the dominant masculinity; Luke Skywalker and the Jedi Knights did. Through the major male characters, Lucas created a gender hierarchy for his universe that realigned hegemonic patriarchal masculine identities and the changing performances of masculinity in North America. In the *Star Wars* canon, this is represented through one's development within and use of the Force. Jedi Knights represent the good side of the Force and the dominant masculinity in Lucas's universe, yet they are associated with qualities that are not traditionally classified as masculine in the patriarchal schema. However, these qualities or characteristics that the Jedi Knights personify, the importance of non-violence, peace, cooperation, connection to and serving others, are reappropriated as hegemonic masculine qualities in Lucas's gender schema. In contrast, those, like Anakin or Darth Vader, who fall to the Dark Side of the Force, represent a hyperbolic realization of conventionally dominant masculine traits. Both of these identities present a path to achieve power, but the appropriation of positive and negative qualities to each of them is a signal to viewers that Luke and the Jedi are the ideal "generalized others."

Notes

1. The regular Imperial personnel represent a very narrow performance of military masculinity. They are characters with limited subjectivity because they are not fully developed outside of the stereotype of officers following orders.

2. See Paul Charbel's essay in this volume.

3. There has been much controversy and debate regarding which Anakin is redeemed at the end of *Return of the Jedi* due to edits made to the 2004 release of the original trilogy that replaced Sebastian Shaw's image with Hayden Christiansen's as a Jedi spirit alongside Obi-Wan and Yoda. Shaw being replaced with Christensen satisfies the image of Anakin from *Attack of the Clones* and *Revenge of the Sith*, but it is Shaw, the unmasked Darth Vader, from *Return of the Jedi*, who represents Vader's full transformation, redemption, and gender development within Lucas's re-imagined masculine schema. It is through this development that Vader ultimately returns balance to the Force by rejecting the Dark Side. This is best represented by Shaw's image.

4. See also Gregory E. Rutledge's essay in this volume.

5. Space prohibits a reading of Chewbacca, Solo's "Indian" sidekick, who speaks non-English, is nearly nude, and uses a bow and arrow. Solo's "uncivilized" link is further enhanced with his connections to the vast alien/non-human underworld, of which he freely maneuvers.

6. The re-reading of the Han/Greedo sequence has thus become a hotbed of fan controversy. See Michael Fuchs's and Michael Phillips's chapter in this volume.

7. Leia also refers to Lando Calrissian as a "scoundrel" in *The Empire Strikes Back*, but she is not romantically interested in him because she is already in love with Han and because she does not trust Lando. Her instincts are correct as Lando betrays all of them to the Empire and is responsible for Han being frozen in carbonite.

8. Though Luke and Leia are twins and share a familial bond, they have very little to do with each other after *A New Hope*. They appear together in the opening and closing scenes of *The Empire Strikes Back* and he rescues her and their friends and tells her they are siblings in *Return of the Jedi*. However, Han has all of the screentime with Leia, which helps develop their relationship. Further, Luke concedes the competition for Leia's affections to Han. Even if they were not related, Luke would not be able to bring a heterosexual relationship to its fruition or he would succumb to the same passions and violations of the Jedi tenets that led to Anakin's downfall.

Works Cited

Canby, Vincent. "A Trip to a Far Galaxy That's Fun and Funny…" *New York Times*. 26 May 1977. Web. 2 Mar. 2015.

Connell, R. W. *Masculinities, 2d ed*. Berkley: University of California Press, 2005. Print.

_____. *The Men and the Boys*. Berkley: University of California Press, 2000. Print.

Devor, Aaron H. "Becoming Members of Society: Learning the Social Meanings of Gender." *Rereading America: Cultural Contexts for Critical Thinking and Writing, 6th ed*. Eds. Gary Columbo, Robert Cullen, and Bonnie Lisle. Boston: Bedford St. Martin's, 2004. 424–432. Print.

Gordon, Andrew. "'The Empire Strikes Back': Monsters from the Id ("L'empire contre-attaque": les monstres du Ça)." *Science Fiction Studies* 7, no. 3. Science Fiction and the Non-Print Media (Nov. 1980). pp. 313–318. JSTOR. Web. 6 Mar. 2015.

_____. "Star Wars: A Myth for Our Time." *Literature/Film Quarterly* 6.4. (Fall 1978): 314–326. Web. 6 Mar. 2015.

Kershner, Irvin, dir. *Star Wars Episode V: The Empire Strikes Back*. Twentieth Century Fox, 1980, DVD.

Lucas, George, dir. *Star Wars Episode I: The Phantom Menace*. Twentieth Century Fox, 1999. DVD.

_____. *Star Wars Episode II: Attack of the Clones*. Twentieth Century Fox, 2002. DVD.

_____. *Star Wars Episode III: Revenge of the Sith*. Twentieth Century Fox, 2005, DVD.

_____. *Star Wars Episode IV: A New Hope*. Twentieth Century Fox, 1977. DVD.

Marquand, Richard, dir. *Star Wars Episode VI: Return of the Jedi*. Twentieth Century Fox, 1983, DVD.

Pennington, Ron. "'Star Wars': Read THR's 1977 Review." 28 Nov. 2014. Web. 3 Mar. 2015.

Savage, William W., Jr. "Introduction." *Cowboy Life: Reconstructing an American Myth*. Ed. William W. Savage, Jr. Norman: University of Oklahoma Press, 1975. 3–16. Print.

Smith, Henry Nash. *Virgin Land The American West as Symbol and Myth*. 1950. Cambridge: Harvard University Press, 2001. Print.

Waller, Marguerite. "Poetic Influence in Hollywood: Rebel without a Cause and Star Wars." *Diacritics* 10, no. 3 (Autumn 1989): 57–66. JSTOR. Web. 1 Mar. 2015.

White, Timothy. "'Star Wars': Slaves to the 'Empire.'" *Rolling Stone*. 24 July 1980. Web. 2 Mar. 2015.

Winkler, Martin M. "Classical Mythology and the Western Film." *Comparative Literature Studies* 22, no. 4 (Winter 1985): 516–540. JSTOR. Web. 4 Mar. 2105.

Wright, Will. "The Empire Bites the Dust." *Social Text* 6 (Autumn 1982): 120–125. JSTOR. Web. 27 Feb. 2015.

Jedi Knights and Epic Performance

Is the Force a Form of Western-African Epic Mimicry?

GREGORY E. RUTLEDGE

"One of the significant things that occurred to me is I saw the western die. We hardly knew what happened, one day we turned around and there weren't any westerns anymore."
—George Lucas, *Rolling Stone* (1977)

Although in August 1977 Lucas stated that *Star Wars*, a sci-fi Western extending all the way back to Homer's epics, combines his careful study of "culture as a living organism" and belief "that the [American] kids were really lost" (Scanlon 43), scholars seldom address questions like "What to the child is *Star Wars*, an epical space Western?" and "What to her or him is the meaning of 'Western,' a term denoting genre, space, and cultural practices?" This is because, when it comes to thinking about art, literature, and culture, even when we engage issues of oppression that have global implications, the default reader/audience/subject to which we address our concerns and about which we are concerned is too often the fully realized adult. Even when the critical lens is astute and the scholar reveals the explicit and hidden forms of racism, sexism, classism, homophobia, fundamentalism, and the like within a work of art or product of culture, the presumed Western Subject—an Individual—situates the fully *formed* adult at the expense of the *forming* youth. This is true notwithstanding the *Brown v. Board of Education* (1954) decision that ordered the desegregation of public schools for the benefit of "colored" children notwithstanding Martin Luther King, Jr.'s famous 1963 "dream[s]" that "my four little children will one day live in a nation where they will not be judged by the color of their skin but by the content of their character" and "one day ... little black boys and little black girls will be able to join hands with little white boys and white girls as sisters and brothers" (104–105).

In other words, the methodology used by scholars is one that defaults to the end, the adult individual, and marginalizes processes of formation that are ongoing. Children represent this process of formation, but so do all (adult-led) cultures: children and cultures continue to evolve and grow, but both have a limited duration because humanity is the process of change forever outstripping any one person or group. Nevertheless, the children/adult divide is more than just a slighting of children because of adult myopia. For centuries if not millennia, the child/adult divide or binary represented Western ways of thinking about societies deemed pre-modern, uncivilized and child-like on the one hand, and those considered advanced, civilized, *European* modern societies on the other. The former had folklore in the form of oral (pre-literate) trickster tales while the latter produced lengthy heroic epic myths, a prerequisite for modern literate nations.

The *Star Wars* franchise is central to all the issues associated with this topic, for the group most impacted by George Lucas' broad imagination—combining knights and princesses to outer-space epic battles—are the billions of children around the world who would, in one way or another and at some point, identity with Jedi Knights and the Force. To them, an impressionable lot swept away by the vast vistas and fast actions of *Star Wars* on movie, television, and now videogame screens, what does the franchise represent as an ongoing process that contains deeply coded cultural values imbedded within? In one sense, this is a relatively easy question of direct affect, of a child's dawning consciousness overwhelmed by the big screen imagination of Lucas. Lucas acknowledges the "responsibility" directors have as a consequence, especially since he was the sole creator-owner (Wetmore 8–9), however the child(ren)/adult binary, once you expand it into its centuries-old meaning of savage/civilized, East/West, oral/written, and colored/white, becomes far too complicated a problem for the responsible *individual*. Since children are born into and influenced by such experiential frames, then adults and their cultures have been and are conditioned, too, by processes that are centuries old. Is Lucas, in this regard, a creator whose inspiration is inseparable from the multiple cultural processes that shaped how he perceived the world, and conceived of creativity? Moreover, for centuries Western modernity has proceeded not simply as a modern parent guiding undeveloped infants, but as a cultural space based on economies of appropriation, exploitation, and imitation. The relationship has not simply been founded, in other words, on slavery and colonialism, of West dominating the non-West (East or Other). Instead, it relies on a cultural economy in which the rich cultures and resources of the

Other were and are exploited and expropriated and then re-performed as Western ingenuity. This exploitation/expropriation and imitation dynamic is so inherent to the mode of domination that it has become the *natural*, darkened part of a creative process that is taken for granted. Race functions, for Lucas and America, as the defining cultural metaphor and trope.

In this context, and with children in mind, I would like to raise a fundamental question about the racial and cultural processes in *Star Wars* that is critical and personal. What is the significance of race in defining *Star Wars* as a process that should be understood from the perspective of, say, an impressionable African American boy who saw *A New Hope* (Episode IV), in 1978? What are the ironies to be extracted from his experience of seeing it with a crowd of moviegoers at the Desoto Square Mall Theater, a premier shopping venue named after Hernando Desoto,[1] a Spanish conquistador? When he literally stumbled out of his seat toward the exit as the credits rolled, his legs wobbly and head woozy because he had identified so deeply with Luke Skywalker that he nearly flew as co-pilot in the cockpit of the X-wing starfighter as Luke attacked the Empire's Death Star with Darth Vader's TIE fighter in hot pursuit, what was the lesson for him? To be heroically rebellious like Luke (or cool like Han Solo) and not blackly evil like Darth Vader (or forceful like James Earl Jones' voice)? To pursue one's bliss and be a Force-wielder even if it means becoming like Darth Vader? And be creative and technologically inventive like Lucas, the creator-screenwriter-director?

That boy, if you had not suspected it, was me. A mere ten-year-old kid, I was in the process of forming my adolescent identity when *Star Wars*, impacting me in a way no movie had then or has since, literally sent me stumbling dizzily from the movie theater. I had not "reframed and reinterpreted" and thus neutralized the Eurocentrism, as suggested by Christopher Deis (90–92), but been overwhelmed by it. Years later, motivated by my longstanding interest in the heroic—super hero comics, sword & sorcery fantasy novels, television serials like *Lost in Space* (1965–1968) and *Star Trek* (1966–1969), and cinema—my own graduate-school and doctoral work in African-American literature and culture put my formative years in a different context. In the process of writing *The Epic Trickster: From Sunjata to So(ul)* (2013), I had to: depart from my initial grad-school interest in Afro-futurism (sci-fi authored by African Americans); part ways with my classical-hero orientation, a Manichean perspective which essentially led me to see (epic) *heroes* as do-gooders who fought "evil"; and, finally see heroic West/Central African epics as cultural performances charged with the rich wisdom of their respective cultures, the epic protagonists themselves being cautionary tales against their own powers, not generic outlets for the (classical) heroic personality of the archetype or monomyth.

Now, with the racial backlash over a black stormtrooper (Afro-British actor John Boyega) still relatively fresh in our 24/7 news cycle, if only this episode is attached to the forthcoming and much-anticipated *The Force Awakens*, it shows these questions have not gone away. Should a black (man) be a stormtrooper, a "black stormtrooper?" However important this question is to racism, when we place it within the child(ren)/adult binary a sense of urgency is unavoidable. There are at least three reasons for the urgency. First, and most obvious, children are most vulnerable to the insidious influences of racism encoded within U.S. society and its sublime stories. As I watched *A New Hope*, for example, notwithstanding my community-taught concern with racism against African Americans, the whiteness of the heroes—Luke, Han, Princess Leia Organa, Obi-Wan Kenobi, and the Britishness of C-3PO's accent—defined my experience. For years afterwards, like many American boys I am sure, I had a deep, abiding crush on Carrie Fisher (Princess Leia). In 1994, nine years after high school, five years after college, and two years after law school, I sketched Princess Leia from the dust jacket of Kathy Tyers' *The Truce at Bakura* (1993), an early "Expanded Universe" novel I read. Second, the debut of the *The Force Awakens* in 2015 will inaugurate an event that looms even larger than the customary anticipation surrounding the release of a *Star Wars* film. Since the *Star Wars* franchise was sold along with Lucasfilm to the Walt Disney Company in 2012, it now belongs to an even more massive corporate, child-focused entertainment empire. Disney's total cultural presence was already one of the few brands—because its animated features appeal to males and female children equally—that compares with the reach of *Star Wars*.[2] Third and last, the urgency has global reach

My March 1994 sketch of Princess Leia.

because the act of defining the child/adult binary as a global relationship is central to defining the identity of the West(ern). Specifically, understanding the child/adult binary leads us on a quest to seek the past cultural processes that underlie the making of U.S. modernity and *Star Wars*.

Central to the child/adult binary is the hero-centered mythology which is, as is commonly known, the driving force behind the *Star Wars* franchise; the epic-myth "monomyth," described by Joseph Campbell in *The Hero of a Thousand Faces* (1949), was the script Lucas read, literally, as he completed the draft of *A New Hope* (Lawrence 22). But whereas the "monomyth" hero is a ready-made adult (notice the absence of children from *Star Wars*, except for *The Phantom Menace* [Episode I], even though Lucas approached his movie in the franchise as a "family-oriented movie" [Wetmore 129]), a performance- and process-oriented approach to mythology reveals how complicated are the cultural forces involved in the creation of *Star Wars*. Because of Europe's centuries-long fascination with classical heroic epics and the U.S.'s New World epic, much of American culture reveals a contradictory racial impulse. It is classically oriented toward a Greco-Roman and Christian epic tradition epitomized by Homer, Virgil, and Jesus on the one hand, as antithesis to the Other, but also co-opts the epic potency of exceptional minorities to drive ingenuity and cultural hegemony, on the other. Both the classical epic tradition and the native epic traditions constitute a form of what I call *epic mimicry*, the selective borrowing and mimicking of exceptional identities from cultures only marginally understood, if at all. The original Trojan War oral tradition upon which Homer's epics are based, along with all of its cultural performances, is forever inaccessible. Whereas the *Iliad* begins *in media res*, nine years into the war between the Trojans and Greeks, this formal feature, elevated into the canon as sublime literary strategy, runs afoul of the tendency for many of the world's epics—compare Hercules, the greatest Greek mortal/demigod—to begin with the childhoods of the epic protagonists. Hence the French term *l'enfant terrible*, which refers to an epic-child protagonist who is the bearer of terrible, destructive power. Implicit here is the epic individual, still in the process of becoming, and the common sense of the community, which should be duly concerned with what such power could become (self-destructive) and the healthy processes needed to contain it.

Redefining the Problem

The consideration of racial misrepresentation or under-representation in *Star Wars* assumes a default position based on adult interests. This is understandable to the extent that the concern is with individual actors who are symbolic representatives for their ethnic groups. But this is a problematic model, for it places the individual leader/celebrity as the legitimate and authorized representative for the community. Along with reinforcing individualism and uncritically conflating individual rights with much broader and older issues, the focus on the individual adult defaults to political matters of voice. Adults and adult actors can agitate (petition, protest, take legal action) for access to Hollywood, whereas the child—actual minors and also the "child" as the symbol defining the relationship between "undeveloped" cultures and also new modern nations—is largely unrepresented.

The postcolonial and cultural studies treatment of *Star Wars* in scholar Kevin J. Wetmore, Jr., *The Empire Triumphant: Race, Religion, and Rebellion in the* Star Wars *Films* (2005) is a case in point. Wetmore uses the seminal theory and methodology of Frantz Fanon, the Afro-Martinique psychiatrist whom many call the father of postcolonial studies because of his works *Black Skin, White Mask* (1952) and *The Wretched of the Earth* (1961). Following the lead of Fanon, a French-trained colonial subject who called for the colonized people to reclaim their indigenous identities and violently rebel against their empires, Wetmore masterfully frames *Star Wars* as a postcolonial rebellion against the Empire, *sans* the urgency of the colonized colored people. "In the case of the *Star Wars* films," he writes, "the Empire remains at the center, as do white males. The rebellion does not exist to achieve liberation for the oppressed indigenous peoples—it seeks to restore the previous privileged to power" (38).

Even though Wetmore proceeds to engage the specific absence of people of Asian and African descent, using his postcolonial frame to give additional depth to the widespread knowledge that Lucas drew significantly upon Japanese cinema and that the Force parallels Eastern spirituality (chapters 2 and 3), and to give voice to the absence of African Americans (chapter 4), the default subject for his analysis is Lucas as the fully mature creative intellect, albeit one vulnerable to the cultural codes that unconsciously shaped that intellect. Given his implication Lucas was and *is* a child of that culture, Wetmore's recognition of the importance of cultural studies, specifically his awareness that *Star Wars* and other films "can shape the real world perceptions of young viewers" (6–7), is critical. It allows him to grapple with art-in-cultural context issues marginalized by Andrew Howe and Christopher Deis in their examinations of race in the franchise. Nevertheless, in light of the fact that he knows European colonialism proceeded on the premise of natives' cultural *tabula rasa* ("blank slate" like children) (22) and that Lucas' target demographic is children under fourteen, Wetmore's marginalization of the child in his analysis is both striking and not—since it is a common oversight among academics discussing issues of identity and oppression.

The Empire Triumphant is, most likely and deservedly, the definitive study of race in *Star Wars*, a politically astute analysis that articulates the role of cultural ideology,[3] but Wetmore emphasizes the oppression within culture without ever asking what cultures and cultural processes make up American culture. The politicized field of inquiry that characterizes postcolonial theory no doubt explains this, for even the indigenous culture is a static decolonial tool to be wielded, or appropriated, as Lucas did with regard to Japanese film culture, Eastern spirituality, Campbell's monomyth, and even Tunisia as filming site. But the dynamism of culture, a performance that centers the child as a growing individual and each society as a "child" that is subject to geo-political cultural processes far larger and older than itself, is conspicuously absent. With an emphasis on the political, Wetmore cites the cultural events unfolding from the writing of *A New Hope* to its release as consisting of

> Nixon's presidency and the final days of the Vietnam War: "A very powerful and technological superpower trying to take over a little country of peasants was big on my mind," claims Lucas. In 1977, Jimmy Carter was in the White House. It was the height of the Cold War. High inflation and spiraling oil prices were the norm, affecting the economy and the lives of the average American, and the television miniseries *Roots* dominated American popular culture. Egypt's Anwar Sadat went to Israel as part of an ongoing peace process in the Middle East [2].

Some pages later, Wetmore discusses how *Star Wars*, like Lucas' *American Graffiti* (1973) before it, is a "nostalgia film" created in response to American audiences' "reactionary politics" and desire for a "return to a simpler time, with a less complex world" (7). The consummation of Wetmore's logic, a critical 1960s-era contextualization, is missing at this moment just as it is missing much later when he discusses African Americans' absence in *Star Wars*. This absence—or, in the case of James Earl Jones as Darth Vader's voice, the presence that emphasizes absence and reinforces European-American racial phobia[4]—is a consequence of Lucas' decision not to cast a black Han Solo and Asian-American Princess Leia because it would suggest an interracial romance, à la *Guess Who's Coming to Dinner?* (Wetmore 128–131).

Wetmore's and Andrew Howe's political, postcolonial critiques of the symbolic meaning of Darth Vader and Lando Calrissian (Billy Dee Williams) are both insightful and necessary, but nevertheless insufficient. Perhaps because he uses the postcolonial frame, which has political (national) independence from Western empires as its objective, Wetmore almost entirely overlooks cultural processes. Howe cites the inseparability of "cultural products from their context" and reads Vader's mask via Fanon, but ultimately exempts Lucas from cultural influence: Vader is not 1970s culture, but Lucas' *choice* to use stock cinematic symbolism (12–17). Whether the frame is the political context in 1977, the "nostalgia" for the past, or black phobia, Lucas' choices are both relevant and, importantly, irrelevant. Lucas is certainly a creator whose decisions should be credited to him, but Wetmore almost entirely—and Howe entirely—empties cultural processes of their depth and breadth. From a postcolonial, adult-rights-oriented approach, Lucas the *individual* creator omits minority presences, or selectively uses them. However, from a culture-based approach that recognizes basic tenets of cultural anthropology and cultural studies, and temporal differentials represented by older "parent" cultures and newer "child" cultures, the absence/presence inquiry proves to be far too simplistic. Culture is not a flat monolith available as resource for the creative individual, the free-thinking adult artist whose abilities advance the culture, although it is that, too. In addition to being a resource, we are conditioned by the culture, nurtured by codes we encounter as children that become to us like "air" so natural they are (Kitayama 320). In these cases, some individual choices are also—and probably first—authorized by the cultural logic. The existence of pre-authorized cultural artifacts makes possible an important extrapolation: Cultural productions can be assemblages or repackagings of archetypes, deep-set beliefs, official histories, cultural practices, stock storytelling narratives (often inclusive of intercultural contact and ethnic/national conflict), important events, and material icons, inter alia, in manners that are distinct from notions of artistic originality. Is Lucas a "craftsman," as he himself maintains, or an artist, as Wetmore holds (11)? Based on the role of culture as something discrete and as a shifting process, the complicated answer is either/or, neither/nor, and both: *either* an artist/author *or* craftsman, *neither* an artist/author *nor* a craftsman, and *both*.

The critical racial question with regard to *Star Wars*, then, is not what the absence or presence of *individual* (minority/colored or majority/white) thespians means, with classical racial politics of assimilation into the nation centered, but what is the fundamental cultural logic speaking through one of its exceptional creators? Admittedly, Wetmore knows that the unveiling of racial/racist "messages and ideologies" is not simply about the absence of "nonwhite performers" or their depiction as aliens, and that these practices represent "larger trends in American popular culture in which racist depictions of people of African and Asian descent are on the increase in American popular culture, while *other* cultures are mined for their novelty in American culture" (10) (italics mine). However, the nature of the challenge is not representation and borrowing from other (Asian) cultures, but a performance in which both of these first happen, and continually unfold, in the national core: "other cultures" and "their novelty" were and have always been part of American culture-mining and nationalism. Wetmore flattens U.S. culture and its dynamism and posits cultureless "people of African and Asian descent," an oddity since the U.S. textbook rhetoric is that it is a country of immigrants, and he critiques *Star Wars* for "erasing cultural difference within the Empire" and thus negating the possibility that the Rebellion is for real national liberation (53). Yet, the indigenous societies and the manifold cultural legacies ranging from names (they were first called "Americans"), crafts, and political thought (influential on the U.S. Constitution) (Loewen 111), disappear into Wetmore's postcolonial national framework.

Since race/racism and white supremacy address, fundamentally, the politics of exclusion that are rooted in colonial American laws and the U.S. constitution, perhaps the better course is to approach this through the centuries-old European cultural performance of exceptionalism. This exceptionalism is more compatible with a European/American culture steeped in Greco-Roman supremacy, Judeo-Christian fundamentalism, and inter-racial cooptation and exclusion. Is the parent of *Star Wars* the millennia-old cultural logic of American exceptionalism, and is Lucas one of the most exceptional storytellers of this common lore? As evidenced by the racial controversy related to the first trailer for *Star Wars: The Force Awakens*, racial representation and the cultural underpinnings of race are not interchangeable. In spite of the symbolism represented by Boyega, Samuel L. Jackson as Jedi Master Mace Windu, Billy Dee Williams as Lando Calrissian, and James Earl Jones as Darth Vader's voice, the recurring North African landscape is the most consistent and expansive "black" and minority presence. Along with the California dialectic between whiteness and Mexican-American labor Curtis Marez excavates in Lucas's sci-fi universes, a vast (sub)Saharan cultural landscape also lies at the heart of *Star Wars*.[5] It can be summed up with a question: Given that "the Force" is the *sine qua non* of *Star Wars*, why is the first Jedi knight ever seen, Obi-Wan Kenobi (Alec Guinness), so similar to West Saharan and West Sudan epic myth bearers? In other words, the underpinnings for *Star Wars* mythology—championed by mythologist Joseph Campbell in *The Power of Myth*—are not only provided by Tunisia, filming and topographical site for much of the franchise, but also unfold within the trans-Atlantic economy of African expropriation and cultural exchange. The Force and its Jedi Knights have precursors that—as Marez's argument of Lucas' expropriation of the Other as resource indicates—reveal how much of *Star Wars*'s creative force is a derivative or correlative of African cultural geographies. Boyega is *not* a black stormtrooper, Jackson is *not* a black Jedi Master, Williams is *not* a black Lando Calrissian, and Jones is *not* a black voice for Darth Vader as much as *Star Wars* is—to borrow from Eric Lott's seminal study, *Love and Theft: Blackface Minstrelsy and the American Working Class* (1995)—a sci-fi based form of blackface minstrelsy. Through cultural processes, this sci-fi blackface is indexed to the mystical soulfulness of African "folk," extended to African Americans and commodified as a manageable and reproducible cultural resource for artistic expression. Just as Lott argues blackface minstrelsy was a means by which the white (male) working class— in competition with the irresistible forcefulness of enslaved African American's culture and working-class potential—lampooned and thus subordinated blacks by expropriating and elevating a caricature of black culture, a similar dynamic works with regard to epic performance. Epic minority figures who stoked America's deepest fears can also appeal to its very desire for epic centrality: for example, the Apache warrior Geronimo, the most feared man in America, then became—once he surrendered and turned performer—one of its greatest objects of admiration (Rutledge 246–47). Likewise, the 1960s Black Power/Arts Movement introduced African culture that, in the form of black militancy soul power, similarly impacted the cultural imaginary of the middle-class world Lucas inhabited.

Blackface Minstrelsy, Epic Mimicry ... and All That Jazz

While racial supremacy and fear are central to understanding the European/American phobia toward the Other, especially African blackness, historically and anthropologically the cultural process has not been characterized by a monolithic racial recoil that tends toward absence. Racial supremacy cannot account for other parts of the cultural process and critical contexts. Not all Western European "white" countries were ranked equally: The Irish were enslaved and colonized by Great Britain, and elites in Europe looked down upon the American colonies, just as the colonial elites—the founders' class— subjugated yeoman whites. The original 1789 U.S. Constitution, which studies now show to be steeped in Homeric/Virgilian epic poetics, not just legal principle, was also shaped by Native-American culture even though it denied Native Americans (Loewen 109–112; Phillips 72–96; U.S. Constitution 1.2). Moreover, the European/American elites, from the twelfth century until the beginning of U.S. nationhood in 1789, literally debated whether the Ancients (Greek and Roman) were greater than the Moderns. This debate also took place between the Moderns: Was the cultured Old World of Europe better than the hinterland of the New World, or was the New World full of greater achievement and possibility than the corrupted, culturally stagnant Old? (Rutledge 87–88, 96–97, 113–114).

First as a settler colony and then a nation, the U.S. elites were often at the butt end of the Ancients vs. Moderns comparison, hence a cultural inferiority complex that made it even more inclined toward a virulent racial superiority complex. This dynamic is national, deep-seated, and contradictory. Although customarily a term most associated with political science, the latent "fantasy" dimension that governs the core U.S. political mythology makes exceptionalism a proper rubric for understanding the contradictions (Pease 1–17).[6] Exceptionalism defines this cultural performance, and the white Homeric epic hero(ine) has served as one of its most recognizable cultural emblems, for the classically-trained founders most directly and, by extension, to their subjects depending on their social distance from elite white-male status. The movement down this socioeconomic and racial/ethnic chain of being does *not* correlate with a diminution of the will to be exceptional, for the existence of a culture of, or dedicated to, exceptionalism also works as a catalyst that motivates the most despised.[7]

Blackface minstrelsy, I argue, emerged as a natural expression of the American exceptionalism of the late-eighteenth and early-nineteenth century. This theatrical performance of perceived blackness resulted from the millennia-old practice of caricaturing enslaved people's culture intertwined with the complexities of exceptionalism: White elites owned slaves and held a status so far above working-class whites that the latter were not much better off than slaves, in fact; the white (male) masses were intermediaries who were socio-economically, legally, and culturally in close proximity to, if not always contact with, the enslaved; enslaved "noble Negroes" and geniuses—a highly literate prince from West Africa, Abdul-Rahman Ibrahim, was enslaved in Mississippi, and literary genius Phillis Wheatley, the colonial-era poet brought as an illiterate child from West Africa, was enslaved in Boston— were often given their freedom, because they were exceptional at a time when slavery was rapidly expanding in the U.S. as a cultural economy; and, importantly, while elite and non-elite whites' racial mythology secured their belief in their qualitative racial superiority, the fact that slaves far outnumbered whites at this time in many places meant this massive quantity of slaves had undeniable qualitative (cultural) force. This cultural force, combined with an inferiority complex born of exceptionalism, establishes the centuries-old context for the 1830s U.S. emergence of blackface minstrelsy as a combination of racialized love and theft, mimicry and *marketry*—artful marketing.

Hence, since "during this stretch of American cultural history the intercourse between racial cultures was at once so attractive and so threatening as to require a cultural marker or visible sign of cultural interaction," Eric Lott focuses on how blackface minstrelsy expresses this phenomenon, which is rooted in "white male obsession with black (male) bodies" (3, 6). Lott's significant contribution to cultural studies is his demonstration that the appeal of popular culture has historically and broadly encompassed racial aversion and ambivalence, which are mutually reinforcing. The material reality of blackface minstrelsy for him was a newly performed racial economy in which "there were in fact contradictory racial impulses at work" (4).[8] The creative and marketing economy of blackface then and now stems from racial recoil, love of certain aspects of black culture, and then theft and re-performance of them in a new market specifically designed for its valuable exhibition. The widespread presence of enslaved people from New England to the South explains why it was the "most popular entertainment form of the nineteenth century" and why it "has been so central to the lives of North Americans that we are hardly aware of its extraordinary influence" (Lott 4). For Lott, then, blackface minstrelsy is the visage of U.S. popular culture because it intersects major historical trauma, racial fantasy, art, ritual, and market economies in ways significant to cultural anthropologists. Hence he invokes Victor Turner and this discipline when he states that "cultural performance originates in 'social drama' … and continues to draw force and meaning from it, constituting, in essence, 'performances about performances.'" In this framework, the original dramas "held such a complicated mix of racial impulses, interracial imitations, and economic facts." Lott writes the development of blackface emerged out of "primarily working-class rituals of racial interrogation" suggests blackface reproduced a "structured relationship" between the races, reinforcing racial difference as well as black cultural forms. The blackface mask becomes a "configuration of the commodity, a sort of trademark assigned to the 'black' images white people paid to see" (Lott 48–49).[9]

Although Lott's insights here are pegged to material performance economies—blackface as "working-class rituals"—realized by broad cultural practices that push aside heroic myth, it is important to keep in mind his invocation of Turner's conception of "social drama" as "performances about performances." In other words, cultural performances in the context of a governing social drama are always imbedded with one another. Blackface performance is, at the very least, a result of another preceding performance and its governing principles of racial domination and expropriation. Ultimately, the social drama is situated in a mythological performance of racial supremacy shared alike by the "white" working class and elites—and, perhaps most devastatingly, by "blacks." Mythological *belief* is also real, although it is the internalized force that governs behavior and material (re)production. In this sense, blackface minstrelsy is indexed to epic mythology—the ancient genre and political economy of exceptionalism—as exemplified by Homer's epic heroes. Achilles and Odysseus/Ulysses embodied the European/American sense of how "white" heroic manhood should be manifest, while blackface minstrelsy performances represent the given belief that such racial exceptionalism— inclusive of Helen's imagined beauty—was impossible for people of African descent. Africa, famed philosopher G.W.F. Hegel wrote out of Germany, a leading producer-consumer of Homeric content in the nineteenth century, was a land of "no history" that could thus produce no epics (Hegel 1046–48).

Contrary to Lott's American frame, which allows him to assert the "odd view" of "blackface minstrelsy as an African-American people's culture" (16), the absence of an objective and heroic sense of blackness and the existence of West African cultures and enslaved Africans' resistance imply an opposite reality beneath that which is staged. The *masking* by blacks—a harsh necessity where a slave's expression of subjectivity could get him or her sold "down the river"—implies, as W.E.B. Du Bois famously writes in 1903, an America based on the existence of "two worlds." In America a black person has a "peculiar sensation … of always looking at one's self through the eyes of others." Importantly, Du Bois articulates the existence of an African sublime he knows "has a message for the world": "The shadow of a mighty Negro past flits through the tale of Ethiopia the Shadowy and of Egypt the Sphinx" (5, 11).

The various forms of masking—historians' veiling of this African past, blackface minstrelsy, blacks' use of it for self-protection, and the very idea of Darth Vader—all have bearing on one of the most disturbing, fascinating, and child-unfriendly scenes in *Star Wars*: The events unfolding in the Mos Eisley Cantina on Tatooine to the accompaniment of music played by Figrin D'an and the Modal Notes. In the first-ever dramatic display of Jedi Knight action, stereotypically fitting for a "pirate city," Obi-wan (Ben) Kenobi (Alec Guinness) demonstrates his Jedi prowess literally and figuratively with the flash of his lightsaber; the actual violence is not shown, but the moment is nevertheless realistic and graphic as two psychotic intergalactic criminals' encounter with Kenobi results in a collapsing body, a disturbing inhuman wail, and a severed, bloody arm. Likewise, Han Solo (Harrison Ford) enters the story (with Chewbacca) and establishes his *Millennium Falcon* as the fastest ship in the galaxy and proves his wit and skills against a bounty hunter. These men and their actions are spliced into a context that seems most ordinarily strange—just right for a galaxy far, far away. Viewers see a frightening multitude of aliens, hear exotic instrumental music, witness anti-droid discrimination, and see Kenobi bargaining with Solo for passage to Alderaan. The action and the rich backdrop are so engrossing that adults as well as children are oblivious to the *masking* here: Jazz, an African-American cultural form, is both the music and the character of the space. Blacks are absent here, but the white imagining of their jazz culture is a presence that fills the space. The cantina is a jazzy-dark space revealed by the cutting camera to include a nightmarish set of aliens, including a dark silhouetted creature, two furry one-eyed aliens cackling with one another, and a werewolf-like monster with red, beady eyes. This display, culminating literally with a long-shot of a grinning devil, is a 1970s nostalgic imagination that amply demonstrates why Du Bois and other elite blacks, in the early decades of the twentieth century, disdained the blues and jazz. They knew the white Judeo-Christian imaginary, made public by the media, associated this music with black criminality, hyperviolence, hyper-sexuality, and the dark arts. Although the grinning, red-faced *jazz*-devil with two large black horns jutting upward and out of frame validates Du Bois' concern, the irony, as with the culture phenomena of blues and jazz, is that the "Cantina Band" and "Cantina Band #2" compositions are part of a musical phenomenon that went platinum in the U.S. In other words, the music—composed by John Williams based on his interest in 1920s to 1950s jazz (Williams)—and the scene resonated with audiences' apparent orientation toward *coolness*.

Jazz erupts out of this scene in ways too paradoxical and complicated to be framed by the democratic, interracial principles of jazz and the phobic racial recoil against the juke. Jazz is not just the music proper, born of the "bad man" blues roots of 1870s America that led to rock 'n' roll's emergence in the 1940s. Instead, it is a psycho-social form working at multiple levels in U.S. culture—*raced* music, a formal music, psychological catharsis, jazz innovation as individual freedom, racial rebellion, sexual vitality—and, just as importantly for *Star Wars*, internationally. The Japanese Shogun culture that fascinated Lucas was infected with blackface fever by the U.S. in the early 1850s, when Commodore Matthew C. Perry forced open Japan to U.S. relations and his crew performed an "Ethiopian Concert" minstrel show (Bourdaghs 170), and jazz in the 1920s. This jazz was a form of minstrelsy, too, for it was not that of the originators, but Paul Whiteman's orchestrated "jazz," which was the cultural and racial ambassador deemed fitting as an expression of American culture in East Asia (Atkins 351). One of the most popular bandleaders of the day, Whiteman feminized and gentrified the music in the early 1920s by "making a lady out of jazz." Like blackface, Whiteman extracted aesthetics from African-American culture in a manner than demeaned, lampooned, and lessened the original formal expression. But that form is child of an older cultural heritage. Thus, the Cantina Band draws potency from Tunisia (exterior of the Cantina) and the cultural interior of jazz coolness, which scholarship—as I'll discuss below—links to African epic performance.

In other words, Lucas could not have imagined that Shogun Japan, in its waning days, was jazzed up, doubly blackfaced by minstrelsy and Whiteman jazz, but also nevertheless shaped by the cultural forms of African influence. The coolness of the Mos Eisley Cantina results in significant part from two key juxtapositions, with jazz providing the sounds and the dangerous character for both: Kenobi is Samurai/Knight/mystical epic hero and Solo is crack pilot/gunslinger/"scruffy" epic hero. Like the Homeric innovator par excellence, Odysseus, Kenobi and Han Solo emerge from this jazz underworld not with jazz as pure opposition, but with their feats in the cantina now inseparable from their own characters as the movie proceeds. Unlike the bright-eyed, bright-clad Luke Skywalker (Mark Hamill), who is too innocent, too shrill, and too "square," Kenobi's cool lightsaber and Solo's cool but deadly suaveness are properly nourished with jazz chords.

The Conquest of Afro-Coolness: Star Wars and African/American Epic Mimicry

Since it is the definitive novelty of Star Wars, a form of spirituality for many (Davidsen 24), and is first seen in action in the Mos Eisley Cantina, no examination of the racial, exceptionalist, and cultural underpinnings of this franchise can sidestep the question, from whence comes the Force-wielding Jedi Knights? Clearly, insofar as Lucas the *adult* artist or craftsman is concerned, the consensus is that the Force is not Christian in origin and is most analogous to Buddhist conceptualization of the interconnected universe, and Eastern spirituality generally. Considering that the Force is indexed to monomyth-inspired epic *warriors*, however inclined they are to peace, it is not surprising that Lucas has acknowledged the Buddhism-Force parallels but said "'it's a notion that's been around before that'" (Wetmore 82). After all, the Joseph Campbell-inspired Lucas had, from Campbell's *The Hero with a Thousand Faces* (1949), a description of the precursor to the Force. Bill Moyers, in his famous conversation with Campbell about Star Wars, recognized the parallel between it and "similar descriptions of the world navel, of the sacred place, of the power that is at the moment of creation" (Campbell 179). However important these specific choices may have been, the cultural context of Lucas's formative days is important as well. Wetmore foregrounds the Buddhist Tao in this regard, noting that Lucas's early career in the late sixties and early seventies coincided with the rising popularity of Eastern spiritualities in the U.S., particularly in California. "Many critics and scholars see a good deal of Asian religions present in the doctrines of the Jedi. Either a general Eastern spirituality or Zen Buddhism specifically are cited as the most similar real-world equivalent of the Force" (82). Julien Fielding, citing the work of Steven J. Rosen, goes yet further to ask whether Sanskrit defines much of *Star Wars*. Yoda, according to Rosen, means "zeal and hard work" and is comparable to "yuddha" in Sanskrit, which means "war." He is a chivalrous warrior of sorts, by this reasoning. Maybe the source is the Bhagavad-Gita, "in which we find a guru-disciple relationship, an emphasis on overcoming desire and anger, and the idea of a 'Force' pervading the universe" (Fielding 27).

Important here is the fact that Lucas would approach Buddhism (and Sanskrit) as an *American* male, as evidenced by his Jedi *Knights*. His Americanness, and its centering of the rugged individual hero, is itself a significant force that conditions his engagement with Buddhism. Buddhism would be but a small part of the American cultural landscape that helped give shape to Lucas' imaginary. Notwithstanding the relevance of Sanskrit and Buddhism, the 1960s and 1970s context, for most people, automatically brings to mind the social unrest of the times. Lucas created his Rebel Alliance at a time when rebellion literally dominated the U.S., and a cultural revolution became a force distinct from the formal Civil Rights Movement led by the Rev. Dr. Martin Luther King, Jr., and the NAACP. Cesar Chavez actively promoted fair labor practices for Mexican-Americans in Central Valley California (Marez 90–94), and the Oakland headquarters of the Black Panther Party (BPP) served as ground zero for a Black Power movement that epitomized socio-political rebellion and a radical cultural shift. Although the revolutionary spirit central to mainstream American identity provides a rhetoric that gave substantial cultural heft to the underdog Rebellion of *Star Wars*, the Black Power iconography of the critical formative period for *Star Wars* was a countercultural revolution in strikingly audiovisual ways.

The public and televised presence of black-leather coats and gloves, dark shades, and large Afros of rifle-toting BPP members, who were quoting Karl Marx and Fanon, exposed the self-fashioned rhetoric of rebellion and *realpolitik* of American exceptionalism to national and international scrutiny during the era of Cold War hysteria. In California, the highly publicized trials of BPP co-founder Huey P. Newton and member Angela Davis are evidenced by iconic photographs showing BPP members and Latino- and Asian-American solidarity with it. In conjunction with the Black Power political movement, the Black Arts Movement (BAM) sought to advance equal rights through cultural nationalism. Inspired by Fanon, BAM undertook a revolutionary arts program whose primary goal was to topple the European/ American/Western cultural hegemony that represented *mental* enslavement. The Afro-centric explosion of artistic expression by authors and other artists, repudiation of "slave names" for West African ones, insistence on self-definition as *Black* instead of *Negro* and *colored*, and rejection of classical Western aesthetics, myths, and canons spread across the country among young, urban blacks. Significantly, BAM was very consciously designed to publicly unfold in the streets and occupy street corners. Indeed, it was a sonic broadcast in the form of *soul* music like James Brown's "Say It Loud—I'm Black and I'm Proud" (1968) and "I'm Superbad (Part 1–3)" (1970). The new *Black* movement, inspired by old cultural forms of West Africa, is described by Robert Farris Thompson as an "aesthetic of the cool" (1966). So potent was this Black Power/Arts movement, Nixon's "law and order" platform and FBI director J. Edgar Hoover's COINTELPRO program quietly (the Cold War stakes were high) collaborated with local law enforcement to specifically target the Black Power leadership and chapters for total eradication.[10]

The late 1960s Black Studies programs that started in California, as a direct result of the Black Power/Arts Movement, help us to better understand and link the African/European cultural contact in the colonial era and the 1960s. Perhaps because the post-colonialism of the 1960s liberated suppressed African culture, new scholarship brought to the attention of U.S. readers revealed a fact still shocking today: West Africa had its own heroic epic performance traditions, as the 1960s and 1970s print versions of these documented.[11] Moreover, works like Lawrence W. Levine's *Black Culture and Black Consciousness* (1977) revealed the then-neglected breadth and depth of cultural continuities from West Africa to the U.S.[12] This research strongly indicated that within the U.S. there was a centuries-long presence of traditional African epic culture dating back to the slave culture *and* mainstream culture of the colonies. This African epic performance heritage includes, scholars indicate: Epic Mali's architectural and textile skills (Thompson, *Flash* 193–223); the soulful rhythms the slaves gave to the spirituals (Roberts 121–166)[13]; the jazzy accents of language and rhythm (Cartwright 37–38)[14] that were the forerunners of blues and rock 'n' roll; and, the confluence of percussive rhythm and verbal felicity that characterizes rap (Rutledge 32–38). The famous ancient Malian epic (Sunjata)[15] would have been suppressed by the surveillance regime of slavery, but the fact that tens of thousands of literate Muslims—among them royal elites like Abdul-Rahman—were enslaved means that "the Sunjata was almost certainly told throughout the American colonies in the early days of the slave trade" (Cartwright 36). Indeed, and despite the basic logic of white-over-black logic of slavery, the two cultures were mutually reinforcing through the close contact between the European/American dominant culture and the ancient, deeply rooted culture the slaves brought with them, including the West/Central African epic performance heritage.

But the significance of the African epic scholarship is not that the mythologized, immaterial reality of Western belief ran counter to the fact that Africa has an ancient epic sublime. Contra dead epic traditions like the Homeric epics or Beowulf, these living epic traditions enabled scholars to understand the complex cultural processes of performed art, and see the *adult* protagonist not only as the Epic Hero but often as a *child* who survives and matures against overwhelming odds that deform him. Far more than the hero-centered, fighting-oriented odyssey of *modern* Western epic ideology, which centers individualism, the West African epic performances also reveal epic traditions to contain: Points of cultural contact and exchange in which good/evil gives way to more complex understanding of power; heroes who, while capable of extraordinary physical battle, become epical because they can negotiate powerful mystical forces; cautionary stories of heroic excess—often with imperialistic and ecological ramifications—associated with the epic hero's god-sized ego; women in critical roles as sorceresses equal to or greater than the protagonists, war-mongerers, and victims of greed whose mistreatment is symbolized by the wasteland motif; and, expert epic storyteller-performers who can adapt the mythical stories to racial morality tales that make real-world postcolonial critique.[16]

In the context of a young nation that prides itself on being exceptional, above the logic of the Old (European) World and the natives' infantile lore, this begs several anthropological questions. What happens when, indeed, an exceptional slave is encountered, male or female? What happens when this exceptional slave is combined with a demographic context in which a local culture is dominated by the sheer mass of the enslaved Africans relative to the people of European descent? How does a culture of exceptionalism complicate or exacerbate this local dynamic while, nevertheless, reinforcing the national logic of exceptionalism? One answer to this last question is through the critical function of the marketplace, a crossroads space signaling the intersection of female and male energies *inside* the epic story and *outside* in the real world of the epic tradition. Citing a famous scene from the *Sunjata* epic,[17] Keith Cartwright points out how Sunjata's mother's and sister's presence in a market allows them to acquire critical information they need to initiate the return of Sunjata from his distant exile: "It is this market scene that probably best points to the function of the epic itself.... The epic reinforces what its audiences share—linguistic, cultural, and historical identity" (35). The market here is not simply a capitalist symbol, but representation of anthropological processes. Under the market exchange lies the more fundamental processes of cultural cohesion and (re)production: The dissemination of information in the story, heard by the audience that identifies with the mythical figures, also connects the audience to other members of the audience and the culture.

Similarly, the Mos Eisley Cantina episode is a culturally complex performance—ranging from R-rated racial undertones to exotic and horrifying visuals set to weird music—whose ability to arrest our infantile selves is proven by its success. The Mos Eisley Cantina is a marketplace crossroads where cultures intersect, information flows, and secret transactions occur. No respectable mother or sister would be caught dead in this place, the logic of the scene implies, but the feminine force of jazz, sinuous and playful, coy and (in this case) corrupt, defines this space. It is the consort to the cantina's male violence, a feminized and erotic instrumental voice giving sultry contour to its interior in ways that continue to reverberate in the franchise and culture. Kenobi's Jedi action and Solo's gun-slinging, representing Eastern and Western heroics, are paralleled and complicated by the cultural range of the jazz. It is pirate-city music, a sci-fi minstrelsy for discerning viewers and listeners; it is the democratic multiracial potency of jazz that revolutionized U.S. and world music cultures; and, it hearkens back to centuries-old Western-African sensibility that resists racial minstrelsy. Figuratively and geographically, Mother Africa is also Eastern vis-à-vis the West. Hence, although Mos Eisley jazz works at the conscious level as a complement to piracy, it carries an aesthetic of the cool—the "broke-legged rhythms" of "American jive-cats and hip-cats" Cartwright finds to be derivative of West African epics (37)—that undertones the minstrelsy.

From this vantage point, the "ubiquitous, cultural common coin" that made blackface minstrelsy the defining conduit for the movement of black cultural expression into mainstream America from the 1840s to 1920s (Lott 4, 6–7), can be more fully understood. Implicated here is *sublime* anxiety/fear/hate, on the one hand, and *sublime* love/desire/admiration, on the other. Blackface minstrelsy is a working-class stand-in for a preceding social drama that implicates elites and working-class people, males as well as females, and blacks as *infants* subject to the *mature* white (male) gaze. The booming market for blackface minstrelsy operated in manifold ways: As real currency, as real theater, as ubiquitous printings of blackface caricature, and as performances undergirded by exceptionalism. But minstrelsy implies another dimension, a fearful recognition and *love* of black excellence—an *epic mimicry*—that had no broad cultural marketplace for expression and emulation.[18] Even if a black American was exceptional, white emulation that recognized and (culturally) marketed her or him was generally not possible in the slavery-based U.S.

But the period from 1920 to 1960, initiated by the retreat of blackface minstrelsy as popular culture during the "vogue" of jazz and blues, as Langston Hughes famously quipped in 1926, began to create space for another *theft* of blackness. As the demeaning minstrel images faded, notably after jazz and blues revolutionized U.S. markets with songs that sold 8,000 "race records" a week for months (Jones 100), theft of blackness evolved from a lucrative 1920s "vogue" to a 1960s, TV-era countercultural coolness. This was the cultural marketplace into which *Star Wars* was born. Indeed, in his influential study, *The Conquest of Cool* (1997), Thomas Frank suggests counterculture was not only defined by conservative political reaction to 1960s excesses, or youths' genuine cultural rebellion against oppressive conformity, but also by a "business history [that] has been largely ignored in accounts of the cultural upheaval of the 1960s" (6–7).

Frank, writing a cultural history of the innovative practices of markets, highlights the role of the immensely dynamic advertising companies. He suggests Madison Avenue advertising firms were not mere "company men," soulless automatons who opposed the counterculture, but were perhaps drivers and co-opters of it. Consequently, he argues, it is virtually impossible to discern "between authentic counterculture and fake," as demonstrated by the "developments in mass culture (particularly the arrival of the Beatles in 1964)." Frank traces countercultural cool to the 1950s and Normal Mailer's "The White Negro" (1957), which called on people to mimic the "Hipster," the antidote to postwar "conformity" (7–8, 12). Although Frank's point of countercultural reference is limited by his non-engagement with serious racial critique—would middle-brow Londoners or the Bohemian Mailer be considered countercultural against the backdrop of the FBI-surveilled Black Power[19] and Arts movement of the 1960s?—he nevertheless articulates the guiding framework for the 1960s/1970s mimicry of racial exceptionalism. If in antebellum America it was blackface minstrelsy and a "Negro vogue" during the New Negro Renaissance (circa 1914 to 1929), then it was the "conquest of coolness"—an *epic mimicry* following the policing of the Black Power/Arts countercultural potency—that characterized the mainstream "love" and "theft" of 1960s and 1970s soul culture.

Madison Avenue could and would not market the Black Panthers,[20] of course, but their black leather and dramatic shootouts with police impacted 1960s America like no ad ever could. Moreover, the Panthers' Oakland, California, headquarters was literally in the county next door (Alameda) to Lucas' home of Modesto (Stanislaus County). Lucas' close proximity would explain both the ambivalence Lott highlighted for white (male) fear of black cultural presence, the nostalgic mode Lucas' Modesto-based *American Graffiti* inaugurated, and, I argue, the epic mimicry creating and linking the Fonz and Han Solo. The nostalgia and epic mimicry are two elements of exceptionalism working together in a manner that enables Lucas to re-envision the American Revolution and project its ragtag colonial rebellion into a futuristic *galaxy far, far away.*

Lucas' conquest of cool and nostalgia can readily be seen by the early 1970s, the height of the BPP, through the continuities between *THX 1138* (1971), *American Graffiti* and the *Happy Days* television series (1974–1984) it inspired, *Star Wars*, and Lucas' *Raiders of the Lost Ark* (1981), first written in 1973 by Lucas as *The Adventures of Indiana Smith* screenplay.[21] Consistent between these productions are worldly older men (leather-clad *solos*) and the All-American naïve hero, or, in Indiana Jones, the combination of both—*Indiana* suggests the heartland, where he holds a professorship, but his World War II-era leather bomber jacket makes him an adventurous, anti–Nazi solo.[22] Lucas' anti-totalitarian futuristic thriller, *THX 1138*, lies outside of this trend, but THX (Robert Duval) is yet another white male rebel who represents what the potential fate of the other characters in a fascist world that is multicultural (blacks *are* disturbingly *present* in this film). *THX 1138* aside, the actors and characters of these nostalgic productions are interchangeable: Luke Skywalker is another take on Richie Cunningham (Ron Howard) of *Happy Days*, just as Han Solo is interchangeable with Arthur "the Fonz" Fonzarelli (Henry Winkler). The coolness of The Fonz/Han Solo no doubt owes its vitality in part to James Dean's signature performance in *Rebel Without a Cause* (1955), and Elvis Presley's own rock 'n' roll cool, but the realism of Dean's and Presley's roles—or Elvis's own debt to black rockers—cannot account for the mythological force associated with the Fonz and Han Solo.

Arthur Fonzarelli, from a mere third-tier character when *Happy Days* started, became the most popular character. Unlike Dean's or Elvis' characters, the Fonz represents a radical break made possible by 1960s Black Power and soul. The fear of a soulful, black-leather wearing, gun-toting, hyper-masculine black man can be neutralized: Not by formal slavery and blackface caricature, but by massive state policing and an epic mimicry that transfers black potency to whites. As in antebellum America, this epic performance occurs in the marketplace of monetary exchange, cultural (re)production, and now ad-men cooptation. Nostalgia is natural and essential to this marketry since exceptionalism itself relies on partial identification with an Ancient Heroic Age that is point of reference and contrast for the greatness of one's own culture. Nostalgically, then, the Fonz has authentic and original *white* soul power—in the 1950s happy days before Black Power. Women swoon, technology obeys his [knuckle] rap (especially the juke box), and wise males back down.

The nostalgia of exceptionalism is also paired with progressivism and futurism, since the assumed greatness of one's culture is measured quantitatively by its length and qualitatively by its achievements. This explains the Fonz/Solo pairing, of nostalgia projected into the future, and how *THX 1138* anticipates *Star Wars*. Nineteen Sixties America would have presented obvious challenges to the purist logic undergirding American exceptionalism, and it shows up in *THX 1138*, whose protagonist confronts a world clearly indicative of Lucas' reaction to Black Power/Arts culture. Marez, attuned to the race- and labor-based logic of the film, describes a critical moment involving "State-controlled housing," imprisonment, black holograms, and homosexual predators. This coincides with an earlier scene, "as a sign of his debasement within a mass society, THX masturbates while watching the hologram of *a naked black woman dancing to the sound of drums*" (95; italics mine). As Marez points out that the film implies "the State uses illusory racial representations to control the white hero in ways that alienate him from himself and from 'real' human relationships, defined as heterosexual relations with his white wife" (95).

This hyper-sexual primitivism is consistent with a white-male perception of the dramatically changed cultural milieu of central California and the nation. Thus, *THX 1138*, in an important way, inaugurates Lucas' nostalgia for both films, as he said by way of comparing it to *American Graffiti*, rely on "'an old hokey American point of view'" which, he "'discovered to be true,'" indicates that a spirit of determination leads to success (Marez 94). *THX 1138* is nostalgic and future-oriented, and provides a marker for measuring how Lucas evolves his aesthetic. Real phobic black people are present in *THX 1138* while they are absent in *Star Wars*, except abstractly as cool counterculture and as a disembodied voice used for the total projection of evil into a black form—Darth Vader—cinema had never seen *and* heard before. "Vader's utter blackness performs his evil," as Howe argues, and "it also reveals his potency and dominion over a galaxy that is largely white" (16), but Black Power culture is an audiophonic presence. James Earl Jones' deep baritone vocalizes black (male) power, and its use a complex and contradictory performance of stock symbolism (black-is-evil), absence of black actors, and presence of black culture as a form of epic mimicry.[23] Though Vader's mask was inspired by Japanese *kabuto* helmets and *mempo* faceplates (Fielding 31; Wetmore 118–119), the Black Power culture's shades (sunglasses), black leather, and black skins, combined with the potency of Jones' voice, situate Darth Vader as a 1960s cultural product resonating deeply within the American psyche.

Just as Vader represents black (power) phobia, Solo is a countercultural, intergalactic Fonz by virtue of his black-clad coolness. Solo's coolness symbolically distinguishes him from the All-American/Jedi goodness of Luke—akin to the Fonz's relationship with Richie Cunningham, the protagonist of *Happy Days*—and aligns him with the too-suave, too-charming, slick-haired, and *cool* Lando Calrissian. If one is inclined to object on the grounds that the Fonz has magical, epical mojo whereas Solo does not, or one is at least interested in how this critical difference can be reconciled, one must keep in mind the associational logic of the sidekick of 1970s America. Notwithstanding the Fonz's cool abilities, an imperial Anglo-Roman-American coolness because Arthur Fonzarelli is a 1960s immaculate conception of pure and potent Arthurian-Italian stock, he is not and can never be the protagonist-proper of 1950s *Happy Days*. Solo, a swashbuckling gambler without a cause, eventually becomes closely associated with, and a *believer* in, the Force. Both the Fonz and Solo are sidekicks to the protagonist-heroes, and Lando Calrissian, the friend of Solo, is the sidekick of the sidekick.

But the most important consideration here is how the obvious cool/blackness of Solo vanishes when scholars focus on Lucas' *choice*—using East Asian names, places, and philosophies—at the expense of the *presence* and *influence* of culture. In this regard, Julien Fielding's discussion of the East Asian etymological roots of Han Solo, Lucas' "anti-hero gunslinger," is illustrative. Fielding's detailed suggestion for the Han forename—*Han* perhaps, he argues, references China's Han Dynasty (206 BCE to 220 CE), or Japan's "Zen monasteries" (30)—is perfectly sensible, but Han Solo commands a non-Eastern, black-clad rebellious flair who mimics Black Power cool. Like the Fonz, Solo is the mainstream 1970s counterculture sci-fi rebel that makes the *look* of Luke Skywalker's rebel ways passé even by 1960s standards, although it is 1950s racial nostalgia that actuates Lucas' lens. This quasi-Frank, quasi-Wetmore perspective on Solo must be taken yet further because the intersection of counterculture, marketing, and race is given specific shape by the Fanon-influenced Black Power/Arts cultural dynamism of the 1960s/1970s. If, to use Fanon's diagnosis of colonialism, the native rebellion must overcome the *black skin, white mask* of internalized inferiority, within the sphere of Lucas' Rebellion Solo's *white skin, Eastern forename*, and *black power cool* is another form of colonialism. The significant presence of Afro-Asianness in Solo and *Star Wars* and the erasure of the African/American cultural influence reinforce the colonial construct where a white (civilized) core draws unto itself the most valuable resources of the colonized. Critics have enabled this by ignoring cultural processes, ignoring the Afro-Asian presence, and, by ignoring the significant African/American cultural presence while highlighting Eastern influence, have reinforced global strategies of divide and conquer.

The ultimate Black Power icon also vanishes as a potential cultural influence on *Star Wars* and, specifically, on Luke Skywalker. No figure during the 1950s to 1970s activism epitomized the threat of Black Power more than Malcolm X. Although never a member of the BPP, his role as the brilliantly analytical and articulate spokesman for the Nation of Islam threatened 1950s white security like no one else. This gifted student and son of a minister who was lynched by the Ku Klux Klan went astray—in a dysfunctional environment created by his father's murder and mother's growing insanity—and also, symbolically, suffered a lynching death himself. Malcolm Little progressed from juvenile delinquent to hustler, thief, and eventual felon, only to be resurrected from prison as an Islam-enlightened spokesman who "X"-ed out his *Little* American-slave identity and effectively debated intellectuals on race and U.S. politics, capitalism, Christianity, and culture. Thanks to him, the X arguably became the most recognizable icon of revolution and counterculture.

This Black Power X is directly associated with *Star Wars*. Lucas' protagonist, Skywalker, pilots an X-wing starfighter, the signature craft of the Rebellion. This coincidence alone is not significant, but in the Star Wars Extended Universe, Skywalker's X-wing is officially a T-65 model. For the children and adults who are fans, audiences, and product-consumers world-round this means nothing, but T-65 is, in fact, a highly suggestive alphanumeric designation. Malcolm X, the most dynamic and controversial black rebel of 1960s America (and perhaps the world), was assassinated in T-65: that is, Time 1965, specifically on February 21, 1965. In other words, *Luke* the fair-haired, fair-eyed farm boy from Tatooine with a Bible-Belt name may seem to have none of Solo's older-man, gun-slinger coolness, but his *ride*—the T-65 X-wing starfighter—seemingly references the most iconic rebel of the era and, quite likely, the twentieth-century. Solo is the emblem for Black Power *culture*, but the X-wing associates Luke with *the* Malcolm X, the most potent and iconic of all the Black Power figures. Literally, in Luke's case, there is far more to him than meets the eye, since this X marks him as "the one." In the logic of epic mimicry, Luke is not just any typical rebel, but a culturally black rebel whose *white* epic potency can include this 1960s X-blackness while remaining nostalgically and progressively white.[24] Like Han Solo, the characterization and presentation of Luke Skywalker shows Lucas engaged in the epic performance of race, culture, and marketry that dates back at least to its first popular expression in 1830s blackface: in other words, a countercultural white guy who conquers (the black) *cool* sells big in U.S. popular culture imagination and markets.

As this discussion suggests, *Star Wars* is the premier form of marketry in U.S. entertainment because it sits in the center of American mainstream culture and counterculture, both the recognized and, importantly, racially disavowed. Its internationalism is matched by its temporal scale from heroic past *a long time ago* to futuristic *galaxy*. The postcolonial frame makes sense, not through Fanon or subsequent postcolonial theorists concerned with the Developing World, but that of the mainstream American Revolution narrative. They were colonies which eventually fought against the overwhelming might of the British Empire. The Britishness of Lucas' Empire, its officers' quaint accent and the stormtrooper uniformity both nostalgic (Red Coat uniforms) and futuristic, makes plenty of sense. Though premature since *The Force Awakens* has yet to be released, a black stormtrooper is just as much out of place as, nostalgically, blacks and Native Americans are to the American Revolution cultural logic. Crispus Attucks, the Afro-Indian and the first person killed in the Boston Massacre in 1770, died for a revolution in the process of inaugurating an empire of white supremacy and slavery. Through the official Founding narrative of the American Revolution, which combines epic, exceptionalism, rebellion, liberty, and individualism, but not race and cultural imperialism, it is right to read Darth Vader—as Joseph Campbell did—as someone who "has not developed his own humanity. He's a robot. He's a bureaucrat, living not in terms of himself but in terms of an imposed system. This is the threat to our lives that we all face today" (178).

However much Campbell can be forgiven for not really reading or understanding the movie and offering this "reductive reading" (Lawrence 26), both he and Lucas (and Bill Moyers) demonstrate the white (male) privilege of reading the world outside the real, tangible cultural processes and brutal histories associated with the heroic myth. The danger of a monomyth or archetypal approach is that it centers the ideology of the exceptional mind or creator who can command a world of mythology and distill the essence. However, the cultural processes are complex for any given culture, and the epic performances are often large-scale cultural encyclopedias. Monomythic or archetypal theory reduces and flattens the artistry of the performance and the lessons of the myth. When Campbell speaks of "the dark side" as the important principle that "evil power is not identified with any specific nation on this earth means you've got an abstract power, ... not a specific historical situation" (177), it reinforces the global violence of the last several centuries. A generic "evil" allows the specifics of oppression to be overlooked. Much of the myth and lore were specifically learned by European colonial administrators for the purpose of disruption and conquest. Hence, François-Victor Equilbecq, a French colonial administrator in West Africa (1902–1932) and publisher of a three-volume set of West African folk tales, said: "it is necessary to know those whom one wishes to dominate." Moreover, the absence of awareness of cultural violence blinds one to the operation of certain insidious archetypal myths within oneself. In this sense, Campbell's and Lucas' interests in heroic myth are deeply imbedded in their perceptions of what is right in the world. Campbell and Lucas are *not* outside of myth at a safe, objective distance, but are part of a myth-driven, West-dominated modern world where, in fact, some native epic storytellers strike back against Western mythical hegemony.

Thus, the great danger is that his monomyth theory is itself an abstraction, one that runs counter to living epic hero traditions attuned to an epical force and that flattens the complex workings of mythological performance. Even if the "world navel," Buddhism, or Sanskrit were selected by Lucas, and Japanese director Akira Kurosawa's *jidai-geki* samurai films gave him his Jedi Knight name and tradition (Fielding 28; Wetmore 102–111), one could and should turn to West African epic continuities as African-*American* culture. Living epic performance traditions vivify the monomyth, providing a critical lens for evaluating the Force, and reveal an American cultural process of epic mimicry. Because epic potency implicates fear and envy by its very nature—whether a member of your tribe or your enemy's, the epic hero's ability and willingness to do anything creates ambivalence—a contest-copycat reflex principle is involved. Even when Achilles had slain Hector and dragged his body in the dust around Troy, for example, the Greek soldiers were amazed at Hector, *first*, and *then* stabbed the body with their spears; likewise, in the *Ozidi Saga*, a heroic epic hailing from present-day Nigeria, Ozidi's epic bravado engenders copycats who come forth to (con)test the young epic hero's mettle. The danger Ozidi reveals that Homer's adult-already epic heroes cannot is the "epic trickster": The child protagonist who is in the weakened, deformed position of the trickster at the beginning of the story, and who survives through trickster-wit and epic potency, becomes not just an Epic Hero proper, but an *epic trickster* who combines the remarkable range of both (Rutledge 18–20).

Hence the African ambivalence toward the epic protagonist (envy and fear), for the mystical powers associated with him are forces of creation and destruction. The Pandora's Box cautionary principle common to epic warrior traditions from ancient Africa to ancient Greece to the ancient First Nations of the Americas is, anthropologically speaking, quite sound. The critical point is that epic-scale destruction is not necessarily bombastic, spectacular, and thus readily avoidable or surgically removable. "Epic agony" can be a self-inflicted socio-cultural wound that can become, if not ritually purged, a cancer that copycats itself within the cultural code of the entire body-politic (Rutledge 51–59).

The *djeli* (*jeli*) epic bards who retell and perform the epic of Sunjata, the West/Central African epic hero, are part of a living tradition of force-wielding, robe-wearing warriors—*Jeli* Knights?—akin to the Jedi Knights. This tradition is already part of American history and culture, and thus parent to Lucas' imagining. The 1960s decolonization of Africa and the Black Power/Arts made it more prevalent by highlighting African lore: The cultural context for Ursula K. LeGuin's *A Wizard of Earthsea* (1968), which shows the influence of living epic traditions (Sunjata included), the *dominance* of the cautionary principle associated with epic, not just its presence, and a brown-skinned epic protagonist (Rutledge 209). LeGuin's epic sense and sensibility demonstrates that these "child" cultures, knowing the dark side of epic-oriented individuality because of colonialism and white supremacy, would force us to query Campbell's myth-inspired urge "To pursue your bliss." Just as the *nyama* soul-force of the Sunjata epic is complex and infinitely full of pitfalls, LeGuin's Sparrowhawk—one of the names associated with Sunjata—has to learn this painful lesson, too. Wanting too much power, or using a small power too long, tapping the wrong power, and not knowing well enough that power, can all separately or collectively lead to absolute ruin. So with this and the stereotypes against colored-people time in mind, I wrote:

> If, then, to Obi Wan Kenobi's spiritual injunction that he "use the force," Luke Skywalker had rightfully asked, "But which one? And how much," *Star Wars IV: A New Hope* would have had to be re-subtitled "A Really, Really, Really Thoughtful—and On-Time—Response, We Hope …" And if the Jedi—*jeli*?—master had said, simply, "you follow your bliss" …, as Joseph Campbell enjoined US in *The Power of Myth* (1988), would not this counsel, in the logic of *nyama*-excess and the movie, create a Dark Knight-Jedi, a second, sorcererous Darth Vader? [Rutledge 34].

The answer to my own question is as clear as the Western European and U.S. past/present: The blissful pursuit of the power of myth, in the U.S. and globally, has given us a galaxy of (epic) heroes, and brutal slavery, colonialism, and massive cultural indoctrination.

And yet in spite of all of this I am, still, a *Star Wars* fan, a child subject to its magical Western influence. So is my nine-year-old son, who will be—with the circle now nearly complete—about the same age I was in 1978 when we see *The Force Awakens*. Unlike me at his age, and yet because I think of me at that age, he knows of and has read some African epics, knows of Achilles and Odysseus, Sunjata and Ozidi, and culture. Knows Helen's fair exceptionalism. Listens to, likes, and *digs* jazz, and a host of world music, not in opposition to "classical" music—he enjoys playing the piano—but as a complement. Already, his young mind reaches out with the force of cultural critique. Thus, when I explained to him that *Gone with the Wind*, a musical, was showing in South Korea beginning in February 2015, he said, "Why would they show that in Korea? It's like tricking Koreans." Or, when we see the occasional Hollywood or Hallyu blockbuster, "Nothing but blue eyes…" and "All that whiteness…" Even as he enjoys a lightsaber fight, *l'enfant terrible* who beats down his Darth Vader dad, his African Americanness, his Korean-Americanness, his Humanity, won't be flattened by exceptionalism, be it white, black, yellow, red, or any place on the rainbow of sexuality and gender. Or his own. He will never play Cowboys 'n' Injuns as I naively did, or celebrate Gen. George Armstrong Custer's imperial bravado and (Disney's) *Davy Crockett*, "King of the Wild Frontier." We've read Twain's *Huckleberry Finn* together and laughed heartily at Huck's adventures: "Jim said bees wouldn't sting idiots; but I don't believe that because I've tried them lots of times myself, and they wouldn't sting me."

Is it enough? Is it too much? Will he have, compared to me and his peers of the same age, a better answer to the question, "What to the child is *Star Wars*, an epical space Western?" Perhaps, perhaps not. I can only try, and try my best. And hope. But I know that it is far more than what the vast majority of the other 99.9 percent of boys and girls—no matter the hue or nation or socio-economic status of each one—will get around the world. They will instead get: Movie trailers and then screenings, a galaxy of commercials, lightsabers, video games, Halloween costumes, greeting cards and birthday party invitations, blasters, wallpapered rooms and computer screens, action figures, DVDs, Blu-ray discs. This cool marketry makes the very epical *Star Wars* franchise also a tragedy, we adults a Farce, and the following exhortation a real old school but epical lesson for those tens of millions of children audience-consumers: "May the Force be with you."

Dedicated to my father-in-law, Boum-Woon Lee,
born 26 August 1927 (lunar calendar), died 28 June 2015,
a Korean gentleman, and to Markus … my new hope.

Notes

1. His surname is also spelled "de Soto." He is not credited with founding Florida (Ponce de Leon has that distinction), but is one of the conquistadors who helped defeat the Incan Empire in Peru.

2. Wetmore thinks *Star Wars*' influence is even greater. See Wetmore 21–22.

3. Wetmore observes that whether "Lucas is racist" intentionally is not relevant because the role of racial ideology in culture is critical (9). His first chapter details the long history of racial ideology in science fiction, and its rise from colonialism. See Wetmore 19–36.

4. Wetmore cites Homi Bhabha's perspective on Fanon here.

5. See also Paul Charbel's essay in this volume.

6. Donald Pease broadens exceptionalism, relying on Freudian notions of "fantasy," and applies it to American Studies and the governing U.S. national fantasy. See Pease 1–17.

7. For example, that ninety percent of all Washington surnames belong to African American surnames (Washington) reveals the depth of the post-slavery self-identification either with George Washington or Booker T. Washington, the famed—and controversially conservative—black leader from 1895 to 1915.

8. Lott acknowledges that his view of the origins of blackface minstrelsy as distinct from "an age-old racism" and "racial aversion" is in the minority view among experts of blackface (6).

9. Lott quotes from Victor Turner's *The Anthropology of Performance* (New York: PAJ Publications, 1986), and Susan Willis, "I Shop Therefore I Am: Is There a Place for Afro-American Culture in Commodity Culture?" in *Changing Our Own Words: Essays on Criticism, Theory, and Writing by Black Women*, ed. Cheryl Wall (New Brunswick: Rutgers University Press, 1989), 173–95, at 189.

10. These both worked together with the nascent drug war and sudden outsourcing of blue-collar jobs to fashion the prison-industrial complex that was specifically designed to criminalize black—especially male—potency. There are many excellent studies of the BPP and local and federal efforts to simultaneously discredit them as "radicals" and "militants" in the popular media and eradicate them through use of the justice system (to litigate the BPP out of existence). The authorities even targeted members like Fred Hampton, the charismatic social justice activist who, as the 21-year-old head of the Chicago BPP, was shot to death in his bed by local police.

11. Most famously, D.T. Niane's *Sundiata: An Epic of Old Mali* (1965), a novelized version of the famous, centuries old Malian epic. G.D. Pickett translated it into English in 1977.

12. The seminal text for this is Lorenzo Dow Turner's *Africanisms in the Gullah Dialect* (1949), a study of Gullah communities in Florida and Georgia.

13. The appeal of the Old Testament epics to the enslaved African Americans because they paralleled West/Central African traditions, as noted by Roberts, coincides with the understanding that Christianity appealed to the enslaved for similar reasons. Black Christianity is a syncretic form between West African and Western Christianity.

14. Cartwright traces epic culture from Mali to Alex Haley's *Roots: The Saga of an American Family* (1976) to Toni Morrison's fiction. Cf. Wetmore's reference to Haley's *Roots*.

15. *Sunjata* is spelled in various ways that reflect its oral heritage, e.g., Son-Jara, Sundiata, Soundiata.

16. For detailed discussion of this, see Rutledge 16–66.

17. Cartwright actually relies on John William Johnson's *The Epic of Son-Jara: A West African Tradition* (Bloomington: Indiana University Press, 1986), a translation of Fa-Digi Sisòkò's storytelling performance. Since Son-Jara and Sunjata are two spellings for the same figure, I use Sunjata to avoid confusion.

18. Exceptional slaves like Frederick Douglass could and did author slave narratives—e.g., his *Narrative of the Life of Frederick Douglass* (1845)—that were best-selling adventure stories. Douglass was regarded as lion-like by Wendell Phillips, Esq. (10), the

famous abolitionist, and *Narrative* was compared with the scale of Homer's *Iliad* and *Odyssey* by the Rev. Ephraim Peabody (62), another abolitionist, but there was no cultural marketplace that generated and supported white desire to be Douglass.

19. Except for a brief reference to the Black Panthers in association with *Forrest Gump* (1994) as an example of 1960s excess, Frank does not weigh in on how advertising-driven or Beatles counterculture compares with the Black Panthers. See Frank at 4.

20. FBI Director J. Edgar Hoover called the BPP "the greatest threat to the internal security of the country," and sought to destroy it and its enablers. For example, government records reveal that actress Jean Seberg, a BPP sympathizer who provided monetary support, was specifically and viciously targeted—and probably blacklisted—by the FBI, which used many of the same COINTELPRO techniques against her that it did against BPP members and other prominent black equal rights activists.

21. It can also be seen in the controversial figure Jar Jar Binks, a digitally created character Lucas successfully targeted towards his massive audience of children. The immense racial backlash against Binks conforms, Pete Lee notes, to my analysis of minstrelsy. Indeed, although I chose to focus on the cultural climate for the 1977 film, the West-Indianness of Binks conveys a reggae-minstrelsy both by speech and flappy ears that recall Jamaican dreadlocks. Reggae, like jazz, also represents Afro-hybridity in the West(ern). But whereas jazz often connotes violence in the mainstream imaginary, reggae in the same often connotes lackadaisical style and irresponsible self-parody—a commodification of original West African cultures, brutally transformed by slavery and now sanitized by Western entertainment culture. Binks is *cool* reggae marketry in this regard, a nostalgically innocent and child-friendly caricature that is futuristic, racially/ethnically marked, and, by virtue of the limits of the digital animation Lucas deployed, *broke-legged*.

22. The World War II backdrop also, of course, invokes nostalgia that also fits 1970s cultural experience: Indiana Jones' 1930s leather jacket let Lucas remove the cool of 1960s black potency back to the days of white American male heroism.

23. An audiophonic mechanical device, it turns out, Jones' Darth Vader voiceover is not Anakin's organic voice, as Pete Lee astutely observed. It is constructed by and emanates from a black suit that channels black power in deeply resonant ways—visually, vocally, electronically, morally, futuristically, racially—*not* indexed to the anti-racism political and cultural objectives of the Black Power movement.

24. Consider also, in this regard, the singularly important role played by Luke's friend, Wedge. As Pete Lee commented, "Wedge's X-wing (with ample screen time for a minor character) destroyed the second Death Star."

Works Cited

Atkins, E. Taylor. "The War on Jazz, or Jazz Goes to War: Toward a New Cultural Order in Wartime Japan," *Positions* 6.2 (1998): 345–392. Print.

Bourdaghs, Michael K. "Japan's Orient in Song and Dance." In *Sino-Japanese Transculturation: Late Nineteenth Century to the End of the Pacific War*. Eds. Richard King, Cody Poulton, and Katsuhiko Endo. Plymouth, UK: Lexington Books, 2012. 167–188. Print.

Brode, Douglas, and Leah Deyneka, eds. *Myth, Media, and Culture in* Star Wars: *An Anthology*. Lanham, MD: Scarecrow Press, 2012. Print.

Campbell, Joseph, and Bill Moyers. *The Power of Myth*. Ed. Betty Sue Flowers. New York: Anchor-Random House, 1991. Print.

Cartwright, Keith. "Reading Roots—From Sunjata to Kunta Kinte to Milkman Dead." *Yearbook of Comparative and General Literature* 43 (1995): 31–51. Print.

Deis, Christopher. "May the Force (Not) Be with You: 'Race Critical' Readings and the *Star Wars* Universe." In *Culture, Identities and Technology in the* Star Wars *Films:*

Essays on the Two Trilogies. Eds. Carl Silvio and Tony M. Vinci. Jefferson, NC: McFarland, 2007. 77–108. Print.

Du Bois, W.E.B. *The Souls of Black Folk.* 1903. Eds. Henry Louis Gates, Jr., and Terri Hume Oliver. Norton Critical Edition. New York: Norton, 1999. Print.

Fielding, Julien. "Beyond Judeo Christianity: Star Wars and the Great Eastern Religions." In *Sex, Politics, and Religion in* Star Wars: *An Anthology.* Eds. Douglas Brode and Leah Deyneka. Lanham, MD: Scarecrow Press–Rowman & Littlefield, 2012. 25–46. Print.

Frank, Thomas. *The Conquest of Cool: Business Culture, Counterculture, and the Rise of Hip Consumerism.* Chicago: University of Chicago Press, 1998. Print.

Hegel, G.W.F. *Aesthetiks: Lectures on Fine Art.* Trans. T. M. Knox. Oxford: Clarendon Press, 1975. Trans. of *Vorlesungen über die Aesthetik.* Ed. Heinrich Gustav Hotho. 3 vols. 1835–38. Print.

Howe, Andrew. "*Star Wars* in Black and White: Race and Racism in a Galaxy Not So Far Away." In *Sex, Politics, and Religion in* Star Wars: *An Anthology.* Eds. Douglas Brode and Leah Deyneka. Lanham, MD: Scarecrow Press–Rowman & Littlefield, 2012. 11–24. Print.

Hughes, Langston. "The Negro Artist and the Racial Mountain." *The Nation* 122 (23 June 1926): 692–94. http://www.thenation.com/article/negro-artist-and-racial-mountain.

Jones, LeRoi. *Blues People: Negro Music in White America.* 1963. New York: Harper-Perennial, 2002. Print.

Kitayama, Shinobu. "Cultural Psychology of the Self: A Renewed Look at Independence and Interdependence." In *Psychology at the Turn of the Millennium, Vol. 2: Social, Developmental and Clinical Perspectives.* Eds. Claes von Hofsten and Lars Backman. East Sussex: Psychology Press, 2002. 305–322. Print.

Lawrence, John Shelton. "Joseph Campbell, George Lucas, and the Monomyth." In *Finding the Force of the* Star Wars *Franchise: Fans, Merchandise, and Critics.* Eds. Matthew Wilhelm Kapell and John Shelton Lawrence. New York: Peter Lang, 2006: 21–33. Print.

Levine, Lawrence W. *Black Culture and Black Consciousness: Afro-American Folk Thought from Slavery to Freedom.* New York: Oxford University Press, 1977. Print.

Loewen, James. *Lies My Teacher Told Me: Everything Your American History Textbook Got Wrong.* New York: Simon & Schuster, 1996. Print.

Lott, Eric. *Love and Theft: Blackface Minstrelsy and the American Working Class.* New York: Oxford University Press, 1995. Print.

Marez, Curtis. "Cesar Chavez, the United Farm Workers, and the History of Star Wars." In *Race After the Internet.* Eds. Lisa Nakamura and Peter Chow-White. New York: Routledge, 2012. 85–108. Print.

Peabody, Ephraim. "Narratives of Fugitive Slaves." *The Christian Examiner* 4th ser. 12.1 (1849): 61–93. Print.

Pease, Donald. *The New American Exceptionalism.* Minneapolis: University of Minnesota Press, 2009.

Phillips, Wendell. "Letter from Wendell Phillips, Esq." 1845. In *Narrative of the Life of Frederick Douglass, an American Slave, Written by Himself.* By Frederick Douglass. Eds. William L. Andrews and William S. McFeely. Norton Critical Edition. New York: Norton, 1997. 10–12. Print.

Roberts, John W. *From Trickster to Badman: The Black Folk Hero in Slavery and Freedom.* Philadelphia: University of Pennsylvania Press, 1989.

Rosen, Steven J. "Yoda and Yoga." *Beliefnet* 2005. Web. 25 July 2015.

Rutledge, Gregory E. *The Epic Trickster in American Literature: From Sunjata to So(u)l.* New York: Routledge, 2013. Print.

Scanlon, Paul. "George Lucas: The Wizard of Star Wars." *Rolling Stone* 25 Aug. 1977: 40–48, 50–51. Print.

Takaki, Ronald. *A Different Mirror: A History of Multicultural America*. New York: Back Bay–Little, Brown, 2008. Print.

Thompson, Robert Farris. "An Aesthetic of the Cool: West African Dance." *African Forum* 2.2 (Fall 1966): 85–102. Print.

_____. *Flash of the Spirit: African & Afro-American Art & Philosophy*. New York: Vintage–Random House, 1984. Print.

Washington, Jesse. "Washington: The 'Blackest Names' in America." *The Huffington Post* 21 Feb. 2011. Web. 25 July 2015.

Wetmore, Kevin J., Jr. *Empire Triumphant: Race, Religion and Rebellion in the Star Wars Films*. Jefferson, NC: McFarland, 2005. Print.

Williams, John. Liner notes. *Star Wars: Original Soundtrack*. 20th Century Records, LP, 1977.

Deconstructing the Desert

The Bedouin Ideal and
the True Children of Tatooine

PAUL CHARBEL

After escaping certain destruction from the Empire, two intrepid droids crash land on the nearby planet. One on a mission to find a new hope for a princess, the other anticipating a doomed future, they observe their new environment. A crane shot descends on the droids, highlighting their isolation in the sand dunes of Tunisia. As Threepio, the humanoid-robot liaison, actor Anthony Daniels sweated in his fiberglass costume in 132-degree heat as he comments on the desolate surroundings. The camera captures his perspectives and the audience agrees.

To say that desert life is harsh would be an understatement and one that hardly encapsulates its characteristics. But when was the last time we really thought about how life must necessarily be if we chose to live in the desert? There are numerous ways to die in a desert, so the choices one must make to eke out an existence in such a place are difficult. Comfort or survival? The individual or the community? These are crucial questions that define desert life. The scarcity of drinking water, the sweltering days, and the frigid nights all make for a life few would actively choose. The person who not only lives this life but thrives in it possesses qualities which we, as members of a relatively comfortable society, find admirable if not downright amazing. The person produced from this lifestyle is necessarily hard-edged and severe, but that does not make them culturally or socially devoid. In fact, desert societies are widely known for their lively culture as well as unrivaled hospitality to guests, even strangers. We need not delve too far into world history to discover the richness of desert societies—most notably, the Bedouin tribes across the Middle East.

The image of a strong, stoic figure surviving this lifestyle has much cultural capital. Classic Bedouin figures, as alien as they may initially appear in contemporary Western culture, have analogues in archetypal American heroes. Sandra Mackey, using the Saudi citizenry as an example, lays out a distinct comparison of the Bedouin hero to someone far more familiar in Western eyes. She writes:

> Psychologically, the Bedouin represents to the present-day Saudi what the Western cowboy folk hero represents to an American. And like Americans, the Saudis have created from the Bedouin, idealized as a desert warrior, a powerful prototype that influences their value system and their patterns of behavior. No matter how much the various geographic regions of Saudi Arabia may differ or how far a Saudi is removed from the desert, the Bedouin ethos is the bedrock of the culture [105].

This idealization of the Bedouin lifestyle is vital to understanding what is happening in the *Star Wars* universe as portrayed in the films and other media. This connection is worthy of exploration as we shall see the similarities in Tatooine's natives with how these "cultural ideals of proper behavior ... are judged against the Bedouin hero" (Maisel and Shoup xxv). The desert planet Tatooine has the appearance and cultural capital to represent many of the themes we associate with cowboys or desert heroes, and this is what creator George Lucas seemingly wishes to portray. It is a desert world which elicits ideas of strength and fortitude in the face of a harsh and inhospitable environment. The people who inhabit this world are necessarily tough, and the heroes and villains of Tatooine, who have gone on to shape the galaxy at large, are the stuff of legends. Lucas' portrayal of these characteristics, however, is only superficially accurate. In fact, as we analyze the relationships between his story's main protagonists and the archetypes they represent, we will find the films appropriate the values of rich and complex cultures but present us instead with an elaborate facsimile.

Let us look to those protagonists, Anakin and Luke Skywalker, and their connection to Tatooine. These figures, which the greater mythology revolves around, are both raised on this planet. Both have been a part of significant events with personal and galaxy-wide ramifications. In multiple ways, they represent the Bedouin ideal in their heroism. Who, then, are the real natives of Tatooine? Anakin's and Luke's experiences illustrate the planet's two dominant lifestyles. On one hand, Anakin represents the more urban centers of Tatooine; not only is he a slave, but his youth is characterized by interactions with a wide variety of people/alien races via the spaceport of Mos Espa. This spaceport, like any trading hub, exposed Anakin to the comings and goings of a small but busy economic waypoint. On the other hand, Luke, being raised by Owen and Beru Lars, was a moisture farmer that grew up much further away from the urban centers of Tatooine. Both protagonists represent two distinct heroic motifs: the street-smart child and the restless teenage youth. These are unique tropes which we understand to have easily relatable characteristics, but they both belie a deeper understanding of what is happening on Tatooine. From Anakin's perspective, audiences are made privy to the trade and commercial centers of cities, and from Luke we become aware of the simple day-to-day life of farming, but although their livelihoods differ, they both represent a settler or colonist population on Tatooine.

While we may normally consider the two vastly different lifestyles Anakin and Luke occupy to be the main fixtures of this planet, in truth, they are both foreign constructs and encroach upon a land that is not their own. Regardless of the films' plots centering on them, this fact remains: humans are not natives to this planet. Truthfully, the vast majority of alien races we encounter on Tatooine are not native to it. The true natives of Tatooine are the Jawas and the Tusken Raiders, and their civilizations most accurately embody the Tatooine landscape and what we associate with desert cultures. In fact, the dreaded and feared Tusken Raiders, or "Sand People," might have much more in common with the Bedouin ideal than either Skywalker protagonist, which runs counter to the symbolism Lucas attempts to evoke by using Tatooine as the story's staging ground.

While we can understand the diverse range of inhabitants in places like Mos Espa or Mos Eisley are the result of trade and the transportation of goods across the galaxy, Anakin's step-siblings and Luke's guardians, the Lars family, represent a pioneer population trying to homestead in a foreign and inhospitable land. They clearly are not natives, and their vitriol for the Tusken Raiders suggests a long history of violence and struggle. Both names for this species can be viewed as pejorative in that they imply either outright banditry or a simple racial epitaph. The use of the term "Sand People" is a dangerously familiar stereotype associated with peoples of Arab or Middle Eastern heritage. Not coincidentally, this moniker has been continuously applied for decades with seemingly little attention paid to it. From this context, the crux of my argument emerges: George Lucas feeds the audience these stories of heroes with arduous backgrounds who come from a harsh environment imbued with a cultural cache represented by the desert world of Tatooine. But it is a false association as the idealized image of a Bedouin hero is best personified by the Tuskens—not Anakin or Luke. I ask us to consider with all sincerity: what is the Lars family doing on Tatooine? They are colonists, carving out an existence in a frontier-like territory while coming into direct and violent conflict with its native population. For the most part, the non-native inhabitants of Tatooine are colonists, criminals, or both. The film avoids a larger reality between the Lars family and other off-world settlers and their encroachment on someone else's land: that of the indigenous Jawas and the Tuskens.

The first question we need to address is why would George Lucas choose a desert world as his ultimate framing device? The motif of the desert hero is one Lucas appears to be well aware of, and it stands to reason that his intention was to capitalize upon this cultural imagery. For Americans, the desert has cultural associations as a gritty Western-style motif or perhaps the sweeping, foreign epic as portrayed in films like *Lawrence of Arabia* (1962). But scholars seem to have missed this reference, or at least self-reflection, that illustrates just how important this motif is to the *Star Wars* ethos. Much has been written about Lucas's use of Joseph Campbell's heroic cycle with its clear delineation of a hero's journey from beginning to end. But I suggest Lucas has additionally poached the motif of the desert hero inherent in many Middle Eastern cultures, as manifested by the reverence for the classic Bedouin or desert warrior/hero in series such as Frank Herbert's *Dune*, Hergé's *Tintin*, or even the real life rescue of Antoine de Saint-Exupery by a Bedouin caravan after crash landing in the Sahara in 1935. Lucas readily cites and lauds Campbell's work for his influence on his filmic mythology, but there is a noticeable lack of credit given to the desert setting Lucas uses as a framing device. Campbell's heroic cycle is abstract enough to allow writers and filmmakers the breathing room to play with the form. Although Lucas does credit *Lawrence of Arabia* as a source of inspiration, very literal and very overt uses of Middle Eastern culture appear in these films with little to no reference of them (Taylor 111).

Lucas tends to paint his characters in broad strokes, and the connection between the complexities of the Bedouin ideal and his characters from Tatooine may initially seem like a stretch. But classically, the Bedouin character is comparable not only to the American cowboy, but many other character tropes. In fact, the Bedouin "is not revealed as an individual composed of various human traits, but rather as an emblematic figure painted in the hard monochromes of abstract Bedouin virtue" (Kurpershoek 25). This monochromatic nature is what defines much of Lucas's work, and we can explore plenty of analyses in this vein. What is worse is it appears Lucas is also perpetuating common stereotypes of Arab culture. This problem is twofold: first, the appropriation without credit given, and, second, the perpetuation of cultural stereotypes from the very source being appropriated. In many ways, this appropriation and simultaneous mocking has parallels beyond the Arab world such as the white co-opting of African American musical styles performed in minstrel shows.[1] That Tatooine is the focal point for many of the crucial events throughout the *Star Wars* universe is enough to clue the average observer in to the importance of desert cultures and themes. To help illustrate just how these themes pervade the mythology as well as how they have been improved upon by other contributors, we shall explore the significance of the true natives of Tatooine and which *Star Wars* character most accurately embodies the desert hero possessed of the Bedouin ideal.

JawaScript Not Supported

The junk dealers of Tatooine, the Jawas, are given little attention in the film universe. They are diminutive in nature, robed, hooded, and hide their facial features. What we can ascertain from their first appearance in *A New Hope* is that dark hair covers their claw-like hands, the only fully exposed part of them. The most distinct feature of the Jawas is their glowing, amber colored eyes. Overall, they are modestly garbed for desert survival. Their cloaks and hoods protect them from the worst of the suns' rays, but this is a wasteful method of dress as it allows for too much exposure to the desert elements. The Jawas make up for this "wardrobe malfunction," however, as they rarely travel in the open desert without their enormous Sand Crawlers—massive vehicles that shield them from the worst effects of the environment. These Sand Crawlers appear to simply be mobile scrap yards: a place to gather valuable salvage from the desert wastes, repair them, and ultimately resell them to customers like the Lars family. Their portrayal is typical of a community of scavengers: they are viewed as dealers and, oftentimes, swindlers. Illustrating this, we needn't look any further than the Jawas' interaction with Owen Lars and Luke in *A New Hope*. After one of the droids Lars purchases malfunctions, he lashes the Jawa seller for trying to pull one over on him. This seems like a harmless enough exchange, but there is a notion of the shifty or untrustworthy Arab in the Jawas' portrayal, a ready motif Western audiences find in the adventures of James Bond or the antics of Bugs Bunny and Popeye. Additionally, their untranslated language equates it with worthless gibberish in the eyes of the average viewer—a common practice when portraying Arabic in film and television.

This is not the only instance of this particular stereotype in *Star Wars*. Some critics have also pointed to the portrayal of Watto, a slave-owning underhanded businessman from *The Phantom Menace* and *Attack of the Clones*, and his "foreign-sounding" accent. In her article, "Racial Ventriloquism," Patricia J. Williams writes, "[Watto] speaks in a gravelly Middle Eastern accent. Although a number of groups have protested that Watto is an insulting Arab stereotype, he struck me as more comprehensively anti–Semitic—both anti–Arab and anti–Jew." In these cases, between Watto and the Jawas, the portrayals of Tatooine traders and businessmen have distinct Arab stereotypes underlying their behavior and appearance. The other natives of Tatooine have a far more complex role in the *Star Wars* universe, and they are consistently portrayed as very real threats.

What We (Should) Talk About When We Talk About Tuskens

The Tusken Raiders or Sand People are perhaps the most overt Arab stereotype in these films. First of all, being referred to as "Sand People" instead of anything approaching an understanding of nomenclature and cultural respect or sensitivity is reminiscent of contemporary American views of Arabs, Muslims, or Middle Eastern peoples in general. In regards to their dress, Tuskens represent a combination of typical desert dweller and Islamic stereotype. The males are covered from head to toe, but this should not raise any eyebrows as the conservation of moisture is paramount to any desert dweller. It is the female Tuskens and their costumes, which appear as poorly disguised versions of the burqa found in Islamic cultures, that should give us cause for concern. This is perhaps the most overt reference to Islamic culture so far in the films, and it is presented immediately prior to Anakin Skywalker's murderous rampage of a Tusken community in *Attack of the Clones*. We shall return to the significance of Anakin's murders shortly.

The Tuskens are repeatedly referred to as a primitive society, but what does that exactly mean in the context of this universe? They do not use spacecraft as far as we know—they prefer to ride giant beasts rather than use the humans' land speeders or the Jawa's Sand Crawlers—but they are familiar with weapons technology and overland vehicles, as discussed below. The Tusken Raiders have also had a consistent presence, having appeared in the first film and the prequel trilogy. Aside from the movies, the official canon has expanded the Tuskens' presence in various comics, games, and IOS mobile applications. Most recently, a scene of Tusken corpses, apparently dispatched by Darth Vader himself, end the first issue of the new Marvel comic, *Star Wars: Darth Vader*, created by Kieron Gillen and Salvador Larroca, which takes place between *A New Hope* and *The Empire Strikes Back* (46). The *Star Wars Databank*, which has canonical descriptions/explanations of just about every facet of the universe, only provides the following brief entry about the Tusken Raiders:

> Fearsome desert savages inhabiting the rocky Jundland Wastes, Tusken Raiders are the foremost reason Tatooine colonists do not wander far from their isolated communities. Extremely territorial and xenophobic, Tusken Raiders will attack with very little provocation. They have even gathered numbers large enough to attack the outskirts of smaller towns like Anchorhead ["Tusken Raiders"].

This article basically sums up what the modern canon and casual movie-goers can readily infer from the visual elements about Tusken civilization: "Sand People" are savages and, therefore must have a primitive intelligence. With this slant in mind, let us begin by analyzing their presence and portrayal in the aforementioned films.

First by its date of release, *A New Hope* introduces the Tusken Raiders in what would become their most iconic portrayal. Luke is incapacitated by them after venturing far from the Lars family homestead in search of R2-D2. While they would later be frightened off by Obi-Wan Kenobi, there is a glaring question when analyzing this scene. If the Tuskens are renowned for their ruthlessness and brutality, why do they spare Luke? After knocking him out, they seem more concerned with what they could salvage from his land speeder rather than take the speeder itself. The boy is not killed, and this gives Obi-Wan Kenobi enough time to scare them off. Wouldn't they have dispatched him first if they were such mindless killers? This perspective calls into question what has been the traditional rationale for the action in this scene. Their brutality, (suggested in the harsh, guttural sound of their language, their aggressive behavior, and John Williams's musical shift to heavy drum beats), may be renowned, but it falls short of its own hype. Also, the untranslated language of the Jawas' is mirrored in the portrayal of Tusken speak. It is equally characterized as incoherent gibberish: their sounds beings "derived … from barking mules" (Veekhoven). The language of a hitherto mysterious people is, in this universe, nothing more than the annoying or jarring braying of a mule. Further solidifying this point, the lack of translation when it comes to Tusken speech is just another means to deny them agency especially in the context of their slaughter by Anakin in *Attack of the Clones*:

> If language is an attribute of intelligent beings, then to deny a person or group language is to place them outside or beyond the pale of acceptability. Thus, when Anakin confesses his crime to Padmé he declares, "They're like animals and I slaughtered them like animals." Incapable of communicating with them it is easier for Anakin to exile the Tusken raiders from a community of rights-bearing citizens. In this way, they can be treated as subhuman and therefore not entitled to the normal protections of the rule of law [Cronin 128].

Since there is no real attempt in any of the films to understand who or what the Tuskens are, we as an audience are allowed to discount their existence and minimize their importance on Tatooine.

The first and last of the prequels provide us with few examples to work with in terms of the Tuskens as a society. In the Boonta Eve podracing scene in *The Phantom Menace*, the Tuskens shoot at podracers for no apparent reason beyond what looks like sadistic enjoyment and a heavy handed piece of "fan service." In *Revenge of the Sith*, they are merely mentioned by Chancellor Palpatine, to whom Anakin apparently confided his past deeds (a faint Tusken roar/mule bark is heard during this exchange). But it is precisely those past deeds that are most central to understanding the Tusken condition in the *Star Wars* universe. *Attack of the Clones* offers us our first brief but in-depth look at Tusken culture that the films have ignored up to this point. Lucas had painted the Tuskens in broad strokes of animalistic violence and sub-human or sub-sentient mindlessness, and this film initially offers more of the same. Anakin's nightmares lead him to believe his mother, Shmi, is in danger, thereby compelling him and Padmé to return to Tatooine. Anakin meets the Lars family and, his stepfather, Cliegg Lars, lays out the details of her capture by Tusken Raiders. Anakin proceeds to track down the Tusken encampment and infiltrates it without drawing attention. However, the area he enters is not the den of mindless killers, it appears to be a small village. The film does not go to great lengths to demonize the Tuskens in these scenes; instead, we are made privy to what a typical evening in a Tusken village looks like.

But what are we to make of this extremely brief segment in *Attack of the Clones* that shows *normal* Tusken village life right before Anakin massacres them all? We can plainly observe Tusken men, women, and children as well as domesticated hunting animals, yurt-like homes, and guards watching over the tent housing Shmi Skywalker. Up until this point, in the fifth installment of six films, we have nothing but negative associations with the Tuskens. However, in mere seconds, all we had previously associated with them is called into question. Lucas portrays them, for the first time, as innocents. While some may be guilty of the kidnapping and torturing of Anakin's mother (as discussed below), this does not condemn an entire community to violent execution. Indeed, it seems that, apart from skirmishes with the human settlers, this "pioneer and Indian" parallel does not seem to extend to episodes of wholesale slaughter between Tatootine's inhabitants. Lars says as much when he gives up Shmi for dead; both sides reject mob-like posses or vigilantism. Anakin disrupts these codes of conflict. In fact, the moment when Anakin begins his slaughter is marked with the startled reactions of the Tusken women and children to his presence.

Watching that scene, the viewer is supposed to be observing Anakin's behavior with disgust. As we observe the aftermath, we can trace this moment as the beginning of his fall. But the transformation of Anakin into Darth

Vader is actually one of the selling points of the prequels. There were more than a few fans excited by this scene and others like it because his growing anger signaled this impending transformation. In this view, Lucas does worse than deny the Tuskens agency as in the original trilogy; he uses them as a sacrificial lamb and does it so poorly their slaughter is met with little more than raised eyebrows. He attempts to humanize the Tuskens just long enough to have Anakin murder them, but this moment becomes an empty gesture because the Tuskens "deserved" it for killing "Ani's" mom. The action quickly jumps to Anakin's returning to the Lars' homestead and Shmi's funeral. Lit by the twin suns, the settlers' mournful expressions draw more audience empathy than the demise of anonymous Tusken "savages" in the near-pitch black recesses of Tatooine.

How does the average viewer observe the massacre of a Tusken community? When first watching this scene, I was more interested in Anakin's fall than with the repercussions of the massacre of mostly innocent villagers. After numerous discussions, other viewers seemed to observe this scene with little more than a shrug in terms of the Tuskens. Anakin's actions and, essentially the entirety of the prequels, "capitalize on the power of the villain.... We root for the flailing heroes, but we often identify with the complexities of villains" (Brown). In fact, Anakin's admission of this massacre to Padmé is met with sympathy and understanding if not downright ambivalence. Despite her characterization as a humane senator—and the many discussions she had with Anakin that with great power comes great responsibility—she turns a blind eye. No one, not even the viewer, feels it necessary to hold Anakin accountable for these actions.

So while Lucas tries to ham-handedly add a bit of depth to the Tuskens in order to make their slaughter "mean something," we are left with the validation of their sub-human portrayal instead. Since Padmé treats his actions with ambivalence, the stereotype that Tuskens are incapable of possessing humanity has been reinforced. The fact is Lucas lets Anakin get away with murder long before his "official" transformation in *Revenge of the Sith*, and yet we are still expected to cheer for this hero and find his fall from grace tragic. If the film was portrayed from someone else's perspective (the cosmopolitan senator Padmé or the wise Obi-Wan), we might have gotten more of an objective struggle over the consequences of this act. But since we are watching this unfold mostly from Anakin's perspective, we tend to sympathize with him as protagonist of this story. The film relegates the wanton destruction of a native community to a mere footnote in Anakin's fall, and thereby cheapens the lives of those men, women, and children. His later massacre of the human/non-Tusken "younglings" at the Jedi temple in *Revenge of the Sith* is viewed as the most abhorrent act he commits, particularly in the scene where Obi-Wan informs Padmé. Unlike her sympathetic understanding of the Tusken massacre, she then finds this piece of information too gruesome to stand and sets out to ask Anakin personally. One would assume that a person who has committed a massacre before and who is currently being accused of another would manifest themselves to an observer as having a pattern. But still, Padmé finds this particular accusation unbearable. The reality her reactions illuminate is this: Republic lives—in the case of the younglings, overwhelmingly white humans—matter more than Tusken lives. Her subsequent confrontation drives the end of her story arc: Anakin nearly kills her, she then gives birth to new hopes to atone for the father's sins against the younglings, and then dies.

The Passion of Shmi Skywalker: A Case Study

The basis for much of this stereotyping is not only present in the Tuskens' film appearances but also in the stories and lore that other Star Wars characters have circulated media outside of the films. But before we venture into the Expanded Universe and to better understand the complexity of the Tusken question we are dealing with here, let us first take the example of Shmi Skywalker's death in *Attack of the Clones* as a case study. Her capture and treatment by the Tuskens should provide us with insight into their characteristics and social behavior. First of all, why is Shmi alive? She was obviously attacked and captured, but, like Luke, she was not killed, nor is she being held for ransom since Cliegg Lars makes no mention of that to Anakin. I think it is safe to say the Tuskens are not keeping Shmi as a bargaining chip or even as bait. So why do the Tuskens spare her life? The fact that she is alive could indicate a few things, so let us address the worst scenarios first.

It is possible that Shmi Skywalker is being compelled by her captors to labor as a slave again. If she is being forced to work in some capacity, her treatment would have been congruent with many real-world civilizations. Numerous cultures, including the Greeks, Romans, Mongols, Persians, and Ottomans, just to name a few, have harbored the practice of enslaving their captives in war. In this scenario, Shmi is again enslaved but not by the Hutts or Watto and not for any financial gain or the settling of monetary debts. Instead, as a settler perhaps encroaching on Tusken territory, her ordeal evokes early American "captive" narratives from pioneer women abducted by Native American tribes. Within this framework, this colonization on Tusken land pits the indigenous Tuskens against the settlers in a perpetual war for territory.

Most alarmingly, there seems to also be a suggested rape scenario being played out with the way Shmi is positioned and bound. The blocking of this scene tacitly suggests to the viewer that something is being forced upon her. Indeed, an observer might quip: why else would these "animals" be keeping her alive? This could echo another cinema stereotype of Arabs in their portrayal as always lusting after Caucasian women, causing them to hunt and capture the unsuspecting and virtuous white woman. The essay "Aladdin, Al-Qaeda, and Arabs in U.S. Film and Television" explores this common film trope of Arab men not only being thorough libertines but especially fond of white or European women:

> In a common mise-en-scene, opulent, palatial interiors reveal a cruel, bloated pasha reclining on cushions and surrounded by harem maidens. The pasha possesses an unquenchable appetite for the flesh and requires sensual handmaidens and harem girls to appeal to his lascivious desires. However, as in the movie *Samson Against the Sheik* (1962), the Arab harem maidens don't attract the pasha's attention as much as the blonde European girl does, so he must abduct and ravish her against her will [Blauvelt].

Applying this scenario to Shmi provokes troubling connotations, but Lucas complicates the implied rape with her earlier connections to a Christ-like figure: in *The Phantom Menace*, she states she gave birth to Anakin without a father—a clear parallel of the Virgin Mary. If the Tuskens channel a Middle Eastern stereotype, then Shmi's capture/rape damns the "infidels" for their horrific violation of the Christian church's Mother. Indeed, Shmi's torture, as depicted in the blocking of this scene, condemns *Star Wars*'s Middle Eastern "others." Besides exhaustion, her hands are bound, her wrists are red with welts, and her face is cut in two places. What exactly the Tuskens are doing to her is left vague, but she has clearly sustained some injuries and, according to Cliegg, she has been gone for a month. Her exhaustion would imply she has potentially been raped; forcibly made to labor; been deprived of sleep, food, or water; or some such combination of these. While deplorable in any combination, these actions do not necessarily make the Tuskens mindless or sub-human; in fact, they are all too familiar human practices. These do represent the worst case scenarios based on what is presented in the film, but let us play the devil's advocate and see if we can determine other, valid reasons as to why the Tuskens captured Shmi but also spared her.

First, the Tuskens may have attacked her for a socio-political reason known only to them. Her picking of mushrooms off moisture vaporators might have been an innocent, habitual practice to human eyes, but it does not mean that these areas were not part of a Tusken system of borders of which she or other settlers were unaware. Choosing to capture her over killing her, similar to Luke's experience in *A New Hope*, indicates some manner of mercy or, at the very least, restraint in deference to a set of laws or codes. We are led to believe these are qualities no settler on Tatooine can believe the brutish Tuskens have. The very idea of mercy is perceived as something beyond the capabilities of these primitives, and this alone demands a closer look at this scenario. Secondly, her capture could indicate a debate within this specific tribal group. Of course it is easier to eliminate her, but perhaps there are those within the Tusken tribe who do not view her as a threat. The fact that she is kept alive could signal a larger Tusken debate over what to do with her, and, by extension, a complex political system in Tusken civilization. This would explain why there are two Tusken men guarding the entrance to Shmi's tent. It would seem unlikely two armed men would be posted at the entrance of a tent to guard a bound and near-death farmer. Instead of preventing this incapacitated woman from escaping, could they be instead guarding against someone from within the tribe? This, in and of itself, is a quality we hope to encounter in every society—the importance of individual lives and the realistic consideration over whether or not to take that life. The tribe could be struggling over dissent and the greater relationships with the human settlers. This possibility humanizes the Tuskens far more than the limited view from the settlers, or the films, thus far.

While it may have been devised as simply a plot device to have Anakin's mother die in his arms in order to send him over the edge, why, then, does Lucas portray the Tusken habitat like a normal village? Women, children, pets—these are not facets of life present in Lucas's depiction of the feared Tuskens up until this point. There is noticeable warmth amidst those Tuskens around the fire as their hunting animals squabble and the children play under the supervision of their mothers and fathers. These elements are clearly presented, but it is difficult to fully grasp why we are made privy to these moments. Even though Lucas may have played up this sentiment to magnify their horrific fate at Anakin's hands, audiences do have, however fleeting, a glimpse into a culture that the settlers of Tatooine have forgotten. We see the Tuskens are indeed a rational, sentient race—one with a cultural tradition which they have chosen to ignore or subvert.

For both the Jawas and the Tuskens, their characteristics represent a collection of Arab and Islamic stereotypes repackaged to varying degrees. Their depiction in film, while some might attest to being alien or otherworldly, have clear parallels in the depiction of Arab and Islamic culture throughout cinema's history. Driss Ridouani outlines the myriad depictions of Arabs and Muslims in the movies, writing:

Ever since the camera began to crank, the unkempt Arab has appeared as an uncivilized character, the cultural Other, someone who appears and acts differently than the white Western protagonist, someone of a different race, class, gender or national origin. The diverse Islamic world is populated solely with bearded mullahs, shady sheikhs in their harems, bombers, backward Bedouin, belly dancers, harem maidens and obsequious domestics [4].

In the films, we clearly see the Jawas and the Tuskens portrayed as shady, primitive, and dangerous desert dwellers. Their motivation has been simply to exploit the colonists/settlers of Tatooine or to kill them.

What is most troubling about the colonist/native dynamic on Tatooine is the sheer ignorance of the colonist population—ignorance of how they might have offended or endangered Tusken society, the lack of insight into why the Tuskens would continue to attack them, and general ignorance of Tusken history/civilization as a whole. This realization is at the core of my analysis. How are we, as movie-goers, to empathize with the systemic oppression of a native population? Lucas and his successors in the Expanded Universe present this stereotype as an easy feat: simply portray the natives from one perspective, and keep your characters from any representation apart from that of unfeeling monsters. As seen in the original trilogy, the Tuskens are shown as a force seemingly beyond the labels of good or evil—something more akin to nature and the natural environment of Tatooine. By deeming them such, Lucas denies them agency in the fate of their world. Because they are treated like other Tatooine fauna such as womp rats or banthas, they are denied the intelligence and reasoning human beings or other "normal" alien species possess. In fact, this relationship's portrayal is reminiscent of myriad other colonial relationships—the colonist taking on the "white man's burden" to fight for their existence on Tatooine. This way of thinking makes it easy for the colonists to act as though Tusken cultural practices are sub-human and, therefore, unimportant or expendable in the modeling of the planet for their own purposes. It also makes it easier for us as viewers to accept their oppression as merely a common scenario where human beings are once again exerting their control over a natural environment.

We could almost ignore these signs as we watch the original trilogy. For all intents and purposes, the Tuskens only play a minor role as a dangerous feature of the environment in *A New Hope*—something to be avoided like quicksand or a predator. It is in the prequels that we get our first real glimpse into Tusken society, and it does not end well. But let us take a step back for a moment and put the colonist/native relationship in perspective. Can we imagine the first settlers who landed on Tatooine? Perhaps they were ill-equipped and/or dangerously naive. It is conceivable that, in times long since past in this universe, the Tusken people were at least curious about the settlers and even ventured so far as to help them. To develop this hypothesis, we must turn to the lore beyond celluloid. The Expanded Universe has done much to broaden our understanding of the motivation of Tusken peoples and why they are such a hostile force against Tatooine's other populations.

Expanding the Tusken Universe

Much of the Expanded Universe serves to expound on the various peoples, worlds, and storylines of the *Star Wars* universe that are not central to the Skywalker family and their role in galactic politics. In many works, particularly the *Star Wars: Legacy* and *Republic: Outlander* comic series, writers and artists have gone to great lengths to explain and give insight into Tusken civilization and their history on Tatooine. Even video games like *Star Wars: Knights of the Old Republic* have entire side quests players can choose to perform that are dedicated to the understanding of Tusken history and customs. The most notable contribution to the history of Tusken society is found in this game, and it establishes the Tuskens used to refer to themselves as the "ghorfa" before the name "Sand People" or "Tusken Raiders" stuck. Additionally, a shared ancestry between humans, Jawas, and Tuskens is suggested. This storyline within the game, while considered conjecture or a spotty Tusken oral history at best, attempts to at least put Tuskens and Jawas on equal footing with humans. But to truly understand the Tusken in terms of the Bedouin ideal and to better debate the Tuskens and Skywalkers' roles as heroes in this nature, we must first define more clearly what the Bedouin ideal is and that set of characteristics which desert heroes often possess. According to John Renard in his seminal work, *Islam and the Heroic Image: Themes in Literature and the Visual Arts*, "The typical Bedouin heroic figure was the man or woman of great courage, generosity, spontaneity, and loyalty, who put all his or her strength and virtue at the service of the tribe" (43). This hero or heroine would commit selfless acts and would not serve personal gain or glory; instead, their efforts serve a greater purpose. But their greater goals do not necessarily have to be galaxy-changing. More often, these heroes help correct small-scale or local injustices felt by marginalized or poorer populations, and these are the stories which are told, retold, and mythologized into folk heroes.

Since Tatooine is our cultural staging ground, it would seem natural to gravitate towards the Skywalker family, particularly Anakin and Luke, as representative of this Bedouin ideal in their heroic deeds. And one would be correct in that assumption up to a certain point. However, I offer a different perspective on a better representation of the desert hero embracing Bedouin ideals in this universe: the human Hett family of Tatooine. This family first appeared in *Star Wars: Republic: Outlander*, a comic book series printed by Dark Horse Comics in 2009. Starting with Sharad Hett, his wife K'Sheek, and son A'Sharad Hett, this family would play a pivotal role in both Tatooine and the galaxy's history. Like the Skywalkers, the Hetts were transplants to Tatooine. Unlike the Skywalkers, they were concerned with the state of lawlessness perpetuated by gangsters like Jabba the Hutt as well as the marginalization of Tatooine's native populations. The most important characteristic of this family is that, while they were technically human, the Hetts were fostered and initiated into a society of Tusken Raiders. Their story would introduce new facets of Tusken civilization previously unexplored. Perhaps deliberately on the part of creators, the series even played up their connection with Bedouin and Arab characteristics simply in their names. To explain, the name of the paragon of Bedouin heroism and chivalry, 'Antarah ibn-Shaddād al-'Absi, shall serve as an example to reflect this linguistic and cultural connection (Hitti 95). In this name, "ibn" means "son of" while "al-" indicates "of the," so the name translates roughly to 'Antarah son of Shaddād of the 'Absi. In the Hett family, the names Sharad and A'Sharad (son of Sharad) deliberately hearken to this Arab naming structure. The impact of the Hett family as told in the Dark Horse comic series *Star Wars: Republic* and *Star Wars: Legacy* redefined the nature of Tuskens as a people and gave Tusken society a depth and breadth not afforded in other mediums.

The patriarch of this family, Sharad Hett, was one of the greatest Jedi Knights the Order ever had, and his exploits in the name of the Galactic Republic earned him such nicknames as the "Howlrunner," the "Champion of Krmar," the "Defender of Kamparus," the "Hound of Worlds," and the "Tamer of Tyrants" (Omnibus 131). Indeed, Sharad Hett was the most renowned Jedi Knight in the galaxy for the thirty years before the events of *The Phantom Menace*. But after the death of his family during a civil war on his home-world, Hett began to question and ultimately reject many of the restrictions put on Jedi Knights, particularly the stigma against familial connection. "Suddenly, things seemed very clear: despite all my training, all my acts of bravery, all my years of service," reflected Hett, "my whole life has been a sham! What use are a Jedi's powers, Ki, if he cannot use them to save his own family?" (218). Detailed in *Star Wars: Republic* issue #9, Hett, steeped in grief, turns his back on his legacy and fame and enters a self-imposed exile beyond the reach of the Republic. He crashes on Tatooine and starts a new life as a member of the Jundland Tuskens after intense trials and initiation

(Omnibus 219). Hett marries K'Sheek, another human adoptee in this Tusken society, and she gives birth to their son, A'Sharad. K'Sheek perished when A'Sharad was a baby, and Sharad soon takes his son as his Padawan and trains him in the ways of both the Jedi and the Tuskens. In this story arc, we learn much about Tusken culture. Among the many revelations, one can easily observe the connection between the Tuskens and their mounts (banthas) as a direct analogue of the Bedouin connection to the camel. And while this story is a familiar trope of the exile being adopted by a native or tribal people in order to find his/her "self" (see the films *Dances with Wolves*, *Lawrence of Arabia*, *The Last Samurai*, or *Avatar*, just to name a few), it is vital for shedding light upon the accepted "heroism" of Anakin and Luke Skywalker.

As father and son, the Hetts would soon organize and lead their tribe against both settlers and criminals, challenging the hegemony of Jabba the Hutt. This kind of warfare appears brutal and savage to the outside observer, and, suspecting something more at play, the Jedi Council dispatches Jedi Master Ki-Adi-Mundi to investigate (Omnibus 133). Meeting up with Sharad Hett, Mundi learns the broader perspective the rest of the galaxy lacks about the Tuskens' struggles against outsiders. After showing Mundi numerous Tusken burial mounds, Sharad explains, "Someone started attacking Tusken camps ... poisoning wells ... leaving disease-infected food for the Tuskens to find ... and contaminated toys for our children! The tribes of the Jundland wanted retribution ... and I was not inclined to stop them!" (Omnibus 221). Sharad points out the current conflict between Tusken and off-worlders was precipitated by Jabba the Hutt's desire to liquidate outdated weaponry to the scared and hapless settlers. This commitment to justice for the Tuskens, and the downtrodden, represents a deeper acceptance of Jedi principles than the Jedi Council's through their inaction and ignorance and also reflects the nature of Bedouin justice in this scenario. The Bedouin have an unwritten code of laws, and one such code is referred to as 'Al 'Orf. The nature of this code "is tough as life in the desert and blood calls for blood" to which Sharad, as war leader, abides by (Bedouin Law). The comic book asks whether a society like the Tuskens can set aside tribal differences to rally around a single leader like Sharad, but precedence for this issue is again found in Bedouin culture. Even when led by a single tribe or leader, Bedouin groups still maintain tribal demarcation, but "they are prepared to fight for one another ... they exact vengeance for one another; and members of a co-liable group assert that they will stand by any of their number who becomes involved in a dispute, and will contribute equally to blood-money" (Marx 182). Sharad is not provoking a bloody campaign for his own personal gain or glory, but he is serving the collective tribes, fulfilling the laws of Tusken society.

On Tatooine, a native population is being terrorized and killed for exploitative reasons, but the Republic and the Jedi Council are not moved to take action until Sharad Hett's involvement is suspected. Both of these governing bodies have tacitly accepted gangster rule on this outer rim world, and Hett and the Tuskens are the only ones willing to do what is right—challenge tyranny and injustice when the Jedi and the Republic are unwilling to do so. This characteristic puts Sharad and A'Sharad on a higher moral level than Anakin or Luke; while the Skywalkers both became great and influential Jedi, neither of them sought to fight against any of these injustices on their home world. Whether it came in the form of slavery, exploitation, or marginalization—tragedies which both Anakin and Luke are intimately familiar with and which the Jedi are *sworn to fight against*—neither would impact any positive change on Tatooine. In fact, we see the Skywalkers as more comfortable with keeping business as usual instead of taking on the encroaching settlers, criminals, or gangsters.

Sharad's experience illustrates some key insights about Tusken society only hinted at in the movies. First, Tuskens willingly take in outsiders, but, like many nomadic or desert cultures, they must prove themselves useful to the tribe. Hett states, "The mortality rate among Tuskens is high and their numbers are few. Thus humanoid adoptees are occasionally taken in, in hopes that their blood will be compatible with the Tuskens' own" (Omnibus 219). Secondly, we learn from Sharad the Tuskens subsist primarily on "hubba gourds" and are fundamentally vegetarians (Omnibus 213). This insight disproves many of the monstrous or cannibalistic associations often perpetuated by the settlers about Tusken society. This is not to say vegetarianism is equated with docility, but here is another instance where Tusken stereotypes are far from the truth. Lastly, it is the simple commitment to justice, not a perceived wanton slaughter, that further "humanizes" this society. Sharad Hett and his son, as members of a Tusken tribe, were willing to challenge a real injustice committed against this native population. This is a trait we find absent in the portrayal of Anakin and Luke, but this exact correcting of injustice at the local or tribal level is part of what defines the Bedouin ideal and a desert hero. It is interesting to note an exiled and nearly-forgotten Jedi without any assistance from the Jedi Order was still living out its creed even though the Order was unwilling to do this work itself. In the conclusion of this story arc, the tribe is lured into a trap, and Sharad Hett is killed in battle but makes Ki-Adi-Mundi take A'Sharad with him to train at the Jedi Temple on Coruscant. The tribe is defeated and scattered, and the Tusken resistance would dissolve overnight, but these events would not be forgotten, and A'Sharad would continue his father's work in the years to come.

Playing the Sith's Advocate

While the story of Sharad Hett is an interesting and important one in terms of Tusken society, his son's story challenges the perception of a hero and what a true Bedouin hero's work entails. As detailed in the issue "Enemy Lines" of *Star Wars: Republic*, A'Sharad returns to Coruscant to train as a Jedi—the first human Tusken to do so. He would play a pivotal role as a general during the Clone Wars and even come into contact with another famous hero from this era, Anakin Skywalker. The meeting of these two heroes, in the issue "Enemy Lines," deserves careful scrutiny. A'Sharad, dressed in his traditional Tusken garb, fights alongside Anakin, but, after both are trapped behind enemy lines, tensions boil over. Unaware of Anakin's deeds in the Tusken village, A'Sharad repeatedly brings up comparisons and recollections of Tatooine, which put Skywalker visibly on edge. Seeing A'Sharad simply dressed as a Tusken is enough to put Anakin in straits, and this begins to manifest itself in his openly derogatory attitude toward A'Sharad and Tuskens (Ostrander 5). When Hett compliments Anakin's prowess, saying, "You would have made a good Tusken," the reader can clearly observe the anger festering in Anakin's dark stare (9). Later, when briefly separated from each other, Anakin is ambushed while reflecting on the death of his mother and subsequent massacre. His ambushers transform into Tuskens in his mind's eye, and he slaughters the "stinking animals," screaming for more as he cuts through them (13). Anakin even attacks A'Sharad who manages to subdue this unexpected wrath. In the midst of this bloodlust, Anakin admits his crime and the vengeance he sought against the Tuskens who captured his mother. In this moment, A'Sharad has the evidence to discredit and perhaps cause the expulsion of Anakin Skywalker from the Jedi order, but he instead chooses to forgive Anakin, removing his head coverings for the first time to reveal that he is also human underneath it all (16). At the end of their journey, Hett states, "You must first accept that what you did was wrong. And you haven't done that, yet. Tuscans are animals to you, aren't they? In your heart you believe they deserved to die. Perhaps they do. But did you have the right to kill them? Would you do it again?" (23). After Hett leaves him to ponder this question, Anakin simply says "yes." Since the events of that massacre on Tatooine, Anakin is finally forced to face his actions. Luckily for Skywalker's future as a Jedi, A'Sharad chooses to keep his secret out of duty and loyalty to the Jedi code. This meeting would have galaxy-wide ramifications since Anakin misses a chance to atone for his actions and grow stronger from this experience. Nevertheless, even though Anakin still manages to avoid punishment for genocide, his secret was shared with someone other than Padmé, and this potentially has more productive results than Padmé's blanket forgiveness.

When *Revenge of the Sith* first premiered, psychologist Eric Bui, during his residency, began an in-depth analysis on the subject of Anakin Skywalker's possible affliction from borderline personality disorder. He diagnosed Anakin as meeting six of the nine criteria of that disorder—one only needs to match five to qualify as having said disorder (Hsu 2010). While the findings were perhaps not surprising given the character's renowned impulsivity and penchant for anger and violence, Bui and his colleagues were confident his disorder could have easily been treated with psychotherapy. This notion is reflected in Anakin's confession to A'Sharad Hett; this could have been the start of Anakin finally finding absolution for his crimes, taking responsibility for his actions, and avoiding the dark side of the Force to validate his conflicted emotions. A'Sharad performed the most taboo action a Tusken can perform: the display of one's flesh openly, and he did this to help ease the rage within Anakin. If A'Sharad's advice had been followed, his selfless act on Anakin's behalf could have saved the galaxy so much woe and suffering, sparing it from Darth Vader. A'Sharad's self-revelation came to naught, but his acts, are the characteristics we look for in a character representing the Bedouin ideal. Hett possessed courage and spontaneity when he unmasked himself to help Anakin regain his senses, even though he knew this was a line that no Tusken could conceivably cross and return. Hett illustrated generosity and loyalty by sacrificing his heritage and giving of himself to help a comrade in need. The reader can easily deduce just how much more connected to Tatooine and its desert culture Hett is compared to Anakin, and nothing signals that more clearly than when the two meet. Their encounter cements the idea Anakin is not a hero representative of the Bedouin ideal, and the associations he might have with a desert culture are superficial at best.

Years later and upon learning who Darth Vader was, A'Sharad would regret the decision to spare Anakin the full judgment of the Jedi Council. That regret would fuel his actions in the decades after the fall of both the Republic and Empire, contributing to his choice to become a Sith. However, there are two particular events that may explain why Hett's turning to the dark side is still congruent with the Bedouin ideal. Dark Horse's *Star Wars: Legacy* series gives insight into what happened to A'Sharad in the wake of Order 66, the order to execute all Jedi throughout the Republic. Returning to Tatooine, Hett reflects, "Settlers and moisture farmers had been stealing Tusken land and water for years," and A'Sharad, like his father before him, would become the tribes' war leader to rectify this injustice (Ostrander and

Duursema #17, 9). When the tribes arrive at the edge of the Lars' moisture farm, Obi-Wan Kenobi, secretly protecting the son of Skywalker, challenges Hett's mission. Kenobi, without revealing his own duty, demands Hett stop what he and the Tuskens are doing. Hett replies, "These are my people! Will the settlers stop killing Tuskens? Then blood calls for blood! The settlers will be forced to abandon the land—or be buried beneath it!" (12). Echoing the same Bedouin sentiment that demands blood for injustice, A'Sharad champions the downtrodden once again in spite of Jedi interference. His subsequent duel with Kenobi leaves him unmasked and without his right forearm; humiliated and unable to wield the traditional Tusken weapon, he is abandoned by his tribe (17). This defeat is important to note because, again, Kenobi, as the guardian of the defunct Jedi Order, seemingly conflicts with greater notions of social justice. The results of this battle lead to Hett's ultimate disillusionment with the Jedi way.

After his defeat at Kenobi's hands, the exiled A'Sharad Hett becomes a bounty hunter. A'Sharad is enticed by a Sith lord to use the dark side of the Force; this, he felt, would help him in a quest to confront Palpatine and Darth Vader, and right the wrongs he allowed to transpire by sparing Anakin from judgment (Ostrander and Duursema, #18, 2). But shortly after venturing into uncharted space, Hett is captured by the Yuuzhan Vong (soon-to-be invaders of the New Republic) and exposed to a torture device referred to as the "embrace of pain" (4). This device is designed to inflict more pain as the prisoner struggles, but Hett, tapping into the dark side, learns to accept its pain and eventually frees himself. In A'Sharad's time in the embrace of pain, his mastery of this ordeal is linked to his Bedouin characteristics. A crucial component of Bedouin "honor-linked values is self-mastery, one aspect of which is physical stoicism" (Abu-Lughod 90). The bearing of any physical pain or discomfort should be done without complaint, and this is precisely how A'Sharad was able to escape (90). During his captivity, Hett channels the dark side to focus his energy and uses that pain leads to his new vision for the galaxy: "Power without purpose is meaningless. The galaxy is chaotic. Order must be imposed because it will never be chosen.... The Jedi will not do it. A new Sith order must be created in secret" (Ostrander and Duursema 6). Both his disillusionment with the Jedi and experience in the embrace of pain molds A'Sharad's future. He sheds his name, become Darth Krayt, and seeks to establish an order to prevent the corruption and decay that consumed both the Republic and the Empire. This journey to establish a lasting order to long-standing grievances, while through the use of the dark side, is still an admirable desire. We may disagree with Hett/Krayt's methods, but his vision would have brought a Tusken's righteous justice to a galaxy brimming with corruption and intrigue—something the Jedi and the Republic seemed unable or unwilling to accomplish. This ambition to strike a new path on behalf of marginalized peoples when the old ways no longer work is something that separates A'Sharad from either of the Skywalker heroes.

A New Hope?

Lest we leave Luke out of this debate, this adopted son of farmers represents the rural youth seeking adventure in the galaxy beyond. But does that coincide with the heroic Bedouin ideal? Luke is, much like his father, loyal to his friends and possesses courage and occasional spontaneity. His accomplishments in the Rebel Alliance endow him with a reputation and legacy which few would question. But his achievements stem from troubling motivations. The death of his aunt and uncle in *A New Hope* is what pushes him to help Obi-Wan Kenobi; he basically embarks on a quest for revenge against the Empire. Indeed, in *A New Hope*, when Luke and Kenobi come across Jawa corpses and a disabled Sand Crawler, Obi-Wan explains the scene was *engineered* by stormtroopers to look like an attack from Tusken Raiders. If Obi-Wan had not been there to correctly identify those responsible for this slaughter, Luke would have most likely believed his foster parents were murdered by Tuskens. Without Obi-Wan telling him differently, Luke's story could have just as easily been directed towards gaining vengeance from the Tuskens. Revenge is what initially motivates Luke and, while loyalty to family is important, we never hear Luke mention his foster parents again. His wish for galactic adventure is fulfilled at their expense, and the nature of his heroism appears more self-motivated than for the righting of wrongs. This is far from what we would associate with Bedouin or Tusken cultures whose motivation primarily lies with the good of the tribe. Self promotion and ego trips may have a place in settler/colonist society, but they have no place in the dunes of Tatooine.

While we are entertaining possibilities, if Owen Lars had eventually allowed Luke to leave the farm, Luke would have been enrolling in the "academy," specifically, the Imperial Academy which produced stormtroopers and Imperial officers. While seemingly not a fan of the Empire, Luke does seem eager to join them. Beru Lars remarks, "Owen, you can't keep him here forever.... The academy means so much to him" (*A New Hope*). It does not matter what he has to do; Luke wants off the planet sooner rather than later. Does this mindset coincide with a Tusken's connection to the desert? Luke's goal is not to join the academy or become a Jedi to battle injustice or wrongdoing—he desires these things out of boredom: "It just isn't fair!" he whines to the droids. The problem with Luke's character is not that he is evil, but his motivations, which illustrate the kind of person he is, are so far from what a true native of Tatooine would consider important. Indeed, Yoda berates Luke during his Jedi training for not only learning his lessons, but for this escapist mindset: "All his life has he looked away … to the future, to the horizon. Never his mind on where he was. Hmm? What he was doing. Adventure. Excitement. A Jedi craves not these things. You are reckless" (*The Empire Strikes Back*). The discipline and fortitude it takes to simply exist as a Tusken is hard enough to imagine let alone the seeking of so-called adventure. Luke is young and fantasizes about a life away from the mundane. While this is a typical trope of young heroes-in-the-making, it is not representative of the Bedouin hero Lucas positions him and Anakin to be. Like his father, Luke's connection to Tatooine is superficial. Recall the Hett family and their devotion to justice and honor even in the smallest of ways. Those characteristics are representative of the Bedouin ideal and reflect the motivations of a true desert hero or heroine.

Oftentimes, desert cultures and their traditions are co-opted without credit, ignored, or demonized in popular culture. At first, we may think that the Skywalkers are simply characters congenial enough to embody Bedouin symbolism without alienating the average viewer. But the story they co-opt is that of the peoples whom they continue to oppress. Conversely, Frank Herbert's *Dune* series is a testament to the embracing of Bedouin, Arab, and desert themes, and it illustrates the respect for source material that Lucas' stories gloss over. Tusken civilization in the *Star Wars* universe has been appropriated by the colonial powers encroaching on their land, and positing Luke or Anakin Skywalker as the desert Bedouin hero in these tales is a travesty that eats at the heart of this franchise. The honor and accolades put on Luke and Anakin for their bravery, spontaneity, and loyalty are exactly the qualities found in the traditional Bedouin and desert hero, but after confronting these characters with more authentic representations, we now know who the true children of Tatooine are.

Note

1. See Gregory E. Rutledge's chapter in this volume.

Works Cited

Abu-Lughod, Lila. *Veiled Sentiments: Honor and Poetry in a Bedouin Society*. Berkeley: University of California Press, 1999. Print.
"Bedouin Law." Bedawiwww. Ganub Sina: El Manshia El Gedida, 2007. Web. 3 June 2015. http://www.bedawi.com/Law_EN.html.

Blauvelt, Christian. "Aladdin, Al-Qaeda, and Arabs in U.S. film and TV." *Jump Cut: A Review of Contemporary Media* 50 (Spring 2008). Web. 5 May 2015. http://www.ejumpcut.org/archive/jc50.2008/reelBadArabs/#n.

Brown, Douglas. "Villains like Vader Captivate Us by Channeling our Darker Sides." *Denver Post*, 19 May 2005. Web. 10 June 2015. http://www.denverpost.com/entertainment/ci_2742107.

Cronin, Michael. *Translation Goes to the Movies.* New York: Routledge, 2009. Print.

Gillen, Kieron, and Salvador Larroca. *Star Wars: Darth Vader,* 1. New York: Marvel Comics, LLC, Feb. 2015. Print.

Hitti, Philip K. *History of the Arabs: From the Earliest Times to the Present,* rev. 10th ed. New York: Palsgrave Macmillan, 2002. Print.

Hsu, Jeremy. "The Psychology of Darth Vader Revealed." Livesciencewww. 4 June 2010. Web. 28 May 2015. http://www.livescience.com/10679-psychology-darth-vader-revealed.html.

Kershner, Irvin, dir. *Star Wars Episode V: The Empire Strikes Back.* Twentieth Century–Fox, 1980. Film.

Kurpershoek, P. Marcel. *Oral Poetry & Narrative from Central Arabia 2: The Story of a Desert Knight: The Legend of Šlēwī Al- A āwī and Other 'Utaybah Heroes.* Leiden: E. J. Brill, 1995. Print.

Lucas, George, dir. *Star Wars Episode IV: A New Hope.* Twentieth Century–Fox, 1977. Film.

_____. *Star Wars Episode I: The Phantom Menace.* Twentieth Century–Fox, 1999. Film.

_____. *Star Wars Episode II: Attack of the Clones.* Twentieth Century–Fox, 2002. Film.

_____. *Star Wars Episode III: Revenge of the Sith.* Twentieth Century–Fox, 2005. Film.

Mackey, Sandra. *The Saudis: Inside the Desert Kingdom.* New York: W. W. Norton, 2002. Print.

Maisel, Sebastian, and John A. Shoup. *Saudi Arabia and the Gulf Arab States Today: An Encyclopedia of Life in the Arab States, Volumes 1 and 2.* Westport, CT: Greenwood Press, 2009. Print.

Marquand, Richard, dir. *Star Wars Episode VI: Return of the Jedi.* Twentieth Century–Fox, 1983. Film.

Marx, Emanuel. *Bedouin of the Negev.* Manchester: Manchester University Press, 1967. Print.

Ostrander, John. "Enemy Lines." *Star Wars: Republic,* 59. Milwaukee: Dark Horse Comics, Dec. 2003. Print.

Ostrander, John, and Jan Duursema. "Claws of the Dragon." *Star Wars: Legacy,* 14–19. Milwaukee: Dark Horse Comics, July 2007-Feb. 2008. Print.

Renard, John. *Islam and the Heroic Image: Themes in Literature and the Visual Arts.* Macon: Mercer University Press, 1999. Print.

Ridouani, Driss. "The Representation of Arabs and Muslims in Western Media." *Ruta* 3, 2011. Web. 20 May 2015. https://ddd.uab.cat/pub/ruta/20130740n3/20130740n3a7.pdf.

Star Wars: Knights of the Old Republic. Casey Hudson, dir. LucasArts. 15 July 2003. Video game.

Taylor, Chris. *How* Star Wars *Conquered the Universe: The Past, Present, and Future of a Multibillion Dollar Franchise.* New York: Basic Books, 2014. Print.

Truman, Timothy, et al. "Outlander." *Star Wars Republic Omnibus: Emissaries and Assassins,* 7–12. Milwaukee: Dark Horse Comics, 2009. Print.

"Tusken Raiders." *Star Wars: Databank.* Web. 2 May 2015. http://www.starwars.com/databank/tusken-raiders.

Veekhoven, Tim. "Tusken Raiders: Meet Tatooine's Menacing Desert Dwellers." Starwarswww. 9 Jan. 2015. Web. 20 Apr. 2015. http://www.starwars.com/news/tusken-raiders-meet-tatooines-menacing-desert-dwellers.

Williams, Patricia J. "Racial Ventriloquism." *The Nation.* 17 June 1999. Web. 20 May 2015. http://web.archive.org/web/20060920011550/http://www.thenation.com/doc/19990705/williams.

Periodizing a Civil War
Reaffirming an American Empire of Dreams

PETER W. LEE

"Another Galaxy, another time" (Lucas 1).

In 1976, those four words introduced the *Star Wars* Universe. The prologue of this modest book adaptation of an unreleased film outlined the history of a long-lived, prosperous Republic. However, "as often happens when wealth and power pass beyond the admirable and attain the awesome, then appear those evil ones who have greed to match." Accordingly, this regime withstood external threats to its borders, but it "rotted from within" as "restless, power-hungry individuals within the government, and the massive organs of commerce" elected a ruler who promised to bring peace with honor and restore freedom to all (Lucas 1). Isolated from his constituents and surrounded by bootlickers, a tyrant's personal ambition overthrew the traditions of good government. Now a war tore the galaxy asunder.

This excerpt, taken from *The Journal of the Whills*—a fictional chronicle in a make-believe saga—did not take place in a land so long ago or very far away.

It happened in America. Right there and then.

Of Evil Empires and Allied Forces

The Gerald Ford and Jimmy Carter administrations did not redeem the Watergate-soaked presidencies in the eyes of disillusioned Americans (Perlstein). By 1976, an unofficial network of Americans expressed their anger: they were mad as hell and weren't gonna take it anymore. A deep popular yearning of nostalgia—an "invisible bridge" linking the nation to a perceived innocence of earlier times—became the stomping grounds of politicians. Ronald Reagan most effectively exploited this longing using his folksy charm, homespun tales, and carefully-cultivated magnetism derived from the seemingly "good ol' days" of Golden Age Hollywood, radio, and sports. *Star Wars* would likewise reflect this narrow construction of history: its good/bad narrative valorized Americanism with a celebratory portrayal of continual progress and—despite Lucas's claims of a mystical Force overcoming monstrous technological terrors—American mechanical prowess.

Director George Lucas eagerly tapped into the American narrative. Although the director had specialized in experimental films during his studies at the University of Southern California and his feature debut, *THX-1138* (1971), depicted a dysfunctional future, he soon went "commercial" in mainstream cinema. His smash hit, *American Graffiti* (1972), evoked an idealized past within living memory of baby boomers. The film's tagline, "Where Were You in '62?" rhetorically relegated audiences back one decade to the pre–Kennedy assassination era, devoid of Vietnam escalation, militant Civil Rights and feminist movements, Watergate, and the other paradigm-shaking epochs that sent America spiraling downward. Lucas started drafting *Star Wars* during the production of *American Graffiti*—the two became linked with Luke Skywalker as an extension of hot-rodders Steve and Laurie. "I wasted four years of my life cruising like the kids in *American Graffiti* and now I'm on an intergalactic dream of heroism," Lucas divulged. "In *Star Wars* I'm telling the story of me" ("The Making of Star Wars" 20).

Lucas's turn toward nostalgic fantasy presented an alternative narrative to the unpleasant present. Film historian Ann Lloyds, writing soon after the decade ended, noted the films of the 1970s celebrated "a refreshingly new and wide cultural experience, and an awareness of a new, young audience" (7). Directors, including Martin Scorsese and Steven Spielberg, fresh out of film school rather than the deceased studio system, transferred a grim and gritty America on the silver screen. Pictures such as *Taxi Driver* (1976) explored the hypocrisy of the American melting-pot and social cosmopolitan harmony As historian Bruce J. Schulman points out, *Fun and Dick and Jane* (1977) lampooned the title of the staid '50s educational primer as the titular pair robbed banks, gave the finger to the police, and defied the Establishment twenty-four frames per second (149).

Lucas denied his projects mirrored the same angst-ridden realities in the United States his contemporaries depicted. He told *American Film* magazine, "Rather than do some angry, socially-relevant film, I realized there was another relevance that is even more important—dreams and fantasies, getting children to believe there is more to life than garbage and killing and all that real stuff like stealing hubcaps" ("George Lucas Goes Far Out" 13).

The director added, "Young people today don't live a fantasy life anymore; not the way we did. All they've got is Kojak and Dirty Harry. All these kids are running around wanting to be killer cops because the films they see are movies of disasters and insecurity and realistic violence" ("The Making of Star Wars" 13). In an oft-repeated statement, he proclaimed, "The reason I made *Star Wars*—I want to give young people some sort of far away, excitement for their imaginations to run free." He echoed the promise of a previous generation left unfulfilled, specifically, a return to the energizing Kennedy years of a martyred president who wanted young people to ask what they could do for their country. Lucas wanted "to get beyond the basic stupidities of the moment and think about colonizing Venus and Mars" (Goddard 89). The *New York Times* also described the galaxy far, far away as having "their own landscapes, housing, vehicles, weapons, religion, politics—all of which are variations on the familiar." Not the least being "dark times have fallen upon the galactal empire once ruled, we are given to believe, from a kind of space-age Camelot" (Canby 66). Actress Carrie Fisher added to the yearning for a lost sense of outer-space wonder in hard times. She told Twentieth Century–Fox's publicity department, "I think people are getting jaded. It's sort of easy now to do all that fantasy stuff on the street without drawing too much attention to yourself. Which is a shame" (Dingilian).

In crafting his space opera Camelot, Lucas certainly borrowed the King Arthur tropes of errant knights, princesses needing rescue, and climatic battles. But he also embraced the earliest motifs from the science-fiction genre. Rather than reflect the "message" pictures of *The Day the Earth Stood Still* (1952), *Forbidden Planet* (1956), or converse with the booming number of Trekkies, Lucas evaded the adult-oriented fare and retreated into space rockets and monsters—the "kiddie" motifs Gene Roddenberry deliberately avoided (Shatner and Kreski 31).[1] Instead, Lucas cited the *Flash Gordon* serials from the 1930s "with all the trimmings" as inspiration (Wright 21).[2] He had attempted to film the franchise, but the costly copyrights made the project unfeasible. Still, the forty-year-old exploits of Buster Crabbe and Jean Rogers on screen and Alex Raymond's artwork in the funny pages had a built-in audience among sci-fi aficionados and underground film nerds. Actress Jean Rogers expressed surprise at the homage *Star Wars* paid to her work and, even though she admitted having not seen it two years after its release, she conceded, "I can't think of anybody who is not interested—you just gotta be" (Sullski 56–59). The film's pressbook encouraged exhibitors to sponsor a "space fantasy quiz" to entice patrons into the theaters. The first question asked: "Ming was the evil nemesis of this space adventurer" (Star Wars pressbook). Answer: Flash Gordon. "It was an old-fashioned Saturday matinee on a Thursday and as much fun as you remembered it," the *Los Angeles Times* sighed affectionately ("'Star Wars' Out of This World" B8).

Flash Gordon and his cohorts aptly played into the 1970s nostalgia. The comic strip hero had simple plots between absolute good and evil. Gordon's creator, Alex Raymond, drew inspiration from the Yellow Peril—a long-standing fear of "oriental" pollution from the east into the American mainstream (Said; Frayling). Like his contemporary Buck Rogers, the bleached-blond Crabbe protected an Anglo-American universe from various the merciless Ming, an Asiatic cousin to the "devil doctor" Fu Manchu (also making a comeback in the 1970s popular culture in kung fu films and comic books); both easily-identifiable villains who found Cold War analogues in commie-duped Korea, Vietnam, and, in underground cells, the United States.

Star Wars's binary forces of "light" and "dark" sides thus paralleled log-lived notions of American righteousness against an "Other." In 1941, before the twentieth century was halfway over, publishing powerhouse Henry Luce dubbed the last tenth of the millennium the "The American Century" because "it is for America and for America alone to determine whether a system, of free economic enterprise—an economic order compatible with freedom and progress—shall or shall not prevail in this century" (65). Luce's description of a world rotating on American ingenuity and economic/political prowess proved irresistible rhetoric. In the decades following, catchphrases such as Containment, the New Frontier, and the Axis of Evil highlighted an antithetical outside force threatening the "American Way"—a term hard to define, but as familiar as Mom and Apple Pie.

Unfortunately, by 1977, the American experiment seemed to have fizzled out. "The Establishment," "The System," and "The Man"—unpopular euphemisms for the bloated bureaucracy of the United States—suggested a government out-of-touch with the common citizen. At worse, conspiracy theorists proliferated; films such as *Chinatown* (1974) and *Winter Kills* (1979) speculated on the corrupt nature of venerated institutions riddled with shadow players engaging in clandestine activities. Conflicting reports over Nixon's erased Watergate tapes, the "magic bullet" and missing gunmen in the Kennedy assassination, and the daily activities of the Central Intelligence Agency increasingly blurred the lines between blind patriotism and paranoia (Uscinski and Parent).

In *Star Wars*, the Empire's fondness for gloomy colors and the anonymity of its uniformed soldiers contrasted sharply against American individualism. In 1981, President Ronald Reagan would successfully tap into this mindset with his slogan "Government is not the solution to our problems, government is the problem" in his first inaugural address. Despite Lucas's claims of not wanting to present a social commentary, his film had the same post–Watergate slant. The villains need no introduction: the music halts to allow Darth Vader's mechanical breaths to fill the theater as he observes the dead freedom fighters around him, prompting audiences to boo. Luke Skywalker's early scenes further hinted at the morally bankrupt state: he bemoans his application's forced withdraw from "the academy," but our hero soon embarks on a celebratory battle against a strict military indoctrination. Indeed, Grand Moff Tarkin (Peter Cushing, of whom one magazine noted "as moviegoers the world over will tell you, there's no actor quite so suited to on-screen villainy" ["Who's Who in Star Wars" 53]) elaborates how the unforeseen Emperor has liquidated the Senate, sweeping aside the remnants of the Old Republic. Not only would fear keep locals in line, but the demise of the legislative branch places a stranglehold on freedom of speech as Vader chokes non-believing dissenters. The scene added little to the plot in 1977 except to establish a political context of the Galactic Empire—tangible evidence of the totalitarianism the Allies struggled against. The Grand Moff's casual derision of the Force as an ancient religion of long vanished from sight further enhanced the bureaucratic state as cold, dark, and mechanical, all embodied by Darth Vader, the unworthy survivor of humanistic spirituality. But more important, audiences recognize the Empire as a *temporary* government sandwiched between the Old Republic and, by implication, a "New" Republic in the making. Like Reagan, who had hinted at the need to clean-up a problematic, bloated government, the Rebels would likewise restore the "good times" of yore. The Death Star's destruction and Vader's spinning into the horizon may have set the foundations for a sequel, but the concluding ceremony, with its glorious pomp and circumstance, hinted at the splendor around the corner after the Empire's presumed fall.

Indeed, the visual and audio cues referring to "Allies" batting "stormtrooper" establish a parallel linking the Emperor to the Third Reich—the latter lasting far short than its projected "thousand years." However, the nomenclature signified a collective American consciousness that had valorized World War II—the "Good War" fought by the "greatest generation" in contrast to the draft dodgers and televised atrocity reports in Vietnam (Ramsay 61–62). In 1972, Nathan Perlmutter, vice president of Brandeis University, argued the social and political angst caused by Americans "over there" in 'Nam besmirched the "trophies of national and personal freedom" from 1945. Troubled, Perlmutter mused over "the moral conviction and physical courage that marked the act of enlistment in World War II has [sic] its counterpart today," namely, "those who refuse to serve" (47). On the literary front, historian William Manchester's 1979 account of his experience in the Pacific theater, *Goodbye Darkness*, similarly betrayed the author's perception of an unfortunate decline of patriotic fervor among disillusioned youths and his own peers who turned into "docile old men who greedily follow Dow Jones averages" (Bodnar 50–51). Even though Lucas and baby boomers did not experience the Second World War, they grew up immersed in plastic G.I. Joes and recalled television fare such as *Twelve O'Clock High* as pop culture references linked to a "simpler" time.

Star Wars transferred the rhetoric of World War II-era to the seventies. Alongside the space opera visuals, composer John Williams's sweeping sound-track reinforced the revival of a triumphant golden age for aging veterans and movie aficionados. One fan magazine applauded Williams return to the use of a full orchestral score, which was "ignored by most of today's com-posers in favor of more atonal clashes mixed with seasoned realities more reflective of the times." Unlike the music utilized for the more post-apocalyptic futures of *Planet of the Apes*, *Star Wars* represented a musical restoration of "Royal" feeling. Nor was this accidental: the critic detected the influence of composer Erich Wolfgang Korngold, who scored many of Errol Flynn's swashbuckler epics in the 1930s and 1940s. "This is not surprising, considering that Flynn's movies usually took place around the throne of England" (Darrow 26–27). Another critic approved, "More Errol Flynn than John Wayne"—the cowboy Cold Warrior of the pro–Vietnam Green Berets paling beside the dashing Flynn's Sherwood Outlaw (Garris 32).

Longtime moviegoers linking Skywalker to Flynn under the umbrella of nostalgia was not lost on Hollywood. As Twentieth Century–Fox prepared to pull *Star Wars* from theaters to build up the anticipation for a sequel, the studio went all out to saturate the airwaves with a media blitz. The *Los Angeles Times* noted "*every* prime time" program would air tailor-made *Star Wars* commercials (comedic in tone for *Barney Miller*, action-oriented for *Black Sheep Squadron*) during the July 19–21, 1978, weekend. One studio publicist also commissioned a new *Star Wars* poster to appeal to the "Saturday matinee, popcorn-eating fun kind of thing reminiscent of the Errol Flynn days." He explained, "We haven't been all that successful with the over-35 crowd. Some see it as a picture just for young people, others feel science-fiction isn't their bag, many are turned off by the word 'war' or the long lines" (Rossman 1). By expanding the marketing campaign to evoke the "good old days," he tem-pered the negative connotations of the implied Vietnam "war" with the "good" conflict of the Errol Flynn days.[3]

Star Wars's throwback to Hollywood's "Golden Age" made for good ad copy. *New West* magazine observed Lucas employed a "liberal use of favorite situations from popular movies of the thirties, forties, and fifties," finding parallels from the droids' predecessors in *Metropolis* (1926) to Luke Skywalker ala James Doolittle from *Twenty Seconds over Tokyo* (1944). Lucas "cheerfully admits" he did: "these are scenes you've seen hundreds of times in dozens of movies" (Nolan 69). The film's successful blend of science-fiction and political nostalgia helped bring science-fiction into the mainstream as a celebration of American progress and technology. Just as Flash Gordon enjoyed a revival, Hollywood threw open its studio vaults to drum up ticket sales. Paramount slapped *The War of the Worlds* (1953) and *When Worlds Collide* (1951) together as a vintage double feature—both pictures feature apocalyptic scenarios from outer space threats and the human (American) response. The *Los Angeles Times* shrewdly noted, despite the changes in moviemaking, the older flicks "have a straight-clad simplicity, an unabashed squareness that seems impossible to achieve in these cynical, tongue-in-cheek times. But that's what nostalgia is all about and why, after more than 20 years, these pictures are such a pleasure" (Thomas 11).

Nostalgia and the re-affirmation of American heroics propelled *Star Wars*, leaving its competition in the space and memory lanes. Universal's *Smokey and the Bandit* came the closest to matching *Star Wars*'s box office, albeit ran behind by over $330 million ("Star Wars" online). The movie was a feel-good Burt Reynolds vehicle about beer smugglers who pick up a hitchhiking bride and run from a Southern sheriff and a teed-off groom. Unlike Lucas's space opera, Smokey stayed rooted in the anti-establishment terra firma of American law and disorder. The film earned a respectable North American gross, and Universal—which had produced *American Graffiti* and turned down *Star Wars*—implored audiences to come take a look: "What? You've never heard of *Smokey and the Bandit*?" one advertisement asked incredulously. The ad copy admitted, "More importantly, perhaps, *Smokey and the Bandit* would appear to be the second most popular American film of the year, topped only by *Star Wars*. Some attention should be paid." To explain why, the publicity department enthused, "It's the sort of movie that's talked about at cocktail parties," a line which might have discouraged the masses on Main Street (Universal Pictures 8).

At a Department Store Near You

Star Wars's success did not remain confined to the movies. The big screen translated to big bucks in a marketing blitz as the Empire stormed its way into department stores in the form of clothes, models, and assorted knickknacks dubbed as "collectibles." Action figures alone constituted "one of the most popular and largest grossing toy lines in the history of the toy industry," as one lawsuit from Twentieth Century–Fox alleged against an accused copyright pirate ("Star Wars Rage in Court" C6). The "Buycentennial" the previous year had exploited patriotic sentiment as a pro-capitalist boon for the sagging economy. "The $pirit of '76" included red-white-and-blue garbage bags and $30,000 silver replicas of the Mayflower. The *Los Angeles Times* excused such sentiment as "only following the energetic example of the old Yankee traders, who did a good job working the territory themselves." But naysayers argued such commercialization cheapened the Founding Fathers and "its meaning somehow destroyed" ("The $pirit of '76" C6).

The hoopla over *Star Wars* memorabilia extended beyond fanboys. In 1979, a culture of materialism and narcissism pervaded the United States (Latsch). This inward materialism as an expression of self-identity became a catharsis for a disenchanted populace dropping out and tuning out the mainstream. For science-fiction aficionados, long confined in the closet of geekdom, *Star Wars* made their hobby relevant in popular culture. The derogatory "monster magazine" had long "aimed at kids whose voices hadn't even started changing." Now, high-glossy 'zines, such as *Fangoria* and its sister publication *Starlog*, targeted adult consumers, including the publisher's "older, sophisticated friends," who could splurge on the $1.95 price tag. Although the magazine "does not tell you about the Mideast crisis"—OPEC was in the midst of its embargo—the editor offered a luxurious commodity defying the shrinking purchasing power of the dollar (O'Quinn 4). Lucasfilm would similarly target fans with disposable income: the Star Wars Fan Club offered its members inclusion in a group identity, privy to "exclusive content" such as *Bantha Tracks*, a newsletter which integrated fans in a close-knit community with Lucas's productions, *Star Wars* knickknacks, and each other.

The masses' indulgent cultural consumerism and personal identification with the film translated into a gold mine. Initially worried over the poor prospects of tie-ins, Lucas's signed a last-minute toy deal with manufacturer Kenner for a board game and a small line of action-figures, reduced in size to a cheap ($1.97 each) 3¾ inches to fit vehicles and playsets. When Kenner could not make the Christmas deadline, they offered an "empty box" with a voucher for four action-figures for ten dollars. The box, marketed as an "early bird certificate package," became an instant collectible, especially in the prized unopened "mint" condition. In 1978, over 26,106,500 figures sold; by the time the line folded in 1985, Kenner offered 111 individuals, not counting "variants" of different figures, with 250 million sold (Samsweet and Neumann 9–10). On the high-priced end, one magazine cataloged the expensive "life-size masks of the Wookie[sic], Darth Vader, See-Threepio, and a stormtrooper" available for forty dollars each (with an order form on the magazine's back page), before *Star Wars* marked its first birthday ("A Flash of Light" 23). On the black market, pirated versions the film netted $1500 per bootlegged copy ("'Star Wars' Is Hot Item" 6). *Newsweek* calculated Lucas's novelization sold over 3 million units, 1.3 million copies of the soundtrack made their way into homes, and even 130,000 "disco" versions tripped the light fantastic in its first week of sales (Schwazz 77–79), and, as Tom Zlabinger notes in his essay, music adaptations continue today. As one fan of Marvel's comic book series enthused, *Star Wars* "is a cultural experience" (Franklin).

Fractured Narrative: A Joyless Holiday Special

Star Wars capitalized on its mass appeal, but the cultural experience itself differed accordingly per viewer. The fracturing of the Cold War consensus during the counterculture and social movements of the late 1960s and 1970s colored the terms "good" and "evil" in shades of grey. Interpretations arose depending on the questions probed. Critics, encouraged by the "long time ago" title card's implication that the film was a documentary of sorts, re-evaluated the picture as social commentary through different lenses. However, *Star Wars*'s affirmation of a narrow mainstream American narrative generally excluded alternative interpretations.

Reading current hot-topics into *Star Wars* complicated the light versus dark narrative. When the issue turned towards civil rights, a melee emerged in newspaper letter columns. Critics Dorothy Gilliam and Raymond St. Jacques accused Lucas with populating his galaxy via segregation, with the "Dark Lord" as the notable exception. Gilliam complained, "Why, in the Force's name, must our film creators continue to perpetuate the terrible destructive ideals that put man against man, brother against brother and nation against nation?" (G1, G8; Jacques R2).[4] One cineaste excused the lack of minority characters *because* of the nostalgic angle: "*Star Wars* is billed as the film that combined the best of the movies we enjoyed in the 1950s" and, therefore, "it should come as no great surprise that *Star Wars* (maybe in the interest of authenticity?) has followed this practice of excluding blacks and other minorities" (Wall O36). In this light, the film's channeling the past made the film immune to contemporary social criticisms.

That *Star Wars* was susceptible to the 1970s malaise upset many fans who preferred the movie remain detached from the real world. One teenager, perhaps experiencing the backlash affirmative action generated (*Regents of the University of California v. Bakke* was one year in the future) insisted minority quotas should not extend to casting agents (MacIver O36). Another fan groused, "Since the movie makes no pretensions to social relevance and does not represent any future (let alone Earth's), it is unfortunate that *Star Wars*, offering itself as a space fantasy, should be maligned for its lack of 'relevance' and George Lucas attacked as 'worse than any racist'" (Keiser O32). Despite this fan's assertion, his roused anger signified the film *did* carry social significance. Nor did the issue die down. Another complained about the film's lack of female characters: Princess Leia attained her Senate seat "only because she's someone's daughter" (Buzzell O36). As Mara Wood's essay demonstrates, the debate over gender lines carried into the sequels, prequels, and the Expanded Universe—a fan-driven continuation of the storyline initiated in 1978 with Alan Dean Foster's *Splinter of the Mind's Eye*.[5] In the immediate years, however, *Star Wars* itself came under fire; the first filmic follow-up, the *Star Wars Holiday Special* (1978), represents a misstep when the infant saga veered off-course from its roots in American culture.

"When a movie succeeds, television usually isn't far behind," sighed a columnist for the *Washington Post* in 1978 (Laurent TV7). The newspaper referred to the then-upcoming television special for the Christmas holidays. Dubbed *Star Wars Holiday Special*, the ninety minute variety show revolved around Chewbacca's attending a "Life Day" celebration with his family on his home planet. To pad out the running time, the producers peppered the plot with recycled movie effects, staged musical numbers, a cartoon sequence, and what one scripter called "a soft core porno that would pass the censors" (Digiacomo). Audiences hungry for more adventures of Luke Skywalker ate up the offering and it came in second in the ratings; only *The Love Boat* outpaced the *Millennium Falcon*'s run in the Nielsen points. For Lucas, television allowed his saga to remain in the public consciousness while he planned *Star Wars II*.

The television special would not become the advance teaser Lucas had hoped for. Instead, it seemed like the Empire had striked back at the Good Guys, leaving the producers, actors, and fans with black public eyes. One fan magazine politely suggested the original director, David Acomba, left due to "artistic differences" (Millar 50). Decades later, Acomba recalled, "For me, there was no center. I couldn't seem to grasp it," concluding, "and it was hell" (Digiacomo). From a production standpoint, the limited special effects failed to operate correctly, the costumed actors suffocated in the extreme heat, and the heroic stars—Ford, Fisher, and Hamill—looked more comfortable in the Death Star's garbage compactor than among Chewbacca's relatives. The untranslated Wookiee speak left audiences in the dark for minutes at a time during dialogue sequences. An embarrassment since its original airing, the television show has remained locked in the studio vaults for nearly forty years.

Star Wars Holiday Special's banishment in popular memory reflected the original film's successful integration with American exceptionalism. The production snafus aside, the extravaganza misfired from a fundamental standpoint. If *Star Wars* had affirmed the timelessness of the American experience, anchoring the television show in the contexts of the 1970s tragically tied Lucas's universe to the dearth of American malaise. The guest stars, including Bea Arthur, Art Carney, and Harvey Korman, had gained famed for challenging the staid American status quo, not for celebrating its past. Arthur had wrapped up *Maude*, a spinoff from *All in the Family* about an outspoken liberal woman who supports abortion and civil rights; Carney had gained fame for portraying Ed Norton on *The Honeymooners*, a series about the unglamorous working-class in gritty New York; and Korman had starred in Mel Brooks' satiric *Blazing Saddles* (1974) and *High Anxiety* (1977) which had mocked American filmic tropes. Unlike the veteran actors Alec Guinness or Peter Cushing, *Star Wars Holiday Special* did nothing to immerse their celebrity cameos within a galaxy supposedly far away from American troubles. Instead, Arthur, Korman, and company brought Mos Eisley right into American living rooms as they've always done: lampooning American (and now, *Star Wars*) motifs with comedy sketches rather than transplant audiences into a theatrical space saga. The format itself was a misstep cementing the special's doom. The "variety" format was near extinction: Korman's *The Carol Burnett Show* had just concluded its last season after an eleven year run. While *Star Wars* had worked as an uplifting episode of nostalgia, its television follow-up was no *That's Entertainment!*. The "modern" musical segments failed to evoke the old song-and-dance spirit of early television, let alone the "Golden Age" of film; guest-starring band Jefferson Starship lacked the appeal of Flash Gordon's rockets or Busby Berkeley-esque choreography.

Trapped in the mire of the 1970s, *Star Wars Holiday Special* appropriately vanished alongside the 1970s. In 1994, fan magazine scribe John Bradley Snyder, looking back at aged bootlegged recordings, found it "silly" with its antiquated feel and now-culturally irrelevant guest stars—even Luke Skywalker's "worst haircut ever" screamed the '70s, cementing the chronological chains. The program "will forever be stuck in 1978, which is great nostalgia if you were there, great history if you weren't," he told fans, fewer of whom were there as time progressed (42, 44). Snyder missed the more important point: even fans in 1978 did not consider it "great nostalgia," as they soon whitewashed it from cultural memory and the filmic canon. Lucas himself seems content to let the television show whither in the receding past: unlike the continuously updated versions of his trilogy, *Star Wars Holiday Special*'s 1970s artifacts defy modernization in the twenty-first century. Indeed, in 1997, actor Mark Hamill, keeping tabs on the then-upcoming "special edition" re-releases, told fans: "They've actually redigitized my hairdo because that was the only thing that really dated the film" (Guttman 22). His 'do in *Star Wars Holiday Special* will have no such luck.

Fractured Narrative: Battling for Endor

After the television debacle, George Lucas re-directed *Star Wars* back to form with the superlative *The Empire Strikes Back* and *Return of the Jedi*. After the trilogy wrapped, the director again toyed with television. Lucasfilm teamed-up with Korty Films to produce *The Ewok Adventure* (re-titled *Caravans of Courage*), as a TV movie devoted to the cuddly warriors who won the land battle on Endor. Producers aimed the film at young children, rather than attempt another variety program for mass audiences. The plot: the teddy bear-like creatures help two stranded children rescue their parents from some oversized trolls who, frighteningly, prey on Ewoks. The older boy learns a lesson about responsibility and his kid sister looks cute for the cameras. Despite the project's limited scope, mixed reactions abounded in the press. "Star Wars it isn't," one critic scoffed. "Star Weary is more like it" (Margulies F12).

Anticipating hostility, director John Korty took steps to emphasize his Ewok adventure was *not* actually *Star Wars*. Like the ill-fated Christmas show—which he left unmentioned—the Ewoks clashed against the established filmic narrative. Although coming-of-age stories was an American story-telling trope, Lucas's saga had emphasized technological progress as a central component to storytelling, as discussed below. Indeed, for *Return of the Jedi* and its climatic battles, Industrial Light and Magic filmed a hi-tech orgy, bestowing the Rebels and Imperials with new spacecraft (A-wings, B-wings, TIE Interceptors) to excite moviegoers and toy manufacturers. From speeder bikes chases to "super" Star Destroyers, *Star Wars* morphed into a showcase for special effects and, through technology, eye-candy action sequences.

Stepping into this industrialized light and magic, John Korty almost apologized for his quiet Ewok venture. The film had theatrical bookings in foreign markets, but not in the U.S.A. He explained, "Otherwise people would regard it as the next *Star Wars* chapter even though it was shot on a budget that's a small factor of what a *Star Wars* movie costs." The lack of funds meant fewer special effects; therefore, Korty rationalized, "you can't compare *The Ewok Adventure* to the films. Even if it made a lot of money, the audiences would feel cheated" (Goldberg 27). He emphasized the movie "has very little violence, just a couple of fights toward the end" (Goldberg 28).[6] *Screen International* noted the theatrical poster played up to the "youth market with the young heroes [featured] much more prominently than the adults." Lucasfilm assured the Star Wars Fan Club the movie did not extend the completed trilogy. The studio issued a leaflet and promotional packaging "designed so as not to mislead anyone into thinking this was a *Star Wars* film," one reporter noted. The Ewok feature "was made as a separate film and in no way a follow-on" (McFarling F12).

Despite the director's warnings, audiences compared *Caravans of Courage* with their established *Star Wars* experience. Ironically, one critic thought the Ewoks "propagate[ed] the sort of [bland] '50s mentality that sent many people scurrying to science fiction in the first place." Lucas had repeatedly claimed *Star Wars* evoked a simplified past, but by the 1980s, this blend of nostalgia had become a battleground for minorities, feminists, and other activists who found the domestic containment of the period oppressive. As a gentle kid's show, the "fifties mentality" dampened Korty's story into a soggy mess: "Endor is a place where monsters have rubber teeth and the good guys are sweeter than Twinkies dipped in chocolate." The obvious moral lesson, in which the boy learns to appreciate his parents, rescues them, and becomes a man in the process, ran smack of a dull "suburban middle class" (Mitchell E1 and E4). In addition, the 1970s materialism that made *Star Wars* memorabilia a marketing bonanza now reflected a cynical attitude toward an over-saturated crass materialism. "Lucas's priority seemed to have changed," observed one writer. Her disillusioned seven-year-old agreed: "I bet they come out with a whole new bunch of Ewok toys now" (Margulies F12). The loss of *Star Wars*'s roots had morphed the mixture of Flash Gordon and *Triumph of the Will* to "Triumph of the Till."

Caravans of Courage did well enough to spawn a sequel—initially *Ewok II* or *Son of Ewok*, but finally settled for *The Battle for Endor*—and an animated series (Warwick Davis, who played Wicket, did not voice his animated counterpart). Answering some of the critics, and Korty's own admission, the film became more *Star Wars*-esque, as implied in the final combat-oriented title. Warwick Davis observed, "There's far more action in it, and it's a longer storyline—it's more like *Star Wars*. It has many battles and things like that" (Pirani 29). As if to amend for the first film's gentleness, the sequel embraces the dark side, including killing off the parents and the older boy at the hands of some skull-faced "Marauders." Despite the attempts to *Star Wars*-ize the

Ewoks, critics remained wary. "TV audiences may have found a few aspects of 'Ewoks' somewhat lacking," *Variety* confided. "They're used to stronger, more involved storylines, and not so used to submerging themselves in the kind of innocence required to enjoy the adventures of the teddy-bear like Ewoks" (Bier 75, 80). Audiences agreed: when compared to *Caravans of Courage*'s placing second among ninety programs a year earlier, *The Battle for Endor*'s Nielsen rating dropped twenty-five percent, ranking twelfth among thirty-two competitors (Bierbaum). Although Lucasfilm has included parts of the Ewok movies and *Star Wars Holiday Special* in their three-volume 2008 encyclopedia (Sansweet and Hidlago), Disney's "ultimate" 2015 volume streamlined the narrative, erasing the Expanded Universe entirely, killing off Chewbacca's Life Day, and rendering the battles over Endor pointless (Barr, Bray, Windham, and Wallace).

When Twentieth Century–Fox released *Star Wars II* as *The Empire Strikes Back* in 1980, Lucas tagged the numeral "Episode V" onto the opening introductory crawl. The original movie, re-released in 1981 as "Episode IV," signified the series was no longer about the "Adventure of Luke Skywalker" but instead encompassed a broader narrative: the numbering alone required prequels in the future. This retrofitting did not apply to the orphaned productions; despite an official DVD release of both Ewok movies, the definition of the "trilogy" necessitated an abandonment of the non-theatrical productions. In a larger cultural milieu, the films were never *Star Wars* in the first place.

Ray-Shielded America: Shooting Down the Evil Empire(s)

The Battle for Endor's action-packed story tried to undo the errors of *Caravans of Courage*, but the all-ages approach met with mixed success. *Star Wars* had already affirmed "the American Way" and relegated the Empire to short-lived aberration. The trilogy's increasing reliance on special effects thrilled audiences as they relegated the human coming-of-age stories as "kiddie fare." The movies' integration with American narrative themes of progress coincided with Ronald Reagan's presidency: the former actor's ascent to leader of the Free World presented the apex of Hollywoodized Cold War nationalism. Both the President and *Star Wars* centered technology as a bulwark of Americanism. When Reagan proposed his Strategic Defense Initiative, the ensuing "Star Wars" debate signified the controversy over the U.S's role in international politics and its own sense of history.

In March 1983 President Ronald Reagan publicized a plan to protect the Free World from Soviet nuclear attack (Desloge). Although Reagan did not give specifics for his Strategic Defense Initiative (SDI), naysayers dubbed the program "Star Wars."[7] In part, their derision stemmed from what they perceived as an anti-technological message showcased in the movie. "It was a day when you needed a Social Message like an overcoat," moviegoer Ellen Goodman asserted in 1977, settling in for an afternoon's escapism (Goodman A15). But before the show ended, she uncovered such a moral: a warning against technology. The United States had long ballyhooed science and engineering feats as keystones in promoting its superiority on the world stage: the twentieth century began with the U.S. flaunting its know-how in constructing the Panama Canal, but the Vietnam quagmire bogged down the American war machine (Adas chapters 4 and 6). Goodman deplored an overreliance on a mechanized computer age "run by people who are run by Social Security cards, automobiles." In blowing up the Death Star—by relying on mystic energy, no less—the "good technocrats win the day, and that's not a bad fantasy for the summer of '77" (Goodman A15). Another commentator saw the popular droids as mechanical Stepin Fetchits, who care more about their masters than themselves: "The American Dream come to life" with "a permanent, mechanical repairable and replaceable Mommy that has to love us above life itself, and we never even have to say thanks" (Schaaf G8).

Challengers to technological progress found homes in Earth Day celebrations and the nascent environmental movement. But as America started "going green," rejecting technology proved difficult. One close friend wrote to actor Alec Guinness and assured him the movie's "idea of magic overcoming science and technology is splendid." However, Guinness, who did not enjoy making the movie (he called the constantly-revised dialogue "rubbish ... and *none* of it makes my character clear or even bearable"), admitted the filmic technology impressively overwhelmed the human performances. He gave "full marks for the creation of two adorable mechanical objects": the droids stole the show (Read 507).[8]

Reagan capitalized on the nation's fascination of mechanical wonders in his outline for SDI. Later details involved establishing orbital platforms in space and counterparts on the ground to intercept Soviet missiles. Aside from the technological feasibility of such a project, critics detected a fallacy from an overreliance on technology. "A classic example of misplaced faith in the promise of technological salvation," scoffed Sanford Lakoff and Herbert F. York (vii). They lambasted the "hopeless and dangerous adolescent fantasy," and cited Reagan's own beliefs in myth-making: while in Hollywood, he had starred in *Murder in the Air* (1940), a near-wartime thriller about G-men safeguarding an anti-aircraft "inertia protector" from communists (7, 101). Equating the Iron Curtain with Darth Vader's iron fist, congressman Tom Downey (D-NY) declared, "The only thing the President did not tell us last night was that the Evil Empire was about to launch a Death Star against the United States" (FitzGerald 210). The Union of Concerned Scientists called SDI an attempt to recapture a pre-atomic past: "an illusion that science can re-create the world that disappeared when the nuclear bomb was born" (Union of Concerned Scientists 5). The combination of technological hope and ideological fear in the Cold War would "undermine national security, not enhance it" (151).

The naysayers' rhetoric did not produce desired results. Even as critics rejected the Empire's moon-sized space station as technology run amok, they had no qualms about the "good guys" using the same gear, albeit on a smaller scale.[9] Film scholar Will Brooker observes *Star Wars* presented a cold, mechanical Empire in contrast to Luke Skywalker's warm desert suns, but the final space battle—the actual "star wars"—emphasized a technological triumph of a nascent military regime. Brooker points out the Rebels adapt the precision and discipline of their enemies, including code names like "Red Squadron" (28). Despite the occasional human slang, the Rebel pilots beat the Empire's at their own game. Film scholars James Chapman and Nicholas J. Cull point out the Rebels's dehumanization: Leia had "no time for sorrows" as she prepared for her last stand. The princess's choosing not to mourn the death of her adopted planet spoke to the desire to escape from the "historical trauma so readily apparent to contemporaries in America at the moment of its making" (161). Nevertheless, by not shedding tears, the Rebels' lack of emotion renders the Alliance as mechanical as the Empire they abhor.

The science that created the ultimate battle station and also allowed for its defeat was not an accidental parallel to American conflicts in Southeast Asia. Despite the many references to World War II, from the "stormtroopers" to the special effects unit mimicking 1940s combat footage, Charles Lippencott, advertising and publicity director for Lucasfilm, admitted "most people have no realization" that the movie was "about a Vietnam situation" (Hoagland 111). Although Lucas later asserted his film contained an anti-'Nam message about freedom fighters battling a larger empire, such "dovish" readings contradicted the American national myth of ascending progress. Since *Star Wars* affirmed this nostalgic narrative, it also acknowledged a deeper cultural agreement with the "hawks" and the Domino Theory. Indeed, Lippencott flipped the roles to read the Galactic Empire as a stand-in for Communism. In the 1980s, Rambo would make a red-blooded living doing the same thing— the lone commando's trilogy struck box office gold by revisiting American "failures" and completing the job bungled by hapless desk-jockeys and bureaucrats (Shaw 275). What Sylvester Stallone accomplished in the jungles, Luke Skywalker did above the Death Star trench. For those too dazzled by the special effects, the *Washington Post* elaborated, pointing out the starfighter dog-fighting was "a harrowing re-creation of what flak suppression and bombing missions over North Vietnam must have been like for U.S. Air Force and Navy pilots" (Hoagland 111). The Death Star's destruction saved the Rebels on Yavin—literally the "Free World."

Unlike the American quagmire, this narrative concludes with a happy ending. In a grand ceremony, the princess welcomes the heroes, placing medals of honor around her suitors' necks, paralleling the more glamorous homecomings of Vietnam prisoners of war as a confirmation of their sacrifice on behalf of freedom. According to Brooker, the silent sequence exemplified the Rebel Alliance-turned-Empire, as the rebels adhere to strict decorum (aside from the principal actors winking and grinning throughout) in a staging reminiscent of Leni Riefenstahl's use of spectacle and pageantry on behalf of the Third Reich (79).[10] For Lucas and Luke, the triumph of the Force persevered through sheer power of will. For audiences, the glorified homecoming spoke to the media fanfare for returning Vietnam soldiers. As historians have documented, however, this symbolic homecoming belied a darker representation of 'Nam. The traumatized, disfigured, and dissenting veterans received less attention (Nicosia). Fittingly, the alien Chewbacca didn't receive a medal, either, much to fans' disconcertment (Gerrold 33).

The film's celebration of technology as Americanism coincided with Reagan's entrenched belief in technological prowess and the President refused to compromise on SDI. Some experts thought the Commander-in-Chief devised the project "as a bargaining chip, even if only as a bluff," to gain diplomatic concessions from the Soviets (Eisendrath, Goodman, and Marsh 137). But the President refused to budge on nuclear defense. For SDIers, the project continued an American tradition of technological advancement against overwhelming odds. This spirit, reflected in "can-do" or "know-how" phrasing, had long roots in celebrated inventors, ranging from Alexander Graham Bell, Henry Ford, Thomas Edison, to the Americanized Albert Einstein. One SDI enthusiast observed Reagan's "Star Wars" merely extended a military tradition from World War II's atomic fission. The final frontier represented "a 'second wind' in the critical home stretch of the Cold War" (Bascom 197–198). Edward Reiss argues *Star Wars* offered a cinematic counterargument to the Strangelove-ian imagery Cold War critics liked to invoke. Rather than portray the blustering incompetents in a War Room, *Star Wars* offered a combination of "distancing, sanitizing, beautifying, fictionalizing war" with its thrilling special effects and handsome heroes, which Reiss terms a "wargasmic" release for audiences (161, 164). One critic had attacked the President's program and the movie, stating Lucas's film depicted war "not so much as a human tragedy as a full-screen, live-action video game" (Mische 20). But for SDIers, the filmic connection made for great advertisement. Two weeks before Reagan announced his vision for nuclear defense, he spoke at Walt Disney Epcot Center, extolling the nascent video game culture as a signifier of technological ascent. "The air force believes these kids will be outstanding pilots should they fly our jets," he beamed. "The computerized radar screen in the cockpit is not unlike the computerized video screen. Watch a twelve-year-old take evasive action and score multiple hits, while playing *Space Invaders* and you will appreciate the skills of tomorrow's pilots" (357). *Star Wars*, as an intermediary between Buck Rogers-era ray guns and the modern role playing computer platforms, continued the glorification of war for children and adults. Noting the multi-billion-dollar industries marketing tech-war toys, video games, and movies, historian Howard Bruce Franklin contends, "To be against militarism and the reign of weapons is to be perceived by some as un-American" (4).

As a colorful piece of technological eye-candy, *Star Wars*'s impressive special effects made the space fantasy realistic, and, perhaps, scientifically feasible outside the celluloid reels. Various national surveys linked the words "Star Wars" with SDI, and although public fickleness flip-flopped in its support for Reagan's plan, the film maintained a close link with the president's space lasers and shields ("Public Attitudes"). Even the Roman Catholic Church expressed uncertainty: a council of bishops recommended continuing "Star Wars" research, but "defense spending as a whole" should not "absorb a morally disportionate percentage of the federal budget" (Witham 164). The bishops walked a fine line between national security and the potential to escalate an arms race. They ultimately decided to support "Star Wars," but not its deployment.

In public, Ronald Reagan and George Lucas deplored the name-association between their two franchises, believing the other cheapened their respective grandiose visions. Although the Reagan had referenced SDI as "a new hope" against an "Evil Empire," he claimed he wanted to distance himself from the movies (Desloge 60). During a news conference on January 9, 1985, when a reporter asked if the President would negotiate with the Soviets on "Star Wars," the Gipper griped, "I wish whoever coined that expression would take it back again" (Reagan 24). For his part, Lucas initiated a lawsuit to bar his trademarked term from appearing in SDI television commercials, but lost; U.S. District Judge Gerhard A. Gesell ruled the advertisement did not constitute a commercial use of Lucas's saga ("Move to Halt" A7).

Film scholar Peter Krämer sees Reagan's use of *Star Wars* as a way to balloon the military budget during a time of wide public apathy to nuclear weapons (67). In addition to the moral rhetoric invoked against the "Evil Empire," the media-savvy Great Communicator recognized *Star Wars*'s name recognition linked his and Lucas's respective works to a larger story of American progress. The Department of Defense did its part, issuing a full-color, high-glossy pamphlet *The Soviet Space Challenge*, which portrayed the United States as the perpetual underdog against the Soviet Union's "laser program" which "is larger than the U.S. efforts and involves over 10,000 scientists and engineers," costing an equivalent of nearly $1 billion a year (Department of Defense 15). The Soviet juggernaut obviously threatened American interests, since the U.S. is "more heavily dependent on space than any other nation" including "civil and commercial activities" alongside the "globally employed military forces in peace time, crisis, during contingency operations, and, most importantly, during conflict" (20). Given the obstinacy of cheating, lying, stalling Soviets and other wannabes "*from outlaw countries*," the United States needed a peace shield to protect the innocents. "President Reagan's Strategic Defense Initiative offers our *best hope of a safer world*," underlined a White House briefing, for both "our security and that of our allies would no longer rest on deterrence through the threat of mass annihilation" ("AVH-192" emphasis in original).

President Reagan continued to underscore the American experience as one based on technology. On the one hundredth anniversary of football legend Knute Rockne's birth, Reagan reminisced about his performance in a biopic of the acclaimed sportsman, and then tied it to the cosmos. "This Soviet progress is no threat to the United States as long as we do what is necessary to develop our own system," he asserted ("Remarks: Observance"). While preparing a draft for Reagan's radio presentation, Director of the Office of Public Liaison Mari Maseng urged speechwriter Tony Dolan to counter the anti–SDI rhetoric with patriotic banter. "A possible suggestion for inclusion in the radio address would be: 'When you hear self-anointed scientific "experts" claim that SDI "can't be done!"—don't believe them. Our country's history is that of one technological achievement after another!'" (10 July 1986). The President himself needed no such reminders. He signed his name to an op-ed piece which originally stated, "To those who counsel us to bargain away the Strategic Defense Initiative, I say they have no vision." Deciding to punch up the language, speechwriters added a flourishing rewrite: "To those who counsel us to give up before we've begun on the Strategic Defense Initiative, I say, you lack vision, courage, and faith in American ingenuity. To those who look at this initiative as a chip to deal away in negotiation, I say, you are playing free and easy with out children's future." Therefore, "SDI is not just for America—it is for all people and for all time" ("OPED Piece").

As public support for SDI waxed and waned, Reagan relied upon the shared legacy of American know-how as a first line of appeal. "It seems as if every month, scientists are finding answers to problems that critics called insoluble a month before. In the age of technology, that good old American know-how is a force for progress, the likes of which this world has never seen," another speech read ("Taping: Coalition for SDI").[11] Six months later, Reagan reiterated the same point: "In SDI, as elsewhere, we've put technology that almost boggles the mind to work ... the relationship between freedom and human progress has never been more apparent" ("Remarks by the President at a Briefing on the Strategic Defense Initiative"). Maseng informed speechwriters, "Opponents of SDI lack the vision necessary to deal with the long-term nuclear arms race and the de-nuclearization of the US-Soviet relationship. The President's proposal is in fact visionary as it attempts to bring about a much needed change in the course of superpower history" (5 Aug. 1986). On SDI's fifth anniversary, Reagan again blasted those he thought lacked such vision. "It's sometimes easier to bring into being new technology than it is to bring about new thinking on some subjects. Breakthroughs in physics are sometimes easier than breakthroughs in psyches." For Reagan, all he could do was "make sure that technology becomes the ally and protector of peace—that we build better shields rather than sharper and more deadly swords" (Institute for Foreign Policy Analysis).

The American narrative, backed by the weight of history and the glamour of moviemaking, coalesced into a project that continued to find support. In the 1990s, National Missile Defense (NMD) circled as a hot topic among scientists, politicians, and the public. Despite the name-change from SDI, the link to *Star Wars* remained prevalent in rhetoric. In 1999, just as George Lucas's first prequel hit theaters, Congressman Lloyd Doggett (D–TX) lambasted NMD, declaring, "As we speak folks are lined up around the block across America to see the new *Star Wars* movie. Just like the original movie, this bill puts a tractor beam in the Capitol Dome and aims it right at the wallets of the American taxpayer to support this defective system" (Mitchell 251). Like the rise of Senator Palpatine, the phantom menace of SDI refused to dissipate in the public consciousness. As James Abrahamson, the director for the Strategic Defensive Initiative Organization, proclaimed during a 1985 interview, "I say that the Force is indeed with us" (Mitchell 103, 61n).

A Next Generation

In 1978, President Jimmy Carter described the nation's State of the Culture as "healthy and vigorous. In music, art, literature, social customs, theater, and television, we are a strong country, a vital and dynamic country—and so will we remain." Filmic fanfare such as *Star Wars* and *Close Encounters of the Third Kind* "demonstrate once again we need not lean on foreign imports and that Hollywood remains, as it has always has been, proud and free" (Rosenblatt A21). As "loud applause" filled the room, Carter temporarily basked in his own mythmaking.

But the clapping soon died. Like oil imports, Hollywood relied on foreign entanglements and big-budget blockbusters to carry profits as ticket sales continued to decline. American malaise had set in, which would soon sweep Carter from office. The dearth of the nation would lead one critic to back-handedly praise *Star Wars*'s simplemindedness: "*Star Wars* hasn't an idea in its head" and had "no statements on the past or future or anything" (Hemniger). Such allegories, he felt, should remain the purview of dense science-fiction prose ala Isaac Asimov, not the technological eye-candy of the silver screen.

But the critic was wrong. *Star Wars* brought the past into the present for the future. The first film originally confirmed the revamped mythic tradition of a hero's journey, and also re-affirmed the United States' narrative concerning American exceptionalism, even for fans living in Moscow sporting "I'm not a tourist, I live here" sweatshirts (Kline B1). Given the uncertain times facing the nation, nostalgia became an easy escape valve. "It's hard to escape the feeling of facing backwards these days," the *Washington Post* sighed. "Maybe because sometimes it's easier to look over one's shoulder than straight ahead…. Lucas isn't kidding about the 'long time ago'" (Kriegsman E1).

Consumers not only looked over their shoulders, but at the Jedi-related collectibles on the shelves. Twentieth Century–Fox publicity director Bob Dingilian described the motion picture as a sales tool—the most "magnificent toy ever invented for grown men to play with and express their fantasies, to project their nightmares and dreams and to indulge their whims and secret desires." *Star Wars* "is a world people on this earth have never been to, but it's a world they may have encountered when years ago they dreamed about running away and having adventures that no one else ever had" (Dingilian). Director George Lucas originally targeted these youngsters, noting he aimed *American Graffiti* at teenagers of driving age and *Star Wars* to fourteen-year-olds "and maybe even younger than that" ("George Lucas Goes Far Out" 10).

But as time progressed, Lucas's saga narrowed its affirmation of Americanism. Its increasingly sophisticated action scenes and emphasis on technological violence echoed the vigorous rhetoric Reagan championed as a cultural catharsis for the "Vietnam Syndrome" and, as Erin C. Callahan notes in her essay, the films' gradual softening of "hard" men like Han Solo. As

Karin Hilck's and Mara Wood's essays note, the masculine-orientation directly impacted the trilogy's sole substantive heroine. Director Richard Marquand, who helmed *Return of the Jedi*, felt audiences had enough of the "delicate, clean princess with underarm deodorant and everything's beautiful in my life" depiction of Princess Leia. Her stints as a slave for Jabba the Hutt and an idol for Ewoks reflected what Marquand called, "for a lack of a better word, feminine." Although wary of offending the women's movement, the director "was very anxious that she [Leia] should finally unfold and to a certain extent demonstrate her femininity, her womanhood, which is something that coincided exactly with what Carrie Fisher wanted herself; she felt ready for that" (Tuchman).

Princess Leia's warming her frosty-Hoth persona passed muster in the Age of Reagan. The reheated Cold War rhetoric aptly tied the Strategic Defense Initiative and *Star Wars* through Americana. In contrast, the botched *Star Wars Holiday Special* flopped not only because of faulty production techniques, but its close association with the troublesome 1970s stripped the film of its charmed timelessness. The Ewok movies aimed at younger kids—the fourteen-year-olds and those "younger than that"—but, by then, Lucasfilm's attempt to cater to pre-teen children created a low-tech, low-budget production no longer considered *Star Wars* among the fans. As for President Carter's luckless presidency, the state of *Star Wars* seemed healthier than his administration. One magazines told Lucas when "the President of the United States pouted because his daughter Amy had a birthday party and invited her friends to see *Star Wars* and he didn't get an invitation, you know you've done something right" (Ackerman 50). Plagued by malaise, the President readily succumbed to a chronicle of a more glamorous and uplifting American experience.

The author would like to thank Jenny Romero and the staff at the Margaret Herrick Library, Academy of Motion Picture Arts and Sciences; Ned Comstock and the staff at the Cinematic Arts Library at the University of Southern California; Ray Wilson and the staff at the Ronald Reagan Presidential Library; and Robert Chin for the use of his vintage science-fiction magazines.

Notes

1. Series designer Matt Jeffries accumulated Buck Rogers-style rocket ship imagery and declared, "There, that's what I will *not* do."
2. Lucas seldom mentioned the various space-themed "cops and robbers" television series in the 1940s and 1950s. *Captain Video*; *Tom Corbett, Space Cadet*; and, later, *Lost in Space*, would seem more relevant for nostalgia purposes to aging baby boomers in

the late 1970s than the Flash Gordon serials, although the television shows lack the larger name-recognition of the older spacemen.

3. Hollywood appealed to the "over-35" crowd with a revival of its "Golden Age." *That's Entertainment!* (1974), MGM's sweeping valentine to its history, pandered to nostalgic good times. The compilation of film clips proved popular enough to inspire several sequels. Other films cashed in the trend: the biopics *Gable and Lombard* (1976), *W.C. Fields and Me* (1976), and *Won Ton Ton, the Dog Who Saved Hollywood* (1976) all cashed in on the collective memory of the industry's sunnier days.

4. Some critics compared *Star Wars* to *Logan's Run* (1976), which had a youthful, largely white cast, but the film deliberately signified a dystopia through its lack of ethnic minorities.

5. Foster recalled Lucasfilm intended the book to become a low-budget film sequel if *Star Wars* bombed at the box office.

6. He also noted the small budget prohibited recreating the Ewok village in the trees, as shown for *Return of the Jedi*. Instead, Wicket and company lived on the ground floor.

7. Critics were not the first to dub a potential defense system "Star Wars." As early as 1977, Lt. Colonel Robert M. Bowman wrote a report to the Pentagon mentioning the possibilities of x-ray lasers for medical and emergency usage. Bowman conceptualized "laser battlestations" and "new capabilities [that] come right out of *Star Wars*. They probably will never have any defensive capability but they have awesome offensive capabilities." Should both sides of the Iron Curtain obtain such weapons, Bowman thought a stand-off "would probably mean inevitable nuclear war" (Mitchell 50).

8. Guinness appeared in the sequels because "it would have been mean of me to refuse" and not out of sentiment for "the Force or any phony philosophy." He characterized his "couple of dreary days" in the "horrible *Star Wars III*" as a "rotten dull little bit."

9. Senator Edward Kennedy made the first connection, attacking Reagan for "misleading Red Scare tactics and reckless Star Wars schemes" (Krämer 65).

10. According to Brooker, Lucas denied association between the award ceremony in *Star Wars* and *Triumph of the Will*. Lucas claimed he was not aware of Riefenstahl's work, despite his many references for film history.

11. The dinner was cancelled and this speech was never read.

Works Cited

Ackerman, Forrest. "George Lucas, Our Hero." *Famous Monsters Star Wars Spectacular '77* (1977): 50. Print.

Adas, Michael. *Dominance by Design: Technological Imperatives and America's Civilizing Mission.* Cambridge: Belknap Press, 2009. Print.

"AVH-192: 4/21/1988-remarks by President, White House Issue Brief: SDI-The Soviet Space Challenge." Box 30. White House Office of Correspondence: Records Series II. Ronald Reagan Presidential Library. Print.

Bascom, Donald R. *The Origins of SDI, 1944–1983.* Lawrence: University Press of Kansas, 1997. Print.

"Bicentennial Celebration: Charges of Commercialism are Expected to Proliferate as 1976 Approaches." *New York Times* 11 Mar. 1974: 17. Print.

Bier. "Local TV Reviews." *Weekly Variety* 4 Dec. 1985: 75, 80. Print.

Bierbaum, Tom. "CBS Edges NBC For Top Spot in Ratings." *Daily Variety* 27 Nov. 1985: 8. Print.

Bodnar, John. *The "Good War" in American Memory.* Baltimore: Johns Hopkins University Press, 2010. Print.

Booker, M. Keith. *Alternate Americas: Science Fiction Film and American Culture.* Westport, CT: Praeger, 2006. Print.

Barr, Tricia, Adam Bray, Ryder Windham, and Daniel Wallace. *Ultimate Star Wars.* New York: DK Publishing, 2015. Print.

Brooker, Will. *Star Wars.* New York: Palgrave Macmillan, 2009. Print.

Buzzell, Linda. Letter. "More 'Star Wars' Skirmishes." *Los Angeles Times* 31 July 1977: O36. Print.

Canby, Vincent. "'Star Wars' a Trip to a Far Galaxy That's Fun and Funny." *New York Times* 26 May 1977: 66. Print.

Chapman, James, and Nicholas J. Cull. *Projecting Tomorrow: Science Fiction and Popular Cinema.* London: I.B. Tauris, 2013. Print.

Darrow, Geoffrey. "The Music of the Stars." *Space Fantasy Film Classics* 1 (1977): 26–27. Print.

Department of Defense. *The Soviet Space Challenge.* Washington, D.C.: U.S. Government Printing Office, 1987. Print.

Desloge, Nick. "*Star Wars*: An Exhibition in Cold War Politics." *Sex, Politics, and Religion in* Star Wars: *An Anthology.* Eds. Douglas Brode and Leaj Dyneka. Lanham, MD: Scarecrow Press, 2012. 55–62. Print.

Digiacomo, Frank. "The Han Solo Comedy Hour!" *Vanity Fair* Dec. 2008. Web. 15 Mar. 2015.

Dingilian, Bob. "Carrie Fisher Loves Acting, Like Fantasy of Star Wars." N.d. "Star Wars [20thCentury-Fox, 1977]," Core Collection Files. Margaret Herrick Library, Academy of Motion Picture Arts and Sciences. Microfiche.

_____. Production Notes. N.d. "Star Wars [20th Century-Fox 1977]," Core Collection Files, Margaret Herrick Library, Academy of Motion Picture Arts and Sciences. Microfiche.

Eisendrath, Craig, Melvin A. Goodman, and Gerald E. Marsh. *The Phantom Defense: America's Pursuit of the Star Wars Illusion.* Westport, CT: Praeger, 2001. Print.

FitzGerald, Frances. *Way Out There in the Blue: Reagan, Star Wars and the End of the Cold War.* New York: Simon & Shuster, 2000. Print.

"A Flash of Light: *Star Wars*—The Sudden Popularity of Science Fantasy." *Science Fantasy Film Classics* 1 (1977): 18–23. Print.

Franklin, Elbert B. Letter, *Star Wars* 8 (Feb. 1978). New York: Marvel Comics. Print.

Franklin, Howard Bruce. *War Stars: The Superweapon and the American Imagination.* New York: Oxford University Press, 2008. Print.

Frayling, Christopher. *The Yellow Peril: Dr. Fu Manchu and the Rise of Chinaphobia.* London: Thames & Hudson, 2014. Print.

Garris, Mick. "John Williams and the Music of Star Wars," *Science Fiction Horror and Fantasy* 1 (1977): 32–33. Print.

"George Lucas Goes Far Out." *American Film: Journal of the Film and Television Arts* 206. "Star Wars [20th Century-Fox 1977]," Core Collection Files. Margaret Herrick Library, Academy of Motion Picture Arts and Sciences. Microfiche.

Gerrold, David. "State of the Art." *Starlog* Feb. 1979: 32–33. Print.

Gilliam, Dorothy. "The Black Heavies." *Washington Post* 11 Sept. 1977: G1, G8. Print.

Goddard, Donald. "From 'American Graffiti' to Outer Space." *New York Times* 12 Sept. 1976: 89. Print.

Goldberg, Lee. "John Korty: Director of the Ewok Adventure." *Starlog* Jan. 1982: 27–29. Print.

Goodman, Ellen. "A Star Wars Fantasy Fulfillment." *Washington Post* 30 July 1977: A15. Print.

Guttman, Monika. "Where Are They Now?" Star Wars: *The Official 20th Anniversary Commemorative Magazine.* New York: Topps Co., 1997: 22–34. Print.

Hernniger, Daniel. "Star Wars: Androids, Laughs, and Dazzle." N.d. "Star Wars" clipping file. Cinematic Arts Library, University of Southern California. Print.

Hoagland, Jim. "The Politics of 'Star Wars.'" *Washington Post* 11 Dec. 1977: 111. Print.

Institute for Foreign Policy Analysis, folder "SDI [1 of 5] (Gilden)(Hayes), March 14, 1988." Box 386. Speechwriting, White House Offices of: Speech Drafts, 1981–1989. Ronald Reagan Presidential Library. Print.

Keiser, Larry. Letter. "The Blacklash Over 'Star Wars.'" *Los Angeles Times* 24 July 1977: O32. Print.

Kline, Kevin. "'Star Wars' in Moscow." *Washington Post* 22 Nov. 1977: B1. Print.

Krämer, Peter. "Fighting the Evil Empire." *Sex, Politics, and Religion in* Star Wars: *An Anthology*. Eds. Douglas Brode and Leaj Dyneka. Lanham, MD: Scarecrow Press, 2012. 63–76.

Kriegsman, Alan M. "Escaping the Present." *Washington Post* 19 June 1977: E1. Print.

Lakoff, Sandford A. *A Shield in Space? Technology, Politics, and the Strategic Defense Initiative*. Berkley: University of California Press, 1989. Print.

Latsch, Christopher. *The Culture of Narcissism: American Life in an Age of Diminishing Expectations*. New York: W.W. Norton, 1979. Print.

Laurent, Lawrence. "O'Brien: 'Basketball Ratings will Go Up.'" *Washington Post* 12 Nov. 1978: TV7. Print.

Lloyd, Ann, ed. *Movies of the Seventies*. London: Orbis, 1984. Print.

Luce, Henry. "The American Century." *Life* 17 Feb. 1941: 65. Print.

Lucas, George. *Star Wars: From the Adventures of Luke Skywalker*. New York: Del Rey Books, 1976. Print.

MacIver, Bill. Letter. "More 'Star Wars' Skirmishes." *Los Angeles Times* 31 July 1977: O36. Print.

"The Making of *Star Wars*." *Screen Superstar* 8 (1977): 13–20. Print

Margulies, Lee. "Ewoks Take Spotlight in Own Movie." *Los Angeles Times* 24 Nov. 1984: F12. Print.

Maseng, Mari. Memorandum to Tony Dolan. August 5, 1986. folder "Dropby Briefing on SDI [2 of 3]," Box 285. Speechwriting, White House Offices of: Speech Drafts, 1981–1989. Ronald Reagan Presidential Library. Print.

_____. Memorandum to Tony Dolan. July 10, 1986. folder "RR Radio Address on SDI, 12 Jul. 1986." Series IV: Events. Box 37. Max Green Files. Ronald Reagan Presidential Library. Print.

McFarling, Tim. "20th Fox to Captialise on 'Star Wars' with 'Caravan.'" *Screen International* 15 Dec. 1984, "Caravan of Courage [Lucasfilm, 1984]." Core Collection Files, Maragret Herrick Library, Academy of Motion Picture Arts and Sciences. Print.

Millar, Natalie. "'Star Wars' Invades TV." *Starlog* Feb. 1979: 50. Print.

Mische, Patricia M. *Star Wars and the Stake of Our Souls*. Minneapolis: Oakgrove Press, 1985. Print.

Mitchell, Elvis. "Lucas' Ewoks Ready to March into Your Home." *Los Angeles Herald-Examiner* 25 Nov. 1984, E1 and E4. Print.

Mitchell, Gordon R. *Strategic Deception*. East Lansing: Michigan State University Press, 2000. Print.

"Move to Halt Use of 'Star Wars' In Defense Plan Ads Blocked." *Los Angeles Times* 14 Nov. 1985: A7. Print.

Nicosia, Gerald. *Home to War: A History of the Vietnam Veterans' Movement*. New York: Crown, 2001. Print.

Nolan, Tom. "The Way They Were." *New West* 20 June 1977: 69. Print.

"OPED Piece: SDI (Myer/Cane), 15 Mar. 1985." Folder "Magazine Publishers (3/14/1985) 2 of 2. Quebec City." Box 194. Speechwriting, White House Offices of: Speech Drafts, 1981–1989. Ronald Reagan Presidential Library. Print.

O'Quinn, Kerry. "Standing Alone." *Fangoria* 5 (1980): 4. Print.

Perlmutter, Nathan. "War Is Getting a Bad Name." *Washington Post* 18 Apr. 1972: 47. Print.

Perlstein, Rick. *The Invisible Bridge: The Fall of Nixon and Rise of Reagan.* New York: Simon & Schuster, 2014. Print.

Pirani, Adam. "Warwick Davis—Return of the Ewok." *Starlog* Dec. 1985: 29–31. Print.

"Public Attitudes Towards [*sic*] Arms Control and the Strategic Defense Initiative Prepared for the White House," 20 Jan. 1987 (1)-(3). Box 35. David Chew Files, Ronald Reagan Presidential Library.

Ramsay, Debra. *American Media and the Memory of World War II.* New York: Rutledge, 2015. Print.

Read, Piers Paul. *Alec Guinness: The Authorised Biography.* New York: Simon & Schuster, 2005. Print.

Reagan, Ronald. *Public Papers of the Presidents of the United States: Ronald Reagan, 1983, Book 1—January 1 to July 1, 1983.* Washington, D.C.: U.S. Government Printing Office, 1984. Print.

_____. *Public Papers of the Presidents of the United States: Ronald Reagan: 1985 Book 1–January 1 to June 28, 1985.* Washington, D.C.: U.S. Government Printing Office, 1988. Print.

Reiss, Edward. *The Strategic Defense Initiative.* Cambridge: Cambridge University Press, 1992. Print.

"Remarks: Observance of Knute Rockne's 100th Birthday, Notre Dame University, South Bend, IN, March 9, 1983." Folder 3. Box 63. Anthony "Tony" R. Dolan Files, Ronald Reagan Presidential Library. Print.

"Remarks by the President at a Briefing on the Strategic Defense Initiative, August 6, 1986. Drop-by Briefing on SDI [1 of 3]." Box 285. Speechwriting, White House Offices of: Speech Drafts, 1981–1989. Ronald Reagan Presidential Library. Print.

Rosenblatt, Roger. "The State-of-the-Culture Address." *Washington Post* 13 Feb. 1978: A21. Print.

Rossman, Martin. "Recall the 'Star Wars' Hype? You Ain't Seen Nothin' Yet." *Los Angeles Times* 18 June 1978: 1. Print.

Said, Edward. *Orientalism.* New York: Vintage, 1979. Print.

St. Jacques, Raymond. Letter. "Correspondence." *Los Angeles Times* 17 July 1977: R2. Print.

Sarnsweet, Stephen J., and Anne Neumann. *Star Wars.* New York: Abrams, 2010. Print.

Sansweet, Stephen J., Pablo Hidalgo, Bob Vitas, and Daniel Wallace. *The Complete Star Wars Encyclopedia.* New York: Lucas Books, 2008.

Schaaf, Miv. "'Star Wars': Era of Uncle Robotism." *Los Angeles Times* 3 Oct. 1979: G8. Print.

Schulmann, Bruce J. *The Seventies: The Great Shifts in American Culture, Society, and Politics.* New York: Da Capo Press, 2002. Print.

Schwazz, Tony. "Sons of *Star Wars.*" *Newsweek* 29 Aug. 1977: 77–79. Print.

Shatner, William, and Chris Kreski. *Star Trek Memories.* New York: HarperCollins, 1993. Print.

Shaw, Tony. *Hollywood's Cold War.* Amherst: University of Massachusetts Press, 2007. Print.

Snyder, John Bradley. "The Star Wars Holiday Special." *Star Wars Insider* 23 (1994): 42–44. Print.

"The $pirit of '76." *Los Angeles Times* 13 Nov. 1975: C6. Print.

"Star Wars." *Boxoffice.* Web. 19 Apr. 2015.

"'Star Wars' Is Hot Item On Black Market, Too." *Wall Street Journal* 9 Sept. 1977: 6. Print.

"'Star Wars' Out of This World." *The Los Angeles Times.* 4 Jun. 1977: B8. Print.

Star Wars pressbook, "Star Wars [20th Century-Fox, 1977]," Core Collection Files, Margaret Herrick Library, Academy of Motion Picture Arts and Sciences. Microfiche.

"Star Wars Rage in Court Over 'Stars' of Smash Movie Hit." *Los Angeles Times* 18 Jun. 1978: C6. Print.

Sullski, Jim. "An Exclusive Interview with Jean Rogers: The Girl who was Dale Arden." *Fantastic Films* 2:2. Jun. 1979: 56–59. Print.

"Taping: Coalition for SDI (Gilder)(Timmons)(Cancelled) February 28,1986." Box 258. Speechwriting, White House Offices of: Speech Drafts, 1981–1989. Ronald Reagan Presidential Library. Print.

Thomas, Kevin. "The Star Wars of an Earlier Era." *Los Angeles Times* 7 Sept. 1977: 11. Print.

Tuchman, Mitch. Interview with Richard Marquand, December 12, 1982; 14 Dec 1982. f. 43. Mitch Tuchman interview transcripts, Margaret Herrick Library. Academy of Motion Picture Arts and Sciences. Print.

Union of Concerned Scientists. *The Fallacy of Star Wars*. New York: Vintage, 1984. Print.

Universal Pictures. Advertisement. *Daily Variety* 3 Jan. 1978: 8–9. Print.

Uscinski, Joseph E., and Joseph M. Parent. *American Conspiracy Theories*. Oxford: Oxford University Press, 2014. Print.

Wall, Thomas Edward. Letter. "More 'Star Wars' Skirmishes." *Los Angeles Times* 31 July 1977: O36. Print.

"Who's Who in Star Wars." *Screen Superstar* 8 (1977): 53–62. Print.

Witham, Larry, "Catholic Bishops Add SDI to List of Immoral Weapons." *Washington Times* 27 June 1988: 164. Print.

Wright, Douglas. "The People who Made *Star Wars*." *Science Fiction Horror and Fantasy* 1 (1977): 21–32. Print.

An Elegant Weapon for a More Civilized Age

Star Wars, *Public Radio and Middlebrow Cold War Culture*

JESSICA K. BRANDT

In the June 2011 issue of *GQ*, Devin Friedman branded the cultural phenomenon of "middlebrow" as "the taste that dare not speak its name." There is a wealth of cultural baggage behind that term, to be sure. Earlier that same year, in *The New Yorker*, Macy Halford felt moved to clarify her usage of the word in a previous column, assuring her readers she meant it in "a positive sense." Even more recently, film critic A. O. Scott deemed the middlebrow "a semantic shoe that belongs on someone else's foot." In a colorful history dating back to the 1920s, literati have struggled to define the vast cultural terrain between high and low, and to understand (and sometimes apologize for) its appeal. It is no great surprise that today's twitterati should do the same. For nearly a hundred years writers and cultural critics have staked their claim on a position somewhere in the continuum of brows. But in the early 1980s, the rocky ground in the middle became a fertile field for the exposition of Cold War fears and aspirations. Middlebrow cultural affinities served to soothe anxieties, and to nurture the optimism that had nearly died with Vietnam. Perhaps above all they filled the gap of what Tom Engelhardt described as "storylessness": an insecurity born of a time when victory was no longer certain and ultimate destruction seemed all too possible (266).

Engelhardt draws particular attention to the *Star Wars* films as an attempt to combat the era of storylessness. It takes no great analytic finesse to mark the *Star Wars* film franchise as an emblem of the middlebrow. It had broad appeal, attempted to resurrect a popular genre that had fallen out of favor, and capitalized on its own success in every possible way, all aspects of middlebrow behavior. One specific episode in the growth of the *Star Wars* universe, however, stands as an allegory of the struggle for cultural value in a time of uncertainty. In 1979, George Lucas made an unexpected move for a successful Hollywood producer: he offered the rights to the *Star Wars* story to KUSC-FM, the National Public Radio (NPR) affiliate station at his alma mater, the University of Southern California.[1] Public radio, it would seem, was the elegant weapon that would hearken back to a more civilized age. And, in the process, would redeem *Star Wars* from the cultural taint of commercial success. The radio production would employ a nostalgic throwback medium to emphasize high-minded, anti-capitalist ideals. Just as Luke was instructed to let go and "see" the drone in his lightsaber training, the listening audience would be entrusted to do the work of "seeing" an expanded *Star Wars* by engaging in imagination and fantasy. At the same time, Lucas hoped to provide the audience with proof of the high artistic value of his space opera, and of the cultural value of public radio in the face of a conservative assault.

A Question of Brows

Let us first take a closer look at what it means, or meant, to be middlebrow in the twentieth century. All later critics of middlebrow owe a debt of eloquent gratitude to Virginia Woolf. She penned a scathing letter, which she never sent, to *New Statesman* in 1932 (it was, in fact, a response to a review of one of her books). In a screed that establishes her own highbrow bona fides, Woolf marshals all of her biting rhetorical skills. She establishes the real cultural evil in British society is neither the haughty highbrow, nor the grungy lowbrow, rather, it is the "pernicious pest who comes between" (184). It is precisely their in-between-ness she found so insufferable. While the high and the low each pursue life with a certain pure purpose, the former the pursuit of an idea and the latter the pursuit of a living, the middle do not pursue much of anything, other than money and power. She relishes the natural bond between highbrows and lowbrows, who, she says, need and respect each other. Those in the middle are pretenders, claiming to be the lowbrows' friend yet wanting desperately to have a seat at the highbrows' table. They are not particularly good at anything, but they are not particularly bad at anything, either. They are eternally, hopelessly "betwixt and between" (180). Woolf accordingly deems the BBC the "Betwixt and Between Company," since, as a government broadcasting outlet, it must operate with the middlebrows' interests at heart (184). Thus, from the very beginning, we have a connection between public broadcasting and the supposed cultural blight of the middlebrow.

When the question of brows is taken up by American critics, it is with much the same disdain for the middle, but also with greater nuance. This is born of the fact that the United States, particularly in the twentieth century, is a nation of the middle. Lacking the kind of rigid class system that Great Britain has struggled with for centuries, Americans tend to see themselves as "middle class," whether they are or not. The post-war years saw an explosive growth in the middle class, as wages grew, working conditions improved, and higher education became more available. While middle class is not synonymous with middlebrow, there is a certain symbiotic relationship between the two. We then see this relationship teased out by American cultural critics. The first prominent example was Russell Lynes, whose "Highbrow, Lowbrow, Middlebrow" essay for *Harper's* in 1949 follows closely in Woolf's footsteps, but with a lighter touch. He makes clear the highbrow in American society is not based on wealth or family prestige, but on "high thinking" (146). So, while Woolf's highbrow pursues ideas *instead* of a living (that's left to the lowbrow), Lynes's pursues ideas *for* a living. The American highbrow is, to Lynes, the atomic scientist, the literature professor, the writer or commentator, all "thinkers of global thoughts." His brow classifications reflect the influence of the Cold War and the budding atomic age. He also introduces the important sub-categories of upper-middlebrow and lower-middlebrow, since the middle is really too vast to be encompassed in one term.

His essay was accompanied by an illustrated chart in *Life* magazine, explicating (in a consciously tongue-in-cheek manner) "Everyday Tastes from High-Brow to Low-Brow." The telling entries for "Entertainment" range from ballet for the highbrow down through theater, musical extravaganza films, and culminate in western movies for the low (154–155). The film industry, or the "middlebrow moneybags of Hollywood" (152), is seen by the high as a corrupting influence on the low. He also identifies a particular tension for the middle that will play out in the *Star Wars* radio saga—a sort of "muses or masses" problem (153). The middlebrows are strivers. They continually look up, in terms of taste, and hope to elevate themselves by adopting the tastes of those above, the muses. They also, however, look to raise old and forgotten cultural elements from below, breathe new life into them, and share them with the public, the masses (who may or may not be lowbrow). As a byproduct of the economic success of the mid-twentieth century, the middlebrows are often looking for ways to make and spend their money in cultural outlets. Thus, as the middlebrows become more active in the arts at all levels, they must constantly confront the question whether they are serving the community, or just pandering to popular tastes. And is there a difference? These questions underlie the unique radio project on which Lucas embarked.

Star Wars *for the Middle*

As Twentieth Century–Fox was preparing to release *The Empire Strikes Back*, the much-awaited second installment in the *Star Wars* saga, reports emerged of a pending radio series. The early discussions about the project touted it as a co-production of National Public Radio (NPR) and the British Broadcasting Corporation (BBC), and an opportunity for both networks to infuse new life into their dramatic productions, and perhaps cultivate a new audience ("Radio Star Wars").[2] Public broadcasting was prepared to look to the stars to generate interest here on earth. After roughly thirty years of the dominance of television, this endeavor would, they hoped, resurrect the radio star, and prove the Buggles wrong.[3] The rendering of a Hollywood blockbuster as radio drama also hearkened back to shows like *Lux Radio Theatre*, which aired from the 1930s to the 1950s, and adapted popular films in one-hour condensed versions for the radio (Verma 24). This nostalgic glance backward at an almost-forgotten art form was classic middlebrow.

The first series, *Star Wars: The Radio Play*, began airing in March of 1981 on 244 NPR affiliate stations across the country. The original two hour film was expanded to approximately six and a half hours, to be broadcast weekly in thirty-minute episodes (Lindsey). The listening audience would be served the same climax as those in the theaters—triumphant destruction of the Death Star, Darth Vader's escape, and a slightly awkward medal ceremony. Production of *The Empire Strikes Back* then began quickly and it aired two years later, in February of 1983, in the heart of the first Reagan administration. It was a more streamlined production, only ten episodes, but still considerably longer than the original. The final installment of the trilogy, however, would remain in public radio limbo for more than a decade, the victim of an array of fiscal and political woes. *Return of the Jedi* for radio only became viable in 1996 as a sort of promotional tie-in for the release of the digitally re-mastered films. Although it aired on NPR, it was produced by Highbridge Audio, a commercial venture.

Coinciding with the production of the *Star Wars* radio series, NPR was entering into a severe fiscal crisis. In the published recollections of those involved in the radio dramatizations, the source of this crisis lay firmly at the feet of the newly-inaugurated President, Ronald Reagan. He had been sworn into office on 20 January 1981, just over a month before the first radio series premiered, but the former governor of California had made his feelings about federal funding for public broadcasting known before his election, so cuts were clearly on the horizon. And so the two key figures who indirectly squared off against each other through the public airwaves were the moviemaker and the Great Communicator. Their relationships to this moment in the late Cold War were curiously parallel. Both had early, formative connections to radio, both were sincerely aggrieved at the loss of optimism in American society, and both engaged middlebrow sensibilities to combat the "end of victory culture" (Engelhardt).

Ronald Reagan spoke of listening to the first commercial radio station, KDKA, when it was still in its infancy, and he began his entertainment career as a radio announcer (Reagan Ch. 6–7). In his autobiography, he uses the oft-heard epithets for early radio—it was "magic," it was "theater for the mind" (59). At the time, radio was still the democratic upstart of the media world, promising to level many playing fields by providing information, education, and entertainment to all. This type of mass accessibility rendered it a lowbrow medium in the eyes of early cultural critics. It was a natural jump from radio to film, and Reagan's reputation as a Hollywood actor was really forged at the pinnacle of victory culture, when the United States was on the verge of "saving" Europe for a second time in thirty years. In the postwar years, he transitioned from movies to politics as the nation's star was on the wane, and his new career persona was grounded in a promise to reestablish American prestige. After Vietnam, he doubled down on the messages of peace (through strength), security (through defense), and optimism (through sheer, American pluck).

George Lucas was only just born at the height of victory culture, and his childhood tracks the explosive growth of the middle class. By the time he was in his teens, being a "teenager" meant something specific, and in his case, it was fed by rock 'n' roll radio and escapist fiction and fantasy. He became active professionally during the Vietnam era, and started to look back creatively, reliving the turning point between carefree teenager and somber adult in *American Graffiti* (1973). By the beginning of the Carter administration, Lucas was consciously looking to affect American hearts and minds through his artistic products. The country was still reeling from defeat in southeast Asia, the world had plunged into an energy crisis, and nuclear buildup continued apace.

Against this backdrop of very real financial and political strife, Lucas demonstrated a nostalgic faith in the power of radio to tell a story in a way the young audience of the late 1970s and early 1980s had never really experienced. He was inspired by the cliffhanger serials on radio during his childhood, and perhaps saw this as a chance to resurrect the genre for a new generation (Lindsey). He had also expressed in interviews an interest in the relationship between teenagers and radio, and the power of radio as fantasy (Farber 6). Through *American Graffiti*, he drew attention to the unique relationship between the disc jockey, like Wolfman Jack, and the young listener. Whether tuning-in in the bedroom or the car, radio had become a private experience in the post-war years, and had helped to foster the new phenomenon of "teenage" culture. Lucas saw his own youth of the 1950s and early 1960s as a time of optimism, though he was a bit self-conscious about it. "It's all that hokey stuff about being a good neighbor, and the American spirit and all that crap. There *is* something in it" (Farber 8). With *Star Wars*, he sought to reinvigorate the American optimism that had been lost after years of quagmire in southeast Asia and massive nuclear proliferation. The movies themselves, as westerns in outer space, were already a throwback genre to a simpler time in the early Cold War years. By now converting them to radio drama, he engaged even more firmly with this seemingly golden age.

Those foundational days of the *Star Wars* radio project spurred their own romanticization of the place of *Star Wars* in American culture around 1980. Brian Daley, science fiction author and the writer of the radio scripts, described the radio licensing as the "brass ring" at a time when "*Star Wars* tie-in rights were like a license to print money" (4–5). By giving these rights to a public radio station, of all things, Daley indicates Lucas's deep-seated philanthropy. We are meant to believe that, were Lucas as crass and uncouth as his box office success would suggest, he could certainly have taken his radio rights to a commercial broadcaster, and thus, to the bank. The fact that he didn't is testament to a higher artistic purpose. By separating the radio project from the blockbuster success of the films, Lucas and Daley both attempt to nudge this particular version of *Star Wars* out of the lowbrow world of space westerns. In this reading, Lucas generously offers his extremely valuable asset to the masses, and thereby helps to alleviate America's doldrums. And once again, the need to convey higher value on a popular piece of entertainment would signal to cultural observers the insecurity of the middlebrow.

This cultural striving has an important hint of noblesse oblige about it as well. The radio version was cast in the role of a cultural safety net, providing the less fortunate with an opportunity to experience what those with means saw in the cinema. In an interview with *Starlog* magazine on the premiere of the radio play in 1981, Mark Hamill focused on the financial advantages of radio: "It appealed to me because it wasn't money-oriented. It sprang purely from the desire to help revitalize interest in radio" (Brender 23). He went on to talk about the kids who couldn't afford the *Star Wars* toys, or even a movie ticket, but who would presumably be brought into the fold through this public radio product. In sympathy with their impoverished plight, he asserted confidently, "there is no budget on imagination." There is only a tinge of irony in the fact that the interview took place at a gala premiere event for the radio broadcast held in the planetarium of the Griffith Observatory in Los Angeles. And behind the scenes, NPR was counting on this production to bring much-needed revenue into its coffers.

The auditory medium of radio presented unique demands as well as opportunities. Much of the action in the film is, naturally, visual, so the radio script required a good deal of subtle explanation to indicate something as simple as a character entrance or exit. At the same time, the lengthened script allowed for more backstory. The listener was treated to additional scenes exploring Luke's relationship with his friends on Tatooine, Princess Leia's relationship with her father, and R2-D2's and C-3PO's ... relationship. One of the keys to the success of the radio version was the decision to allow the radio producers the rights to use any and all of the sound created for the film, from Chewbacca's "voice" to John Williams's unmistakable score. Since a great deal of the "science" in science fiction can be conveyed with sound, the radio series was able to evoke the appropriate distant galaxy and time in much the same way that the movie had.

One of the expanded scenes in the radio play is a telling example of the disdain Daley, and presumably Lucas, wanted to express toward any notion of financial gain. Once aboard the *Millennium Falcon*, after Luke's first lesson in lightsaber handling and the Force, Han Solo (Perry King) engages Obi-Wan/Ben (Bernard Behrens) about faith in the Force versus the virtues of luck and money:

> BEN: *(LAUGHS)* You're quite a paradox, Captain Solo. You prize above every-thing else the cardinal freedom of star travel, yet you're held back from it by something as trifling as money. Come to think of it, there are entire worlds in just that same predicament.
>
> CHEWIE: ROARS ANGRILY
>
> HAN: You said it, Chewie! *(TO BEN)* So money's "trifling," huh? Well just *you* try getting along without any!
>
> BEN: Oh, but I do!
>
> HAN: Wha... [230].

Ben, a cave-dwelling ascetic warrior monk, not surprisingly responds he has indeed gotten along without money, and suffered not the slightest inconvenience for "quite some years now." Han refuses to concede, however; as the *Millennium Falcon* approaches Alderaan, he delivers a parting philosophy on free enterprise as the established norm: "you measure your freedom in this life in *cash*, old man. If you have enough, you can go as far and as fast as you want" (230). Just as the Empire has literally enslaved worlds, their economic structure has done the same: the length of the purse strings determines individual self-worth.

Ben's student, Luke, agrees with his teacher. As Han leaves, Luke has the final word in this exposition on greed, as he assures Ben, "all the money in the Empire" wouldn't stop him from helping in this quest (231). In the film version, Han's need to clear his debts, without engaging in the just cause of the Rebellion, is certainly made clear. But this particular scene in the movie focuses on his skepticism with regard to the Force. Here, the not-so-subtle dig at "entire worlds" who sacrifice freedom for the pursuit of wealth is a timely reference to the general threat, as Lucas, Daley, and others saw it, of a conservative Republican administration, and the specific woes of public radio. They suggest America has misplaced its priorities—when art must be profitable, artists sacrifice their freedom, so the government should be more involved in supporting the arts, not less. And wouldn't we all be happier if we took a step back from worrying about paying our bills or buying a new car and just enjoyed some good old-fashioned fun?

This is one of the sticky problems with middlebrow—it wants to have fun, but it should be impressively intelligent fun. In his introduction to the radio script for *Star Wars*, Brian Daley likens the radio drama to Tom Stoppard's 1966 play *Rosencrantz and Guildenstern Are Dead* (3). He is referring to the fact that his radio play introduces several scenes not in the movie. Like Stoppard's (or Shakespeare's) hapless messengers, the two droids become the center of the action more frequently in the radio version, and their relationship is more fully fleshed out. Daley's choice of Stoppard for comparison is telling on another level as well. *Rosencrantz* is certainly a comedy, but one that relies on higher-than-middlebrow sensibilities. It is meant to challenge, but to allow those who "get it" to feel they belong to an exclusive club of "insiders," that humor is acceptable in art, but it should be difficult. *Star Wars* is really anything but difficult. But presenting it this way allows Daley to showcase a deeper cultural meaning.

Star Wars *for the Mind*

As the only two major characters to reprise their roles in the first radio dramatization, Mark Hamill and Anthony Daniels became the voices of publicity for the new project. Hamill was frequently quoted in periodicals and trade publications, waxing nostalgic for a time he himself admits he never quite experienced (Lindsey; Brender 23). He emphasized the sheer fun he had in working on the radio play and the way this medium, the dramatic serial, reflected George Lucas's original inspiration. Daniels asserted that listening to radio drama takes effort, but that in itself was what made it so enjoyable—listeners had to work to create the images in their minds ("The Making of *Star Wars*"). Television actor Perry King was brought on to play Han Solo, and he, too, focused on the link between radio acting and childhood through the mental exercise of fantasy and imagination (Lycan). Just as Reagan had, they all adopted the view of radio as theater for the imagination.

In fact, the publicity surrounding the development of the radio plays overflows with references to storytelling and the imagination. The promotional special, which was aired on public radio stations in February of 1981, bore the title "The Making of *Star Wars* for Radio: A Fable for the Mind's Eye."[4] Mental imagery and the ability of sound to inspire and guide it were presented as the keystones of the project. In this way, the producers built on the already vast terrain of media theory concerning radio. Richard Toscan, the executive producer of the radio series, declared that, when he saw the movie, he was struck not by the visual, but by the sound, and believed it "could be a highly successful vehicle in a purely auditory format." The special included extended interview material with John Madden, the director of the radio plays, and Ben Burtt, the sound designer for Lucasfilm. Madden reinforced this view, expressing his hope this production would "awaken people to the idea of what radio can do with the dramatic form." He echoed Daniels, saying auditory memories were so vivid because "you've done the work … it lives in your imagination." Burtt, meanwhile, looked to the particular challenge of competing with visual media. It wasn't enough to simply recreate old-time radio drama, or to play the soundtrack of a movie, as though audiences in a cinema could experience the story with the projector turned off. By the 1980s, the audience had to be engaged in a special way in order for them to find value in the act of listening.

Part of that engagement included a promotional poster designed specifically for the radio production. It featured a gleaming C-3PO poised before a stand microphone. Wearing headphones and with one hand raised to his ear, he mimicked the radio announcers of old. In the background is the obligatory spacescape, but two TIE fighters appear to be circling C-3PO, suggesting the ever-present threat of the Empire (reproduced in Daley *Star Wars* 2). The image is unmistakably an element of the *Star Wars* franchise, but it also is largely meaningful only to those who have *seen* the movie. Even after listening to the full radio series, one would most likely not have conjured exactly that image of a protocol droid, and certainly would not recognize the difference between the small attack forces of the Empire and those of the Rebel Alliance.

The poster was designed for the initiated. Of course, given that *Star Wars* was already, by 1981, within the top five highest attended films of all time, it was reasonable to expect most of the listening audience had, in fact, seen the movie. Nevertheless, the poster made the assumption listeners would easily link the image of Threepio with Anthony Daniels's character. With little context, some may have thought the robot represented the mechanical Darth Vader.

This issue was aptly expressed by M. R. Montgomery for the *Boston Globe* in 1994, when the two radio series, *Star Wars* and *The Empire Strikes Back*, were being re-broadcast: "Re-creating a movie creates a small problem for those of us who have not seen it. Either we know what a Wookiee looks like or we don't, and little on the radio version will help us imagine it" (84). This lack of faith in the power of the imagination is a telling response from the mid–1990s. In its golden age, radio's magic supposedly lay in its ability to fire the imagination. Montgomery's response, although it was most likely the minority, suggests the limits of the radio enterprise in a video-saturated world. But what matters is Lucas and others involved in the project *believed* that radio could still wield that magic power, if only given the chance.

Even when the *Star Wars* series premiered in 1981, the press messaging included warnings about Reagan's impending cuts. In an article for the *New York Times* just before the premiere, Robert Lindsey reported on NPR's concerns, citing a proposed 25 percent reduction in budget expected to begin the following year. The article asked a pivotal question, from the perspective of public radio—can a production such as *Star Wars* attract a larger, and more importantly, younger, audience? Lindsey assists NPR in asserting Reagan's policies would "jeopardize innovative ventures" such as these, thereby stifling the voice of NPR, and preventing the youth of America from joining the public broadcasting enterprise. In the Lucas universe, Reagan's conservative empire posed a lethal threat to public radio's only hope.

The problem with this characterization of events is it elides the very real problems already plaguing National Public Radio at the time of Reagan's election, and disregards the fallout of NPR's own attempts to address its financial crisis. *Star Wars* was already in the can, a lavish production by radio standards.[5] Costs were estimated at $200,000, a significant outlay for a total of six and a half hours of programming (Lindsey). By comparison, NPR's 24/7, 365 day a year classical music programming at the time cost approximately $700,000 (McCauley 56). *The Empire Strikes Back* for radio would ring in at $275,000 (McLaughlin). The network prided itself, as it should, on being able to provide in-depth news and cultural programming at a national level, while most public broadcasting, particularly television, was still very locally oriented and controlled. The down side to this arrangement was that NPR had been, since its inception in 1970, primarily dependent on federal funding, while its public television counterparts relied more heavily on viewer support and corporate contributions raised locally (Schwartz). It was ill-equipped to take on massive spending for individual projects, however promising the potential return.

By most accounts, the production of *Star Wars* for radio was successful in luring a video-centric audience away from its televisions. NPR logged approximately 50,000 telephone calls and letters about the series, nearly all of them positive (Daley *Empire* 4). Further, more than 600,000 people over the age of eleven listened to *Star Wars* each week, approximately double the number that listened to public radio in an average week (Giovanonni "How Public Radio" 1). Arbitron ratings showed a total of 750,000 people altogether heard some part of the broadcasts. Frank Mankiewicz, the President of NPR at the time of the *Star Wars* broadcasts, claimed a 40 percent growth in listenership as a result of the project (McLaughlin, Daley *Empire* 4). In the retelling, nearly everyone involved in the first series depicted a glorious triumph.

However, as devotees of the trilogy know, in order for the plot to move forward and the Jedi to return, the empire must strike back. That is exactly the characterization of events favored by Mankiewicz, Daley, and others when attempting to explain the much shorter adaptation of *The Empire Strikes Back*. And that characterization lays the groundwork for the failure to produce *Return of the Jedi* as anything more than an afterthought. As the first series was receiving praise and accolades for resurrecting radio drama, the financial situation at NPR was already precarious. While expectations were growing for *The Empire Strikes Back* for the radio, the rhetoric issuing from the network and the artists involved in the series focused on what they saw as the draconian attitudes of the new commander-in-chief. In an interview with Steve McKerrow for the *Baltimore Sun*, Brian Daley stated simply: "Ronald Reagan eviscerated public radio funding" (6E). He also emphasized "Reaganomics cutbacks" in his introduction to the published radio script for *The Empire Strikes Back*. This second series premiered on radio on Valentine's Day, 1983. The process of recording this installment was quite different from the first, however. Where *Star Wars* for radio had been recorded in Los Angeles, *The Empire Strikes Back* was recorded at A & R studios in New York. Brian Daley and Mark Hamill made note of the different feel conveyed by "doing radio" in New York. Hamill, who had already described radio acting as a kind of "time warp," now wished he could "be wearing a 40s suit and a fedora" and "stroll on over to Lindy's with Fred Allen" (Collins). Once again, the series was connected to radio's golden age and a simpler time.

The "Public" in Public Radio

Nineteen eighty-three was a watershed moment for every major player in this story. It was the nadir of the fiscal crisis at NPR. It marked the emergence of an upstart competitor for the public airwaves, a rebel alliance, of sorts, called American Public Radio. And in March of that year, while *The Empire Strikes Back* was still airing on stations across the country, President Reagan first publicly introduced his Strategic Defense Initiative (SDI). His speech to the nation on 23 March was a direct appeal to support his defense budget. At the end of this speech, he proposed a "means of rendering these nuclear weapons impotent and obsolete." The theoretical defensive weapon would intercept ballistic missiles, destroying them in the sky long before they can reach their targets. Senator Edward Kennedy quickly and dismissively dubbed the project "Star Wars," hoping to invalidate the President's plans with the rhetoric of Hollywood fantasy (Kennedy 3). Many have criticized Reagan for confusing his acting roles with real life, but Reagan himself consistently focused on his strategic defense policy as the conservative way to end the crippling fear of mutual assured destruction. The two sides squared off over the issue for years to come, battling for the claim to represent the true path to security and peace.[6]

Battle lines were drawn on numerous fronts. Reagan was still Public Enemy No. 1 at NPR, but now they also had to confront the possibility of losing their place as the sole provider of public radio programming nationally. At the same time, the conflict between the left and the right in government deepened, as this new defense plan would dramatically increase military funding, while enforcing significant cuts to arts and cultural programs. And George Lucas found it personally offensive for his space-age western to be associated with a weapon of massive destructive potential, regardless of its stated intent. In this environment, even as the climax of the trilogy was about to premiere in theaters, talks concerning production of *Return of the Jedi* for radio came to a halt.

The U.S. General Accounting Office was asked to review NPR's financial operations after the network had been forced to seek a $7 million loan from the Corporation for Public Broadcasting (CPB) to cover its shortfall in fiscal year 1983 (U.S. GAO). NPR had engaged in an ambitious plan late in 1981 to wean itself of federal funding entirely by 1988. NPR President Frank Mankiewicz dubbed it Project Independence, and through it, the network earnestly pursued new ventures in technology, broadcasting, and funding to meet this goal. NPR has never lacked vision. Unfortunately, in the early 1980s, it did lack business sense. Their goals included a much greater emphasis on listener support and corporate sponsorship, as public television already enjoyed. The essential problem was that, almost as soon as the initiative began, the leadership at NPR began behaving as though it were already successful. According to the GAO report, the network simply did not have the management structure in place to navigate the expansion it was aggressively pursuing. As a result, decision-making was severely compromised. There was then confusion over the budget, as plans for a new financial management information system had not yet been implemented. Thus, people were spending without knowing how much they had to spend. It was clear no one understood that their new fundraising efforts had not yet generated the revenue they expected they eventually would. Perhaps the most egregious example of this unregulated spending was the issuance of American Express cards to approximately one quarter of all employees, with little regard for supporting documents to manage the accounting afterwards (U.S. GAO Attachment 1 p. 26). The internal disarray led inevitably to Mankiewicz's resignation.

This is not to say that NPR appeared to the listener to be suffering. The early 1980s were, in fact, a time of great development in content and style for the network. The audience was growing, and real programming hours increased by 62 percent between 1977 and 1982. Unfortunately, in the same period, expenditures nearly quadrupled (McCourt 53). Although costly, the *Star Wars* and *The Empire Strikes Back* radio productions were essential to the fundraising efforts of stations across the country. Meanwhile, a subset of public radio stations was coalescing around the idea that they could provide a cultural product that NPR did not.

American Public Radio began as the brainchild of William Kling, the president of Minnesota Public Radio, and a founding member of the NPR board. Minnesota Public Radio was a loose affiliation of NPR stations within the state that had banded together to support production of their flagship program, *A Prairie Home Companion*. Kling wanted to bring *Prairie Home* to a national audience and approached Frank Mankiewicz about making such an arrangement with NPR (McCauley 53–54). Mankiewicz's response made clear the very classist associations people tend to make with certain types of entertainment, and the inability to recognize when that middlebrow shoe belongs on one's own foot. Mankiewicz refused, demonstrating utter disdain for APR and *Prairie Home*, which he characterized as a "great little weekly program for yuppie listeners who live in the suburbs, enjoy country music and refuse to admit it" (McDougal Part 3). Kling then sought to establish a nationwide network of stations in major markets that would pay fees to cover the cost of syndicating *Prairie Home*. This became American Public Radio.[7] Mankiewicz firmly believed NPR was doing the real work of broadcasting in the public interest, while APR was an elitist organization providing, as McDougal termed it, "white wine and meringue to the nouveau riche." Mankiewicz added that comparing the two would be "like comparing apples to quiche." He rightfully took pride in NPR's reputation as the premiere national broadcast news and information outlet, the "*New York Times* of radio." He further pointed to NPR's original mandate, as a federally-funded broadcaster, to "attempt to reach everyone." But his criticism failed to acknowledge NPR's own actual audience, which was in fact composed largely of the same "yuppie listeners." As Giovanonni's research demonstrated, public radio listeners were (and are) well-educated, and well-educated people make more money ("The Critical Distinction" 1, "The Cheap 90" 11).[8] So, while claiming lowbrow mass appeal, Mankiewicz ignored the fact that his outlet really served the middlebrow, exactly the target audience for *Star Wars*.

How does this little internal war affect our hapless *Jedi*? Arguably the single most important figure in compiling the final product for both *Star Wars* and *The Empire Strikes Back* for radio was the independent sound producer, Tom Voegeli. Brian Daley's scripts adapted the stories to an audio format, and director John Madden elicited the performances in the studios, but Voegeli then undertook the painstaking work of assembling the new voice tracks with the actual sound effects and score from the movies. Since the radio plays were significantly longer, and with necessary changes in various scenes, that was not as simple as running the movie sound track in the background. He was responsible for the final product that drew listeners, and kept them, in the hundreds of thousands. And Tom Voegeli frequently worked with Minnesota Public Radio. When NPR was in the throes of financial distress in 1983, Voegeli realized they were unlikely to come up with the funds to produce *Return of the Jedi*. They were on the verge of having to give up their flagship news productions, so another fanciful trip to outer space was out of the question. So Voegeli approached American Public Radio, which believed it could generate the funding from its affiliate stations by having them pay an advance broadcast fee. The only hurdle was the fact that NPR still held the rights. And NPR would not let them go. APR's proposal included a one-time broadcast option for its member stations for the entire trilogy, after which all of the rights would revert back to NPR. Expressing simply a belief that they could work things out in time, NPR's new President, Douglas Bennett, declined the offer (McDougal Part 2). To be fair, they did work things out, just at a decade's-plus remove from the film's release and the scope of this essay, and with little relevance to larger cultural trends (though one could perhaps argue *Return of the Jedi*'s radio adaptation was thus just as disappointing as the movie had been, but that is a story for another day).

Conclusion

In 1980, the writing was on the wall regarding Reagan's cuts to cultural outlets, like public radio, so George Lucas offered his most valuable commodity to his alma mater's public radio station. The production of *Star Wars* for radio was a feature draw for fund-raising campaigns (pledge periods, "begathons") at stations across the country. One has to wonder, though, if Lucas really wanted to help public broadcasting, he could have donated a lump sum, or even wiped out NPR's debt, rather than offer this literal artistic license. He chose instead to create a new artistic product that would combat the American malaise. As an "artistic expression," radio would elevate his franchise and American culture to highbrow sophistication. Yet these very productions became sources of strife for public radio. The events point to the difficult position of public radio—it views itself as a purveyor of culture to the masses. In so doing, it provides a service that should have no price, as far as its practitioners are concerned. But this very willful ignorance of price was exactly part of the underlying problem for NPR's contradictory public image with the actual demographics of its listeners.

This brings us back to the choice of public radio as the outlet for the radio *Star Wars*. The audience for that set of stations was inclined to seek the kind of trapping of high culture Woolf described and to recognize the social value of trying to reclaim an art that was considered lost. By reclaiming it, they elevate it. Radio, in its original incarnation, was deemed the lowest of cultural output. But radio drama in the 1980s was not the radio drama of the 1930s and 1940s. It was now relegated to a niche audience in the high middle. Radio was not exactly "popular" entertainment anymore. Despite its invocation of the "public," National Public Radio was, and still is, not a "popular" outlet in the sense of one crafted for the broadest appeal to the greatest audience, regardless of socio-economic status. In theory the network strived to be such an outlet, but from the time that the network began collecting audience research, it was clear the majority of its listeners came from more educated and affluent households than those who tuned in to radio dramas in their heyday.

There is now a movement to claim (or reclaim) the middle. Friedman's *GQ* piece on the lure of middlebrow is self-deprecating and snarky, but it is also an invitation to others (of whom he knows there are many) to join him in his confession. Yes, he is making fun of them, too, but in a good-natured way. He has constructed a Venn diagram of the various brows and their intersections, an updated take on Lynes's chart from 1949. Friedman also supplements the diagram with a list of what he sees as the top fifty markers of contemporary American middlebrow. Topping the list in a comfortable slot at number one—NPR. The network's very raison d'être is to bring the high within the reach of the middle (because, let's not kid ourselves, NPR isn't really reaching out a hand to the low, except in very rare circumstances). The audience for NPR is, like it or not, predominantly a well-educated, sophisticated, culturally aware elite. These are the people who wouldn't be caught dead admitting to watching *America's Got Talent*, unless it was in reference to a piece they heard on *Morning Edition* about Howie Mandel's struggles with Obsessive-Compulsive Disorder. But make no mistake about it, a lot of them (us) do watch *America's Got Talent*.

Star Wars has always attempted to straddle two poles, so to speak: the commercial and the artistic, the futuristic and the nostalgic, the yet-to-be and the long-gone, the material and the ideal. Lucas once described himself as "a very bad cynic," and the *Star Wars* franchise attests to that (Farber 8). His efforts to protect the *Star Wars* name from the soiling association with Ronald Reagan's defense policy were themselves further evidence of the murky middlebrow. They reflected a valuing of his cultural product as art, as something highbrow, yet the legal pathway he employed was designed to protect a commercial interest. Little could be more middlebrow than using the courts to enforce the artistic quality of one's creative output. Virginia Woolf would surely relegate such behavior to the irredeemable sense of insecurity felt by those in the middle.

Tom Engelhardt describes the prevalent American attitude for much of its existence, up through the early twentieth century, as emblematic of "victory culture." Generations of striving and success had created an ethos in the United States that was characterized by confidence, if not downright certainty, of success. Scientifically, economically, militarily, the American people had repeatedly encountered challenges and threats, and repeatedly overcome them. As a result, by the beginning of the twentieth century, there was a certain expectation of positivist progress. Engelhardt contends that cracks in this confidence began to show during World War II, and it began to crumble shortly thereafter. The tragic embarrassment of Vietnam ensured its ultimate demise.

The Carter years were a real trough in American cultural and political life. In their aftermath, and while the filmmaker may have shuddered to admit it, the two standard-bearers for middlebrow America at the time were George Lucas and Ronald Reagan. Each conceived of an elegant weapon to return a beleaguered America to some semblance of a civilized age, free of the looming threat of the Cold War. Reagan put himself forward as the leader to get us out of this funk. Lucas put his movies forward to do the same. Much to the former's chagrin, George Lucas and Ronald Reagan were essentially engaged in the same project, the reassertion of a bygone age of American security and comfort, brought to you through the pleasing tones of your Philco. It is not important whether such an age truly existed, merely that both Lucas and Reagan, along with millions of other Americans, believed that it did. Rather than making a valiant stand against the heartless Cold Warrior, Lucas in fact obligingly fed the public the same comfort food. And most of us wouldn't have it any other way.

Notes

1. The offer was technically a sale—for the grand sum of one dollar. See Daley *Star Wars*.

2. Great Britain had a history of treating radio as a respected vehicle for fiction that was originally written for other media. From the earliest days of the BBC, several British novelists were actively involved in adapting their works for broadcast (Riley 7–8). Among these was H. G. Wells, whose *War of the Worlds* would shake the airwaves of the U.S. in 1939. Further, however, the BBC also took radio drama seriously as its own genre, separate from the stage, or eventually, film.

3. The Buggles's version of "Video Killed the Radio Star" was released as a single in 1979, a synthpop expression of the late twentieth century's concerns about media in modern lives.

4. The title seems to be a nod to the 1978 novel by Alan Dean Foster entitled *Splinter of the Mind's Eye*, published by Ballantine. That work was one of the first examples of the Expanded Universe, adding to the story between *Star Wars* and *The Empire Strikes Back*.

5. In his introduction to the published radio script for *The Empire Strikes Back*, Brian Daley takes pains to parse the expense of the *Star Wars* radio venture by breaking it down to the cost-per-listener. Given the large audience, he touts the cost of 3.6 cents per audience member per episode.

6. As far-fetched as the "Star Wars" anti-ballistic missile plan may have seemed at the time, and despite the gallons of ink spilled in questioning its feasibility, we have now arrived at a point that the government is once again seriously pursuing the possibility. China has successfully launched anti-satellite missiles deeper and deeper into space, possibly threatening our own missile-warning satellite system, which is based in deep geosynchronous orbit, but is basically a set of "sitting ducks." See "The Battle Above," *60 Minutes*. CBS. WCBS, New York, 26 Apr. 2015. Television.

7. The five original member stations were WNYC in New York, WGUC in Cincinnati, KQED in San Francisco, and, interestingly, KUSC in Los Angeles. In 1994 the network changed its name to Public Radio International (PRI).

8. According to the 2012 News Consumption Survey at the Pew Research Center, 54 percent of NPR listeners have a college degree, while only 29 percent of Americans overall do. Likewise, 43 percent have a family income greater than $75,000, compared to 26 percent of the general population.

Works Cited

Brender, Alan. "Star Wars' Latest Incarnation: It's a Radio Play!" *Starlog* June 1981: 23–24. *Internet Archive*. Web. 6 June 2015.

Collins, Glenn. "Metropolitan Diary." *New York Times* 16 June 1982: C2. *ProQuest*. Web. 3 Mar. 2015.

Daley, Brian. *The Empire Strikes Back: The National Public Radio Dramatization*. New York: Ballantine, 1995. Print.

_____. *Star Wars: The National Public Radio Dramatization Based on Characters and Situations Created by George Lucas*. New York: Ballantine, 1994. Print.

Engelhardt, Tom. *The End of Victory Culture: Cold War America and the Disillusioning of a Generation*. Rev. Ed. Amherst: University of Massachusetts Press, 2007.

Farber, Stephen. "George Lucas: The Stinky Kid Hits the Big Time." *Film Quarterly* 27.3 (Spring 1974): 2–9. Print.

Friedman, Devin. "Middlebrow: The Taste That Dare Not Speak Its Name." *GQ* June 2011: n. pag. Web. 15 May 2015.

Giovanonni, David. "The Cheap 90. Public Radio Listeners: Supporters and Non-Supporters." Washington, D.C.: Corp. for Public Broadcasting, 1985. ARAnet On-Line Library of Public Radio Research. Web. 31 May 2015.

_____. "The Critical Distinction between Public and Commercial Radio: The Audience's Point of View." *Long Range Planning and Legislation*. Washington, D.C.: National Public Radio, June 1980. ARAnet On-Line Library of Public Radio Research. Web. 31 May 2015.

_____. "How Public Radio Gained Two Million Listeners." ARAnet On-Line Library of Public Radio Research. Web. 31 May 2015.

Halford, Macy. "On 'Middlebrow.'" *The New Yorker* 10 Feb. 2011: n. pag. Web. 15 May 2015.

Kennedy, Edward. "Address of Senator Edward M. Kennedy, The Brown University Commencement Forum: The Nuclear Freeze and Arms Control, 4 June 1983." ted-kennedy.org. Web. 7 May 2015.

Lindsey, Robert. "Will 'Star Wars' Lure Younger Listeners to Radio?" *New York Times* 8 Mar. 1981: D34. *ProQuest*. Web. 3 Mar. 2015.

Lycan, Gary. "Stellar Cast Reunites for Play." *Orange County Register* [Santa Ana, CA] 17 Nov. 1996: F32. *ProQuest*. Web. 12 Mar. 2015.

Lynes, Russell. "Highbrow, Lowbrow, Middlebrow." Rpt. *Wilson Quarterly* Autumn 1976.

"The Making of *Star Wars* for Radio: A Fable for the Mind's Eye." *Midday*. MN Public Radio. 6 Mar. 1981. *American Archive of Public Broadcasting*. Web. 3 Apr. 2015.

Martens, Todd. "Star Wars Celebration: Capturing the radio spirit of the late '70s." hero-complex.latimes.com. Web. 12 Apr. 2015.

McCauley, Michael P. *NPR: The Trials and Triumphs of National Public Radio*. New York: Columbia University Press, 2005. Print.

McCourt, Tom. *Conflicting Communication Interests in America: The Case of National Public Radio*. Westport, CT: Praeger, 1999. Print.

McKerrow, Steve. "Even on radio, 'Star Wars' has the force." *Baltimore Sun* 9 July 1993: 6E. *ProQuest*. Web. 12 Apr. 2015.

McLaughlin, Jeff. "Short Cuts; Tuned In; That Galaxy Far, Far Away Is Coming through the Airwaves Again." *Boston Globe* 10 Feb. 1983: 1. *ProQuest*. Web. 4 Apr. 2015.

Montgomery, M. R. "Radio 'Star Wars' Misses its Sights." *Boston Globe* 21 May 1994: 84. *ProQuest*. Web. 4 Apr. 2015.

"Radio Star Wars Series Planned." *Globe and Mail* [Toronto] 30 Apr. 1979: 18. *ProQuest*. Web. 4 Apr. 2015.

Reagan, Ronald W. "Address to the Nation on Defense and National Security March 23, 1983." *The Public Papers of President Ronald W. Reagan*. Ronald Reagan Presidential Library. Web. 7 May 2015.

_____. *An American Life: The Autobiography*. New York: Simon & Schuster, 1990.

Reagin, Nancy R., and Janice Leidl. *Star Wars and History*. Hoboken, NJ: John Wiley & Sons, 2013.

Riley, Donald W. *Handbook of Radio Drama Techniques.* Ann Arbor: Edwards Brothers, 1939. *HathiTrust Digital Library.* Web. 1 June 2015.

Rubin, Joan Shelley. *The Making of Middlebrow Culture.* Chapel Hill: University of North Carolina Press, 1992. Print.

Schwartz, Tony. "National Public Radio at 10: Excellent, but in Danger." *New York Times* 16 Apr. 1981: C31. *ProQuest.* Web. 18 Mar. 2015.

Scott, A. O. "The Squeeze on the Middlebrow." *New York Times.* 3 Aug. 2014, New York ed.: AR1. Print.

Shaw, Tony. and Denise J. Youngblood. *Cinematic Cold War: The American and Soviet Struggle for Hearts and Minds.* Lawrence: University of Kansas Press, 2010. Print.

Thomas, Thomas J., and Theresa R. Clifford. "AUDIENCE 88: Issues and Implications." Washington, D.C.: Corp. for Public Broadcasting, 1988. *Public Radio News Directors Guide.* Web. 3 June 2015.

United States General Accounting Office. *Statement of Fredrick D. Wolf, Director, Accounting and Financial Management Division Before the House Subcommittee on Oversight and Investigation of the Committee on Energy and Commerce on National Public Radio, 10 Feb. 1984.* United States Govt. Accountability Office. Web. 20 Apr. 2015.

Verma, Neil. *Theater of the Mind: Imagination, Aesthetics, and American Radio Drama.* Chicago: University of Chicago Press, 2012. Kindle file.

Woolf, Virginia. *The Death of the Moth and Other Essays.* New York: Harcourt, Brace, Jovanovich, 1972. Print.

Part of Our Cultural History

Fan-Creator Relationships, Restoration, and Appropriation

MICHAEL FUCHS *and*
MICHAEL PHILLIPS

In his recent study of fan responses to Disney's acquisition of Lucasfilm, William Proctor writes that "without *Star Wars*, I would not be sitting here writing this article as an academic" (198). Attributing one's career choice to a science fiction saga may seem a bit extreme, but if you're reading this book, chances are you can understand where Proctor is coming from. In the past forty years, *Star Wars* has arguably exerted a stronger influence on the lives of its viewers and fans than any other media text. Indeed, it is rare to find a person born in the last sixty years who does not have some sort of a relationship with what Matt Hills has called the "cult blockbuster" ("*Star Wars*") that is *Star Wars*. The proliferation of pop cultural references to the saga testifies to its unparalleled cultural force. When Rachel donned the Princess Leia slave girl attire to fulfill Ross's childhood-cum-adulthood fantasy in an episode of *Friends* or Bart Simpson quipped about returning to 1974 to experience "a world where no one's mad at George Lucas" ("Treehouse"), the respective creators could rest assured that the entire audience would be in on the joke. Indeed, particularly in America, the films have become a kind of unofficial national religion, to the point that when India's Prime Minister Narendra Modi visited New York in the fall of 2014, he closed his address to thousands of spectators with the iconic Jedi farewell, "May the Force be with you."

Beyond the passion of its fans, *Star Wars* shares another characteristic typical of many religions: the presence of a god-like creator figure who inspires a wide range of emotional responses in the members of the congregation. While in the early years, the dialogue between creator and followers remained "measured and entirely friendly" (Brooker, "Internet Fandom" 69), in this essay, we will examine the complex ménage à trois between creator, fans, and text that has played out over the last forty years. After a brief overview of the formative years of this complex relationship, we will examine two events that transformed this civil exchange: the release of the Special Edition of the Original Trilogy in 1997, which sowed the seeds of discontent, and the release of the Prequel Trilogy between 1999 and 2005, which provoked an all-out rebellion. In particular, we will focus on the ways in which, especially in the more recent past, fans have leveraged new technologies to challenge George Lucas's iron grip on the *Star Wars* story.

The Franchise Awakens

From its inception, *Star Wars*'s promotional effort anticipated the cross-channel, multi-media campaign that has become standard for Hollywood blockbusters in the twenty-first century. Among science fiction fans, *Star Wars* had already become a household name by the time the first movie hit the screens. Multimedia presentations and original props from the first movie's production were shown at the 1976 San Diego Comic-Con (back then attended by a mere few hundred fans) and the 1976 WorldCon.[1] Trailers were shown in theaters starting in the holiday season of 1976, with the first movie's novelization being published around the same time and eventually selling more than 500,000 copies by May 1977. A couple of weeks prior to the movie's release, Marvel launched its *Star Wars* comics series.[2] When *Star Wars* was eventually released on Memorial Day weekend of 1977, it was shown in only 43 theaters. By August, more than 1,000 theaters had screened the movie, and in the summers of 1978 and 1979, the movie was again presented in more than 1,000 theaters across the United States.[3]

In the wake of the film's huge success, a flood of spin-offs and merchandise (e.g. posters, t-shirts, buttons, and even a disco version of the score) followed, with Kenner selling 42 million *Star Wars*-themed items in 1978 alone, 26 million of these being action figures. These products not only brought in unprecedented profits, but also helped cement the audience's attachment to the narrative. As media scholar Robert Buerkle has noted, "*Star Wars* was … a meta-experience: the larger experience of how kids revisited, expanded on, and performed the trilogy. … But more than anything else, *Star Wars* was the *toys*" (italics in original). Indeed, the toys may be considered an early vehicle for facilitating fan appropriation, as children around the world (including the authors of this chapter) spent countless hours using the characters and props of the *Star Wars* universe to "bring the *Star Wars* story to life" (Geraghty 127) and, perhaps more importantly, to create their own stories with the beloved characters.

However, these children's mini-theaters, performed in private, were not the only creative license taken with the *Star Wars* galaxy. First, there were the official, Lucas-sanctioned ancillary texts. The documentary *The Making of Star Wars* (1977), for example, was hosted by fictional characters C-3PO and R2-D2, making it an early example of the blurring of borders between the diegetic world, the production process, and the fan experience, which has continued to the present day and, in fact, intensified with the passage of time. A second spin-off, the much-maligned 1978 *Holiday Special*, represented an early, and rare, case where Lucas and the fan base were in complete agreement about the worthlessness of a project, as well as offering a prime example of a *Star Wars* product that Lucas is on record as wanting to erase from public memory. Unfortunately for Lucas, his attempts to suppress this spin-off was rendered impossible due to the circulation of non-sanctioned video copies and, eventually, widespread (again unauthorized) digital distribution on the internet.

Beyond losing control of the official ancillary texts, as early as the spring of 1978 Lucas and company were already engaged in an effort to exert control over the evolving world of unofficial, non-profit fan publications. Asked about his stance toward fanzines, Lucas responded: "Right now we're working out a policy about fanzines. Basically, a problem with copyrights has to be resolved" ("Open Letters"). This early tidbit from Lucas was featured in issue no. 6 of the *Star Trek* fanzine *Scuttlebug*, which also included the following information: "The Star Wars Corp. wants to keep track of what SW zines are coming out. They are not out to hassle, sue, etc., anybody. They just wan [*sic*] to convince 20th Century Fox's legal department that there are more than five SW fans who are interested in publishing zines. Even if you are planning a zine, they would like to know about it" ("Open Letters"). While this sounds friendly and encouraging, around the same time, *Probe* reported that the Star Wars Corporation was starting "to inform [publishers of unsanctioned fanzines] that they are in violation of copyrights" ("Open Letters"). In the summer of 1978, rumors were already circulating that Lucas would allow fan fiction as long as it stayed PG-rated, a policy that was confirmed in the summer of 1981 when Lucasfilm started sending out letters to fanzines which published "x-rated material" informing them that

> a great deal of the infringing material published in small circulation fan publications has been overlooked by Lucasfilm because the costs of stopping such

activities are often out of proportion to the amounts involved. This situation is tolerable to Lucasfilm only so long as the materials published are not harmful to the spirit of the Star Wars saga["Open Letters"].

Interestingly, the letter neither acknowledged the free marketing provided by fanzines nor explicitly mentioned Lucasfilm's tolerance of material written in the spirit of *Star Wars*. Rather, it highlighted that tolerance was not a form of encouragement, but rather based on recognition of the prohibitive legal costs of halting such fan appropriations. In any case, the letter continued to explain that editors

> should seriously consider [their] responsibility to Lucasfilm, the copyright owner of these materials, and to the many loyal fans whose high regard fro [*sic*] the Star Wars saga is based in part on the wholesome character that everyone associates with it. Any damage that [editors and fanfic writers] do to this character hurts both Lucasfilm and the fans, and it would be irresponsible for [editors and fanfic writers] to act without a sense of duty [they] owe to both ["Open Letters"].

Revealingly, the planet-destroying Grand Moff Tarkin and his neck-snapping henchman Darth Vader were apparently included in this category of "wholesome characters," indicating a typically American acceptance of violence. Fortunately, a short time later, Maureen Garrett, then director of the *Star Wars* fan club, sent out notifications to fanzine editors which clarified the real target of Lucasfilm's injunction: "Lucasfilm Ltd. does own *all* rights to the Star Wars characters and we are going to insist upon no pornography" ("Open Letters"; emphasis in original). It is worth noting that, unlike modern-day online fan communities and similar forums, the original fan club was run by Lucasfilm Ltd. and used as a tool for propaganda and fan control. Thus, in a subsequent letter to the fanzine *Warped Space*, Garrett could even lay out edicts from the Grand Leader himself: "The word has come from George Lucas, himself, that STAR WARS pornography is unquestionable [*sic*] unacceptable.... Pornography is directly opposed to the very ideals and the spirit that the STAR WARS Saga embodies" ("Open Letters"). In a rhetorical flourish worthy of a political spin doctor, Garrett later defended this edict in a letter to *Judland Wastes* by explaining that Lucasfilm's banning of "pornography" constituted "an exercise in OWNERSHIP not censorship" ("Open Letters"). In a final step, Garrett clarified in a letter to *Imperial Entanglements* that Lucasfilm "cannot authorize homosexual expression [*sic*] of love.... This controversial subject must remain detached from the world created by Lucasfilm in order to preserve the innocence even Imperial crew members must be imagined to have" ("Open Letters"). After pushback from the fan community, even the Corporation was forced to acknowledge the ethical questions raised by a code of conduct condoning the genocide perpetrated by a group of people while strictly prohibiting any potential homosexual interactions between them. In October of 1981, they finally reversed course and officially approved the first fan fiction containing homosexual content.

Thus, from an early time, three things were clear. First, unlike Gene Roddenberry, Lucas's counterpart in the world of *Star Trek* fandom, who was a regular attendee of conventions and eager to interact with fans, Lucas remained aloof, peering down from his Olympian perch and interacting via vaguely threatening official releases. Second, the injunctions against pornography provide early evidence of Lucas's desire to maintain a "pure" fictional universe suitable for viewers of all ages, which is connected to his inability to understand his audience and to comprehend its composition. And third, like the real universe, the *Star Wars* universe abhorred a vacuum, and with too much time left between primary texts, fans and Lucasfilm licensees alike were ready and eager to fill the void.

The Universe Expands

Whereas at the time *Star Wars* was released, there was no guarantee of a sequel, the situation was entirely different when *The Empire Strikes Back* came out three years later. Even the opening crawl, which labeled the film "Episode V," made it clear that more films were to come and offered the first hint at a much longer history that had preceded the events of the first film. Of course, the movie's conclusion, with its range of unresolved storylines, left fans clamoring for more. Similarly, although *Return of the Jedi* brought a more definitive (if widely mocked) ending, it still raised at least as many questions as it answered, both about the diegetic past (How did Anakin turn to the Dark Side to begin with? What were the Clone Wars?) and the diegetic future (So when we finish singing ridiculous nonsense songs with the walking teddy bears, what happens next?). And indeed, these narrative mysteries, as Jason Scott has noted, generated "fanzine discussion" and led to "developing scenarios that resolve such enigmas" through fan fiction (15). In addition, official tie-ins answered some of these questions, as the *Star Wars* universe gradually evolved into what would be labeled the "Expanded Universe." As a result, by the mid–1990s,

> the *Star Wars* universe was far bigger than it had been twenty years earlier. In the long drought between official primary texts, fans had taken what they could get, and characters like Mara Jade and Xizor had become favorites; they appeared in comic books, on trading cards, and as mini action figures [Brooker, *Using* 70].

The serial (but, at times, also parallel) publication of these stories (and fan productions based on them) not only heightened anticipation for each new publication (and, eventually, film release) but also sustained fan investment, both emotional and financial, in the saga.

In this context, Nathan Hunt has emphasized "the importance of trivia" in science fiction fandom, whereby the seemingly unimportant knowledge fans have accumulated is transformed into cultural capital. As Hunt concludes, "through their use of trivia, fans lay claim to having special access to, and hence dominion over, specific texts owing to their ... superior knowledge of them" (186). As a classic example, one of the current authors was once the proud owner of the *Star Wars* edition of *Trivial Pursuit*, a full-fledged, official release of the wildly popular 1980s game, packed with hundreds of *Star Wars*-related questions. The very existence of such a game pre-supposes a (sizable) customer base of people who have seen the films dozens of times (if not more). Such a game could not have existed in the pre–VCR era. However, the release of *Star Wars* coincided with the emergence of VCR technology and cable movie channels such as HBO, which provided the technological means for undermining Lucas's vision of the fan-text relationship. In a 2004 interview, Lucas expressed his conviction that when he made the original movie, it "was not meant ... to be seen more than once in a movie theater. It was designed to be a large theatrical experience that ... would blow you away" (qtd. in Lyons & Morris 190). Apparently, Lucas not only believed that *Star Wars* should not be seen multiple times, but he was also initially unwilling to show the films on the small screen, as this would diminish the *Star Wars* experience. However, the one-two punch of cable TV and the VCR knocked out this vision of a passive fan experience and fostered an intimate fan-text relationship which introduced a new type of cinephilia that transcended cinema. In the case of *Star Wars*, the combination of mass appeal and technological conditions thus led to the emergence of a passionate fan base with a detailed knowledge of every aspect of the original texts. Add in a creator afflicted with a serious case of Whitman Syndrome (i.e., the irresistible urge to continuously tinker with one's artistic creations after they have already been released to the public), and conflict was inevitable.

One such conflict emerged in the run-up to the release of the Special Edition of the Original Trilogy in the mid–1990s. In 1994, Jason Ruspini set up an unofficial *Star Wars* website. With up to 40,000 visitors per day, it was a hit in the early days of the internet. Yet as Ruspini reported, Lucasfilm "nicely asked me to shut it down, with the implication that if I didn't[,] they would bring in a lawyer or something" (qtd. in Sommer 7B). When Ruspini then posted excerpts from the communication with Lucasfilm on his site, fellow fans grew angry and flooded the company with thousands of emails. In May, Lucasfilm issued the following statement:

> There has been quite a bit of confusion on the internet regarding Lucasfilm's position on Jason Ruspini's web page. Please let us clarify. First and foremost, we are not "shutting down" Jason's website. We are sorry for any confusion that may have emerged from any miscommunication on our part.
>
> Lucasfilm appreciates *Star Wars* fans' support and we want you to be able to communicate with one another. Your energy and enthusiasm makes you an important part of our *Star Wars* family. As you can understand, it is important, as well, for Lucasfilm to protect the *Star Wars* copyrights and trademarks. Since the internet is growing so fast, we are in the process of developing guidelines for how we can enhance the ability of *Star Wars* fans to communicate with each other without infringing on *Star Wars* copyright and trademarks and we hope to make these guidelines available in the near future.
>
> As we prepare for the *Star Wars Trilogy Special Edition*[,] which will be coming to theaters next year[,] and as we begin pre-production on the upcoming "prequels," we are now entering an exciting new *Star Wars* era. Many thanks for your support and interest [qtd. in Brooker, *Using* 167].

As the failure of this early attempt to suppress fan productions shows, the evolution of technology had already empowered the fans. The emergence of the internet provided the perfect vehicle for fans to interact, organize and, ultimately, resist the decrees of the "authorities," an activity which would soon increase dramatically.

Rebellion Brews

Although the then-still-unnamed first episode in the *Star Wars* saga was originally slated for release in 1997, by 1996 it was clear that this release date would not be met. Fortunately (although many fans would disagree with the use of that particular word), "ILM had been brainstorming how they might alter the original movie as early as 1993" (Taylor 309). Since Lucas "became frustrated that the costumes, sets, and other production elements weren't living up to his vision of *Star Wars*" while shooting the original films, as the Lucasfilm-produced documentary *Empire of Dreams* suggests, the creator had always insisted that, in particular, the movie that came to be known as *A New Hope* "was a half-finished movie that just got thrown into the marketplace" (qtd. in Pollock 290). As a result, ILM didn't need to convince the godhead that, in the mid–1990s, changes were no longer merely a possibility for the distant future, but rather a dream whose time had come. So, by the mid–1990s, Lucas had "the energy and the stuff … need[ed] to fix" (qtd. in

Pollock 290) the original movies. Yet beyond "finishing" the "half-finished movie," Lucas rationalized his decision to re-visit the Original Trilogy as follows:

> The most obvious thing that's happened is we've gone back to the original negative, cleaned it up considerably, redone a lot of the optical effects, the dissolves and improved the quality of the film, because it was deteriorating. One of the things I wanted to do was preserve the film so that it could still be a viable piece of entertainment in the twenty-first century.... This one had deteriorated a lot more than anybody expected... The audience will get a brand new print that's very clean and actually better than the original release in terms of technical quality. It's less grainy, it's less dirty, and it's just a better print [*Jedi News*].

Although Lucas claimed that preservation was the primary driving force in creating the Special Edition, he also admitted to adding scenes "that had been cut out due to time and money constraints" (*Jedi News*). If it had been merely about the preservation, or restoration, of the original movies, no one would have probably cared too much (or fans might, in fact, have even embraced the restoration[4]), but among the nearly three hundred changes between *Star Wars* and *A New Hope*'s Special Edition were some that truly caused a stir— in positive and negative ways.

On the positive side (from a "serious" fan's perspective), the Special Edition contained some nods to the hard-core fans of the Expanded Universe. These references "mark[ed] a dramatic shift in the hierarchy between canon and quasi-canon," for certain elements from the Expanded Universe were suddenly "drawn into the primary text" (Brooker, *Using* 71). For example, Dash Rendar's starship *Outrider*, which was introduced in *Shadows of the Empire* (an ancillary text published in 1996), is supposedly seen during one of the inserted panorama shots of Mos Eisley. While the verification of Rendar's existence was, arguably, more of a construction of overzealous fan interpretations, the Special Edition marked the first appearance of Coruscant, the "Imperial City" (Zahn 15) at the center of both the Old Republic and the Empire, which was briefly shown in the celebration scenes at the end of the Special Edition of *Return of the Jedi*.[5] Finally, one further addition that even casual fans noticed was the re-incorporation of a deleted scene in which Luke meets his old friend Biggs just prior to the launch of the attack on the Death Star in *A New Hope*. This scene struck many as being "an important scene," for it emphasized "their friendship" (Walker) and thus deepened the emotional impact of Biggs's death for the audience, which had been relatively minimal, since the scene showing Biggs and Luke bonding at the very beginning of the film was cut.

However, beyond these few exceptions that catered to various audiences, a number of other changes received a less-than-favorable reception from the wider fan base. In some cases, alterations can reasonably be viewed as enhancements. Beyond the simple visual improvements of many scenes and the erasing of matte lines,[6] a legitimate case can be made that changes such as the *Millennium Falcon* rising up from Docking Bay 94 to escape, some digitally enhanced and inserted shots of Cloud City, or CGI shots of the Sarlacc added to the films' visual ambience.

Yet when the camera lingered too long, or when the digital elements became too obtrusive, it crossed a line for many fans. We would posit two reasons for fan displeasure. First, for many fans, viewing *Star Wars* may be compared to a religious ritual, something familiar one returns to time and again for the feeling of stability and comfort. This feeling is inevitably disturbed or destroyed by the introduction of new, unexpected elements. Inserting an unnecessary dewback into a desert scene or some faux-comic slapstick of Jawas falling off a ronto when Luke and company enter Mos Eisley is analogous to a priest performing a Jim Carrey spit take when sipping the wine during a Catholic mass. The second reason for fan resistance we would put forth is the quality of the effects themselves. In the initial release, the new digital effects did not blend in very well with the older footage, and this dissonance only worsened as technology improved in the ensuing years. Comments posted by fans on Drew Stewart's remarkably thorough online breakdown of the Special Edition's digital alterations allude to this issue, as when user Ludvik Herrera comments, "The dewbacks are so CGI fake that I really cannot stand it." Or, as another fan put it, the Special Edition's primary concern seems to be "shoving more shit on the screen to distract" (RedLetterMedia) viewers from the narrative.

While scholars have recently emphasized that digital visual effects may be "used to transmit story information" (McClean 11), the Special Edition's new "spectacular visual effects" clearly do *not* "articulate a range of complex concepts and thematic concerns that are central ... to the narratives of the films" (Whissel 4), but rather merely fetishize the technological apparatus. Tellingly, as Stephen Prince remarks, "Lucas was relatively slow to incorporate digital effects into his own films" (21). While *The Wrath of Khan* (1982) sported ILM-created effects that served as "the era's great industry eye-opener, showing what digital imagining could do for cinema," *Return of the Jedi*, released a year later, "used only a small amount of digital animation to simulate graphics displays" (Prince 21–22). Indeed, in the documentary *From Star Wars to Jedi* (1983), Lucas took down fellow science fiction creators because, in his sweeping generalization of his profession, they were "showing off the amount of work" they had put into the establishment of an environment rather than effectively employing the setting and failed to understand that "special effects are just a tool, a means for telling a story. People have a tendency to confuse them as an ends in themselves.... Special effects without a story is a pretty boring thing." [We pause here briefly to allow you to revel in the amazing irony of this quote.]

Considering the eventual triumph of effects over plot in the Prequel Trilogy, Dan North's point that one of the Special Edition's primary objectives was "making the six films more visually continuous and compatible" (163) is thus endowed with another level of resonance: The Special Edition may be considered a testing ground for the gradual replacement of narrative with spectacle. As North correctly concludes, the Special Edition presented "an irrevocable push towards a digital aesthetic" (165), which was fully realized in the prequels.

Perhaps the premier example of the Special Edition's foreshadowing things to come was the reinsertion of a deleted dialogue scene between Jabba the Hutt and Han Solo using a CGI Jabba. In his video analysis on YouTube, user HelloGreedo succinctly sums up fan reaction to this scene: "Overall, CG Jabba looks like complete shit.... That giant piece of digital shit was really approved to be in the final ... film." In the 2004 DVD release, Lucas attempted to salvage the scene by updating the digital effects, but this misses the point. In this case, the technology was just the tool, but the fans were objecting to how it was employed, for the Jabba-Han dialogue scene touches a fan nerve by altering important characters. First, Boba Fett, who quickly became a fan favorite after his introduction in *The Empire Strikes Back*, appears in the scene seemingly demoted to the job of bodyguard, a departure from his usual role of lone bounty hunter. However, Boba Fett's diminution pales in comparison to what the scene did to Jabba. In terms of physical size, the staging of the scene, which was originally shot with a human actor who was shorter than Harrison Ford, made it impossible to insert a digital figure that would match the scale established in fans' minds by *Return of the Jedi*. Furthermore, no matter how good the digital effects might have been, they could never mask the fact that Han Solo looks down on Jabba and interacts with him casually. Jabba thus sheds the menacing, merciless image from *Return of the Jedi* to become a kind of avuncular godfather figure, complete with slapstick comic tendencies, mediocre bargaining skills, and hollow-sounding threats. Here, Lucas's technophilia trumped his (already limited) sense of character development and his (also limited) directorial sensibility.

Of course, no discussion of Lucas's Special Edition tinkering would be complete without mentioning the most infamous change of all, the notorious "Han Shot First" controversy. Here, we enter the realm of what Dan North has labeled "a more foundational refurbishment of the trilogy" (162) that "disrupt[ed] the text's received interpretations" (163). Since we assume the basics of this issue are familiar to anyone reading this book, we will just summarize briefly. In the original version of the cantina confrontation scene between Greedo and Han Solo, Han engages Greedo in conversation long enough to get his gun out of his holster and then "happily" (or at least without much sign of remorse) shoots him dead. However, in the Special Edition, the scene was edited to make Greedo shoot first, in an apparent effort to provide Han with some sort of "stand your ground" defense. Like the removal of the laser impacts with Imperial officers (i.e., non-stormtroopers), this was clearly not a visual cleaning, but rather a moral cleaning, and the fans were not pleased to see their beloved rogue sanitized in this fashion. Although Lucas would eventually alter the scene twice more (at the time of writing), Han never again shot first. In an illuminating 2012 interview with *The Hollywood Reporter*, Lucas explained his side of the story:

> What I did was try to *clean up the confusion*, but obviously it upset people because they wanted Solo to be a cold-blooded killer, but he actually isn't. It had been done in all close-ups and *it was confusing about who did what to whom*. I put a little wider shot in there that made it clear that Greedo is the one who shot first, but everyone *wanted to think* that Han shot first, because they wanted to think that he actually just gunned him down [qtd. in Bock; our emphases].

This explanation is notable for two reasons. First, it shows Lucas not just trying to set the record straight, but rather to re-write history entirely. The disingenuous suggestion that Greedo shot at all is clearly contradicted by existing evidence, no matter how hard Lucas has tried to suppress it, and supports Will Brooker's assertion that

> Lucas's recent interviews, which obsessively rewrite the history of the production process and the saga's evolution, just as the series of Special Editions and DVD versions rework the detail of the narrative world, overriding and repressing any contradiction, are no longer a reliable document of his authorial intentions or reflections [*Star Wars* 83].

The second, and perhaps more important, point about the Han Shot First controversy is that it highlights Lucas's fundamental weakness in understanding and staging character development. The fans don't want Han to be a cold-blooded murderer; they simply want him to be a likeable ruffian who plays by the criminal code of conduct. By this code, shooting down a fellow criminal who points a gun at you and has just threatened your life isn't cold-blooded murder; it is simply being a good gangster. Waiting for him to fire first, on the other hand, just makes you a lousy gangster and a bit stupid (setting aside the ridiculousness of a bounty hunter shooting at a stationary target from three feet away and somehow missing; unless subsequent edits of Han "dodging" were meant to suggest that Han has Jedi-like anticipatory abilities that allow him to dodge laser bullets, which would be a complete contradiction of everything Han stands for ... but we digress.). In the end, this episode makes one thing abundantly clear: CGI is just a tool, and ultimately, CGI doesn't kill movies, sub-par directors kill them.

Attack of the CGI

If the Special Edition was the first step on the seductive path to the dark side of digital wizardry, the release of *The Phantom Menace* would soon prove that Lucas's transformation was complete. Where the Special Edition was Lucas's attempt at re-writing and re-contextualizing his history as a filmmaker, the prequels were his attempt to claim a place in the pantheon of visionary filmmakers who have influenced the way movies are made. To get an insight into Lucas's mindset about the prequel films, it is helpful to look at the making-of included in the *Phantom Menace* DVD box. This documentary begins with a few snippets taken from a *60 Minutes* interview with Lucas that was originally broadcast in March of 1999, in which he stresses the significance of *auteur* theory. Introduced by François Truffaut in the 1950s, it was American critic Andrew Sarris who distilled what came to be known as "*auteur* theory" from Truffaut's writing by claiming that a movie director assumes three key functions in the filmmaking process: "those of a technician, a stylist, and an *auteur*" (133). While Lucas is laying claim to these aspects (i.e., directing, editing, and, crucially, technical innovations), he is also reviving a point from Truffaut's original work that was omitted from Sarris's discussion—the emphasis on the power of "homme[s] de cinéma" (20), which Truffaut understood as filmmakers directing movies that are based on their own scripts. Lucas's emphasis on being an "homme de cinéma" makes his claim to sole authorship of the entire *Star Wars* series explicit.

For the Original Trilogy, this claim is clearly overstated. During the filming of *Star Wars*, there were people who questioned Lucas's decisions (e.g., the well-known point that the actors repeatedly told him, "You can write this stuff, but you can't say it") and strongly impacted the final shape of the movie. Indeed, as Chris Taylor has pointed out, "The first reel of *Star Wars* was vital—and yet a surprising amount of the credit for it belong to people whose names are not George Lucas" (ch. 11). Alfred Newman had composed the Fox fanfare, a sound that came to symbolize *Star Wars* more so than Fox, in the 1930s; John Williams's Academy Award-winning music sets the tone for the entire movie; and the opening crawl was heavily edited by Brian DePalma and then-*Time* movie critic Jay Cocks. Once viewers virtually enter the diegesis, they are welcomed by ILM's special effects. Add to these aspects the fact that Lucas didn't want Anthony Daniels voicing C-3PO and the importance of the (Academy-Award-winning) editing team, and it becomes obvious that *Star Wars* was a collaborative project. For *The Empire Strikes Back*, Lucas then delegated directing duties to his former teacher Irvin Kershner, provided only the story (which was refined by Leigh Brackett and Lawrence Kasdan), and retreated to the function of executive producer. However, already prior to *Return of the Jedi*, Mike White argues in a fanzine, Lucas "bought into his own hype and felt that he could do no wrong," which led him to once again assume a more active role on the film when he thought director Richard Marquand was not up to the task. Afterwards, his "self-delusion spiraled out of control back at Skywalker … ranch" (White), a process which culminated in the near-total control he exercised over all aspects of the Prequel Trilogy.

Tellingly, in the documentary *The People vs. George Lucas* (2010), Lucas's biographer Dale Pollock notes, Lucas "is beyond a certain level of criticism. He is beyond the idea of true collaboration." *The Phantom Menace*'s making-of supports this idea. After the aforementioned snippets from *60 Minutes*, viewers see a storyboard meeting. On the agenda is deciding which elements of specific scenes will be CGI effects and which will exist in the pro-filmic reality. As Lucas goes through the storyboard, there are several looks of disagreement and utter confusion among the crew members, but no one challenges Lucas. There is complete silence in the room until he mixes up the color codes and, tellingly, begins laughing at himself, upon which the others apparently feel okay joining Lucas in laughing at Lucas. The odd aspect of this making-of is that, assuming that Lucas was involved in its creation, it seems to be Lucas doubling down on his own questionable decisions, as if to say, "Yup, that was my call, and there is nothing you can do about it."

And what did this total control bring about? Since brutal takedowns of the Prequel Trilogy abound (we can recommend the well-known RedLetterMedia review), and our space here is limited, we will restrict ourselves to pointing out two flaws that are most relevant for the discussion below: the excess of CGI and the misguided attempts to maintain the alleged innocence of the fictional universe. Relevant to the former, while the Original Trilogy is permeated by "feelings of ambivalence … towards technology both within and without the film texts" (North 158), the prequels embrace technology on all levels, as is evident in both the selection of production techniques and the technophilia on display in the storyworld. In the diegesis, for example, one need only contrast Vader's famous warning to not be "too proud about this technological terror you have created" with Qui-Gonn's technobabble explanation about the midichlorians behind the Force to see how the very soul of the Original Trilogy has been assimilated by a Borg-like technological sensibility in the prequels. On the production level, from the much-maligned podrace (which, astonishingly, is the edited version—Lucas had initially planned a longer cut, as revealed in the special features on the DVD) to the cartoonish final battle between Obi-Wan and Anakin,[7] the prequels are replete with examples of the very kind of special effects excess at the cost of storytelling Lucas had so decried in his fellow sci-fi directors twenty years earlier.

Yet the most reviled technological innovation of the prequels, which also brings in our second topic of infantilism, is none other than the world's first fully digital actor/character—Jar Jar Binks. In his detailed analysis of this widely detested character, Dan North has pointed out that the character is "inconsistent with the worlds of *Star Wars* because of his interpersonal clumsiness, gesticulatory fervor, and childish persistence" (156). However, North stresses, "in his appeal to the youngest members of the film's audience," Jar Jar "might be a jarring reminder ... that *Star Wars* was always" intended "for kids ... and that merchandise and toy sales by far outstrip the box office takings of the films" (156–157). This explanation echoes Matt Hills's earlier intervention that Jar Jar haters "belong to a certain generation; or, at least, they discursively construct themselves ... as a generationally 'truth-seeing'-section of *Star Wars* fandom" ("Putting Away" 78). As Hills continues, "These fans consistently devalue Jar Jar through articulated discourses: the character is childish and/or for kids, and is also simultaneously 'commercial,' being a case of George Lucas 'selling out'" ("Putting Away" 79).

Since we prefer to avoid prequel-bashing (unfortunately, a near impossibility for a first-generation *Star Wars* fan), we will simply acknowledge the arguments above and suggest one possible twist. Perhaps it is a false nostalgia, but it seems to us that kids back in the pre–*Return of the Jedi* days did not need walking teddy bears and slapstick cartoon aliens to get excited about *Star Wars*. It was a simple story of Good vs. Evil, in which the evil characters were as intriguing as the good guys. For example, one of the present authors' fondest *Star Wars* memories is the plastic Darth Vader costume he wore for Halloween in 1977, and the other spent many glorious hours making his Imperial walkers stomp all over Ewok villages. Either kids have changed a lot in the nearly two decades between the trilogies, or Lucas overshot badly in an unnecessary effort to pander to his perceived next generation of fans, while simultaneously managing to alienate large portions of his older generations of fans. We will leave this question to the child psychiatrists and *Star*

Wars fanatics to debate, but the indisputable fact is the prequels set off a veritable revolt in the *Star Wars* community.

The Fans Strike Back

Despite the intense criticism, most fans were unwilling or unable to reject the prequels completely and have acknowledged that the Prequel Trilogy adds important details to the *Star Wars* experience. Thus, two different methods of making the prequels "watchable" have arisen among fans: identifying a viewing sequence for the complete epic which minimizes the prequels' weaknesses and excising their more offensive parts. To address the former option first, on the surface, there are two possible ways to watch the films. First, Lucas advocates watching them in diegetic chronological order (i.e., episodes 1–6). Lucas has always argued that the saga is the story of Anakin Skywalker's rise, fall, and eventual salvation, in which case this order would make sense. However, for the fans, this entails a few problems. First, the would-be protagonist is clearly not the focus of the Original Trilogy. Second, this order destroys the dramatic tension created in *The Empire Strikes Back* and *Return of the Jedi* revolving around the revelation that Vader is Luke's father and Leia his sister. The "I am your father" moment is so iconic that filming one's children's reactions to this scene has become a genre of YouTube videos, and fans are simply unwilling to give that up. Finally, and perhaps most importantly, fans have pointed out that the prequel films were so horribly executed that Anakin simply is not a sympathetic or even believable character. Buried in digital shenanigans and inept directing and acting, the character becomes little more than a caricature in the first three numeric episodes. Most fans have thus rejected Lucas's argument that *Star Wars* is Anakin's story and stuck to the original fan experience, in which Luke was the first hero we met.

Naturally, complete faith to the original fan experience would mean watching the films in order of original release date. But not even fans blinded by nostalgia can miss the obvious problem with this approach: the prequels simply lack suspense, as it is absolutely clear what will happen to the main characters before even watching the first minutes of *The Phantom Menace* (a fact which, to be fair, one must acknowledge made the challenge of making the prequels interesting not insubstantial). To remedy these problems, *TheForce.net* user Ernest Rister has proposed introducing new initiates (usually kids or new girlfriends) to the movies in the following order: *A New Hope— The Empire Strikes Back—The Phantom Menace—Attack of the Clones—*

Revenge of the Sith—Return of the Jedi. Thus, after Vader outs himself as Luke's father, the Prequel Trilogy functions as an extended flashback to shed light on Anakin's journey to the Dark Side. Rod Hilton has taken this idea a step further in his "Machete Order," for he suggests leaving out *The Phantom Menace* entirely, as the movie is "completely irrelevant to the rest of the series." As Hilton highlights, apart from the fact that "it's almost as if this is somehow the intented [*sic*] order," the decision to exclude the first prequel has a number of advantages, such as "virtually no Jar Jar," "no midichlorians," and "no virgin birth."[8]

While some fans have made peace with the Prequel Trilogy via these alternative viewing orders, others have felt compelled to employ the more radical solution of re-editing the movies to fit their needs. For example, the relatively famous (for fan edits, that is) "Phantom Edit" reduces the runtime of the entire Prequel Trilogy to just over two hours. Here, the only thing that remains of *The Phantom Menace* is the "Duel of the Fates" lightsaber battle (a decision which reveals the deep fascination with lightsaber duels that lurks in the heart of even the most committed narrative critics). Padmé's family is introduced in *Attack of the Clones* (a scene which had ended up on the cutting room floor), the action on Kamino (and, thus, effectively, the existence of the Clone Army) is cut, and the narrative jumps from the Geonosis arena battle to Dooku returning the Death Star plans to Sidious. General Grievous is completely excised from the narrative (suggesting that the aforementioned passion for lightsaber duels contains a purist ethos that does not extend to the protection of duels with droid villains), as is the oft-parodied "Noooo!" at the end of *Revenge of the Sith*. Although this fan edit (in fact, it's merely a cut, not an edit) highlights how many relatively insignificant scenes the movies contain, it also manages to even further flatten the prequels. However, this is ultimately consistent with the project's stated aim of "cutting away all the fluff and focusing on the narrative of how Anakin becomes Darth Vader," that is, reducing the entire flawed prequel to an overblown flashback from the "real" story.

L8wrtr's edits of the three movies, on the other hand, are more involved. By the fan editor's own count, there are more than two hundred edits in each of the prequels, which reduces the first two installments down to 96 minutes each, while *Revenge of the Sith* clocks in at 112 minutes. Each of the three edits opens with a disclaimer that "it is a not-for-profit educational experiment in the use of consumer editing software as a means to offer a critique of the original source as well as explore the means of telling different stories using existing media." Indeed, these versions represent a stronger act of appropriation. *The Phantom Menace* has been renamed *Shadow of the Sith,* and even the opening crawl indicates the fan edit's difference from the original text by highlighting that "[a] thousand years have passed since the Jedi Order vanquished the Evil Sith Lords." The opening paragraph thereby not only sets an entirely different tone to the original text, but also clarifies an aspect the entire Prequel Trilogy never makes explicit—what the Sith took "revenge" for. Indeed, the entire opening crawl evokes more of a *Star Wars* spirit than *The Phantom Menace*'s, as it continues,

> The Galactic Senate has come to rely on the Jedi to settle disputes and maintain peace throughout the Republic.
> Jedi Knight Qui-Gon Jinn and his apprentice, Obi-Wan Kenobi, have been dispatched by the Supreme Chancellor to resolve a dispute between the Naboo and the Neimoidian Trade Federation.
> Little do the Jedi know that a Phantom Menace has been plotting revenge....

By cutting out all of the original text about trade disputes, the revised crawl simply and effectively sets the stage for the events to follow.

Overall, viewers have praised the much tighter pacing of the fan edit in comparison to Lucas's movie. Some scenes were cut entirely (e.g., the longish underwater journey from Gungan City to Theed), while others were trimmed (e.g., the never-ending podrace). Jar Jar is (mercifully) demoted to a background character with little screen time; the Neimoidians no longer appear like cowards who would have never struck a deal with a Sith but seem to have some sort of motivation (that this motivation remains a mystery, indeed, adds to their character); some deleted scenes are re-integrated into the movie (e.g., Anakin fighting Greedo); and the timing in the lightsaber battle just prior to Darth Maul's death has been adjusted such that Obi-Wan no longer telegraphs his plans for several seconds. Finally, in terms of narrative, Anakin no longer just stumbles into heroic acts, but takes an active role in the destruction of the droid ship.

L8wrtr's edits of the other two prequel movies—re-titled to *A Republic Divided* and *Dawn of the Empire*—follow a similar pattern: More effective opening crawls, the cutting of superfluous scenes and irrelevant dialogue, the re-integration of some deleted scenes, and some re-editing of scenes. L8wrtr's edits not only eliminate the midichlorians, but also transform Anakin into a more responsible agent, who, in fact, kills Padmé (rather than the extremely kitschy notion of her dying of a broken heart). Finally, *Dawn of the Empire* also manages to avoid spoiling the narrative twists in the Original Trilogy by showing the birth of Padmé's babies but omitting the scene in which they are named.

Creative fannish interventions such as these fan edits are nothing new and have existed since home video technology became affordable. However, in the digital age, these productive appropriations of cultural artifacts reach a much wider audience, as even casual fans become aware of how "fans make unauthorized and 'inappropriate' uses of cultural texts" and "combine conspicuous, enthusiastic consumption of official texts and spin-offs with their own creative and interpretive practices" (Gwenllian-Jones 172). Especially since these "creative and interpretive practices" have become so visible in the digital environment of the late twentieth and early twenty-first centuries, the public at large has come to understand that *Star Wars* "fans themselves have also contributed to *Star Wars*, not simply as consumers but participating in creating and producing the *Star Wars* culture" (Scott 11). In this way, fans have effectively become (co-) authors of *Star Wars*.

On the Battlefields of Nostalgia

While the prequels, as widely disparaged texts, were viewed as fair game for slicing and dicing, fan resistance to Lucas's tampering with the Original Trilogy has been more complex. Lucas clearly identified the mission of his own "restoration" efforts in a 1997 interview:

> What ends up being important, in my mind, is what the DVD version is going to look like, because that's what everybody is going to remember. The other versions will disappear. Even the thirty-five million tapes of *Star Wars* out there won't last more than thirty or forty years [qtd. in Magid 68].

In the documentary *Empire of Dreams*, made for the 2004 Trilogy box set, Lucas further advanced his agenda of re-writing history. *Empire of Dreams* tells the story of the production of the Original Trilogy, but especially *Star Wars* (when it was just *Star Wars*, not *A New Hope* or *Episode IV*). It employs a somewhat "devious" trick: toward the end of the documentary, the Special Edition is introduced as a kind of climax with a brief synopsis of some of the most explicit changes, such as the dewbacks in the first shots of Tatooine, the digitally added shots of the X-wing formation prior to the approach of the Death Star, and Han confronted by dozens of stormtroopers (and a TIE Fighter in the background) after chasing a small group of them through the Death Star's corridors. The implication is that this is the first time in the documentary that re-vamped scenes are shown, which is, however, clearly not the case.

The most obvious attempt to integrate scenes from the Special Edition into the original production of *Star Wars* occurs when the documentary shows some brief clips of John Williams recording the movie's score with the London Symphony Orchestra in 1977. A jarring discord emerges from the difference between the aged look of the images recorded in London and the

Special Edition's slick images that are digitally projected onto a screen in the background, effectively creating a "special edition" of the 1977 studio recordings. While we do not mean to suggest the documentary implies that these images were projected onto that specific wall on that specific day in March of 1977 (or, at least, we hope it doesn't try to), juxtaposing the crisp images of the Special Edition with the antiquated look of the recording from the 1970s emphasizes the documentary's (and, thus, Lucas's) desire to clean up all confusion and construct a (more or less) coherent narrative. And while there are rather obvious scenes in which Special Edition shots are used in the documentary, there are also moments when original shots more or less smoothly segue into Special Edition shots or vice-versa (such as in the scene in which Red Leader misses his shot in *A New Hope*), whereby Lucas's re-imagination literally supplants the original movies.

In addition to the problem indicated above, neither the documentary nor Lucas himself has been able to maintain the coherence of this constructed narrative. As Graham Lyons and Janice Morris have pointed out, "Lucas's at-times contradictory stance toward his own edits—that is, preserving at once the intended, 'correct' shot and the narrative integrity of the story—completely collapses" (202). After all, upon the Special Edition's release, he proudly proclaimed that this "won't be what I would call the 'rough cut,' it'll be the 'final cut.' The other one will be some sort of interesting artifact that people will look at and say, 'There was an earlier draft of this'" (qtd. in Magid 68). Nevertheless, the Special Edition was revised for the 2004 DVD release and, then again, for the Blu-ray release in 2011, evidence that Lucas will perhaps never be able to leave well enough alone.

Of course, Lucas knew all along that there would be resistance to his efforts to re-write history, as already discussed above. With reference to *Star Wars* fan videos, in 2002, Jim Ward, then vice president of marketing at Lucasfilm, said:

> We've been very clear all along on where we draw the line. We love our fans. We want them to have fun. But if in fact somebody is using our characters to create a story unto itself, that's not in the spirit of what we think fandom is about. Fandom is about celebrating the story the way it is [qtd. in Harmon].

Referring to this statement, Henry Jenkins appropriately quips, "Lucas wants to be 'celebrated' but not appropriated" (*Convergence* 149).

As indicated by Ward's statement, the attempts to regulate the production of fan texts, which had begun in the 1970s with fanzines, continued in the digital age. For example, when Lucasfilm offered free web space for *Star Wars* fan sites and unique content for these sites in 2000, the company only did so "under the condition that whatever [fans] created would become the studio's intellectual property" (qtd. in Jenkins, *Convergence* 152). Likewise, when their subsidiary AtomFilms began hosting official fan video contests in 2003, "Lucasfilm drew a hard line that fan creativity could be parodic but not expansive of the *Star Wars* universe" (Gray 165). The key point here is that parody has a clear legal foundation, and Lucasfilm couldn't keep fans from producing parodic fan vids. Their decision to "allow" such productions and even support them by providing a download library full of sounds, effects, etc., from the movies was ultimately an attempt to convey an illusion of goodwill toward fan producers grounded in Lucasfilm's claim to authorship and authority over the text by "permitting fans to make their own meanings but only within the tightly constrained limits offered up by the producers" (Pearson 92).

However, some fans have always seen through these attempts to re-write history and control fan responses. United by a "faithfulness to and love for the original" (Lyden 777) that endows the unaltered Original Trilogy with a nearly sacred status, fans have been quick to turn Lucas's own words against him to criticize his incessant tampering. When testifying before Congress in a hearing that ultimately led to the introduction of the Film Preservation Act of 1988, Lucas condemned such practices as colorizing classic black and white movies, defiantly proclaiming:

> American works of art belong to the American public; they are part of our cultural history.... People who alter or destroy works of art and our cultural heritage for profit or as an exercise of power are barbarians, and if the laws of the United States continue to condone this behavior, history will surely classify us as a barbaric society.... Our cultural history must not be allowed to be rewritten [qtd. in United States 295–297].

In the court of fan opinion, Lucas has been found guilty of these very crimes. By tinkering with the original films, Lucas destroyed part of the look and feel that made *Star Wars* special. Lucas himself stressed this specific production design ethos in an interview in the early 1980s, "I'm trying to make a film that looks very real, with a nitty-gritty feel.... I like to have that edge of reality because I want the movies to make you believe they are real" (qtd. in Rinzler 105). This is the "old future" look that made *Star Wars* famous. In his BFI companion to *Star Wars*, Will Brooker echoes this point: "Dirt, trash, scuffs, scratches. The desert battered surface of Luke's landspeeder, and the worn, washed-out fabric of his farmer's clothes.... Han Solo's outfit ... and his customised 'piece of junk' pirate ship. This is the aesthetic of the Rebels" (23). Needless to say, some fans did not take Lucas's sanitizing of their cherished texts lying down. Scorning the corporate attempts to encourage them to produce safe, officially sanctioned (and owned) projects and accept Lucas's constant re-writing of history, they set out on a mission to restore the sacred texts on their own by fighting fire with fire—or in this case, technology with technology.

While there are numerous projects in *Star Wars* restoration circles, we would like to briefly focus on two general types of approaches to digital restoration and highlight the important distinctions between the goals and motivations of these approaches. The first kind involves the straight digitization of the best-quality original source copies the project leaders can obtain. To date, this digitization approach has been most successfully applied by Team Negative1, which is converting and restoring the original movies from multiple 35mm Lowfade Positive Prints (i.e., reels that were distributed to theaters during the films' original runs). The group released a first, raw high-def transfer of *The Empire Strikes Back* in December 2014, explaining they had received better prints and thus meant the transfer to function as a very early sample of what *Star Wars* purists can expect. A second project, run by originaltrilogy.com user poita, uses a similar approach, which, however, includes some special selling points, such as the use of a professional-quality Imagica Digital Film Scanner Model 5000 (original price of $400,000, which he got for a bargain price via ebay) as well as a range of high-quality prints. The goal of this project is to (re-)release all three restored original movies before January 31, 2017, as that will mark the date on which the lifetime of the Special Edition will officially exceed that of the original films (if one concedes that the originals "died" when the Special Edition was released).

In terms of ethos, the digitization approach could be considered the most purist exercise in nostalgia. When these projects talk about restoring the "grit" that made *Star Wars* special, they are not only referring to the diegetic grit, but also the filmic grit; that is, the graininess of the actual prints. Here, viewers can really see the film as they might have first experienced it upon its original release. Of course, this claim to authenticity is somewhat false, as fans watch the movies in their private homes, not in the public spaces of movie theaters. In addition, the original source prints themselves have inevitably deteriorated to some degree and the technology used to consume the new versions is entirely different from the projectors of days past. As fans are quick to point out when criticizing the official Lucasfilm efforts, new technologies highlight flaws that were easily overlooked in original, lower-quality versions. In particular, poita's project scans at a resolution of 10k (compared to the typical Blu-ray level of a tad below 2k), which yields a per-frame file size of about 120mb! At this level, you can be sure every tiny error from the original print will leap right off the screen in ways they never would have when buried in the original film.

The second class of restoration approaches involves a more creative and radical re-working of the source material. These approaches once again feature a complex tension between various impulses and raise interesting questions about the "proper" goals of image and audio optimization, the acceptability of changes made for the special editions, and how to maintain consistency. One prime example of this type of approach is "de-specializing," where the primary (stated) goal is to reverse the changes Lucas made in the process of creating his various editions. In this field, Petr Harmacek's (Harmy) project has gradually eclipsed other projects due to its outstanding efforts and results. This high-definition "de-specialization" project has already reached version 2.5 for *Star Wars*, version 2.0 for *The Empire Strikes Back*, and version 1.0 for *Return of the Jedi*. For *Star Wars* alone, Harmy has worked with seven primary video sources and incorporated no fewer than twenty-one audio tracks (including three tracks from the theatrical release and commentary tracks from different releases) in order to "reconstruct ... the 1977 theatrical version of STAR WARS," as he describes it on the originaltrilogy.com forums. For an example of the painstaking effort put into this labor of love, one need look no further than the opening of the first film. Harmy's edition uses a color-corrected 1977-style Fox logo (taken from the *Alien* Blu-ray), replaces the new Lucasfilm logo with the one from 1977 (taken from a 35mm print), and includes a self-made opening crawl recreated on the basis of frame scans taken from a print. In the later stages of the movie, Harmy even goes so far as to re-introduce matte lines and special effects bloopers (e.g., scenes, or even just frames, in which lightsabers are white).[9]

This final point highlights an interesting tension in the de-specializing approach. On the one hand, it embraces some of the technological accomplishments of Lucas's official restoration. As a primary source, Harmy uses the Blu-ray editions, thereby acknowledging the value of the color and sharpness corrections that Lucasfilm achieved in its restoration efforts. On the other hand, re-inserting matte lines and special effects bloopers suggests a nostalgic romanticizing of the limitations of "ancient" technologies and the trivial gaffes which the "true" fans cherish. Here, the fans challenge Lucas's authority to dictate the terms of the films' authenticity. From a fan perspective, the shared knowledge of such trivial mistakes and the production histories behind them are key factors uniting the community. As Timothy Corrigan diagnosed as early as 1991, fan groups frequently "establish a relationship with technology itself," a relationship which is often based on a "secret ground" that is "closer to Pittsburgh [an allusion to the production of *Night of the Living Dead*] and grainy stock than to the glamor [*sic*] of Hollywood" (27). Continuing Corrigan's ideas, Kate Egan has more recently noted that "low-budget production histories ... allow for a sense of closeness and a more intimate access to a film and its makers" (34). That Corrigan and Egan made these statements in reference to cult movies testifies to the cultish origin of the entire multi-billion-dollar *Star Wars* franchise.

Furthermore, Harmy's decision to use his own skills with the technological tools at hand to restore imperfections may be read as an attempt to further undermine the authority of the (former) CEO of the *Star Wars* universe by subtly aligning the project with the front line special effects workers who participated in the films' original production—an alliance made more explicit in *The People vs. George Lucas* when Jay Sylvester, founder of originaltrilogy.com, remarks:

> George Lucas may be the brainchild [*sic*] behind *Star Wars*, he may have come up with the story and all of the characters, but everyone who participated in the making of those films had some type of creative input. I mean, they won an Oscar for Best Special Effects. Some of those effects are stripped out and replaced with "CGI enhancements," if you wanna call them that. I think that that's really disrespectful to the people who worked on those models and did those shots.

To further explore the idea of challenging authenticity and using technology to appropriate the original texts, it is helpful to look at one final example of what we have called the "radical re-editing approaches"—Adywan's "*Star Wars* Revisited." The site's mission statement informs visitors that Adywan set out "to make what he felt the Special Editions *should have been*" (our emphasis) with the goal "to recreate how he remembered watching the film when it first came out." These statements reframe the debate about authenticity by first basing it on an individual's subjective memories and second claiming the authority to dictate the alleged ideal form of the films. As the word "revisited" implies, this project has outgrown the imperative of re-creating the theatrical experience of the 1970s and 1980s.

The real mission of this project is perhaps best captured in the quasi-legal disclaimer that appears on the right-hand side of every page: "All rights and respect to George Lucas, who made this universe for us to play in." The operative word here is "play," for the project transcends mere nostalgia and replaces it with an ethos of creative license, whereby the original text becomes the raw material for the project leader's exploration of the possibilities of modern technologies. Adywan follows his own vision and is not constrained by reverence toward a "sacred" original text. For example, one of the 250 (!) changes listed for *A New Hope* indicates how he inserted a battle droid from one of the prequel films into the Jawa sandcrawler. In some fan circles, this type of inter-trilogy mixing would be considered a cardinal sin, but such actions are consistent with the idea of revisiting (i.e., reconsidering), as opposed to restoring.

Furthermore, Adywan has preempted the criticism one might receive from hard-core fans by inviting them in to play in the *Star Wars* universe with him. By leveraging modern communications technologies, he has fostered a community spirit around the project. The project website features regular updates on Adywan's current and planned efforts, side-by-side video comparisons of the originals and his altered versions, comment sections, where users can offer praise and suggestions, and even the occasional auction, where users can bid on models and other props used as part of the editing efforts. Such measures echo the Corporation's use of behind-the-scenes documentaries, official fan clubs, and newsletters to build a community, but this time in the service of the re-imagined text.

As a final point, the website clarifies that revisiting the Original Trilogy is simply woodshedding to master the technological tools in preparation for a much bigger effort—a complete reworking of the Prequel Trilogy with the goal of enabling a diegetically chronological viewing of all six films which preserves the narrative surprises of the Original Trilogy (i.e., the virgin viewers' jaws should still drop when Vader says, "I am your father"). This will require a herculean effort of digital changes and plot reconstruction, which Adywan says should render the prequel trilogy films "unrecognizable." Thus, Adywan plans to use the power of technology to transform his project into a kind of modern-day video version of fan fiction. However, its goal emerges as far more audacious, for Adywan is working in the same medium as the original, and ultimately, the project outcome should replace the original text for future generations, rather than simply augment it. In this way, Adywan will usurp the authority of the original creator, and the apprentice will become the master.

In Disney & J. J. We Trust?

The writing had been on the wall for Lucas for some time. In December of 2012, Lucas made his own bid to salvage his maligned prequels and prolong his relevance in the universe he had created by commencing the release of his own prequel Special Edition. However, rather than addressing fan dissatisfaction with the technophilia of the prequels, Lucas doubled down on the technology by remaking the films in 3D. Predictably, the release of *The Phantom Menace* in 3D in 2012 failed to generate much excitement and was perhaps a harbinger of events to come.

Indeed, a not-so-phantom menace was already hovering ominously over the fandom like a giant Death Star, albeit sporting two giant mouse ears. As one might expect, news of the sale of Lucasfilm to the Disney Corporation met with widespread suspicion in the fan community. While few tears were shed over Disney's first act, the decision to discontinue the 3D prequel releases and cancel the planned 3D editions, fan suspicions were soon confirmed by the company's decision to retcon[10] much of the Expanded Universe ("As if millions of voices suddenly cried out in terror, and were suddenly silenced."). However, a new hope soon arose with the anointing of J. J. Abrams to direct the then-unnamed *Episode VII*. Speaking for the middle-aged demographic of hard-core *Star Wars* fans, filmmaker Eli Roth (who wrote a scathing review of *The Phantom Menace* a week before its official release) said, "Thinking that George Lucas made 'The Phantom Menace' for me is symptomatic of my entire generation who grew up with Star Wars, because as kids in the 70's and 80's, those films were made for us. We just assumed that would continue in the 90's (and secretly hope it does with J. J. Abrams at the helm of the new ones)" (qtd. in Ryan).

Although the expectations are essentially impossible to fulfill, Abrams's chances of success are at least better than 3,720 to 1 ("Never tell me the odds."), for he is among the current generation of directors whom Suzanne Scott has dubbed "fanboy auteurs." These are filmmakers who draw on their own past experiences as fans and therefore occupy a liminal position between "visionary auteur and faithful fanboy" (440). This is hardly a new trend; after all, George Lucas also emphasized his fanboy credentials during interviews in the 1970s: "Some of my friends are more concerned about art and being considered a Fellini or an Orson Wells [*sic*], but I've never really had that problem…. I'm more drawn to Flash Gordon. I like action adventure, chases, things blowing up, and I have strong feelings about science fiction and comic books" (qtd. in Farber 9).

Also working in Abrams's favor is the fact that he is battle-tested, having already braved the treacherous seas of sci-fi fan expectations when he tackled the daunting task of directing the recent *Star Trek* reboot. In fact, during this ordeal, he even drew strength from the example set by George Lucas, as he expressed in a 2013 interview (months before he became *Episode VII*'s director): "And it is for me a heartening lesson to see that George has had his battles before, during, and after making films. When you see that you can't please everyone, that includes studios, actors, the audience…. You're always trying to do the best you can" (qtd. in Curtis).

Clearly, Abrams has a reasonable perspective on fan expectations. And what are these expectations? The media emphasis on Abrams's own fannish past has certainly baited fans into expecting "stories which reflect the aesthetic traditions and shared tastes of the fan communities from which [he] emerged and which [he] now seek[s] to court" (Jenkins, "Guiding"). The early signs are good (but, then again, so were the signs prior to the release of *The Phantom Menace*). Within days of their release, the teaser trailers for *The Force Awakens* had been deconstructed and analyzed frame-by-frame and sparked wild speculations on an unprecedented level for such texts, a clear sign that *Star Wars* fan culture is alive and well, and thriving like never before in today's era of user-generated content.

We will leave the speculation to the "professionals," such as *IGN*'s orgasmic review of the second teaser trailer, and limit our comments to two points relevant for the present paper. First, there is a complete absence of any slap-sticky, child-pandering comic relief to tempt the digital cutting implements of future disgruntled fans. And second, the visual effects are stunning, yet restrained, and used to support the main mission of the trailer—tempting the audience to speculate on the stories of the many characters (both new and old) featured within. Indeed, regarding production technology, perhaps the most encouraging words came from Abrams himself in a February 2015 interview:

> I feel like the beauty of this age of filmmaking is that there are more tools at your disposal, but it doesn't mean that any of these new tools are automatically the right tools…. And there are a lot of situations where we went very much old school and in fact used CG more to remove things than to add things [Kastrenakes].

One thing is for certain: as with all official releases, the release of *The Force Awakens* is sure to be a major event that is bound to stir up enough emotions and ideas to keep critics, fans and academics (not mutually exclusive categories, of course) busy for years to come. No matter how the final film turns out, it is sure to provide the raw material for countless fan appropriations, deconstructions, and reconfigurations, thereby adding yet another chapter to the never-ending romance between the fans and their beloved fictional universe.

Notes

1. For a pretty interesting retelling of how *Star Wars* came to the 1976 WorldCon, see this *YouTube* video: https://www.youtube.com/watch?v=G7gOYEm1H6I.

2. A move that Jim Shooter (assistant editor and writer at Marvel in 1976; editor-in-chief by 1978) has claimed saved the iconic comic book company from impending bankruptcy (Thomas).

3. Numbers taken from *Box Office Mojo*. In the 2004 documentary *Empire of Dreams*, Alan Ladd, Jr., states that *Star Wars* opened in 37 theaters.

4. See, for example, the extremely positive responses to the high-def restoration of *Jaws*, which presents the film in unadulterated form on Blu-ray; indeed, it even includes the original 1.0 audio track.

5. The first draft of *Return of the Jedi* refers to "Had Abbadon, the Imperial capital planet. It is almost entirely urban, extremely overpopulated and polluted heavily" (Bouzereau 236). Up until the third draft of *Star Wars*, Alderaan was the capital of the Empire.

6. Matte lines, which are typical of older special effects, appear at the intersections between two visual layers when they are combined. In the Hoth battle, for example, the aircrafts were miniature models. Especially in the cockpit scenes, white lines marked the intersections between the aircraft and the background, which were filmed separately.

7. In the making-of the Mustafar scene, stunt coordinator Nick Gillard tellingly remarks, "After three or four minutes in, you get over the initial explosion of the fight, why they are fighting, and all the flashy moves are done."

8. The "virgin birth" has been toned down in the Expanded Universe, as the novel *Darth Plagueis* (2012) strongly implies that Shmi's immaculate conception was a reaction by the midichlorians to Plagueis and Darth Sidious's manipulation of the Force hinted at in *Revenge of the Sith*. In other words, Anakin—the Chosen One who should bring balance to the Force—was practically created by the Dark Side.

9. Harmy has provided detailed photo galleries illustrating all of the changes he made. They are available at https://plus.google.com/u/0/109609428403596349302/photos.

10. "Retcon" stands for "retroactive continuity"; that is, the process by which established facts in the continuity of a fictional work are altered or removed.

Works Cited

Armendarno, Nicolas. Comment to "Image #123." Star Wars *Special Edition Changes HD.* Google+ Photo Gallery by Drew Stewart. Google, 24 Aug. 2014. Web. 30 Apr. 2015.

Bock, Alex Ben. "5 Questions with George Lucas: Controversial 'Star Wars' Changes, SOPA and 'Indiana Jones 5.'" *The Hollywood Reporter.* Prometheus Global Media, 9 Feb. 2012. Web. 19 May 2015.

Bouzereau, Laurent. Star Wars: *The Annotated Screenplays.* New York: Ballantine, 1997. Print.

Brooker, Will. "Internet Fandom and the Continuing Narratives of *Star Wars, Blade Runner,* and *Alien.*" *Alien Zone II: The Spaces of Science Fiction Cinema.* Ed. Annette Kuhn. London: Verso, 1999: 59–72. Print.

_____. *Star Wars.* London: BFI, 2009. Print.

_____. *Using the Force: Creativity, Community and* Star Wars *Fans.* London: Continuum, 2002. Print.

Buerkle, Robert. "Playset Nostalgia: *LEGO Star Wars: The Video Game* and the Transgenerational Appeal of the LEGO Video Game Franchise." *LEGO Studies: Examining the Building Blocks of a Transmedial Phenomenon.* Ed. Mark J. P. Wolf. New York: Routledge, 2014. Kindle.

Corrigan, Timothy. "Film and the Culture of Cult." *The Cult Film Experience: Beyond All Reason.* Ed. J. P. Telotte. Austin: University of Texas Press, 1991: 26–41. Print.

Curtis, Bryan. "J. J. Abrams Discusses His (Until Now) Secret Relationship With George Lucas." *Grantland.* ESPN, 25 Jan. 2013. Web. 19 Apr. 2015.

Egan, Kate. *The Evil Dead.* London: Wallflower, 2011. Print.

Empire of Dreams: The Story of the Star Wars *Trilogy.* Dir. Edith Becker and Kevin Burns. Twentieth Century Fox, 2004. DVD.

Farber, Stephen. "George Lucas: The Stinky Kid Hits the Big Time." *Film Quarterly* 27.3 (1974): 2–9. *JSTOR.* 11 May 2013.

From Star Wars *to* Jedi: *The Making of a Saga.* Dir. Richard Schickel. Fox Home Video, 1995. VHS.

Geraghty, Lincoln. *Cult Collectors: Nostalgia, Fandom and Collecting Popular Culture.* Abingdon: Routledge, 2014. Print.

Gray, Jonathan. *Show Sold Separately: Promos, Spoilers, and Other Media Paratexts.* New York: New York University Press, 2010. Print.

Gwenllian-Jones, Sara. "Phantom Menace: Killer Fans, Consumer Activism and Digital Filmmakers." *Underground U.S.A.: Filmmaking beyond the Hollywood Canon.* Ed. Xavier Mendik and Stephen J. Schneider. London: Wallflower, 2002. 169–179. Print.

Harmon, Amy. "Film; 'Star Wars' Fan Films Come Tumbling Back to Earth." *New York Times* 28 Apr. 2002. New York Times. Web. 11 Apr. 2015.

Harmy. "Harmy's STAR WARS Despecialized Edition HD - V2.5 MKV IS OUT NOW." originaltrilogy.com. originaltrilogy.com, 5 Apr. 2011 [last updated 21 Dec. 2014]. Web. 12 May 2015.

HelloGreedo. "*Star Wars Changes—Part I - Episode IV: A New Hope.*" Online video clip. *YouTube.* YouTube, 27 Sep. 2011. Web. 17 Mar. 2015.

Herrera, Ludvig. Comment to "Image #31." Star Wars *Special Edition Changes HD.* Google + Photo Gallery by Drew Stewart. Google, 9 Sept. 2010. Web. 30 Apr. 2015.

Hills, Matt. "Putting Away Childish Things: Jar Jar Binks and the 'Virtual Star' as an Object of Fan Loathing." *Contemporary Hollywood Stardom.* Ed. Thomas Austin and Martin Barker. London: Arnold, 2003. 74–89. Print.

_____. "*Star Wars* in Fandom, Film Theory, and the Museum: The Cultural Status of the Cult Blockbuster." *Movie Blockbusters.* Ed. Julian Stringer. Abingdon: Routledge, 2003: 178–189. Print.

Hilton, Rod. "The *Star Wars* Saga: Introducing Machete Order." *Absolutely No Machete Juggling.* n. p., 11 Nov. 2011. Web. 13 Feb. 2015.

Hunt, Nathan. "The Importance of Trivia: Ownership, Exclusion and Authority in Science Fiction Fandom." *Defining Cult Movies: The Cultural Politics of Oppositional Taste.* Ed. Mark Jancovich, Antonio Lázaro Reboll, Julian Stringer, and Andy Willis. Manchester: Manchester University Press, 2003. 185–201. Print.

IGN. "Analyzing the *Star Wars: The Force Awakens* Trailer #2—*IGN* Rewind Trailer." Online video clip. *YouTube.* YouTube, 27 Sept. 2011. Web. 17 Mar. 2015.

Jenkins, Henry. *Convergence Culture: Where Old and New Media Collide.* New York: New York University Press, 2006. Print.

_____. "The Guiding Spirit and the Powers That Be: A Response to Suzanne Scott." *The Participatory Cultures Handbook.* Ed. Aaron Delwiche and Jennifer Jason Henderson. New York: Routledge, 2013. Kindle.

Jensaarail. "A Nerd-Rage Rant: The Prequel Trilogy." Online video clip. *YouTube.* YouTube, 13 May 2013. Web. 17 Mar. 2015.

Kastrenakes, Jacob. "J. J. Abrams Has Been Mobbed by Fanboys Over the New Lightsaber." *The Verge.* Vox Media, 6 Feb. 2015. Web. 30 Apr. 2015.

Kwan, Andrew. "*Star Wars* I-III: A Phantom Edit*1080p*." Online video clip. *YouTube.* YouTube, 8 Jun. 2015. Web. 10 Jun. 2015.

Lyden, John C. "Whose Film Is It, Anyway? Canonicity and Authority in *Star Wars* Fandom." *Journal of the American Academy of Religion* 80.3 (2012): 775–786. Print.

Lyons, Graham, and Janice Morris. "The Emperor's New Clones; or, Digitization and Walter Benjamin in the *Star Wars* Universe." *Culture, Identities and Technology in the* Star Wars *Films: Essays on the Two Trilogies.* Ed. Carl Silvio and Tony M. Vinci. Jefferson, NC: McFarland, 2007: 189–213. Print.

Magid, Ron. "An Expanded Universe: Digital and Analog Special Effects Collide in the Retooled Version of *Star Wars.*" *American Cinematographer* 78.2 (1997): 60–70. Print.

McClean, Shilo T. *Digital Storytelling: The Narrative Power of Visual Effects in Film.* Cambridge: MIT Press, 2007. Print.

North, Dan. "Kill Binks: Why the World Hated Its First Digital Actor." *Culture, Identities and Technology in the* Star Wars *Films: Essays on the Two Trilogies.* Ed. Carl Silvio and Tony M. Vinci. Jefferson, NC: McFarland, 2007: 155–174. Print.

"Open Letters to *Star Wars* Zine Publishers by Maureen Garrett." *Fanlore.* Organization of Transformative Works, 1 July 2015. Web. 1 July 2015.

Pearson, Roberta. "Fandom in the Digital Era." *Popular Communication* 8 (2010): 84–95. *Routledge.* Web. 26 Feb. 2013.

The People vs. George Lucas. Dir. Alexandre O. Philippe. Exhibit A Pictures, 2010. Blu-ray.

Pollock, Dale. *Skywalking: The Life and Films of George Lucas,* updated ed. New York: Da Capo, 1999. Print.

Prince, Stephen. *Digital Visual Effects in Cinema: The Seduction of Reality.* New Brunswick: Rutgers University Press, 2010. Print.

Proctor, William. "'Holy Crap, More *Star Wars*! More *Star Wars*? What If They're Crap?'" Disney, Lucasfilm, and *Star Wars* Online Fandom in the 21st Century." *Participations: Journal of Audience & Reception Studies* 10.1 (2013): 198–224. Web. 10 Apr. 2015.

RedLetterMedia. "*Star Wars: The Phantom Menace* Review (Part 2 of 7)." Online video clip. *YouTube.* YouTube, 9 Apr. 2012. Web. 17 Mar. 2015.

Rinzler, J. W. *The Making of* Star Wars: *The Definitive Story behind the Original Film.* Enhanced Ed. LucasFilm, 2013. iBook.

Ryan, Mike. "Eli Roth's Lost 'Phantom Menace' Review: Man, He Really Hated 'Star Wars: Episode I.'" *Huffington Post.* Huffington Post, 28 Mar. 2013. Web. 11 Apr. 2015.

Sarris, Andrew. "Notes on the *Auteur* Theory in 1962." 1962. *Film Culture Reader.* Ed. P. Adams Sitney. New York: Praeger, 1970: 121–135. Print.

Scott, Jason. "*Star Wars* as a Character-Oriented Franchise." *Fan Phenomena:* Star Wars. Ed. Mika Elovaara. Bristol: Intellect, 2013: 11–19. Print.

Scott, Suzanne. "Dawn of the Undead Author: Fanboy Auteurism and Zack Snyder's 'Vision.'" *A Companion to Media Authorship.* Ed. Jonathan Gray and Derek Johnson. Malden, MA: Wiley-Blackwell, 2013: 440–462. Print.

Sommer, Constance. "Hollywood is girding for an assault on the Internet." *The Dispatch* 7 Dec. 1996: 7B. Web. 11 May 2015.

"*Star Wars.*" *Box Office Mojo.* Amazon, n.d. Web. 14 Apr. 2015.

Star Wars—Episode I: Shadow of the Sith. Dir. George Lucas. Ed. L8wrtr. Perf. Liam Neeson, Ewan McGregor, Natalie Portman, Jake Lloyd, Ian McDiarmid, et al.

Star Wars: Episode IV—A New Hope. Dir. George Lucas. Perf. Mark Hamill, Harrison Ford, Carrie Fisher, Alec Guiness, et al. Twentieth Century Fox, 2006. DVD.

Star Wars: Episode IV—A New Hope. Dir. George Lucas. Perf. Mark Hamill, Harrison Ford, Carrie Fisher, Alec Guiness, et al. Twentieth Century Fox, 2011. Blu-ray.

Star Wars: Episode V—The Empire Strikes Back. Dir. Irvin Kershner. Perf. Mark Hamill, Harrison Ford, Carrie Fisher, Alec Guiness, et al. Twentieth Century Fox, 2011. Blu-ray.

Star Wars Revisited. "About Revisited." Star Wars *Revisited News.* WordPress, n.d. Web. 19 May 2015.

_____. "ANH:R Change List." Star Wars *Revisited News.* WordPress, n.d. Web. 19 May 2015.

Taylor, Chris. *How* Star Wars *Conquered the Universe: The Past, Present and Future of a Multibillion Dollar Franchise.* London: Head of Zeus, 2014. Kindle.

Team Jedi News. "Inside the Holocron—*A New Hope* Changes." *Jedi News.* Jedi News, 2 May 2015. Web. 8 May 2015.

Thomas, Michael. "Jim Shooter Interview, Part I." *Comic Book Resources.* Boiling Point Productions, 6 Oct. 2000. Web. 7 May 2015.

"Treehouse of Horror XXIII." *The Simpsons*. Writ. David Mandel and Brian Kelley. Dir. Steven Dean Moore. Twentieth Century Fox, 2012. *Simpsons World*. Web. 20 July 2015.

Truffaut, François. "Une certaine tendance du cinéma français." *Cahiers du Cinéma* 31 (1954): 15–29. Print.

United States. Congress. *Technological Alterations to Motion Pictures: A Report of the Register of Copyrights*. 1989. Web. 22 July 2015.

Walker, Max. "Biggs Darklighter Extended Scene—*Star Wars: A New Hope*." Online video clip. *YouTube*. YouTube, 3 Mar. 2014. Web. 17 Mar. 2015.

Whissel, Kristen. *Spectacular Digital Effects: CGI and Contemporary Cinema*. Durham: Duke University Press, 2014. Print.

White, Mike. "Triumph of the Whills; or, Everyone Knows It's Windu." *Cashiers du Cinemart*. Impossible Funky, 2004. Web. 11 Apr. 2015.

wishnow [Jason Wishnow]. "*Star Wars* or Bust." 1999. Online video clip. *YouTube*. YouTube, 21 Jan. 2012. Web. 17 Mar. 2015.

Within a Minute: The Making of Episode III. Dir. Tippy Bushkin. Twentieth Century Fox, 2005. DVD.

Zahn, Timothy. *Star Wars: Heir to the Empire*. New York: Bantam, 1991. Print.

About the Contributors

Jessica K. **Brandt** is an adjunct instructor of Russian language and culture at Montclair State University. Her work centers on media and cultural history during the Cold War, with a particular focus on non-commercial radio. Her projects include an investigation of the overlapping worlds of Soviet underground publishing and American broadcasting through Radio Liberty.

Erin C. **Callahan**, Ph.D. is a professor of English at San Jacinto College. Her research interests focus on identity construction with a specific focus on gender and the intersection between popular culture and identity, with a special emphasis on film and music. Her projects include study of Don Robey and the history of blues music in Houston, Texas.

Paul **Charbel** is a Ph.D. candidate of history and culture at Drew University, researching the encapsulation of Lebanese culture in Utica, New York. He has written mostly on Arab immigration to the West and how those émigrés use technology to bridge the gaps between the "old country" and their new homes.

Michael **Fuchs** teaches in the Department of American Studies at the University of Graz. He has co-edited three books and authored more than a dozen journal articles and essays on horror and adult cinema, video games, comics and American television. His research interests focus on English and American studies and culture.

Karin **Hilck** is a Ph.D. student at Jacobs University in Bremen, Germany. Her dissertation focuses on the interdigitation of the American spaceflight program as a unique entry point into the gender, technological and political correlations for American social and Cold War history.

Peter W. **Lee** is a Ph.D. candidate at Drew University. His dissertation is on boyhood in early Cold War films. Among his publications are contributions to *Journal of the West*; *Children in the Films of Alfred Hitchcock*; *Learning the Left: Popular Culture, Liberal Politics, and Informal Education from 1900 to the Present*, and McFarland's "The Ages of the Superheroes" series.

Michael **Phillips** is a senior lecturer in the English Studies Department at the University of Graz. He has co-edited *ConFiguring America: Iconic Figures, Visuality, and the American Identity* (2013) with Klaus Rieser and Michael Fuchs;

they are working on various other publications. His research interests include the representation of iconic music stars in various cinematic genres.

Gregory E. **Rutledge** is an associate professor of English and Ethnic Studies at the University of Nebraska–Lincoln. His primary interests lie in African American literature and culture, critical race theory and racial exceptionalism and epic performance. He is widely published in law and cultural studies and is author of *The Epic Trickster in American Literature* (2013).

Mara **Wood** is a school psychology doctoral student in Arkansas. Her research interests include the educational and therapeutic applications of comic books. She podcasts with the Missfits and Talking Shojo. Her blog, marawoodblog. com, focuses on comic research and geek culture.

Tom **Zlabinger** is an assistant professor of music at York College/CUNY in New York where he directs the York College Big Band and the York College Summer Jazz Program. His research has focued on jazz and improvised music in Vienna after Ossiach, music in media and the pedagogy of improvisation and the music industry.

Index

241